"Hollifield & Coffey provide the practical and conceptual foundation students need to become professional media research analysts. This text provides clear demonstrations of how multiple research methods produce key insights within various industry contexts. In doing so, it will distinguish itself as an enduring resource for both students and instructors."
　　—**Matthew Corn, Ph.D.,** *Director of Research, HBO/HBO Max*

"An indispensable resource not only for students of media analytics, but for professionals as well. It provides a comprehensive and detailed study of today's complex media ecosystem and how to effectively reach consumer targets on the right platforms at the right time with the right message."
　　—**Steve Walsh,** *Chief Revenue Officer, Consumer Orbit*

"It is no exaggeration to say that those of us who teach media analytics have been desperate for a book like this. It is comprehensive in terms of the industry sectors, measurement systems, and analytical contexts covered; and best of all, it comes with actual data for students to work with."
　　—**Philip M. Napoli, Ph.D.,** *Director, DeWitt Wallace Center for Media & Democracy, Duke University, USA*

Media Analytics

This textbook takes a case study approach to media and audience analytics. Realizing the best way to understand analytics in the digital age is to practice it, the authors have created a collection of cases using datasets that present real and hypothetical scenarios for students to work through.

Media Analytics introduces the key principles of media economics and management. It outlines how to interpret and present results, the principles of data visualization and storytelling, and the basics of research design and sampling. Although shifting technology makes measurement and analytics a dynamic space, this book takes an evergreen, conceptual approach, reminding students to focus on the principles and foundations that will remain constant.

Aimed at upper-level students in the fast-growing area of media analytics in a cross-platform world, students using this text will learn how to find the stories in the data and how to present those stories in an engaging way to others.

Instructor and Student Resources include an Instructor's Manual, discussion questions, short exercises, and links to additional resources. They are available online at www.routledge.com/cw/hollifield.

C. Ann Hollifield, Ph.D., is Professor Emerita at the University of Georgia, USA, and an international consultant on news media viability. In 2006, she founded one of the first certificate programs in media analytics in the United States. She is the author/editor of more than 50 publications on media economics and management.

Amy Jo Coffey, Ph.D., is Associate Professor in Media Management at the University of Florida, USA, where she also developed the online master's program and certificate in audience analytics. Her published research has focused on media management and economics topics, including audience valuation, advertiser investment in diverse audiences, and media ownership.

Media Analytics

Understanding Media, Audiences, and Consumers in the 21st Century

C. Ann Hollifield and Amy Jo Coffey

Routledge
Taylor & Francis Group

NEW YORK AND LONDON

Designed cover image: ConceptCafe/© Getty Images

First published 2023
by Routledge
605 Third Avenue, New York, NY 10158

and by Routledge
4 Park Square, Milton Park, Abingdon, Oxon, OX14 4RN

Routledge is an imprint of the Taylor & Francis Group, an informa business

© 2023 Taylor & Francis

The right of C. Ann Hollifield and Amy Jo Coffey to be identified as authors of this work has been asserted in accordance with sections 77 and 78 of the Copyright, Designs and Patents Act 1988.

Library of Congress Cataloging-in-Publication Data
Names: Hollifield, C. Ann, author. | Coffey, Amy Jo, author.
Title: Media analytics : understanding media, audiences, and consumers in the 21st century / edited by C. Ann Hollifield, Amy Jo Coffey.
Description: New York, NY : Routledge, 2023. | Includes bibliographical references and index.
Identifiers: LCCN 2022060804 (print) | LCCN 2022060805 (ebook) | ISBN 9781138581036 (hardback) | ISBN 9781138581050 (paperback) | ISBN 9780429506956 (ebook)
Subjects: LCSH: Mass media—Audiences. | Mass media—Economic aspects. | Data mining. | Mass media—Research—Methodology. | LCGFT: Textbooks.
Classification: LCC P96.A83 H65 2023 (print) | LCC P96.A83 (ebook) | DDC 302.23—dc23/eng/20230213
LC record available at https://lccn.loc.gov/2022060804
LC ebook record available at https://lccn.loc.gov/2022060805

ISBN: 978-1-138-58103-6 (hbk)
ISBN: 978-1-138-58105-0 (pbk)
ISBN: 978-0-429-50695-6 (ebk)

DOI: 10.4324/9780429506956

Typeset in Sabon
by Apex CoVantage, LLC

Access the companion website: www.routledge.com/cw/hollifield

To Lee, my fellow adventurer through a lifetime, and to Jessica, Mark, Zadie, and Willa. Thank you all for all you do to make the world a better place.

To Jon, for your abiding love and support, and the meaning that comes from doing life together

Contents

Text website URL: www.routledge.com/cw/hollifield

Data availability

Some data reprinted in the textbook or available on the companion website has been donated by media or research firms for the expressly limited purpose of being used as a teaching tool in the exercises and case studies in *Media Analytics: Understanding Media, Audiences, and Consumers in the 21st Century*. Other datasets in this book or on its companion website were created by the authors to simulate the types of data media analysts might work with in specific media sectors or in analyzing certain problems.

While some of the donated datasets are presented in their original form, others have been adapted or excerpts are used for specific cases and to make the data more manageable for students. In addition, it should be noted that the anonymized Comscore Information in the Textbook/Website represents data, research opinion, or viewpoints published by Comscore as of its original publication date and not as a representation of fact. None of the data or datasets in or accompanying this book are to be used for any purpose other than working the exercises and assignments in this text. Access to and use of the data are available only to individuals who have purchased or rented the book or who have accessed it through a library that has purchased it. Reproducing the data or sharing it with third parties is expressly prohibited.

Acknowledgments

We owe debts of gratitude to so many people, without whom this book and its associated online materials would not have been possible. Over the many years that led up to this project and the several more involved in its actual creation, there has been a community of people who have enthusiastically supported our work and contributed to it in countless ways.

First and foremost, we want to thank Gary Corbitt, retired research director at WJXT-TV/Post Newsweek Stations in Jacksonville, Florida, and Patti Cohen, senior vice president, CBS Television Stations, New York City. It was their idea, in the late 1990s, to try to inspire faculty in universities with electronic media programs to launch academic programs in media analytics. We are beneficiaries of their inspiration and challenge. But we also thank them for the numerous times and ways they helped us over the years by sharing their expertise with our students and by putting us into contact with other media analytics professionals, many of whom became resources for this text.

Heather Birks, executive director of BEA (Broadcast Education Association), has also played a large role in media analytics education efforts. She championed Gary's and Patti's idea of encouraging universities to offer curricula in media analytics and arranged sessions at BEA's annual convention to "teach the teachers" about the profession. She also organized seminars, symposia, and numerous conference calls over the years between media analytics experts and the handful of faculty then teaching in the area. Her efforts made it possible for us to broaden our network of contacts across the profession and to get advice as to how to best prepare students for this rapidly changing field. The impact of her efforts and support is everywhere in this text.

Tom and Wendy Dowden supported this project by endowing the Thomas C. Dowden Professor of Media Research. A cable industry pioneer, Tom enthusiastically supported the need to teach future media professionals about the business of media and the potential value in media entrepreneurship. Through his endowment of the Dowden professorship, he funded the *Media and the Public Sphere* conference at the University of Georgia that launched some of the foundational work on this textbook, as well as much of the research and travel required to complete it. We also thank the University of Florida College of Journalism and Communications for its support of this project, which included a sabbatical that enabled much of the work.

So many others have helped make this textbook possible. Many allowed us to interview them, sharing their expertise and shaping our understanding of the work they do in specific media sectors. Some helped us make contact with colleagues, clients, and friends in the profession who they thought could also help improve this work. Some went to bat helping us acquire real media data for readers to use in building their expertise and skills.

We want to give special thanks to our many former students, many of them now senior-level analytics professionals. So many of them contributed in ways large and small, and we thank them for their support of this project and for all that they taught us in the process.

We are particularly grateful to each of the following individuals and organizations for their contributions to this work:[1] Alliance for Audited Media, Dr. Alison Alexander, Daniel Anstandig, Kelsey Arendt, Dr. Lee Becker, Eric Bruce, Vincent Bruzzese, Mario Callegaro, Mentian Chen, Britta Cleveland, Dave Coletti, Dr. Matthew Corn, Dr. Sarthak Dasadia, Dr. Amanda Felbab, Brian Fuhrer, Dr. Itai Himelboim, Dr. Jiran Hou, George Ivie, Lauren Izzo, Sachin Kamdar, Sarfraz Khan, Rich Kinzler, Dr. Carl Marci, Billy McDowell, Heather McKinney, Joel McLean, Dan Migala, Dr. Philp M. Napoli, Brian O'Shea, Devora Olin, Mary Omachonu, Dr. Pat Phalen, Doug Peiffer, Teresa Perry, Christine Pierce, Podtrac, Kevin Rini, Bruce Rosenblum, Larry Rosin, Jamal Salman, Adrian Segovia, Howard Shimmel, Linda Brooks Thomas, Jim Thompson, Sal Tuzzeo, Dr. Duane Varan, Steve Walsh, Lisa Wegscheider, Reid Williams, Henry Willmore, Jun Xu, and Tania Yuki.

We thank various personnel and their organizations that contributed artwork or specific materials for this text, including Gerard Broussard for the Council for Research Excellence, Daniel Cardiel and Parse.ly, Kimberly Mosley and the Digital Analytics Association, and Michael Sweeney and Clearcode.

Finally, the heart of this book is in the cases it provides readers—the practical experience it offers in thinking critically about real-world media problems through the lens of real-world media data. These offerings would have been impossible without the generous donations of data we received from research companies, media companies, and media entrepreneurs. Not all of the donors or interviewees wished to be acknowledged by name, but we hope they know how grateful we are for the critical support they provided to us and to this project. In particular, we wish to thank the following data providers: Comscore, Kovsky Media Research, Marshall Marketing, MPA—the Association of Magazine Media, Oconee County Observations, and OzTAM.

We also want to thank our editors at Taylor & Francis/Routledge. Linda Bathgate first encouraged us to develop the project. Ross Wagenhofer, Brian Eschrich, and Sean Daly provided excellent guidance over the life the project. Fred Dahl provided skilled editing and Kate Fornadel did an amazing job as production editor. We cannot thank them enough.

Many more people than we can possibly acknowledge contributed to *our* knowledge about and understanding of media analytics over the years, and they have worked to keep us abreast of the many, ongoing changes in the field. We apologize to everyone to whom we owe so many thanks but have not named here. We are deeply grateful.

And, of course, any errors of understanding or explanation in the text are entirely our own.

Note

1. Only individuals and organizations that gave us express permission to acknowledge them are noted here. Where individuals gave us permission to thank them, we have not included their organizations due to space reasons. Organizations have been thanked where individuals requested anonymity but asked that their organization be acknowledged.

Preface

New York City, May 2016
World Media Economics and Management Conference

As often happens, Ann and Amy Jo found themselves sitting next to one another at a conference with other media management scholars and industry practitioners, focused on the challenges of the day. At a morning session, likely involving media measurement . . .

AH: I have a proposition for you. Dinner later?
    That evening . . .
AH: What do you think about a case text on media analytics?
AJC: I think you're out of your mind.
AH: Ever thought about it?
AJC: Yes, for about two seconds. There's a reason there's no text—this space is changing every five minutes. A book?!
    We were too familiar with the lack of a current media/audience analytics text. We'd both taught in this space for years, developed curricula, and had both launched certificates/online master's programs in analytics.
AH: *(Laughs)* True. But what if we could write it in a way that was evergreen and more conceptual? Focusing on the fundamentals, foundations?
AJC: *(Skeptical, perhaps an eye roll)* Ann, this space is not going to see stability for a long time, especially in video. *(Pauses)* But there still is no book, and media/audience analytics courses and programs continue to pop up. This stuff has to be taught . . .
AH: And we could get datasets for the students and finally solve *that* issue . . .
    Media industry data access was a tiresome topic for those of us teaching analytics. The proprietary nature and cost were prohibitive for most. Instructors had lamented it for years and desperately needed a current text on this topic. Most didn't have time to curate their own content and, especially if they didn't teach regularly in this space, preferred a textbook.

> *With our extensive experience founding and running media analytics programs and strong industry connections, we knew we were uniquely positioned to write such a text.*
> AJC: (*Sigh*) It would be a lot of work. Are you sure?
> *Ann smiles, with that glint in her eye. She knew she had hooked the fish. We work well together. Who better to take this adventure with and jump off the cliff?*
> AJC: Let's do it. . . .

The origins of the project long predated that delightful evening in New York, of course. Indeed, this book has its roots in the turn of the 21st century, in the days when media were just starting to be disrupted by digital technologies, and industries were just starting to see data analytics as a potentially valuable management tool.

At that time, many stations hired psychology, sociology, and marketing graduates into their research departments, only to find that while their new employees knew research design, sampling, and data analysis, they were largely clueless about the media industry. That meant those new hires were good at figuring out what the data *said* but not what they *meant*. The teaching curve was too high for already overstretched research directors, and a group of them got together and decided to try to flip that script. They wanted to find people who knew a lot about media and just enough about data.

So two leaders in the field, Gary Corbitt,[1] then Research Director at WJXT-TV/Post Newsweek Stations in Jacksonville, Florida, and Patti Cohen,[2] then Director of Research and Programming at WGCL-TV in Atlanta, Georgia, turned to the Broadcast Education Association (BEA) for help. BEA is the United States' largest association for college and university professors who teach courses and conduct research in video and audio media. BEA's Executive Director, Heather Birks, immediately saw the opportunity, and she, Corbitt, and Cohen began organizing regular sessions at the annual BEA national convention to educate university faculty about the field of media analytics.

When the three began their efforts in the early 2000s, there were no undergraduate or graduate programs in US journalism or communications programs focused specifically on preparing students for careers in media research and analytics. For one thing, US media and communication students are notoriously anti-numbers and math phobic. Media faculty know from experience that a substantial percentage of their students have chosen communications majors at least in part because of the mistaken belief that media are a math-free major and profession.

In reality, media are and always have been among the most numbers-driven industries on the planet. If that's news to you as you read this, plan to spend some serious time with Chapter 2.

But as industry demand for graduates with both media knowledge and skills in data analytics grew year by year, so too did the number of communication programs offering courses, certificates, and even majors in the field. The interest and growth were worldwide.

With this backdrop, this textbook, with its evergreen approach to teaching media analytics, was born. It provides the conceptual foundations that will remain constant, even as the industry evolves, and it reminds students that it's not about the numbers themselves. It's about what they *mean* and about how, as effective media analysts, we can help organizations make solid strategic decisions. So this text addresses two needs: It covers the foundational knowledge media analysts need to succeed and provides case studies and the media datasets required to work them, so that readers can practice basic skills in data analysis, interpretation, and communication.

In researching this textbook, we crisscrossed the country and spent countless hours on phone and video calls interviewing media analysts at many levels and in many industry sectors. Many of them were early alumni from our own media analytics programs, now leaders in their profession and working for some of the largest and most important media and syndicated research firms in the world. We thank each of them for the gifts of their time and expertise.

(And for the record, many of them told us they *still* can't find enough entry-level media analysts to hire—a claim supported by the speed at which our recent media analytics graduates have been snapped up by employers.)

A primary contribution of this text is the valuable datasets accompanying it, which were generously donated by a number of audience research firms, media companies, and media entrepreneurs. The executives and companies who agreed to donate their data did so because they recognized the importance of helping universities fully prepare future media research and analytics professionals. We cannot thank them enough. In some cases, when we could not find data donors, we created our own hypothetical datasets modeled after the types of data that analysts working in those industry sectors told us they use.

We hope you will find this textbook a valuable resource. Above all, our goal for this project is to help the next generation of media analysts and leaders understand the issues and challenges facing 21st century media and develop the critical and analytical thinking skills they will need to solve them.

—Dr. C. Ann Hollifield & Dr. Amy Jo Coffey

Notes

1. Now retired.
2. Now Senior Vice President, CBS Television Stations, New York City.

Introduction

Someone hands you a dataset and asks you to use it to develop a new strategy. Great! Time to start analyzing, right? Wrong. How do you know whether you can trust that dataset? Do you know where the data came from? Were actual humans at work behind the data generation, or might the data have been generated by a robot? Can this be verified? Was the sample representative of the population you intended to measure, and was it large enough?

If yes, great. Now you can start analyzing, right? Wrong again. What is it that you are measuring? Perhaps your client asks you to determine whether there was an "increase in *engagement*" year over year. Better, right? Wrong once more. Why? Because you don't yet know what your client is referring to by the term "engagement." What activities or outcomes constitute engagement? Ask ten different people, and you may get ten different answers. It depends on the platform, the context, and the industry sector, among other factors.

Once you've established your operational definition of "engagement" and have selected the appropriate tools and metrics, you feel you can get to work. For the sake of efficiency, let's say you've done due diligence on all remaining issues and have resolved them, including knowing your research questions and objectives and how to identify the trends and patterns that will help you arrive at the answers. You go to work. Hours or even days later, you admire your output. Done, right? (You know where this is headed.)

The best analysts today—the kind you aspire to be—have just begun. Now you must become an interpreter and translator of the results, one who can identify which findings are both relevant and meaningful and which have implications for your organization. You become a storyteller. What is the story that your results will tell? The most valuable media analysts can take the discovered *insights*, break them down for CEOs and managers alike, and tell them the headlines and takeaways—particularly those that affect the bottom line. Today's most effective analysts are also clear communicators in

DOI: 10.4324/9780429506956-1

oral, written, and visual forms. Telling your organization's stories in clear, concise language and formats for all to understand is an appreciated and valued skill because the recipients—the "hearers" and "readers" of your reports—are also an audience. After receiving praise from their audience for their presentation or report, the very best analysts take the process one step further. Their analyses lead them to more research questions and new lines of inquiry. They dig further and start their processes anew.

The type of analysts just described are rare and in great demand. Not only are there insufficient numbers of analysts to fill a growing number of roles, but not all analysts are prepared to expertly do all that was just described. This is an opportune time to become a media analyst. The scarcity of qualified job applicants not only means more leverage when it comes to salary, it also gives experienced analysts choices in terms of the types of analytics jobs they may want to pursue. (*Wait, I can make good money in these roles?!* Yes, you can! Read on!)

There is a place for you in the media analytics industry whether you find yourself drawn to media content development, selection, scheduling, or pricing; promotion and marketing campaigns; advertising and marketing effectiveness; usability testing or user experience (UX); media branding or rebranding; news selection and development; social media; publication management; political campaign messaging and fundraising; video game development; or trend spotting of all types.

Moreover, the industry needs *critical thinkers* to cut through the metrics clutter to focus on what truly matters. As the many analytics executives we interviewed shared with us, ***what gets measured ends up being what matters***. This can be good, or it can be terrible! Why? Some things are easier to measure because, well, the data is "there." So if the data is easily accessible, why not just measure it and report it? Problem is, once it's measured and reported, it gains importance and becomes the focus—even if it's not helpful. Meanwhile, what might *really* be needed is not being measured at all, and your company spends time and money on things that don't really help. What are your goals? You need metrics to help you measure those things, and you can be the thinker in the room to guide your organization.

It's time to roll up your sleeves and become the most qualified, prepared analyst you can be. This text is designed to help you become that analyst. While the intended audience for this text is analysts-in-training (undergraduate or master's students), we hope that professional analysts will also find it a useful desk reference.

Purpose of the text

Media analytics in the 21st century is a demanding and rewarding field, and it is one that advances rapidly. Because of this, today's analyst must be prepared to adapt to change, including technological and structural change, as industries evolve. Today's professionals are also on the move, often not remaining with a single employer long-term. Therefore, you will need a knowledge and skill set that can "travel" with you, regardless of industry. Analysts move both within and across industry sectors—and industries. For these reasons, this textbook will take a "wide and deep" approach to teaching the art and science of audience and consumer analytics so that you have a proper grounding and the necessary skills, regardless of where your career may lead you. In fact, many people who start their careers in media analytics find that it is a launching pad into other industries, as the companies that hire them see their skills as highly transferrable.

Until now, no single resource has existed to thoroughly address audience analytics in the digital era and the challenges confronting the field, using the broad approach outlined here. By the same token, realize that *media measurement companies, metric names, and tools will change*, even during this text's life span. However, the fundamentals and principles will remain constant and should be the reader's focus because the desired learning outcomes are the same. Technology and industry sectors, even companies and metric names, are always going to be in flux. *Focus on the concepts and principles* presented in this text; these basics are what will remain constant and what are essential to being a good analyst. You'll be able to apply these fundamentals long after certain companies and technologies are gone.

Finally, the best learning happens by doing. That's why this text takes a case study approach to analytics, using actual data and lots of it! We provide a companion website with access to the types of data you'll encounter as a media/audience analyst, and the cases provide the context in which you'll need to analyze data to help your organization make decisions. We devote a section toward the end of this chapter on how to best use the exercises, cases, and the companion website in order to maximize learning. Instructors have access to a full Instructor's Manual, along with solutions to exercises and cases, on the website.

Current issues and challenges addressed by this book

Current issues and challenges within the field of media analytics are plentiful. One of the most pressing issues is the lack of qualified analysts. Companies cannot fill positions fast enough to keep up with the demand for data analysis within their firms. But they do not want to fill these positions with just anyone who can run Excel and compile a few charts; they want data storytellers. More specifically, companies want people who understand the management challenges facing their industry and who can find answers to those challenges in the trends and patterns extracted from datasets—people who can interpret the data and translate findings into meaningful, relevant stories for the various stakeholders within their organization. These stories can then become recommendations for action.

Data quality is also an area of emphasis in this text, as will be further described. Responsible, accurate analysis depends on quality data and careful assessment practices. Measurement challenges abound in the dynamic digital media environment, due in large part to the rapid advance of technology. Measurement is almost always a few steps behind technology. Related to this is the challenge of definitional issues. Common definitions of such basic concepts as "viewing" and "loyalty" are not agreed upon across industry sectors. Even if they were, differences in how audiences for different types of media are measured make achieving comparable audience data across media platforms nearly impossible. Finally, various sectors and companies use different terminology for metrics. Often, the very same construct may have several definitions, or, conversely, the same word (e.g., "engagement") may be applied in dozens of ways, holding different meanings for different industry sectors and users.

Organization of this textbook

This text will describe best practices to overcome the preceding issues and other challenges faced by professional media analysts. The book is divided into three parts: Foundations of Media Analytics, Media Analytics and the Business of Media, and Media Analytics across Industry Sectors. An overview of these parts is provided here in brief, followed by an explanation of how to use this text, the cases, and website for best learning outcomes.

Foundations of Media Analytics, as the title suggests, will lay the conceptual foundations and contexts for the book. You will be introduced to the profession of media and audience analytics, the fundamentals of media economics and management, research methodology, and the art and practice of effectively communicating the insights you develop from your data. Not to worry if you have no experience with any of these processes. This first part of the book is intended to provide you with the basics you need to succeed as you work through the rest of the text. We consider the first four chapters essential reading.

The second part of the text, Media Analytics and the Business of Media, focuses on the economic engines or drivers surrounding analytics today: advertising, consumer behavior, and big data. Because advertising still is the primary method of revenue generation across most media sectors, understanding advertising is critical to understanding the field of analytics as a whole. Consider Chapter 5 essential reading also. Advertising and most content-marketing decisions are made based on consumer behavior, to which we also devote a chapter. No discussion of these topics or any analytics text today would be complete without a discussion of big data.

With the proliferation of data collection across digital platforms expanding at unsurpassed velocity and volume, industries of all types have amassed datasets of previously unimagined proportions. While the potential exists for endless data mining and insights, big datasets must be approached cautiously and responsibly. This chapter will provide an overview of the pitfalls that can occur when utilizing big data, as well as the ethical issues surrounding the use of such data. Best practices for managing and analyzing datasets are offered.

The third part of the text, Media Analytics across Industry Sectors, will delve into the specific details of various industry sectors, their measurement practices and approaches, and best analytics practices. We begin with Foundations of Audiovisual Measurement, which serves as a critical prologue to both the video and audio analytics chapters due to common concepts and practices. Following this, we explore analytics used in publishing, online and mobile, social media, news, and entertainment media.

How to use this text and get the most from it

For best results, we recommend that you read this text in the order presented. While we hope you will read it in its entirety, we know some types of media may be more relevant than others to university programs—and to your personal career ambitions. Thus, in keeping with the increasingly popular media programming strategy of allowing audiences to "Choose Your Own Adventure!," we've done that here. While we strongly recommend that you go systematically through the first five chapters, most chapters after Part 1 are written to be stand-alone so professors and students can focus on those that best fit their specific learning goals. The one exception is Chapter 8, Foundations of Audiovisual Measurement, which should be read as a necessary prologue to both Chapter 9 and Chapter 10.

Following the narrative content within each chapter, you will find discussion questions and exercises to help reinforce ideas, help you think critically, and problem-solve by applying the principles you've learned. We hope you will use them. They are designed to help you practice the most critical skill a media analyst needs: how to *think* about real-world problems and pull together the types of data you need to understand and solve them.[1]

Finally, the centerpiece of this text is the case studies and data related to the concepts presented in the chapter. These are found not in the text itself but on the text's companion website. We learn by doing, and that means playing in the data and applying the concepts in practice. Case studies have the benefit of allowing you to immediately apply what you've learned in each chapter and build your basic skills in data management and analysis. You will not gain the full benefit of this text or learn how to "do" analytics without doing some cases. Your instructor will tell you which case(s) are being assigned to you. Some might be utilized during your class period, and others may require more time and can be worked on incrementally. They could be individual or group projects.

Two important notes: First, many of the case study assignments require you to work with real media data just as you will when you are interning or working in a media analytics position. Most media firms use Microsoft Excel for routine data analysis.[2] Therefore, nearly all of the case studies that require data analysis provide the data in Excel spreadsheets, which is the only software you will need to complete them.

Software training is beyond the scope of this text. If you are not familiar with Excel, we recommend you take an online Excel training course, which many universities make available to students, faculty, and staff for free. If your university does not offer Excel training, no problem! You can easily acquire the Excel skills needed to complete the cases by viewing a few YouTube videos, Googling the specific thing you need to do, using the tutorials built into Excel in the "Help" tab, or even just by teaching yourself through trial and error. We also provide a few basic tips in Case 2.1. That said, Excel is neither a simple nor very intuitive program, and Microsoft frequently updates the program and changes the way different functions work. So if you're not already using the program, we *strongly* recommend that you not wait until an assignment is due to start trying to figure it out. Finally, the analysts we interviewed for this text said expert Excel skills were critical to their work; so consider seeking formal Excel training at some point on your journey into the profession.

Here's more good news: No statistical knowledge required here. If you can add, subtract, multiply, divide, and calculate percentages, you're all set. If you've forgotten some of those skills (percentages, we're looking at you), this is what you need:

- Small number/big number (in most instances)
- Move the decimal point two places to the right
- Round to one decimal point
- Add a percentage sign

There. You're all set for the rest of this course. Being a media analyst is not about math. It's about thinking, pattern recognition, and storytelling.

Finally, in this book, we focus on the secondary analysis of data. Secondary data is data someone else has collected. Most media analysts today work almost entirely with secondary data that has been acquired from professional research firms. While a foundation in research methodology is essential to research and is presented in Chapter 3, one chapter is not a substitute for comprehensive coursework in research methods, which we recommend that you also pursue. Many useful quantitative and qualitative methods are commonly used in primary audience research, such as surveys, experiments, focus groups, and interviews.

And now to the main attraction . . .

What are case studies?

Do you remember story problems from your early math classes? That's sort of what case studies are. Case studies are real-world or hypothetical scenarios that present challenges or problems to be solved by applying the concepts and principles you've learned. They are individual and case based; hence the name "case study." There is not always a right or wrong answer with a case; in fact, there may be multiple ways to think about a challenge and present solutions. The cases in this text are intended to help you apply what you've learned about media analytics in the various industry sectors, along with related topics, and to build your basic skills. In order to answer the questions in some of the cases, you will need to analyze the data provided on the website, some of which will be in existing table or graph formats. In other cases, you will graph the data yourself and learn to build your own data visualizations for analysis, after which you can then answer the case questions. The cases will provide guidance and tips as needed.

Other chapter features

We wish we could go into greater detail on almost everything in this text, but space just does not permit. For this reason, at the end of each chapter, there is a section called Additional Resources. Please take a deeper dive on whatever topics interest you. The resources we list will help get you started. Following this is a Discussion Questions and Exercises section. These are beneficial for in-class discussion and/or homework. Most exercises presented here are brief and can be completed in little time. Throughout the book, while we try to define many terms within the context of each chapter, you may wish to use the glossary, where you can quickly look up a definition. Terms featured in the glossary are *italicized and bolded* throughout the text. You may notice some variation across chapters in how some of these terms are used, and that is due to the media industry sector's application of the term and some lack of uniformity across sectors in term usage; however, the general definition you see in the glossary will be relevant in most instances. Other terms throughout the text are simply *italicized* and, while not in the glossary, are important for you to know. The book's index also serves as a helpful resource for cross-referencing topics and locating the page number(s) in which these topics appear. Finally and certainly not least, we hope you'll agree that the greatest asset of this textbook is the collection of case studies and datasets, which are located on the textbook's companion website. The text and website are to be used in tandem for achieving the learning outcomes needed to prepare future analysts. This password protected website URL is www.routledge.com/cw/hollifield. Once on the website, you will see instructions for how to locate the password.

A final note

This case study approach to analytics is designed to reflect not only the challenges and opportunities you will encounter in real life in your workplace but also the excitement and adventure of the field. Analytics is not really about the numbers in the datasets you examine. It's about understanding what those numbers *mean*. It's about data storytelling and converting your findings into actionable insights and recommendations for stakeholders, whether these are your CEO, sales manager, or marketing team. The best analysts are those who enjoy thinking strategically, who love solving problems, who thrill from knowing before everyone else where things are headed, and who want to know that their daily work has impact on media and society. What kinds of impact? Netflix may decide what its next original production will be based on your team's exhaustive and granular analysis of psychographic trends and preferences across genres, based on its vast consumer data. A presidential candidate in your country might turn to your analytics expertise to create effective messaging and segmentation strategies for her campaign. A major nonprofit agency could tap you to optimize fundraising on its website to help end world hunger.

Changing the world though analytics? It could happen. The practice of analytics is woven throughout most consumer and media sectors today; the strategies developed and decisions made from the analyses have real human implications. More than ever, the field needs qualified analysts— just like the one you are about to become! Best wishes as you embark upon your analytics adventure.

Notes

1. **Note to Instructors**: The discussion and exercises can be used as assignments and case studies in place of the online materials provided, where internet access is a problem.
2. Many syndicated research firms provide their clients with proprietary software to use to analyze the data that the research firm provides. But those software programs are available only to clients, require specific training to use, and vary from one research firm to another. Data scientists managing big datasets and conducting inferential analyses increasingly use *R*, which is an open-source

statistics software package and programming language. As media analysts advance in their careers, learning *R* would prove helpful but requires course-level study in itself. Python is another open-source programming language used for data analysis of large datasets. It tends to be more general purpose than *R* and not used for statistical analysis; however, it is also increasingly being used in audience research. The programs share similarities, and you would want to explore the capabilities of each to decide which would best serve your organization's needs.

Part 1

Foundations of media analytics

1 The industry and profession of media analytics

Ask most professional media analysts what they do for a living, and they'll say, "I'm a storyteller." A media analyst's job, as we heard over and over while writing this book, is to find and tell the stories that are hidden in data. Stories about what people like to watch or read or play, and how, when, and on what devices they like to watch it, read it, or play it. And *why* they like it. Why those bits and pieces of content are important in the lives of the people who use it.

Ask professional media analysts what professional skills a media analyst needs most to be successful, and the answers you hear are virtually unanimous: They need to be great writers; they need to be good storytellers; they need to be able at tell stories visually; and they need really, really excellent people skills. But being an excellent writer is always mentioned first. Does that surprise you? Most people think of media analysts as math whizzes and data nerds—the furthest personality type from storytellers and, usually, the last thing people attracted to careers in media see themselves doing. But in fact, most media analysts today spend their time serving as the liaison between the company's data scientists and top management. The media analyst is the person who looks at the data on audiences' and advertisers' choices and behaviors and figures out what the numbers *mean* in terms of strategy, which media programs or content should be greenlighted and which should be canceled, where the company should advertise its newest film or TV series, which new musical artist should get a recording contract, and which video game should be developed.

In order to do that, media analysts need more than just writing and storytelling skills, of course. They need to have a story worth telling. To have that, the media analyst needs a deep understanding of the media industry—of the *business side* of the media business. That means understanding how media businesses make money, what influences audience demand for content and advertiser demand for advertising time and space around content. It means understanding how the data being analyzed were gathered

DOI: 10.4324/9780429506956-3

or generated—and being able to tell whether you can trust the data enough to use it to make a multimillion dollar recommendation to your boss.

The job of media analyst is incredibly important in the industry and growing more so as the media industry becomes increasingly data-driven. Billions of dollars change hands every year around the world on the basis of the interpretations and recommendations that media analysts make to the top executives in media companies. Their analyses and recommendations shape the success and failure of media companies and what people see and don't see in terms of media content and even news stories.

But the senior executives who depend on media analysts have little time for long research explanations, which is where the need for great writing and storytelling skills comes in. Analysts must be able to condense findings into a few basic sentences, headlines, or bullet points to explain why a particular strategy is recommended, such as why a show should be canceled or a new subscription model offered. And those all-too-important people skills? Senior research director Heather McKinney explained, "My job is to tell my boss that his baby is ugly—and to still have my job when I'm finished."

If a career as a storyteller who influences the most important decisions made in media companies around the world, who helps shape the news and entertainment and marketing content that reaches people appeals to you, then read on. That's what this text is all about.

A growing profession

Type the term "analytics" into your favorite search engine today, and you are likely to get more than a billion results. (Yes, billions). Analytics has become more than a buzzword or frequently searched topic. The industry and profession of analytics have become vast and diverse, and you are likely to get a multitude of definitions for analytics depending on the context. Analytics can refer generally to metrics, but it can also be used in combination to describe specific fields such as business analytics, digital analytics, and the focus of this textbook, media analytics. Let's begin by defining the scope of analytics for this text.

Media analytics refers to the field and practice of media measurement, including the various metrics used in the media measurement industry and the analysis of data. Some well-known media metrics include ratings and shares (used in traditional television and radio); impressions, unique visitors, page views, time spent per page, length of sessions (in online measurement); stream starts or minutes viewed or listened to (used in online video and audio streaming, respectively) or number of downloads (used in podcasting and some video on demand); and circulation (used in the newspaper and magazine industries). Subscription media also utilize metrics, such as total subscribers or new subscribers and cancellations per month (or per quarter or year), also known as churn rate, as performance metrics. Metrics that can be used in the media space but also in the consumer space generally may also include such *key performance indicators* (*KPIs*) as monthly sales, monthly revenue, and the like. The term "KPIs" is often used interchangeably with the term "metrics," typically referring to the indicators or measurements used by a company to evaluate performance.[1]

But we will not just refer to media analytics in this text. *Audience analytics* refers to the broader field and practice of audience analysis and measurement, including the many metrics used. We often use the term "consumer analytics" interchangeably with "audience analytics" because audiences are indeed consumers—of media content or anything else. If you are a business of any kind today, you have an audience; they are your potential consumers, who hopefully will become customers. The art and practice of audience analytics, you will find, has useful application to analytics in other fields. The valuable skill set possessed by an analyst easily transcends industry sectors.

The field of analytics has evolved in multiple ways over recent years, and one particular shift is that analytics as a practice has gone mainstream. Data is[2] no longer the realm of just the company analyst or research director. Most adults are familiar with or at least exposed to analytics in a basic form, whether dealing with metrics from their personal Twitter account, tracking the number of video views on YouTube, or using Google Analytics to monitor the performance of a personal website. Beyond the "mainstreaming" of analytics, most major corporations today are now data-centric, with data being the fuel for strategic decision making. It is common to hear companies talk about being "data-driven" and relying on business intelligence for informed decision making.

Who needs analysts?

Because audience measurement has expanded beyond media content, we often use the more general terms "audience analytics" or "consumer analytics" to refer to this expanding field. Indeed, we are seeing the "datafication" of most business sectors today. Data drives value for companies in a range of areas, including helping them optimize their media mix and gain advertising efficiencies, identify consumers' interests, and help with segmentation strategies (Schlachter, 2016). Nearly 80% of media-, technology-, and marketing-related organizations surveyed in 2018 reported being data-driven at some level. However, the main obstacle for becoming more data-centric for these companies was the current talent gap of data practitioners and analysts (Winterberry Group, 2018).

Because of this talent gap, the media industry began hiring personnel from outside the industry who possessed strong analytics and data expertise in order to help media companies "catch up" on knowledge, skills, data systems, infrastructure, and processes. In the past few years, those personnel have often moved between media companies, transferring skills and making them more endemic to the industry (D. Coletti, personal communication, October 2017; July 2022). If someone possesses core analyst and research skills, many companies are willing to train them in a sector's content area, such as media. The data analytics industry has become a multidisciplinary one because the common skill set that is valuable to so many industry sectors "travels" well. The fundamentals and best practices of analytics, once learned, can be adapted and transferred to other industries, such as financial, travel, medical, retail, or insurance, just to name a few. As a result, those now entering the analytics profession quite literally have the world as their oyster.

Audience analysts vs. data scientists

Many people mistakenly use the terms "audience/consumer analysts" and "data scientists" interchangeably, assuming they are the same thing. They are not. Most audience/consumer analysts are what you might consider standard researchers who know their sector well and know how to perform basic descriptive and statistical analyses using *secondary* or *primary data*. *Data scientists* have more advanced training in how to evaluate and analyze big datasets (Chapter 7) and are usually high-level statisticians, computer scientists, or engineers. Both types of researchers are essential to successful big data initiatives. Most big data teams are multidisciplinary, as not all data scientists and statisticians are going to be familiar with the marketing and sales side that the consumer/audience analyst brings to the table or with the typical performance metrics used in the media measurement industry. Similarly, the typical analyst will not possess all of the computer science and advanced statistical skills common to big data analyses.

In recent years, as data analytics has become more important to media management, advertising, and brand management, large media corporations have started hiring data scientists to manage data analysis. But as you will read repeatedly throughout this text, figuring out what data say—the job of data scientists—is only the first step. What matters is what the data *mean*. Understanding what they mean requires a deep understanding of media economics, strategic media management, media industry trends, technology trends, trends in audience preferences and behaviors, and the creative aspects of media content development and distribution. Bringing expertise on *those* topics to the interpretation of data output is the job of professional media analysts—and the difference between being a media analyst and a data scientist. This book is designed to help prepare people for careers in media analytics. But as media analysts and data scientists continue to work together on big data opportunities, it is important for each to be conversant in the other's "language" and understand their capabilities and expertise areas. That way, each can complement the other and communicate what is needed to successfully undertake a company's big data objectives (Chapter 7).

Industry demand

Demand for analysts is strong, and many employers cannot fill advertised roles fast enough. More than 88% of marketing and media organizations surveyed in 2016 stated that data analytics was the area where they faced the greatest need for "enhanced resources," yet only a third of these companies felt their teams possessed the expertise and training needed to carry out the firm's data-driven initiatives (Winterberry Group, 2016, p. 13). There is a shortage of qualified personnel, so industry experts report that the most significant challenge is "how to develop and nurture a corps of marketing and media professionals who embed certain fundamental data skillsets" (Winterberry Group, 2018, p. 28).

The US Bureau of Labor Statistics tracks job trends and concurs that market research analysts are in high demand. Projected job growth in this role is 22% for 2020–2030, whereas average growth rate for all jobs is 8% (US Bureau of Labor Statistics, 2022). Analyst job titles can significantly vary by industry sector and even by organization, so it's important not to get too caught up in the specifics of any particular job title. The key is to look for which skills and competencies are being requested and then assess whether you believe you are a potential match. If data continues to be generated at the current pace or greater, there is no doubt the future will continue to be bright for those in the analytics profession. There will be more data and more demand for trained professionals to analyze and interpret that data.

Salaries vary based on the nature of the analyst's role, expertise, and experience level, but a sampling of job titles and salaries as reported by Glassdoor US can be found in Table 1.1. The more senior the role (e.g., placing the term "senior" in front of any of these job titles, suggesting a higher experience level), the higher the salary. Also, as noted earlier, the role of data scientist or big data analyst typically requires more advanced training than a typical analyst, which is also reflected in the average salary, usually well over six figures.

Table 1.1 Annual Salaries by Job Title as Reported by Glassdoor (June 2019)

Job title	Salary in US $
Account manager	$65,069
Big data engineer, analytics	$123,558
Brand analyst	$59,992
Brand manager	$96,333
Data analyst	$67,377
Data scientist	$117,345
Digital media analyst	$55,579
Digital media manager	$50,000–$75,000 (est.)
Media analyst	$55,579
Media planner/media supervisor	$51,000–$65,000 (est.)
Market researcher	$52,149
Campaign manager/media buyer/audience development	$65,000–$80,000 (est.)
Market analyst	$60,823.00
Business intelligence analyst	$61,000–$83,000 (est.)
Consumer insights analyst	$62,000–$91,000 (est.)
Social media research analyst	$46,000–$66,000 (est.)
Social media marketing manager	$50,000–$56,000 (est.)

Source: www.glassdoor.com

Where analysts are needed

Within the media and consumer realm, there are endless types of organizations that employ analysts. Among these are major media entities that own diverse kinds of media content units (e.g., The Walt Disney Company, Warner Bros. Discovery, Paramount); social media companies (e.g., Meta/Facebook, Twitter, and Google, including YouTube); research divisions of major corporations such as Amazon, Coca-Cola, Procter & Gamble, and Walmart; brand and advertising agencies; public relations firms; and, of course, measurement companies themselves (such as Nielsen, Comscore, or Kantar Media). Job titles are wide-ranging, but a sampling of actual job titles for analyst roles within the media and consumer realm can be found in Box 1.1. It's important to note that job titles are not always uniform from one organization to the next. For instance, what digital analysts or brand analysts do at one company may not be identical to what they do at another. Nevertheless, these job titles are common ones for people trained as analysts. Similarly, data analysis may not be the primary job in some of these positions, such as "Account Manager." But the basic thinking and skills of a media analyst are still necessary for success in those roles.

Box 1.1 Sampling of job titles in media and consumer analytics

Media researcher	Research analyst
Media buyer	Research insights director
Audience researcher	Brand analyst
Audience analyst	Social media analyst
Audience insights analyst	Digital analyst
Audience development manager	Digital marketing analyst
Account manager	Product development researcher
Brand researcher	Political researcher
Brand manager	Campaign analyst
Market researcher	Data analyst
Consumer analyst	Business analyst
Consumer behavior analyst	Project analyst
Consumer insights analyst	Entertainment industry analyst
Content data analyst	Data visualization analyst

Media analytics industry structure

Before delving into the nature of analysts' work, it is important to understand the structure and major entities playing a role in the broader media analytics industry. There are three primary actors: media researchers, syndicated media research firms, and independent media auditing firms.

Media research divisions

Most large media companies as well as local media outlets have a research department. These are individuals and teams of individuals whose focus is to conduct strategic data analysis on the specific questions that a particular media company needs answered in order to maximize its success and profitability. Examples may include major video streaming services, national television networks, cable entertainment networks, local radio stations or newspapers, Hollywood film studios, video gaming companies, and even book publishers. No matter the media product, media analysts at these firms are interested in optimizing their companies' performance. They use data to identify strengths and weaknesses and, in the case of the latter, to fix the problems.

Syndicated media research firms

Another segment of the media analytics industry involves companies whose job it is to measure media consumption by audiences. Comscore, Nielsen,

and Kantar are examples of *syndicated research firms*. Media organizations rely on valid, reliable measurement of audiences so that advertisers
can feel confident in the audience data used as industry *currency* for transactions with advertisers. Audience ratings, shares, total viewership, total
users, and total listenership are just a few of the types of metrics used to
assess audience size and behavior. In order to remain neutral, syndicated
media measurement firms are independent third parties, and their sole job
is to provide trustworthy data to clients. These firms are in the information
business, and they sell syndicated reports and services to subscribers (such
as TV networks) for a fee. Audience measurement can be an expensive
process, so the informational products sold by these media measurement
firms pay for the cost of data collection, processing, and reporting. Many
of these firms also conduct custom research for clients.

Auditing bodies: Measurement industry oversight

In order to ensure the *validity* and *reliability* of media measurement tools
and processes, a third actor comes into play in the analytics industry,
and these are auditing bodies. They are independent third parties whose
responsibility is to evaluate the quality of measurement by the syndicated
firms. The Alliance for Audited Media (AAM) audits North American publications' claims about their print and digital circulation sizes on behalf of
advertisers. The US-based Media Rating Council (MRC) audits the tools,
techniques, and services, including those used by syndicated research firms,
that are used to measure video, audio, and digital audiences, with successful audits resulting in accreditation.

Many countries around the globe have similar auditing bodies. These
independent bodies will be discussed more later, but submitting a media
measurement tool or service to an audit by one of these services is not
typically required by the media industry of a particular country. Rather,
it is a choice of the media measurement firm. The process can be long and
expensive, but if an audit results in successful accreditation of the measurement tool or service, it increases the credibility of that tool or service
with potential media and advertising clients. Accreditation gives advertisers confidence in their media buying decisions.

Other actors also use media research data, including advertising and
branding agencies, as well as media buyers. These actors work on the "buy
side" of the industry, seeking opportunities for clients who wish to place
advertising and marketing messages within media content, something also
referred to as buying inventory, spots, or placement.

Nature of analyst roles and work

What does a typical analyst do? While there are commonalities to most
analyst roles, actual duties and responsibilities depend on the type of

analyst and the industry. A media analyst/researcher will often examine different types of data and reports, as well as run various analyses to determine media content performance. The assortment of activities for a media researcher is wide, including such things as:

- Analyzing ratings, circulation, and sales reports,
- Conducting a longitudinal analysis of a media company's performance to identify areas of weakness and opportunity,
- Examining syndicated shows within a local market to recommend whether to renew a particular program or audience consumption of particular types of publication or online content to determine whether changes are necessary,
- Analyzing content performance to identify the best placements for a particular advertiser (for the sales team to then pitch for a media buy),
- Forecasting a media company's future revenue stream based on such things as subscriber churn and pricing tiers,
- Identifying trends in consumer preferences for specific types of content, including regional, seasonality, and weather patterns for different parts of the country,
- Preparing reports on any of these topics over a given time period, whether monthly, quarterly, or at some other frequency.

On the digital side, the media researcher may track performance of video or audio streams and downloads, as well as website traffic and metrics. Media analysts should be comfortable interpreting data from all types of media platforms—both linear and digital—in order to understand not only the holistic picture of audience consumption but also how media and consumer behavior fit together. The industry has often been described in terms of its "silos" (video, audio, online, etc.). While those silos are disappearing, they are not gone. A media conglomerate still wants to know how its individual properties perform, whether they are a television network, a website, or a mobile application ("app"), and to know how to optimize the performance of each one. So while breadth of knowledge is critical, analytics experts say it's still important to have depth of knowledge in a given silo or platform. Having someone who is deeply involved in one of these silos (such as mobile or video) is vital to an organization, as he or she can guide the organization and expertly interpret that data in context.

In the consumer analytics realm, roles also vary. A brand analyst or social media researcher might do a *sentiment analysis* on social media chatter to detect trends in consumer opinions about a brand, program, or other types of content and then make strategic recommendations to management on what to do. An analyst working in retail might track online sales for various product categories to see how demand is changing. That information might be used to maximize sales or improve efficiency by shifting inventory. A consumer behavior analyst might design research where data is collected through observing how people shop in stores, what types of packaging and shelf placement capture their attention, or even how they actually use the products they buy in their day-to-day lives.

The nature and challenges of media measurement firms

The syndicated research industry is made up of independent firms that measure and report media consumption and then sell that information to clients. Nielsen, Comscore, Kantar, IBOPE, and Ipsos are just a few examples of the many syndicated research firms that exist around the world. In the complex 21st century media world, large, syndicated research firms need to have expertise in many different areas. They hire engineers to develop technologies and software that can measure media consumption; data scientists and social scientists to develop statistical modeling and analyze the incoming data; sales personnel to deal with clients; and still other scientists to explore how new developments in fields such as psychology and neuroscience might be applied to audience measurement. Many of these companies are global in nature and even do business with regional partners.

In the United States, the syndicated research industry was fairly stable during the last half of the 20th century. Basically, the Alliance for Audited Media[3] audited publications' circulation, while Nielsen measured television audiences and Arbitron measured radio. The advertising and sales side of the industry liked the simplicity of having one provider on which industry advertising deals would be transacted, instead of dueling sets of numbers. But having a sole provider and no competition had its downsides; industry stakeholders often complained that these syndicated research companies did not innovate quickly enough to measure emerging media platforms. Fast forward to today, and, like the technology driving media consumption and metrics, these syndicated providers are also now in flux! Challengers like Comscore have arrived, and others keep coming. Some will survive and others will not.

One of the biggest challenges in the syndicated research industry is balancing the need to stay current with the latest technologies, understand and track audience migration and consumer behavior, and attend to client needs and preferences for measurement tools and services across emerging platforms, all while staying on budget. Not all technologies are adopted by consumers, so some time is typically needed to assess whether a particular media platform will be around long enough to devote resources toward its measurement. Once a decision is made to develop a measurement system and tools for the new consumption device or technology platform, such a process requires research, more time, and significant financial and human resources. As a result, industry demand for measurement often comes sooner than the measurement industry can respond and can cost more than some clients are willing to pay.

Accuracy vs. cost

One point that measurement firms are quick to emphasize is that greater accuracy is almost always possible with current technology, but that, paradoxically, the industry doesn't always want the latest tool. More advanced, accurate, and sophisticated methods have been developed by media measurement firms than are typically adopted by clients, who don't want to pay more, even for better quality data. More sophisticated methods and technologies come with higher price tags for the syndicated reports and for other audience information sold by the media measurement firms, and media companies and advertising agencies are on a budget like everyone else. Most do not want to pay more for metrics than is absolutely necessary. So, despite industry pleas for greater accuracy, many decide—when they see the price tag—that the metrics they already have are "good enough."

Accuracy vs. resistance

Another area of industry pushback when it comes to accuracy, interestingly, is the fear of change in the numbers themselves. With increased accuracy comes a shift in ratings or viewership (or listenership or readership) numbers, with some going up and others going down. In other words, some content providers will be winners, while others will be losers. So, rather than risk being a loser in this scenario, some content companies dispute the new numbers when new measurement systems are released. (Of course, if a company's numbers go up, they must certainly be correct, and there are no complaints!) An example of this industry pushback with clear winners and losers came with the introduction of Nielsen's *People Meter* in the United States in the late 1980s to measure national audience ratings (Barnes & Thomson, 1994) and with the *Local People Meters* in the early 2000s, when the technology was rolled out for local markets (Ahrens, 2004; Cook, 2004; Wired Staff, 2004). Broadcast network ratings declined overall by an average of 4.5 rating points (Adams, 1994) when the meters were first introduced, while cable network ratings rose almost 20% (Adams, 1994). Specialized or niche networks particularly benefitted from the People Meter, which showed advertisers that niche content like sports and music networks delivered more demographically homogeneous audiences. Advertisers had a much clearer idea of whom they were reaching, thus making audience segmentation possible. That made niche networks more popular with advertisers, which brought more revenue to those cable networks (Barnes & Thomson, 1994).

Arbitron's introduction of its **Portable People Meter** (**PPM**) also met resistance with concerns surrounding the measurement of minority audiences. An MRC audit revealed Hispanic and African-American listeners were being undercounted. Among the methodological flaws uncovered was that only half of the sample provided data, and only a subset of that was usable data (Bachman, 2009; Shagrin & Warfield, 2009). Radio stations with high minority listenership, along with their owners, stood to lose with lower, untrustworthy audience figures (Shagrin & Warfield, 2009). This is just one example of how measurement technologies are not truly benign (Napoli, 2010). The metrics produced from the data, if not representative of the audience, can present a distorted view of audience preferences, which in turn, can impact what types of content gets produced and for whom.

Competition vs. single currency

Despite their resistance to change and measurement, industry executives often criticize the big measurement firms for not innovating quickly enough to develop measurement systems and metrics for new, emerging devices and media platforms. Indeed, when a single company is considered the *currency* for the industry (such as Nielsen with television), the lack of competition can be a deterrent to developing new metrics quickly. Historically, having a single measurement provider has kept things simple for transactions, much like a single monetary currency does within a country, but initiatives for new metrics certainly take root. Competitive industry efforts can often apply the right amount of pressure, launching their own initiatives to encourage the larger or established measurement firms to move faster.

Measurement around the globe

Because audience data is the currency of media companies everywhere, media analytics is a growing profession globally. You will find different measurement service providers and methods in various parts of the world, but some form of the industry can be found in most places. Some US-based measurement firms provide services outside the United States, either solely or in partnership with another company. Other countries use their own domestic measurement firms or other global measurement firms that are not found elsewhere. For instance, OzTAM is the dominant video measurement firm for Australia, and IBOPE is a firm that services much of Latin America, as does Kantar Media, along with several parts of Europe and Asia. In addition to Nielsen and Comscore, GfK, Ipsos, TNS, AGB, and Gallup are other companies that provide measurement services in whole or in partnership with others globally. Many audience measurement firms from various parts of the world share best practices and learnings at meetings and through alliances. One such initiative is the Global Alliance for the Measurement of Media Audiences (GAMMA), comprised of firms from France, Canada, India, and Japan. Their objectives include creating a common technical framework for digital platforms, as well as working on common audience measurement initiatives, with goals of greater global standardization and efficiency (egta, 2021).

Industry oversight

Because billions of advertising dollars are at stake in the buying and selling of audiences that can affect the financial survival of media companies, the validity and accuracy of measurement is paramount. The Alliance for Audited Media (AAM) and the Media Rating Council are the two major oversight bodies in the United States. They both exist to audit the tools, technology, and methods used to measure audiences so that the audience data on which millions of dollars in advertising and content rights changes hands each year can be trusted by the parties on all sides.

AAM was the first audience data auditing company established in the United States. It was created in 1914 when a group of advertisers, advertising agencies, and publishers got together to create a nonprofit cooperative to verify publications' circulation claims (Bennett, 1965). Then called the Audit Bureau of Circulations (ABC), the organization changed its name to the Alliance of Audited Media in 2012 to reflect the increasing importance of digital distribution to its membership. The AAM's goal is "delivering authentic, credible data to the market" and "setting universal benchmarks for media transparency and excellence" (Alliance for Audited Media, 2022). AAM and the metrics it uses to audit publishing companies are discussed in detail in Chapter 11.

Established in the 1960s by the US Congress as a means of industry self-regulation, the Media Rating Council (MRC) has three main objectives. According to its website, these purposes are to "secure for the media industry and related users audience measurement services that are valid, reliable and effective; evolve and determine minimum disclosure and ethical criteria for media audience measurement services" and to "provide and administer an audit system designed to inform users as to whether such audience measurements are conducted in conformance with the criteria and procedures developed" (Media Rating Council, n.d.).

The body serves measurement firms that are submitting their measurement tools and processes for review and accreditation, as well as the firms that are members of MRC and financially support it. These members include television networks, cable companies, websites and online content providers, as well as advertising agencies and advertisers themselves, including international members. Media measurement companies—such as Nielsen and Comscore—are not permitted to be members, as these are the companies being evaluated. The MRC is an impartial entity, and this is one way it maintains its neutrality. Media measurement companies are not required to submit their tools and methods to the MRC to be rated—it's voluntary—but for advertisers deciding whether to buy time or space from a media company, it is a big deal whether the audience data were gathered through MRC-accredited research.

Auditing and accreditation

The auditing and accreditation processes are long, arduous and can take months, depending on the case. *Accreditation* refers to the desired outcome of an audit. If accreditation is received, it means that the measurement company has "passed the standards test," receiving what is akin to the Media Rating Council's seal of approval for the product or service being evaluated. It means that a neutral body, the MRC, along with its third-party auditors, have carefully reviewed every detail of the product or process brought forward for accreditation, that they have ruled it to be a valid, acceptable method of testing, and that users can place faith and confidence in the measurement results generated by that product.

An *audit* is the long and detailed evaluation process used to determine whether a product or tool should receive accreditation, i.e., become known as an "accredited service." Even after the initial accreditation, audits can occur again at regular intervals to re-evaluate the product or tool, to ensure that it is still valid and acceptable. It is much like a recertification process. Audits can also be expensive, with some audits costing a measurement firm into the seven-figure range; the lowest price tag is around US $75,000 (G. Ivie, personal communication, June 2022). It should be noted that the MRC does not charge a fee for audits and accreditation services; this is one way it remains a neutral body. Members pay dues to the MRC for its operation. The costs of an audit are simply those costs associated with paying independent auditing firms (who perform the auditing work for MRC) and their certified public accountants (CPAs). Some of the largest audits require the services of several CPAs for thousands of hours of work.

Establishing standards

Another role played by AAM and the MRC, particularly as technology evolves, is one of establishing new standards. For instance, there were no standards for measuring digital audiences in traditional publishing companies and no streaming audio and video measurement standards when the streaming or *OTT* (*"over-the-top"*) industry emerged as a result of broadband technology. Similarly, there were no measurement standards for online advertisements to ensure that they were viewable by users until the MRC stepped in to develop these. The oversight bodies and industry associations have worked together to develop standards for digital measurement that are as consistent as possible across different platforms. These standards serve as guidelines to the industry as to what is expected regarding fair play in the new technological environment, such as what constitutes a valid "count" for content consumption, and whether that count refers to a "view," web page visit, or other. Both oversight bodies provide education to the industry through seminars as well in order to help the industry develop best practices. Such seminars have included topics such as sample design, response rates, digital measurement and compliance, and audit testing and validation. The AAM offers membership to Canadian media companies, while the MRC provides auditing services to measurement firms outside the United States, including China, Mexico, and Brazil. More information about both oversight bodies can be found in Additional Resources.

The oversight procedures for verifying media audience data developed in the United States have gone on to influence the establishment of similar media measurement evaluation bodies in other parts of the world. Indeed, the MRC is looked upon by industry leaders in other countries as providing much needed expertise, and other countries have established and modeled their own accreditation bodies after the MRC. Some examples of these "sibling" accreditation or measurement standards bodies are JICWEBS in the United Kingdom, the Consejo de Investigación de Medios in Mexico, and the China Media Assessment Council in Asia. An international organization of media audit bureaus also exists, known as the International Federation of Audit Bureaux of Certification (IFABC). Similarly, multiple Audit Bureaus of Circulations (ABC) exist around the world. They have traditionally been dedicated to counting and reporting circulation figures of publications; however, these bureaus' roles have now expanded to digital publishing, online readership measurement, and cross-media verification.

The analytics industry and ethics

You don't have to look far these days to find a news story about consumer data hacks, privacy breaches, or use of personal data without permission. With more data access and computer systems seemingly more susceptible to breaches from hackers, it is a legitimate concern. The practice of analytics is a balancing act when it comes to what information and how much of that information is needed and useful for companies. On the one hand, knowing more about a customer enables a company to serve that customer better, to recommend specific content or products to her, to serve her the most relevant advertisements, and to deliver certain offers that could save her money or be timely. Many customers appreciate the relevant *microtargeting* that is made possible by audience/consumer analytics. However, others are less comfortable with such practices and may instead feel stalked by brands' microtargeting efforts. One's personal comfort level with analytics as a part of the consumer experience can indeed vary by individual.

But such an ethical conundrum begs questions in a textbook about analytics: How much information is too much information, and how much is truly essential to serve consumers well? The answer to this question may very well depend on whom you ask. However, one way to think about this is through the filter of the type of information being shared. Health information is more sensitive than most consumer product information and is normally quite protected, yet such information has been accessed without consumer knowledge. *The Washington Post* reported on a popular health app that some women use to track their pregnancies. While this is highly sensitive information, and some women have willingly shared health details within the app in exchange for the benefit of its services, what are the possible consequences of such information being compromised or accessed by the wrong parties? In this case, the woman's employer was able to access personal health information about her pregnancy, much to her shock (Harwell, 2019). Yet some consumer information, if compromised, can have serious consequences as well. Credit card numbers, account information, and even product purchase details can not only violate consumer privacy but result in possible identity theft and financial disaster.

As referenced elsewhere in this book, the European Union has taken a more stringent stance than other parts of the world when it comes to consumer data protection and privacy. The *General Data Protection Regulation (GDPR)* went into effect in 2018 and has altered the way businesses operate online, not just in Europe but around the world, as it applies to any organization handling the personal data of European Union residents, regardless of the company's location (Wolford, n.d.). Other provisions of the GDPR include stronger consumer consent conditions including more understandable language for data usage and privacy policies, mandatory consumer notifications of any breaches within 72 hours, the right for consumers to access their data collected by the company, the consumer's "right to be forgotten" or data erasure, and other provisions. Heavy fines are levied on companies that violate the GDPR (GDPR.EU, n.d.; Wolford, n.d.).

Codes of ethics and analytics professional certifications

In an effort to standardize best ethical practices, codes of ethics for analytics professionals have materialized, as have certifications, which can act as a "seal of approval" by the industry to ensure that analytics professionals operate within these certified ethical guidelines. Organizations offering a code of ethics or professional code of conduct include the Digital Analytics Association (see Figure 1.1) and the Data Science Association. Ethical

The Code of Ethics

As a Web Analyst, my views regarding ethical conduct are my own and do not necessarily reflect the views of my clients/employer. I hereby agree to personally follow the Web Analyst's Code of Ethics regarding consumer data collected on any digital property I work on, with, or for:

PRIVACY – I agree to hold consumer data in the highest regard and will do everything in my power to keep personally identifiable consumer data safe, secure and private. To this end I will never knowingly transfer, release, or otherwise distribute personally identifiable information (PII) gathered through digital channels to any third-party without express permission from the consumer(s) who generated the data. I will also work with my clients/employer where applicable to enforce a cookie and user identification policy that is appropriate and respectful of the consumer experience.

TRANSPARENCY – I agree to encourage full disclosure of my clients/employer consumer data collection practices and to encourage communication of how that data will be used in clear and understandable language. To this end I will work with my clients/employer to ensure that the privacy policy is up-to-date and provides a clear and truthful reflection of our collection, use and storage policies towards digitally collected data. Without divulging proprietary or competitive information, I will be transparent, honest, and forthright regarding the data collected and how it is used to improve the overall consumer and customer experience online.

CONSUMER CONTROL – I agree to inform and empower consumers to opt out of my clients/employer data collection practices and to document ways to do this. To this end I will work to ensure that consumers have a means to opt out and to ensure that they are removed from tracking when requested. Further, I will do my best to use tracking and browser-based technologies in the way they were designed and not otherwise circumvent consumer control over their browsing experience.

EDUCATION – I agree to educate my clients/employer about the types of data collected, and the potential risks to consumers associated with those data. To this end I will make every effort to inform my peers of the commitment to data privacy and to educate staff, especially senior management, of current data collection capabilities, data definitions, and potential data risks. Further, I will educate my clients/employer about how these technologies could be perceived of as invasive.

ACCOUNTABILITY – I agree to act as a steward of customer data and to uphold the consumers' right to privacy as governed by my clients/employer and applicable laws and regulations. To this end I will work with appropriate teams as necessary to ensure that data access lists are up-to-date and that anyone with access to these systems understands how that data can and cannot be used. I will do my best to comply with all practices governing ethical use of consumer data.

Figure 1.1 The Web Analyst's Code of Ethics

Source: Credit: Digital Analytics Association; Eric T. Peterson & John Lovett and refined by numerous members of the DAA, the DAA Standards Committee, and the Digital Measurement community at large

guidelines are also offered by the Institute for Operations Research and the Management Sciences (INFORMS), which also offers an analytics professional certification program (INFORMS, n.d.). Some individual analytics firms have written their own codes as well (Blast Analytics & Marketing, 2019).

Staying current in the industry

Be aware that media analytics as a media profession also has its own professional trade press, including free electronic newsletters. Media-Post's "Research Intelligencer" and "Data Leaders Brief" are two examples. Research companies like Nielsen and Comscore also send out free e-newsletters to clients and others interested in their work. One of the best ways to prepare yourself now for a future role as an analyst, as well as to stay informed and current with happenings in the industry, is to subscribe to these and read the trade publications regularly. Keep in mind that the professionals you read about in these articles are your potential future employers, so knowing who they are and what companies they work for is a great way to start career planning and networking! Also consider signing up for the many free webinars about industry trends and developments. (Hint: These are not only great ways to understand and anticipate where the industry is headed, but, when you are armed with this valuable information, you can be more competitive for that next opportunity.) We recommend some trade publications in the Additional Resources section, but there are many more out there than we can list. Go search.

Summary and conclusion

We often hear from students, "I don't like math." We have good news for you! While numbers are certainly involved, as you have now seen, analytics is more about seeing numbers for what they represent—trends, patterns, and stories that are worth telling—to help media firms and content creators better understand their audiences. It's storytelling with data. What story does your data tell, and what stories do your managers need to hear? What are the key takeaways from the data you analyze, and what *insights* can you glean about your audience? Based on your analysis and interpretation, what recommendations do you have for your managers? What should they do tomorrow, next week, or next month to help the business?

This is a rapidly evolving field due to technological change, which alters audience behavior, preferences, and device usage. Measurement and audience analysis need to keep pace to help the industry thrive. This means not only that the field of analytics is more critical than ever; so are industry oversight and ethical decision making. You can be a part of that process.

Finally, analysts are in demand around the globe and in nearly every industry sector. If you are curious, ask good questions, allow knowledge to lead the way, and possess strong communication and people skills, you are well-positioned for a promising career in the media and consumer analytics industries. With so much data, firms will be ready to welcome you to their team. Let the adventure begin!

Additional resources

Alliance for Audited Media: https://auditedmedia.com/
Media Rating Council: mediaratingcouncil.org
Grady, D. (Ed). (2020). *The golden age of data: media analytics in study and practice*. BEA Series. Routledge.

Suggested trade publications

MediaPost: www.mediapost.com
Cynopsis Media: www.cynopsis.com
Games Industry.biz: www.gamesindustry.biz
Variety: www.variety.com
The Hollywood Reporter: www.hollywoodreporter.com
AdAge: www.adage.com
Radio+Televison Business Report: www.rbr.com
Broadcasting & Cable: www.nexttv.com/broadcasting-cable
Podcast Magazine: https://podcastmagazine.com
Radio Ink: https://radioink.com/

Recommended cases

These cases can be found on the textbook website: www.routledge.com/cw/hollifield

Case 1.1: The Analytics Job Market
Case 1.2 (12.3): Accreditation of a New Media Measurement Tool
Case 1.3: Collecting Qualitative Secondary Data for a Trends Analysis

Case studies, along with accompanying datasets for this chapter, can be found on the text website. We particularly suggest the preceding cases. See the companion website and instructor's manual for detailed descriptions of these and other relevant cases.

Discussion questions and exercises

1. After reading this chapter, what are your reactions? Has it changed your understanding of how the media analytics profession and the syndicated research industries work? What areas of this profession interest you most as a place you would like to start your career? What do you see as the personal strengths you would bring to the job of media analyst? Where do you see your weaknesses, that is, the areas where you would most need to build you skills? What parts of the job do you think you would find most fun? What aspects of this industry and profession most excite you? Concern you? Why? What else would you like to know more about? Make notes of your answers and revisit them after you've finished this class.

2. Audience and consumer privacy has become a major topic of concern and discussion around the world. Yet the field of analytics, at its core, involves gathering data to learn more about audience behavior and preferences. Is it ethical to conduct audience analytics? Should we be gathering information about audiences at all? Why or why not?

3. Many privacy regulations have gone into place in various parts of the world. Conduct some research on a few of these. Suggestions include the European Union's General Data Protection Regulation (GDPR) and the California Consumer Privacy Act (CCPA).

   a. What are some of the major provisions of these laws and regulations? As an individual, do you agree with them? Why or why not?
   b. Now put yourself in the place of an online media content company, online retailer, or other consumer brand that conducts business online. How do you feel about these privacy laws and regulations?

4. *Exercise: Measuring media around the world*

   For this exercise, you will be conducting some online research and writing a brief report. Select a country other than the United States, and do some online research to find out what companies serve as the major audience measurement providers in that country. Your report should focus on video and audio sector measurement, but you are welcome to report on more. Find out all you can about how the audience data is gathered, how often it is gathered, and how it is reported and used in that country's media marketplace.

   Second, conduct research for that same country to find out whether there is an accreditation body like the Media Rating Council (MRC) in the United States. What is the name of it? What does this organization oversee and do? Does it have a formal auditing and accreditation process? What types of media measurement tools and processes does the body review? What is the nature of the review process? Be sure to include proper citations and references for your report.

Notes

1. However, this interchangeable usage is not universal and can vary by organization, as metrics can also refer to something quite specific.
2. The term "data" has historically been a plural noun of the singular form of the Latin word *datum*. In recent years, however, the terms "data" and "big data" have evolved, now increasingly used and accepted as an "uncountable" noun (e.g., water, information), particularly when referring to the singular phenomenon of data or big data. We do so here and elsewhere in the text where appropriate, also giving the term a singular verb ("is"). We may utilize "data" in its plural form when referring to specific data (e.g., when conducting a specific analysis) and give it a plural verb in such instances, although many people now treat data as a singular form in this case as well.
3. Then called the Audit Bureau of Circulations (ABC). ABC changed its name in 2012.

References

Adams, W. J. (1994). Changes in ratings patterns for prime time before, during, and after the introduction of the People Meter. *Journal of Media Economics*, 7(2), 15–28. https://doi.org/10.1207/s15327736me0702_2

Ahrens, F. (2004, June 11). Nielsen sued over TV ratings method. *The Washington Post*. www.washingtonpost.com/archive/business/2004/06/11/nielsen-sued-over-tv-ratings-method/8eacd4d8-c0fe-49b2-9477-4dcc05ff67f0/?utm_term=.bc8410a59cdb

Alliance for Audited Media. (2022). *About AAM: Who we are*. https://auditedmedia.com/about/who-we-are

Bachman, K. (2009, July 14). Florida A.G. files suit against Arbitron. *AdWeek*. www.adweek.com/tv-video/florida-ag-files-suit-against-arbitron-112885/

Barnes, B., & Thomson, L. (1994). Power to the people (meter): Audience measurement technology and media specialization. In J. Ettema & C. Whitney (Eds.), *Audiencemaking: How the media create the audience* (pp. 75–94). Sage.

Bennett, C. O. (1965). *Facts without opinion: First fifty years of the Audit Bureau of Circulations*. Audit Bureau of Circulations.

Blast Analytics & Marketing. (2019). *Blast analytics and marketing code of ethics*. www.blastam.com/code-of-ethics

Cook, J. (2004, June 20). Nielsen under fire for using people meters. *Chicago Tribune*. www.chicagotribune.com/news/ct-xpm-2004-06-20-0406200140-story.html

egta. (2021, June). *Egta insight: Advances in hybrid TV audience measurement*. www.egta.com/uploads/000_publications/2021_egta_insight_vam.pdf

GDPR.EU. (n.d.). *General Data Protection Regulation*. https://gdpr.eu/article-33-notification-of-a-personal-data-breach/

Harwell, D. (2019, April 10). Is your pregnancy app sharing intimate data with your boss? *The Washington Post*. www.washingtonpost.com/technology/2019/04/10/tracking-your-pregnancy-an-app-may-be-more-public-than-you-think/?utm_term=.bbd495c847ba

INFORMS. (n.d.). *INFORMS ethics guidelines*. www.informs.org/About-INFORMS/Governance/INFORMS-Ethics-Guidelines

Media Rating Council. (n.d.). www.mediaratingcouncil.org/

Napoli, P. (2010). *Audience evolution: New technologies and the transformation of media audiences*. Columbia University Press.

Schlachter, R. (2016, November 17). Break down your silos: Unleash the power of data. *IAB*. www.iab.com/news/break-silos-unleash-power-data/

Shagrin, C., & Warfield, C. (2009, October 1). Arbitron's flawed ratings hurt minority radio. *The Hill*. https://thehill.com/opinion/op-ed/61241-arbitrons-flawed-ratings-hurt-minority-radio

US Bureau of Labor Statistics. (2022). *Occupational outlook handbook, market research analysts*. US Department of Labor. www.bls.gov/ooh/business-and-financial/market-research-analysts.htm

Winterberry Group. (2016, September). *The data-centric organization: Transforming the next generation of audience marketing*. www.winterberrygroup.com/our-insights/data-centric-organization-transforming-next-generation-audience-marketing

Winterberry Group. (2018, February). *The data-centric organization 2018*. www.iab.com/wp-content/uploads/2018/02/DMA-IAB-Winterberry-Group-The-Data-Centric-Org-2018-February-2018.pdf

Wired Staff. (2004, April 16). Nielsen 'People Meters' draw fire. *Wired*. www.wired.com/2004/04/nielsen-people-meters-draw-fire/

Wolford, B. (n.d.). What is GDPR, the EU's new data protection law? *GDPR.EU*. https://gdpr.eu/what-is-gdpr/

2 Fundamentals of media economics and management

Media analytics is about solving problems. The problems are managerial and economic problems because the primary job of media managers is to maximize the media company's *profitability* or, if the media organization is nonprofit, its resources. Whether a media manager is managing content development, news, human resources, marketing, promotions, public relations, advertising, or some other business function, all decisions lead back to the central mission of maximizing the organization's profitability or financial sustainability. The media analyst's job is to use data to figure out the best way to support that goal in each area of the media company's operations.

Thus it is critical for media analysts to understand the fundamentals of *media economics* and *management*. This chapter will provide an overview of the key economic and management issues that media analysts must understand. Entire books have been written about media economics and management respectively, so, of course, this will provide only the briefest introduction. But it will give you the basic understanding you will need to work the problems and cases in the rest of the book.

Media business models

The first principle of media economics and management is this: Commercial media companies are not in business to create amazing content, to inform us, to entertain us, or to serve the public interest. Most media companies are in business to make money—that is, *profits*.

So the obvious question is how do media companies make money? That depends on the type of media content a media company produces. Different media industry sectors use different *business models* (Box 2.1). But most media companies use business models that depend heavily on one or more of the following *revenue models*: (1) advertising, (2) subscriptions, or (3) direct sales of content to customers, such as through film ticket sales, downloads, books, etc.

DOI: 10.4324/9780429506956-4

A revenue model refers to each major activity a company does to bring in money. A company's business model refers to the combination of revenue models the company uses. Most companies build their business model around one or just a few revenue models, and those models can change over time as business conditions or the industry changes.

Box 2.1 Primary revenue models for media industry sectors

Medium	Primary revenue models[a,b]
Newspapers	(1) Subscription and direct sales (2) Local and national advertising
Magazines	(1) Subscription and direct sales (2) Advertising
Digital native media organizations	(1) National advertising (2) Local advertising
Local terrestrial radio broadcasting	(1) Local advertising
Satellite radio	(1) Subscriptions (2) National advertising
Podcasting	(1) National advertising
Broadcast television networks	(1) National advertising (2) Program syndication
Local television stations	(1) Local advertising (2) National spot advertising
Cable MSOs[c]/satellite TV services	(1) Cable/satellite TV subscriptions (2) National advertising (3) Local advertising sold by local cable company
Cable/satellite television networks	(1) Revenue from cable/satellite subscription fees from distributors that carry the network (2) National advertising
Premium Cable network services	(1) Subscriptions
Streaming video services	(1) Subscriptions (2) Per-play direct sales (3) National advertising
Film industry	(1) Direct ticket sales (2) Film syndication (3) Product placement (4) Marketing synergies
Recorded music industry	(1) Direct album and song sales (2) Concert and merchandising sales

Medium	Primary revenue models[a,b]
Video game industry	(1) Direct sales (2) Subscriptions (3) In-game sales
Book publishers	(1) Direct sales
Social media platform companies	(1) National advertising (2) Local advertising (3) Sales of user data
Advertising agencies	(1) Per-hour billing for client services (2) Percentage of value of advertisement placements

[a] Based on commercial for-profit media in the United States; information is based on general practices. Revenue models vary among individual media companies within industry sectors.

[b] Reflects the primary historical revenue sources. Most media companies develop important additional sources of revenue, and media industries are rapidly developing new revenue sources.

[c] A cable "multiple system operator" (MSO) is a parent company that owns "local cable system operator" (LSO) companies. Cable TV subscribers buy the service from the LSO that serves their community. MSOs and LSOs are in the business of cable television distribution. But LSOs often control a few minutes of time in each hour of cable television network programming that airs on their system, which they sell to local advertisers.

Television and radio stations, digital-native media organizations, many podcasts, and social media platforms depend almost entirely on selling advertising around their content for revenue. News organizations like print and online get most of their revenue from selling advertising but supplement that revenue by selling subscriptions. Cable and satellite television companies, cable television networks, and magazines do the opposite. They get most of their revenue from selling subscriptions but also get some revenue from selling advertising. Premium cable networks such as HBO and Showtime and some streaming services depend entirely on subscriptions. Finally, film studios, book publishers, and recorded music labels make most of their money from selling individual content products—films, books, songs, and albums—directly to consumers.

Nonprofit media companies, such as public service broadcasters, also have business models. Those usually include some combination of direct subsidies from the government or mandatory user fees collected by the government; donations from the public, companies, and foundations; and sales of merchandise or services. Nonprofit media don't need to maximize profits for shareholders as commercial media companies do, but they do have to compete with other societal needs for donations and government subsidies.[1]

What all major media revenue models have in common is that they're based on audiences. Advertisers buy time and space around media content in order to reach the consumers most likely to buy the product the advertiser is trying to sell. For advertisers, not all audiences are created equal (Chapter 5). That means that to successfully sell advertising, media companies have to produce content that attracts the specific types of audiences that advertisers most want to reach. There are different strategies for doing that, which will be discussed later, but all require that the media company have a very accurate understanding of its *audience's size, demographics,* and *psychographics*, including behaviors.

Subscription revenue models also are based on understanding and successfully attracting audiences. Media companies selling subscriptions have to know what content audience members want. They also have to know how much content subscribers expect to get in return for their monthly payments. If the company fails to meet those expectations, audience members will cancel their subscriptions—known as *subscription churn*.

Media that depend on direct sales of content also must understand their audiences and predict audience size for each piece of content before it's created. The types of content sold through direct sales—films, music, some video games—all take a great deal of time and money to produce. Media analysts help producers understand what types of content are likely to be popular with audiences before the company invests in production.

Even nonprofit and government-funded media organizations are expected to attract audiences and, in some countries, bring in revenue from advertising, subscriptions, and direct sales. Given the growing number of information and entertainment options available, governments and taxpayers are demanding evidence that audiences are using the content being paid for with public funding and are pressuring nonprofit media to find new revenue sources and improve operating efficiency.

In summary, media managers are trying to accomplish the same things regardless of what type of media they manage: maximize audience size and satisfaction, maximize the amount of revenue they bring in, and minimize the costs of producing and distributing content that audiences want.

Given these goals, media analytics is an increasingly important part of media management in all industry sectors. For the analyst, the best advice is simple: Follow the money. Said another way, based on the data, which strategy is likely to grow the company's audiences or its revenues? In most instances, that's going to be the answer top management wants to hear.

Understanding the basics of demand, profitability, and finance terms

If audiences are necessary for media companies to generate revenue and profits, and revenue and profits are the things media companies *must* produce, let's review the basic principles of consumer demand and business finance.

The amount of consumer or audience demand for any product is based on three things: the *utility* or usefulness of the product to the buyer or audience member; the amount of product available (*supply*); and the product's price. The idea of utility is obvious. If something is useless to you or you don't like it, then you won't want it, regardless of its price. But if a product is useful to you in some way, you'll want it, thus creating *demand* for it.

But total demand for a product is affected by price. As price goes up, demand goes down. Some people won't be able to afford it, and others won't think the product is worth its price.

So what affects price? It is the relationship between demand and supply. If there is a lot of demand for something but only a limited supply (*scarcity*), the price goes up as people compete with one another to buy it. Prices, in turn, affect supply. As the price of something rises and selling becomes more profitable, more sellers will enter the market to compete for the business. Think about how as a particular type of content becomes popular—reality shows, superhero action films, or a new type of music—media companies rush to produce some version of the same idea so they can capture a share of the demand for it.

As the new producers increase the available supply of a popular product, they'll lower prices to try to draw buyers (audiences) away from competitors. As price falls, demand will rise at least slightly but not infinitely. No one needs an unlimited supply of any product or content.

If prices fall so much that producers can no longer make a profit, some suppliers will leave the market, reducing the amount of supply available, causing the price to rise again. Eventually, supply, demand, and price become relatively stable.

So what does it take for a company to make a profit? Simple. A company must bring in more revenue than it has to pay to produce and distribute its products. Said another way, customer demand for a product must be high enough that the company can charge each customer more than what it costs the company to produce and distribute the product the customer wants. If the company's total revenues are higher than its total costs at the end of the year, the difference is its profit. It's exactly the same process as balancing your own monthly budget.

Financial terms for the media analyst

To make sure you understand the discussions that follow throughout the book, take a moment to review some basic financial terms in Box 2.2.

Box 2.2 Key financial terms and how they're calculated

Term	Definition	Formula
Revenue or sales	The money generated by business operations	
Expenses or costs	All the things a company has to pay for in order to produce, sell, and distribute its products	
Operating profit or income	The amount left over after expenses are subtracted from revenue but before *income taxes, depreciation*, and *amortization* are subtracted	(Revenues – expenses)
Net profit or income	The amount left after all expenses, including depreciation, amortization, and taxes are paid; often called "the bottom line"	Operating profit – (depreciation + amortization + taxes + other accounting expenses)
Operating profit margin	The percentage profit a company makes from its normal business operations. A measure of management efficiency in controlling operating costs. Comparing profit margins across companies controls for differences in company size.	Operating profit/ revenue = %
Net profit margin	The percentage profit a company makes after all expenses are calculated; a measure of total management efficiency, helpful in comparing management performance across companies	Net profit/ revenue = %
Return on investment (ROI)	The percentage return made from the amount it cost to produce that return	Total profit/total costs = %
Fixed costs	Costs of doing business that management has little control over, such as facilities and equipment costs, raw materials, etc.	
Variable costs	Operating costs over which management has some control, such as salaries, marketing, travel and entertainment costs	

The characteristics of information products

Most media companies produce, sell, and distribute *information products*. Information is an *intangible good*, which means that while it has value and you buy and sell it, it does not have a physical form. It may be packaged in something that has a physical form, such as a book. But the consumer's demand is for the information or content, not the package.

Information products have unique characteristics that are different from *tangible* (physical) consumer products, such as cars, shoes, groceries, etc. These characteristics make managing the profitable production and sale of information products both different and harder than with tangible consumer goods. There are many differences in the characteristics of information products as compared to consumer goods (Karpik, 2010; Priest, 1994; Reca, 2006), but we'll focus only on those that influence the issues media analysts most often work with.

High first-copy costs

Media producers pay almost all the costs of creating content—a film, book, TV series, video game, etc.—up front. That is, they have to pay the complete cost of production just to create the first copy of the content and before the first audience member ever sees it. Thereafter, reproducing that first copy for mass distribution costs the producer almost nothing, particularly in the digital age. That's different from tangible goods like cars, where the producer pays for most of the materials and labor required to make the product only as each item is produced.

Why does this difference matter? For three reasons: (1) With tangible goods, if a product doesn't sell, the producer cuts production and financial losses. With information products, if audiences reject a film, book, or video game, the producer loses almost the entire investment because the costs were paid up front. (2) Because the costs are paid up front, it's critical for the producer to sell as many copies of the information product as possible to recover those costs. (3) Information products' high production/low reproduction cost ratio encourages *piracy* of information products. The pirate pays none of the production costs, and copying the finished film or song costs almost nothing. That means every sale of a pirated film or song represents almost 100% profit for the thief—and a significant loss for the producer, particularly since most audience members consume a book or film only once. So if they buy a pirated copy, the original producer is never able to recover any costs from that consumer.

Different relevance to audiences

Audience members are active consumers of content, choosing what appeals to them and rejecting what doesn't. No one needs to consume news or entertainment to survive, so media consumption is optional and individual tastes in content differ. This makes it hard to predict audience demand for proposed projects such as new films or albums before they're made. But because information products have high first-copy costs, media companies *must* estimate likely demand and revenue for each project before they can set the project's production budget. Making those predictions are the job of the media analyst.

Taken together, these two characteristics of high first-copy costs and different relevance to audiences increases the financial risks of content production. That's why demand for media analysts, who can help media companies use data to estimate and reduce risks, is rising so quickly.

Time costs of consumption

Unlike most consumer products, the "price" of information products includes the *time* spent consuming it. For many people, the time-costs of media are bigger than the actual price. In most cases, there is an inverse relationship between the time required to consume a piece of content (Tolstoy's *War and Peace*, for example, or *serial* rather than *episodic* TV shows) and audience demand.

On-demand and streaming technologies now allow us to consume content when it suits us as opposed to when the media company schedules it. In the audio/visual market, this has created new *binge watching* and *binge listening* audience behaviors, challenging the industry's understanding of how the time-costs of content consumption affect audience demand. It's an issue media analysts are intensely studying. But as of 2022, only about 35% of total TV consumption in the United States was on-demand/streaming, according to Nielsen (Spangler, 2022). Thus it's not yet clear whether binge watching/listening is widespread enough to influence producers' ideas about the ideal lengths for video and audio programs.

Joint commodity characteristics

A joint commodity—also called a *dual product*—is a product that is sold into two different markets simultaneously. Sheep, for example, are sold into the wool market and the meat market. Farmers raising sheep make decisions calculated to maximize total profits across the two markets. Similarly, advertising-supported media—which is the majority of media—sell simultaneously to audiences (the content) and advertisers or underwriters (messaging time or space). So they are selling in a *two-sided market*. Media managers and media analysts must understand both of those markets and manage them separately to maximize total combined profits.

Managing a joint commodity requires careful analysis because actions taken to maximize profits from advertisers can cost a media company audience, and vice versa. If a newspaper or magazine raises its subscription price, some subscribers are likely to cancel their subscriptions. If enough do, advertisers will demand lower prices or stop advertising because they're reaching a smaller audience, so the newspaper may actually lose money because of its subscription price increase. The same thing can happen when a media company increases the amount of advertising "clutter" that it sells around content so as to increase revenue. The clutter increases audiences' time-cost of consumption and will cause some to switch to other content.

Taken together, the time-costs of consumption and joint commodity characteristics greatly affect the types of content that media companies are willing to produce. In the highly competitive market for audience time and attention, content length has become a major issue for producers. Similarly, media companies that sell advertising focus not on creating the best content or even the content that will attract the biggest audiences. They focus on creating content that will attract audiences with the demographic profile advertisers want to reach.

The final two economic characteristics we'll discuss here have major impact on the spiraling competition for audience time and attention that media companies are facing in the 21st century. That competition has played a major role in the financial challenges media companies face—and now look to media analysts to help solve.

Public good characteristics

In economics and management, a public good is a good that is not depleted when it is consumed. If someone buys a bottle of water and drinks it, no one else can drink it while you're drinking it, and when you're done, the water no longer exists for someone else to drink. Not so with media content. If you "consume" an episode of your favorite series tonight, millions of other people can watch it simultaneously, and the program will still be there to be consumed by millions more tomorrow—or 20 years from now.

There are many different types of public goods in every society: roads, firefighters, public education, etc. One of the problems with a public good is that as long as someone pays to create it, it becomes available to others who didn't pay for it. This encourages piracy and what economists call "freeloading"—which is when someone benefits from a public good without helping pay for it. Every student who has ever worked on a group project is familiar with freeloading.

The public good characteristic of media products has several management implications: (1) Once created, an information product can be sold repeatedly. (2) Because public goods can't be depleted, they're not scarce. Value is created by scarcity, so it's hard both to set a price for public goods like content and to recover the costs of their production. That means producers have less of an incentive to produce at all, particularly expensive, high-quality content. (3) Once created, a media product potentially remains in the market indefinitely, continuing to compete for audiences and revenue with newly produced content.

Externality value

Externality value is the value something generates for society that the producer does not get fully paid for by the people buying the product. In other words, it is the ripple effects a product or service has on society that are not built into the price. Positive externalities are positive effects; negative externalities are negative effects.

Textbooks like this one, for example, educate people. More highly educated people have, on average, higher total lifetime income, contribute more to a nation's economic prosperity, are healthier, live longer, and are less likely to wind up in the prison system. But textbook authors aren't paid a share of the total economic value textbooks generate across society through these benefits and savings. Similarly, programs that glamorize violence normalize violent behavior in society. But the producers and media companies that profit from violent content aren't billed for their share of the societal costs their content helps create. Because producers of positive externalities are never fully rewarded, and producers of negative externalities are never fully charged for the effects of their work, socially beneficial content tends to be underproduced and socially harmful content is overproduced relative to their true impacts on society (Helbling, 2020).

Externality values may not be measured in money, but the rewards to those who capture them can be real: fame, popularity, influence, etc. One type of externality has become a major issue for media companies in the digital age. With mobile phone cameras, editing apps, social media, and cheap internet connections, billions of people in the 21st century have become content producers with potentially global audiences. For most, the return on the time and money they spend creating content is not financial— it's recognition from friends and family and the satisfaction of sharing their opinions or photographs. For media companies, however, every moment someone spends watching free user-generated content on YouTube, Facebook, Instagram, or a personal web page is the loss of audience time and attention to a competitor.

Singularities

Information products are *singularities* (Karpik, 2010), which means that most content is individually created one at a time by skilled professionals.

Such products cannot be mechanically mass produced on an assembly line. From a management standpoint, this means media professionals are not interchangeable. A film and its remake will be very different because the creative teams were different, even though the story is the same. An investigative report by one team of journalists will be different from another team's reporting on the same topic. This characteristic creates the "star system" among employees in media companies. It also is leading to a much greater focus on tracking the success metrics and fan bases of individual media professionals from performers to journalists.

Experience good

Media content is an *experience good* (Reca, 2006). Audiences must buy and consume (experience) the content before they know whether they'll like it or find it useful. As content prices rise, so does the audience's risk when selecting which content to buy. For example, as the price of theater tickets has risen, global box office sales have fallen, with more people waiting for films to be streamed or released on TV to see if they like them. In-home viewing and listening also lower the time-costs of consumption for experience goods. You can turn something off when you don't like it or pause it and return later.

Language-based goods

The potential market for any media product is limited to the number of people who speak the language in which the content was produced or translated. Further, with text-based content, the potential market is limited by the audience's literacy rate.

All these characteristics of media put together make it very hard for media companies to predict how people will respond to a particular piece of content, increasing the financial risks of production. Media management and media analytics are all about risk mitigation. The next section outlines some key management and risk mitigation strategies.

Risk mitigation strategies in media management

Let's start with some basic strategies that media analysts should think about as they consider the business issues challenging their company. One of the most basic for media firms is capturing *economies of scale*. "Economies of scale" refers to making it less expensive to produce each unit of a product—say a car—as you produce more units. That lets you spread the fixed costs of production (the basic things you have to pay for just to be in business, such as buildings, equipment, electricity, labor, etc.) across more sales, while also helping you negotiate lower supply costs by buying in bulk.

Think of economies of scale this way: You start your own video production house, creating video commercials for clients. Your total first-year start-up costs for equipment, office rental, insurance, electricity, your own salary, and everything else is $100,000. If you have only one client who wants you to produce one 30-second advertisement for her, you would have to charge her $100,000 just to break even. But if you had 10 clients wanting 30-second advertisements, you could lower your price to $10,000 each and still break even. Capturing economies of scale makes you more competitive by letting you lower your prices and still be profitable. As prices fall, demand rises. As demand rises, you can capture more economies of scale.

Given media's high first-copy costs and low reproduction costs, economies of scale are critical. Media firms must sell enough copies, tickets, or views of each piece of content to cover the initial cost of production—or the company loses money. Once those costs are covered, the revenue generated from every additional sale or view is largely profit. Therefore, generating the maximum audience possible is the goal for every piece of content and is the motivation for many other management strategies such as global content distribution.

Economies of scope are another way to lower costs and risks. Companies get economies of scope when they cut distribution costs by selling different but related products or services through the same distribution pipeline. An example would be cable companies offering video, telephone, and high-speed internet services in one subscription package. If you buy all three services from them, they can deliver them all down one cable to your home and manage your account with one staff member. But if a company is selling a range of unrelated products, let's say cars, shoes, and groceries—they'd need separate facilities and staffs to distribute them.

Media *consolidation*—that is, buying up competitors so that your organization grows and captures more *market share*—can bring economies of scale and scope. Examples would be several different radio stations broadcasting out of a single station building managed by a single management team (scale) or jointly owned broadcast and newspaper companies operating out of the same newsroom and sharing content across platforms (scope).

Another risk mitigation strategy is *branding*. Branding means creating a strong identity for a product so people know what it is and have an image of its price and quality, as soon as they hear the name. *Fox News Channel*'s branding of itself as the conservative voice among news networks in the United States, *Animal Planet*'s identity as the source of nonfiction entertainment related to animals, and The Walt Disney Studios's identity as a producer of high-quality family-friendly entertainment are all examples of media branding. Developing a brand identity is a key way to create loyal and predictable audiences. Loyal audiences reduce the risk producers face from differences in audience taste, while strong brand identities reduce the audiences' risk in selecting experience goods.

Series, *sequels*, and *spinoffs* are now widely used for risk mitigation, particularly in high-cost productions such as films and video games. Series, sequels, and spinoffs help address the problem of the different relevance of content to audiences. If a studio produces a major film based on an original screenplay, it can't know whether the film will be a hit or a failure with audiences. But if the studio produces a film from a best-selling book such as the *Harry Potter* series or a sequel or spinoff from a hit such as *Star Wars*, then at least a small audience of devoted fans can be counted on to show up and buy tickets. That's also the reason TV producers make multiple versions of hit series, such as all of the versions of the reality show *Survivor* set in different locations or based on rematches between previous players or the prequel series *House of the Dragon* from the global television blockbuster *Game of Thrones*.

For the same reason, media companies constantly return to the same small pool of talent in the form of directors, actors, and news anchors, counting on those individuals' personal fan bases to draw audiences. This reduces demand for new talent, such as students interested in media careers. It also increases the pressure media companies put on individual employees to become *influencers*, developing personal social media followings their employers can leverage into loyal audiences. Measuring media personnel performance is becoming another growing role for media analysts.

Related to the use of series, sequels, and spinoffs is the risk mitigation strategy of *marketing synergies*. "Marketing synergies" refers to selling the same basic content through as many forms and platforms as possible. The Walt Disney Company is particularly skilled at maximizing marketing synergies. From a single animated film such as *The Lion King*, sequels, animated serial versions for TV, a Broadway play, a music album, theme park and cruise ship characters, and a wide range of merchandise from stuffed animals to backpacks are created. Perhaps the most striking example of marketing synergies in industry history was Disney's development of the wildly successful *Pirates of the Caribbean* film franchise, which was based on one of its original Disneyland theme park rides.

But while Disney may be best known for capturing marketing synergies, the strategy has been widely adopted across the industry. In some entertainment sectors such as children's television, a producer pitching a new show concept must pitch the marketing synergies to go with it or have no hope of getting greenlighted. Film studios and video game makers now codevelop products—games based on films and vice versa. Broadcast stations and news networks sell coffee mugs, jackets with their logos, and other branded merchandise. Newspapers and magazines sell archived stories, facsimiles of historically important front pages, copies of famous news photographs, and even branded wine clubs and travel packages. In media sectors such as sports marketing, increasing the sales of the merchandise related to a team or sporting event is one of the major parts of a media analyst's job.

Across the industry, risk mitigation strategies evolve constantly, and media executives are always looking for ways to reduce costs and increase revenues and profits. Evaluating the effectiveness of new approaches to risk mitigation is a key responsibility of media analysts in the 21st century.

Understanding audiences

Financial risk mitigation depends on media companies' success in attracting audiences to content and the advertising around it. That's increasingly difficult in a media-saturated world where experts estimate the average American is bombarded with between 4,000 and 10,000 advertisements daily. Moreover, those estimates don't include all the nonmarketing content, social media *posts*, phone calls, texts, and emails that also demand our time and attention (Marshall, 2015; Sanders, 2017).[2]

A new concept has emerged to describe this tsunami of messaging: the *attention economy*. As with traditional economics, the attention economy also operates on the laws of supply, demand, and price. Audience attention is the scarce and valuable commodity being traded. Content that captures more audience attention is more valuable than content that attracts less because audience attention is an increasingly scarce commodity given the number of suppliers competing for it.

Media companies operating in the attention economy face a conundrum. The demand for content and the amount of time each day the average person spends consuming media rose steadily through the first two decades of the 21st century, appearing to level off at just over 11 hours per day in early 2019 (Jerde, 2019; Nielsen, 2019). However, even as total demand for content rises, audience size for each individual piece of content has dropped dramatically due to the *fragmentation* of the audience's attention across exponentially increasing numbers of platforms and content choices. As audience size falls, so does the revenue generated by that content, thereby increasing production risks and reducing future investments in content production. What results is a downward spiral in content quality on many media platforms.

The idea of the attention economy is only one of the frames media managers use to understand and manage audience attention. There are many other ways of understanding audiences, including as *passive*, as *active*, or as a *commodity* (McQuail, 2005).

The perception of audiences as passive, easily influenced recipients of media messages has a long history (McQuail, 2005). Media regulations such as content ratings and restrictions on nudity and bad language are based in the idea of passive audiences. We know media content does influence individuals and societies, although the mechanisms are complex and poorly understood. Most research suggests that media influence is a long-term process, not a "silver bullet" causing immediate effects. However, if media had no ability to influence people, advertising wouldn't work.

Audiences as *active* media consumers is a second concept of audience behavior. Audience members actively choose media content that meets their personal needs and interpret that content through their own frames of reference. Media companies that depend on direct sales or subscription sales for revenue view audiences as active.

The *uses and gratifications* audiences seek when choosing media content have been extensively studied, with scholars identifying a number of different reasons for consuming content (McQuail, 2005): environmental surveillance and decision making; social/cultural information and awareness; entertainment and diversion; and self-learning and self-awareness. But researchers have struggled to find correlations between categories of uses and gratifications and actual individual media use. Because of the differences in relevance of content to individuals, different people will get very different gratifications from the same piece of content. One person may watch a movie for entertainment, while another learns how to solve a problem from the dramatization. But the idea of uses and gratifications is still useful in helping media executives think about how to capture audience attention from competing content. Much of their analytics work focuses on understanding why and how individuals and groups choose and use content.

Another factor in audiences' content decisions is what Dimmick (2003) called *gratification opportunities*. "Gratification opportunities" refers to an audience's ability to access content where and when the individual wants it and on a platform that makes consumption efficient and convenient. Providing audiences with easy access to content has become an increasingly important part of content management.

The final audience concept used in media management is the audience as a commodity, that is, as a product that is created, bought, and sold by media companies and advertisers (Webster et al., 2006). This commodity concept of audience underlies the sale of advertising and is most concerned with the *institutionally effective audience* (Napoli, 2003, 2010). The institutionally effective audience is the audience a media company can monetize because advertisers value those individuals and will pay to reach them. Audiences that advertisers don't care about are basically wasted audiences from the commodity point of view. Overseas readers or viewers cannot possibly shop at the stores and car dealerships that are advertised on a local news site or television station. So while audience numbers might look great, if a local news site or TV station is racking up large numbers of online readers or viewers from other continents, without a subscription paywall, those audiences have little financial value.

The commodity audience also is understood through another important frame: the *predicted audience*, the *measured audience*, and the *actual audience* (Napoli, 2003). The predicted audience is what media companies sell and advertisers buy. The advertising around content is sold before—often months before—the content is released, so the price is set on predictions about the size and makeup of the audience.

The measured audience is, of course, what media analytics is all about. But accurately measuring an audience is difficult and expensive (Chapter 3), is based on estimates, and is subject to a wide range of errors. For example, podcast platforms provide producers with data showing exactly how many copies of a podcast were downloaded and, when streamed, where in the episode each listener stopped listening. But they can't tell the producer with accuracy how many total people listened to the podcast.

As audience size shrinks, accurate measurement becomes harder, and the true size and composition of an audience can never really be known. That creates a problem: What happens when the predicted audience that the advertiser paid for doesn't match the measured audience? For media companies, it's a financial loss either way. If the audience is smaller than the range predicted, the media company provides the advertiser with *make goods* in the form of either a refund or free additional advertising spots. If the audience is larger than estimated, the advertiser gets the extra benefit without paying for it—lost revenue for the media company.

Audiences' centrality to media profitability means media analysts constantly gather and examine data on all types of audience behavior, trying to understand that behavior in the context of the different media management functions—content choice, consumption, *engagement*, advertising consumption and targeting, content discovery and distribution. One of the reasons social media data (Chapter 13) has become so important is because social media posts and responses are made by individual audience members, generating data that give analysts direct *insights* into audience preferences and motivations.

The whole purpose of understanding audiences is, of course, to figure out how best to gain their attention so that attention can be monetized, whether through sales, subscriptions, or advertising. To accomplish that, media companies have developed sophisticated approaches to content management.

Content management

Content management is one of the two primary areas where media analysts work, so it's critical to understand content management theory and practice. The content management process consists of content selection, production, distribution, promotion, and evaluation. Content management theories focus on trying to understand audience behavior as it relates to content consumption, while content management strategies are designed to maximize audiences and revenue and to minimize production risks. Different industry sectors use different content management strategies. In this section, we'll touch briefly on the most important ones in key industry sectors.

Content management is changing rapidly. The development of individually addressable digital technologies such as smartphones and wireless internet services allow audiences to determine where and when they want to consume content. Live sports coverage is now one of the few content types that audiences *appointment view*. Even with traditional print media, subscribers now expect 24-hour access and updates.

This audience expectation of *on-demand* content has disrupted traditional media content management practices and, with them, media business models. Many experts predict that traditional modes of content delivery—such as *linear* broadcast, cable and radio, and printed books and magazines may be entirely replaced by digital delivery in the foreseeable future. Others, however, strongly disagree, believing traditional media platforms are here for the long haul—and are likely to regain at least some of their lost market share because of the efficiencies they offer to audiences.

In the meantime, however, traditional media platforms are still alive and very much in need of media analysts to help them with content management. Additionally, much of what we've learned about content management over the past century also applies in the on-demand world. So let's begin with some of the foundational concepts in media content management (Box 2.3).

Box 2.3 Goals of content management

Term	Definition
Conservation of programming resources[a]	Maximizing the revenue generated by each piece of content
Compatibility[a]	Selecting and scheduling content that matches the audience that is available at a given time
Audience flow[a]	Selecting and scheduling content to keep audiences moving from content to content on your channel, app, or website and not leaving
Habit formation[a]	Creating a preference for your company's brand or content in individual audience members so they come to your company's channel, app, or website regularly
Content discovery	Making audiences aware that content exists

[a] *Source:* Eastman & Ferguson, 2013

Conservation of content resources

One of the primary jobs of a content manager is to conserve the media company's content resources (Eastman & Ferguson, 2013). That means maximizing the company's profits by selecting, scheduling, promoting, and distributing content to the largest possible audiences. If the company is using advertising sales in its business model, then the content must attract audiences that advertisers want to reach. In some cases, that means choosing content that attracts audiences of a narrow demographic or psychographic. Niche content companies, such as *business-to-business* (*B2B*) media or niche magazines and cable networks, use this strategy. In other cases, it means selecting and distributing content that attracts a wide variety of audience types so that the company can sell advertising to as many different types of advertisers as possible. Broadcast networks and online news sites use a broader audience targeting strategy.

Conserving content resources also means using all the legal rights to a piece of content a company has paid for before those rights expire. That's why television networks sometimes replay a movie multiple times back-to-back on the same day or over a weekend "marathon." Repurposing content, such as news stories, that the company already has paid to produce also is a content manager's job. Local television stations have greatly expanded the number of newscasts they program, in part so they can rerun and sell advertising around all of the news stories they paid to produce for the first newscast of the day. They then also post it to their websites and sell ads around it again. Newspaper groups take stories written by the reporters at one paper and republish them in another, whenever they can.

Content managers' final responsibility is to continuously evaluate the effectiveness of content selection, scheduling, promotion, and distribution strategies in maximizing audiences and revenue. That's why media analysts are so central to content management across all media industry sectors. It's also why it's so important for media analysts to thoroughly understand the goals and strategies used in content management.

Strategies for maximizing audiences

Compatibility

To succeed in maximizing audiences, content managers try to schedule and distribute content to achieve three things: *compatibility*, *audience flow*, and *habit formation*. Compatibility refers to scheduling or delivering content that matches the audience available to consume content at any particular time. In television, that means delivering children's programming during after-school hours and serious adult fare in late evening after children are in bed. In radio, it means delivering the best content as people commute to and from work, when radio audiences are largest. With digital media, it means delivering new content at the peak times people are likely to turn to their devices for distraction: early mornings, lunch hours, etc. In the digital age, compatibility means understanding which devices audiences are most likely to be using at each point during the day and then feeding new content to those devices first.

Content compatibility with audiences is different on different media platforms and with different types of content. But in each media sector, audience size and demographics are generally predictable by time of day, weekday, and season. Understanding those patterns is critical, which is where media analysts come in. Content managers avoid scheduling or posting their most valuable content at times when their potential audience is small or less demographically valuable to advertisers. Cheaper and less important content is released when the available audience is smaller or less valuable.

Audience flow

Audience flow refers to selecting and scheduling content in a way that keeps audiences on your company's channel, app, or website, watching program after program in broadcasting and cable television, or moving from item to item on your app or website. Audience flow is achieved by understanding what an audience likes and programming a steady stream of similar content that will be relevant to that person or group. That discourages them from switching to a different content source.

In linear media, audience flow is achieved by placing similar programs or music back-to-back on a television or radio schedule. In digital media, audience flow occurs when content is placed in a "section" or on a "page" of similar content, either through automatic rolls of the next episode in streamed content or through algorithms that "recommend" additional content you might like based upon what you've previously watched, bought, or clicked.

Content managers use a number of specific strategies to improve audience flow. They *block* content, which refers to scheduling the same type of content across most or all of a *daypart* or in topics-based "sections" in publications and online. Blocking tries to ensure that all the content in the block will be relevant to the audience that shows up, so that they flow from program to program, story to story, or game to game. In publications and on websites, blocking takes the form of grouping content into topical *sections* or pages. Content managers try to choose a strong *lead-off*, *lead-story*, or eye-grabbing photograph to attract readers to a content block. Similarly, they try to follow (*lead-out*) each piece of content with something on the same topic or in the same genre to keep the flow going.

Habit formation

Habit formation refers to two things: (1) getting audience members to do appointment viewing or reading, that is, consuming your content at regular or predictable times, and (2) creating a preference for your company's brand so individuals come to your channel, app, or website first. Getting people to download your company's mobile content app has become a critical element of 21st century content habit formation.

Media managers use a number of strategies to encourage habit formation. One is to schedule, distribute, or update content at the same time every day, whether newscasts, tweets, or site updates. In television, this is called *stripping* content, so that audiences know that they can watch a favorite program at the same time every day.

Content discovery

Content managers also have strategies to help with an increasingly important challenge: content *discovery*. Audiences have to know content exists before they can use it. Although content promotion has always been a key content management function, now with trillions of bits of content competing for attention, helping audiences discover each piece of content is a major problem.

Media managers use multiple content placement strategies to help audiences discover content (Box 2.4). Offering content similar to what a media company's primary competitor has up at the same time can help draw off some of the competitor's audience, a strategy known as *blunting*. Running content targeting entirely different tastes from what major competitors are running—called *counterprogramming* in broadcasting and cable media—can attract new, underserved audiences. Identifying what content genres and topics are missing or minimal in the choices available at any given time is called **white space analysis** in media analytics. Another strategy for helping audiences discover new content is surrounding highly popular content with new or less popular material in the hope that audiences coming to a favorite show or author will see and try something new (see *hammocking* and *tentpoling* in Box 2.4).

A key concept in content discovery is *curation of content*. The concept is to create a collection of content in a particular genre or on a particular topic that is likely to appeal to a specific audience segment. When a streaming service promotes a collection of programs as "drama," "comedy," "British TV series," or "spy movies," or a book retailer emails an ad to you suggesting a new book "based on what you've read," that's curation.

Box 2.4 Ten content discovery and programming strategies

Term	Strategy
Lead-off or anchor	The first program or content scheduled in a *daypart* or on a site, designed to capture and hold an audience
Lead-in	The content that comes immediately before the content being scheduled or analyzed; in TV programming, the best predictor of the audience size of the content following, called the *inheritance effect*
Lead-out	The content that comes immediately after the content being scheduled or analyzed
Blocking or stacking	Putting similar types of content together. Blocking is based on the idea that individual audience members have preferred genres of content and are likely to move from one piece of content to another, if the content is of the same type.
Blunting	Scheduling or placing content that targets the same audience that one or more of your competitors is targeting
Counterprogramming	Scheduling or placing content that targets an audience that one or more of your competitors is not targeting
Stripping	In TV, scheduling the same program or series in the same time period every day of the week; helps content discovery
Hammocking	Surrounding a piece of content that is new or has a smaller audience with more popular content; helps audiences find new or less popular content
Tent-poling	Surrounding a piece of content with a larger audience with less popular content; helps audiences find new or less popular content
Curating	Grouping content by genre or topic or using audience consumption data to suggest specific pieces of content to individual audience members based on the content those individuals previously consumed

Understanding advertising management

If content management is one of the two primary foci for media analysts, advertising management is the other. Media companies must understand and respond to what advertisers want just as much as they must understand

and respond to what audiences want. So important is advertising revenue that many analysts work almost exclusively on advertising sales and placement, including consumer behavior analysis.

In fully commercial media systems that depend primarily on advertising revenue, content is developed not to serve audiences but to attract the audiences advertisers want to reach (Eastman & Ferguson, 2013; Webster et al., 2006). In essence, content is the bait on the fishhook that media companies use to catch the "species" of audience member the advertiser wants to buy. The media company is selling the advertiser the audience's time and attention. Advertising rates historically have been set based upon predicted audience size and audience quality.

So what do advertisers want in an audience? On the surface, it's simple:

1. They want *audience size*, i.e., to reach as many people as possible for every advertising dollar spent.
2. They want *audience quality*, i.e., to reach the individual members of the audience most likely to buy whatever they're advertising or whom they most want to influence.
3. They want as high a *return on investment* (*ROI*) or **return on advertising spend** (**ROAS**) as they can get for each advertising dollar spent, That means reaching as many high-quality audience members as possible for as low a per-person cost as possible.

Once past those concepts, very little is simple about understanding what advertisers want. Historically, audience size has been the primary characteristic of interest, and advertising prices are usually based on size. For most media, advertising prices are calculated on the basis of **CPMs**, which stands for *cost per thousand*.[3] An advertising price quote usually refers to the price for every 1,000 people who are expected to see the ad.

So, yes, size matters—but only if all the people an advertiser is being charged to reach are that advertiser's target audience. From the advertiser's standpoint, not all audiences—or media platforms—are created equal. What is a quality audience to one advertiser is wasted money to another.

To better understand this, consider this example: If you watch TV, in most countries you will see ads for companies such as fast-food restaurants, soft drinks, and mid-priced car brands. Such brands find advertising on television efficient. The price they pay for a TV spot is high because the CPM for each spot is multiplied by the thousands or millions of households it reaches in whatever market they buy. The products they are advertising are available everywhere in most cities and affordable to most people who might see the ad. Therefore, a large percentage of the people who see the ads on TV are potential customers.

In contrast, the owner of a corner market or neighborhood coffee shop would be wasting money with a TV ad. Few people will drive across a major city to buy groceries or a cup of coffee, so most of the TV audience those business owners would pay to reach would be *wastage*. Advertising through a local newspaper, direct mail, or some other geographically targeted medium would be smarter.[4]

In the last half of the 20th century, advertisers started demanding more precise audience information so they could target their *ad spends* more precisely—not just by geography but also by personal characteristics. Media measurement companies began gathering audience demographic data. Gender and age are generally seen as most important because demand for many products is based on those factors, and people between the ages of 18 and 49 spend a higher percentage of their income on consumer goods, particularly in households with children. Income also is important, of course, because advertisers want to pay to reach only people who can afford to buy what they're selling.

But even then the concept of audience "quality" is complicated. Media often charge more to deliver audiences that are harder to reach. Sports programming, for example, delivers a larger percentage of younger men to advertisers, a group that generally spends less time with traditional media. People 49+ tend to be wealthier than other age groups, but they also use more mass media and so are easier to reach, and they often have established brand preferences, so they might pay less attention to some advertising. Consequently, advertisers are less interested in advertising to people in that age group. Ethnicity and culture also may affect how audiences are valued. Napoli (2002) found that American advertisers paid lower CPMs for minority audience members than white audience members, even when other factors such as age, gender, market size, and average per capita income in the market were controlled.

In addition to demographic factors, some advertisers use psychographics to define audience quality—the personal characteristics that define people but that are more changeable than demographics. Psychographics include such things as social class, living environment (rural, city-center urban, suburban, etc.), lifestyle, hobbies and interests, religion and political views. Lifestyle differences predict consumer buying behaviors, and psychographically based content preferences help advertisers more precisely target audiences.

Digital distribution allows media companies to develop even more refined psychographic profiles of individual audience members. Every *share* and every "like," "love," or "angry" emoji someone puts on social media posts is cataloged against the content to which they responded, helping media companies develop detailed profiles of each user's likes and dislikes. Advertisers use personality traits to craft messages that will be more effective in influencing the people they're targeting.

As you can see, understanding what advertisers want is complicated. An advertiser's personal psychology (Napoli, 2002) and understanding of advertising practices, consumer behavior, and media habits also play roles. Finally, advertisers' valuation of audiences is changeable and subject to fads, fashions, and "quick-fix" decisions. Part of a media analyst's job is to help her employer stay current on media buying trends—and to measure the actual effectiveness of whatever the "flavor-of-the-month" buying strategy happens to be.

But it also is important to keep in mind that how advertisers value different audience segments has real effects on society. Media companies that depend on advertising produce less content for those audience groups that advertisers don't value or value less. Furthermore, in the increasingly competitive 21st century advertising market, media companies trying to serve "lower value" audience segments, such as specific ethnic or linguistic groups, find it harder to survive financially. While some of this may be changing, when niche audience media companies fail, it further reduces the amount of relevant content available to the audiences they served. Finally, as media analysts develop highly detailed demographic and psychographic portraits of individual audience members in order to keep advertisers happy, questions surrounding the audience's personal privacy become more urgent. The practice of media analytics should never be divorced from a constant and conscious consideration of the ethical implications of media management decisions.

Discovery and distribution management

One of the most challenging tasks for media organizations today is to get their content discovered by audiences. Fifty years ago, media *promotions* was a relatively minor function in media companies, often considered an entry-level position. Today, promotions is a high-powered, highly paid professional specialty. Enormous amounts of research, time, money, and data go into figuring out when, how, where, and to whom media content should be promoted so that audiences can, first, know a piece of content exists and, second, be motivated to seek it out. Different versions of film, TV, and video game trailers and promotions are tested with audiences before a promotional campaign is launched.

Nearly everyone is familiar with the concept of something going *viral*, which, of course, is the holy grail in promotions. But the magic ingredients that make one thing go viral and another disappear without a sound into the attention abyss are still imperfectly understood. So media analysts are tasked with working out effective strategies for promoting content to the audiences most likely to consume it.

Promotions take different forms and now occur across many different platforms. Traditional advertising is still used. But increasingly important are multiplatform content-promotion strategies for turning passive audiences into active "fans," such as hiring "influencers" to boost your content and segmenting potential audiences by their likely uses and gratifications so as to target them with messages based on those motivators. Finally, there are techniques such as *search engine optimization* (*SEO*). SEO requires understanding the *algorithms* that search engines and social media companies use in their search functions. The promotions team then impregnates a piece of content, or a *promo* for it, with the keywords most likely to be used in a search by people interested in similar topics. The goal is for the content to appear at the top of search results. Search engines and social media companies frequently change their search algorithms, making effective SEO a data-driven art form.

Distribution is another increasingly important issue in media management. If you create content but can't distribute it or can't distribute it in the format audiences want, you face total loss of your production costs.

The digital age has created a number of new distribution issues for media management. As more media companies distribute content through digital platforms, the question of who owns those platforms and what types of control they can exert over the content on their platforms becomes critical. Does the government require digital network companies to treat all content distributors equally—something called *net neutrality*? Or are the platforms allowed to discriminate however they wish against smaller content distributors? Discrimination can include making smaller producers pay higher prices to upload content or reducing download speeds so most audiences won't wait around to get independently produced material. Both actions give high-volume, for-profit institutions—and in some countries—government-approved content—a competitive advantage in the attention economy.

Then there is the increasing importance of the flip side of that debate: How do societies balance freedom of speech and the individual's right "to seek, receive and impart information and ideas through any media" (United Nations, 1948) against the dangers both to the individual and to the society of misinformation and disinformation? What responsibility do media platforms have to remove misinformation posted by others onto their sites? Who decides what is and is not misinformation? What if the misinformation is being distributed by a media company? Is that different than if it's being distributed by an individual? Why? Should governments regulate the distribution of misinformation? If so, who decides when the government has started using accusations of "misinformation" and "fake news" to limit free speech and disseminate propaganda and disinformation, and what remedies should there be for government overreach?

Who controls the distribution pipeline and how that entity is allowed to use that control has huge implications for free speech, the citizen's right to know, and the survival of content producers. In the pre-digital era, authoritarian governments often controlled access to newsprint—the type of paper used by newspapers and magazines—guaranteeing that only government-approved content was published. If a high-sales-volume distributor such as Walmart refuses to carry certain magazines or CDs in its stores because their cover art or content violates the retailer's own "community" standards, that has upstream effects on content creation as companies change what they produce in order to protect distribution and sales (Katz, 1997; Wal-Mart: Pop culture gatekeeper?, 2004). Similarly, if a large percentage of audiences start using a social media platform as their primary platform for accessing news content, the people who own that social media company potentially gain enormous control over the information that does— and does not—reach the public.

While these larger distribution issues are critical in 21st century media management, the distribution issues that media analysts are called upon to examine are at a more micro level. These include understanding audience members' choices regarding place, time, and device of consumption, questions that can be understood only through data analysis. As with all distribution issues, the audience's screen of choice for consumption has upstream implications for content development.

Summary and conclusion

Media analytics is first and foremost about solving media management problems. Media management problems are, almost always, grounded in economic and financial issues. There is a temptation while studying media analytics to focus on learning to scrape data, create charts, and track social media posts because those things are easy and fun. But the most important and most fascinating part of media analytics is figuring out what data *mean* in the context of specific media management problems. For that, it is necessary to understand the challenges facing 21st century media companies in terms of economics, business models, audiences, content, advertising, discovery, and distribution. This chapter has tried to present the most important concepts in media management and show how they interconnect and affect the survival and success of media companies.

The role of the media analyst is to define what questions need to be answered, develop the analyses to answer them, and interpret the findings for senior management in terms that connect those findings to the company's success. To pull that off, the analyst needs to be an expert in the media business and in effective communication, with enough expertise in research design, methods, and data analysis techniques to evaluate data quality and vendors and avoid serious mistakes. The next chapter, the Fundamentals of Research Design and Methodology, is designed to give you the foundations you will need to understand research design and evaluate the quality of the *secondary data* research firms provide. The chapter after that, Communicating Insights, will teach you approaches to efficiently and effectively communicating your analysis to different types of media managers and stakeholders.

Throughout the book, you'll constantly be referred back to this chapter to refresh your understanding of relevant economic and management concepts. As you work the discussions, cases, and assignments in other chapters, you will be expected to apply the concepts from this chapter, explaining not just what your data show but also what they mean in terms of the underlying management problem. You'll also be expected to make professional recommendations for realistic courses of action.

Finally, it's worth noting that students often are horrified to realize that, for media companies, it is, as stated at the beginning of this chapter, all about the money. Most mass communication and journalism students have not chosen their field because they dream of spending their lives making media investors rich.

Fair enough.

But as also noted in the chapter, media content has enormous externality value in society—both positive and negative. Democratic governance cannot function without a well-informed citizenry who are making fact- and evidence-based decisions about their own futures. The ability of citizens to do that depends on the quality of the news and information content that reaches them. Entertainment content informs, teaches, and diverts people, as well as reflects images of society, which then shape society. Content soaked in violence exaggerates people's perceptions of how dangerous society is, even when actual crime rate data belie what we see in the media. Perceptions of nations, groups, and possibilities are shaped by what we see—or don't see—on our screens. In short, *media content matters.*

Producing high-quality content and promoting it so that people discover it requires significant financial resources. The ever increasing level of competition in the attention economy is reducing audience size, which means it's also raising the financial risks of production. As profitability falls, so does the quality of the content produced. And media companies that don't survive in the market produce no content at all.

That's why media analysts are now so important in media industries. It's the analyst's job to make sense of all the forces affecting media companies today so those companies can survive and continue to produce content that matters.

Additional resources

Albarran, A. (Ed.). (2019). *A research agenda for media economics.* Edward Elgar Publishing.

Anand, B. (2016). *The content trap: A strategist's guide to digital change.* Random House.

Doyle, G. (2013). *Understanding media economics* (2nd ed). Sage.

Recommended cases

These cases can be found on the textbook website: www.routledge.com/cw/hollifield

Case 2.1: Working with Data and Data Visualization in Excel using TV Financial Data

Case 2.2: Understanding Key Factors in Media Organization Financial Analysis

Case 2.3: Analyzing Personnel Data for Media Organizations

Case 2.4: Calculating the Revenue Potential of a Podcast

Case studies, along with accompanying datasets for this chapter, can be found on the text website. We particularly suggest the preceding cases in the order listed. See the companion website and instructor's manual for detailed descriptions of these and other relevant cases.

Discussion questions and exercises

1. The chapter emphasizes that in commercial, for-profit media, media management and media analytics are all about making profits; that content creation, creativity, and quality are, in most cases, secondary considerations. Is that a surprise to you? What is your reaction to that as a future media professional?

2. What three media companies do you use most often each day? What business model does each of those media companies use? What are the

strengths and weaknesses of those business models? How financially strong and stable are each of your favorite media companies? How does that affect the quality of content they are producing for you? Be sure to provide hard evidence and examples to back your opinions and analysis.

3. Go to the websites of three different news organizations you think are targeting different audiences. What differences do you see in the advertisements placed in those news organizations? Who are the advertisers targeting in terms of the demographics and psychographics of the audiences they seem to be trying to reach? What differences, if any, do you see in the advertisers and advertisements placed with each news company? Are there any differences in the types or focus of the news stories the news organizations are covering that suggest that they are targeting or serving the same audience the advertisers seem to be trying to target? Compare and contrast the news content and advertising across the different news organizations you've selected.

4. *Exercise: Analyzing basic media financial data*
   Use the financial data from the hypothetical media company (Table 2.1) to calculate each problem. Use a calculator or an Excel spreadsheet. Round to the first decimal point.

   a. What is the percentage change in revenues from across the 5 years? (Take the figures from the first year and the last year: [Big number – small number]/[Earliest year number].) If the earliest year number is larger than the more recent year, then the resulting percentage change will be negative.
   b. What was the percentage change in total costs across 5 years?
   c. What is the percentage change in operating profit across 5 years? Operating profit is the best calculation of how well the company's management is controlling costs because variations in income taxes, *depreciation*, and *amortization*[5] can sometimes make it hard to understand what a company's net profit for a year actually represents in terms of management performance.
   d. What was the percentage change in net profit across 5 years?
   e. What was the company's net profit margin in each year (Net profit/revenues)? Profit margin is always expressed as a percentage.
   f. What was the change in net profit margin across the five years (Bigger profit margin—smaller profit margin)? If the earliest year is larger than the more recent year, then the change is negative. The change is expressed *not* as a percentage but as a change in *percentage points* because you already are subtracting one percentage from another.

Table 2.1 Income Statement for Hypothetical Media Company (2015–2019) (figures in millions)

	2019	2018	2017	2016	2015
Revenues	86,206	77,561	73,645	67,966	62,734
Total costs	68,867	55,142	58,292	53,373	49,140
Operating profit	17,339	22,419	15,353	14,593	13,595
Income taxes, depreciation & amortization	6,639	1,681	7,437	7,147	10,056
Net profit	10,700	20,738	7,916	7,446	3,539

5. *Exercise: Reading media company financial reports*
   Go to the Investor Relations website page of several publicly held media companies in different industry sectors. Examples might be The Walt Disney Company, Comcast Corp., Meredith Corp., New York Times Co., Paramount, Springer, etc. In an age of mergers and acquisitions, the company names and configurations change, so you will need to figure out which companies are the publicly traded *parent company* to find the right website. Look up the 3-year or 5-year financial statements for the different companies and compare them. Which media corporations are the largest? Which have the largest profit margins? Which ones have the largest operating profit margins and net profit margins in recent years?

6. *Exercise: Analyzing a television program schedule to understand scheduling strategies*
   Use Table 2.2 to answer the following questions:

   a. What TV networks achieve good audience flow, and which do not?
   b. What are some examples of blocking?
   d. What are some examples of counterprogramming?
   e. What are some examples of blunting?
   f. Are there examples of stronger content being placed between two weaker shows to help discovery (*tentpoling*)?
   g. Are there examples of weaker programs being placed between two stronger programs to help discovery (*hammocking*)?
   h. What is the lead-in for Network 1, Comedy 1B?
   i. Which network wins Tuesday at 9 p.m.?
   j. Which network wins Monday 10 p.m., 18–49?
   k. Which network wins Tuesday night?
   l. Which network wins Tuesday night, 18–49?
   m. Which would a network rather win: the overall ratings for the night or the 18–49 ratings for the night? Why?
   o. If a TV show had low ratings overall but was one of the network's higher-rated shows for 18–49 audiences, how might that influence a network's discussion about whether to cancel or renew the program?

Table 2.2 Hypothetical Example of US TV Network Primetime Ratings Grid

Monday

	8 p.m.	8:30 p.m.	9:00 p.m.	9:30 p.m.	10:00 p.m.	10:30 p.m.
Network 1						
Program	Reality 1A	Reality 1A	Comedy 1A	Comedy 1A	Reality 1B	Reality 1B
Prog. Sub.	Talent	Talent	Single Females	Single Females	Romance Competition	Romance Competition
Lead/Gender	Both	Both	Female	Female	Both	Both
Ratings/Share (18–49)	2.3/11 (1.7/8)	2.5/11 (1.8/8)	1.1/5 (0.7/3)	0.7/4 (0.5/3)	1.5/6 (1.0/4)	1.1/6 (0.7/4)
Network 2						
Program	Comedy 2A	Comedy 2B	Comedy 2C	Comedy 2D	Drama 2A	Drama 2A
Prog. Sub.	Family	Family	Male Singles	Male Singles	Crime	Crime
Lead/Gender	Male	Male	Male	Male	Male	Male
Ratings/Share (18–49)	0.6/3 (0.4/2)	1.0/5 (0.6/3)	0.6/3 (0.4/2)	0.5/3 (0.3/2)	1.4/6 (0.9/4)	1.1/5 (0.7/3)
Network 3						
Program	Dramedy 3A	Dramedy 3A	Drama 3A	Drama 3A	Drama 3B	Drama 3B
Prog. Sub.	Mild horror	Mild horror	City Politics	City Politics	Sci-fi	Sci-fy
Lead/Gender	Male	Male	Ensemble	Ensemble	Ensemble	Ensemble
Ratings/Share (18–49)	1.3/6 (0.8/4)	1.5/7 (0.9/4)	1.8/7 (1.0/4)	2.1/9 (1.2/5)	1.8/8 (1.1/5)	1.6/8 (1.0/5)
Network 4						
Program	Drama 4A	Drama 4A	Drama 4B	Drama 4B	Reality Show 4A	Reality Show 4A
Prog. Sub.	Superheroes	Superheroes	Outer Space	Outer Space	Police	Police
Lead/Gender	Male	Male	Male	Male	Male	Male
Ratings/Share (18–49)	0.5/3 (0.3/2)	0.5/3 (0.3/2)	0.9/5 (0.6/3)	0.9/4 (0.6/3)	0.6/3 (0.4/2)	0.4/3 (0.3/2)

Tuesday

	8 p.m.	8:30 p.m.	9:00 p.m.	9:30 p.m.	10:00 p.m.	10:30 p.m.
Network 1						
Program	Comedy 1B	Comedy 1C	Drama 1A	Drama 1A	News/Info.	News/Info.
Prog. Sub.	Male Singles	Family	First Responders	First Responders	Various topics	Various topics
Lead/Gender	Male	Ensemble	Ensemble	Ensemble	Female	Female
Ratings/Share	1.1/5	1.2/6	1.1/5	1.1/6	1.0/4	0.7/4
(18–49)	(0.7/3)	(0.8/4)	0.8/4	0.8/4	(0.7/3)	(0.5/2)
Network 2						
Program	Drama 2B	Drama 2B	Drama 2C	Drama 2C	Drama 2D	Drama 2D
Prog. Sub.	Military Crime	Military Crime	Military Combat	Military Combat	Espionage	Espionage
Lead/Gender	Male	Male	Male	Male	Female	Female
Ratings/Share	1.2/5	1.4/5	1.7/7	1.7/7	1.1/5	1.1/7
(18–49)	(0.9/4)	(1.0/4)	(1.2/5)	1.2/5	(0.8/4)	(0.8/5)
Network 3						
Program	Reality 3A	Reality 3A	Reality 3B	Reality 3B	Drama 3C	Drama 3C
Prog. Sub.	Talent	Talent	Single Female Lifestyle	Single Female Lifestyle	Crime/Justice	Crime/Justice
Lead/Gender	Ensemble	Ensemble	Ensemble	Ensemble	Ensemble	Ensemble
Ratings/Share	1.6/7	1.9/8	1.5/7	1.4/7	0.8/5	0.6/5
(18–49)	(1.1/5)	(1.2/5)	(0.9/4)	(0.8/4)	(0.5/3)	(0.4/3)
Network 4						
Program	Comedy 4A	Comedy 4A	Dramedy 4A	Dramedy 4A	Drama 4C	Drama 4C
Prog. Sub.	Family	Family	Medical	Medical	Medical/Criminal	Medical/Criminal
Lead/Gender	Both Genders	Both Genders	Male	Male	Female	Female
Ratings/Share	0.8/5	1.0/5	1.5/7	1.5/7	2.0/10	2.2/10
(18–49)	(0.5/3)	(0.6/3)	(0.9/4)	(0.9/4)	(1.2/6)	(1.3/6)

Notes

1. Other types of communication companies such as advertising agencies, public relations agencies, sports marketing firms, political consultants, and syndicated research companies also hire media analysts. But such companies get most of their revenue from the fees they charge clients for the services they provide.
2. Although 4,000–10,000 ads per day are numbers commonly referenced in discussions of the attention economy, credible research does not appear to be the source of those estimates. Therefore, their validity is suspect. However, if you consider all the ads you personally encounter daily through legacy media, digital media, email marketing, billboards, placards on buses, taxis and subways, business signage, product packaging, telemarketing, and even talking gas pumps and brand stickers on fruit in the grocery store, it is clear that regardless of specific averages, people are bombarded with marketing messages daily.
3. The "M" comes from the Latin word for "thousand," which is *mille.*
4. Another illustration is advertising by *business-to-business (B2B)* companies. B2B companies sell products and services to other businesses, such as industrial machines, employer health care policies, high-capacity office equipment, etc. Most B2B companies find advertising in mass media highly inefficient. Specialized media—such as business and financial media or industry-specific trade press—are more efficient advertising vehicles for most B2B advertisers (Chapter 11).
5. Depreciation is an expense that reflects the estimated loss of value over the previous year of the company's tangible assets, such as equipment, buildings, etc., as the result of use and age. Amortization is an expense that reflects the estimated loss of value over the previous year of a company's intangible assets, such as programming rights and content value, due to use and age. Depending on the tax laws of the country in which a media company operates, the company may be allowed to deduct depreciation, amortization, and other taxes it has paid as a business expense.

References

Dimmick, J. W. (2003). *Media competition and coexistence: The theory of the niche.* Lawrence Erlbaum Associates Publishers.

Eastman, S. T., & Ferguson, D. A. (2013). *Media programming: Strategies and practices* (9th ed.). Wadsworth Cengage Learning.

Helbling, T. (2020, February 24). Externalities: Prices do not capture all costs. *Finance and Development.* International Monetary Fund. www.imf.org/external/pubs/ft/fandd/basics/external.htm

Jerde, S. (2019, March 19). The colossal amount of time spent consuming media may finally be flatlining, according to Nielsen report. *Adweek.* www.adweek.com/tv-video/the-colossal-amount-of-time-spent-consuming-media-may-finally-be-flatlining-according-to-nielsen-report/

Karpik, L. (2010). *Valuing the unique: The economics of singularities.* Princeton University Press.

Katz, J. (1997, June 2). Corporate censorship part I: Son of Wal-Mart. *Wired.* www.wired.com/1997/06/corporate-censorship-part-i-son-of-wal-mart/

Marshall, R. (2015, September 10). How many ads do you see in one day? *Red Crow Marketing.* www.redcrowmarketing.com/2015/09/10/many-ads-see-one-day/

McQuail, D. (2005). *McQuail's mass communication theory* (5th ed.). Sage Publications.

Napoli, P. M. (2002). Audience valuation and minority media: An analysis of the determinants of the value of radio audiences. *Journal of Broadcasting & Electronic Media*, 46(2), 169–186.

Napoli, P. M. (2003). *Audience economics: Media institutions and the audience marketplace*. Columbia University Press.

Napoli, P. M. (2010). *Audience evolution: New technologies and the transformation of media audiences*. Columbia University Press.

Nielsen. (2019). *The Nielsen total audience report, Q1 2019*. www.rbr.com/wp-content/uploads/Q1-2019-Nielsen-Total-Audience-Report-FINAL.pdf

Priest, C. (1994). An information framework for the planning and design of "information highways." www.eff.org/Groups/CITS/Reports/cits_nii_framework_ota.report

Reca, A. A. (2006). Issues in media product management. In A. Albarran, S. M. Chan-Olmsted, & M. O. Wirth (Eds.), *Handbook of media management and economics* (pp. 181–201). Lawrence Erlbaum Publishers.

Sanders, B. (2017, September 1). Do we really see 4,000 ads per day? *The Business Journals*. www.bizjournals.com/bizjournals/how-to/marketing/2017/09/do-we-really-see-4-000-ads-a-day.html

Spangler, T. (2022, August 18). US streaming tops cable TV viewing for first time, Nielsen says. *Variety*. https://variety.com/2022/digital/news/streaming-tops-cable-tv-viewing-nielsen-1235344466/#!

United Nations. (1948). *Article 19: Universal declaration of human rights*. www.un.org/en/about-us/universal-declaration-of-human-rights

Wal-Mart: Pop culture gatekeeper? (2004, August 20). *PBS Newshour*. www.pbs.org/newshour/economy/business-july-dec04-wal-mart_08-20

Webster, J. G., Phalen, P. F., & Lichty, L. W. (2006). *Ratings analysis: The theory and practice of audience research* (3rd ed.). Lawrence Erlbaum Associates.

3 Fundamentals of research design and methodology

Media analytics is a garbage-in/garbage-out process. All research is. If your research design, sampling method, or data collection method is bad, then the data you gather are garbage, the analysis you perform on that data is garbage, the interpretation of the data you make from that analysis is garbage, and the advice you give to senior management based upon your interpretation is garbage. It's that simple.

But if, as you read this chapter, you start thinking to yourself that all the challenges of research sound overwhelming or that it all sounds too hard, technical, or boring, know this: Research is *fun!* In fact, virtually all of the professionals the authors interviewed for this text said they love their jobs. They find them constantly changing, constantly fascinating. Their jobs in analytics make them leaders in media industries and the media content of the future. And they wouldn't dream of doing anything else.

Research expertise as a foundational job skill

The job of a media analyst is to ask questions and seek answers—and to advise the most senior managers of media and communication companies about the most important business decisions they make. Research is simply the tool media analysts use to do that. The questions media analysts ask and the answers they produce directly impact the content created for audiences around the world.

Most of the data media analysts work with day-to-day are not *primary data*, or data the analysts collected themselves. Media analysts mostly work with *secondary data*, that is, data collected by third-party, or independent, research vendors such as Comscore, Nielsen, and Marshall Marketing, to name just a few, or by digital platforms such as Google, Facebook, and Twitter that automatically collect data on user behavior. Thus most media analysts only occasionally design and conduct their own research.

Instead, media analysts have three primary tasks: (1) evaluate the quality of the vendors trying to sell them data, (2) evaluate the quality of

DOI: 10.4324/9780429506956-5

each dataset they get, and occasionally (3) commission or design custom research to generate data to answer specific questions.

As discussed in Chapter 1, the syndicated research industry is thriving. As media industries become more data-driven, the number of third-party research vendors vying to sell data to media companies is mushrooming. Audience research vendors are in a for-profit business and therefore have a financial incentive to minimize their own production costs—that is, cut corners—as much as possible.

Thus, one of analysts' primary tasks is to evaluate the research methods a research vendor used to gather the data it's selling. Especially when working with local or specialized research firms, it is entirely up to the analyst to determine whether the data or research offered are worth buying. Being able to critique a vendor's research design, sampling, and data collection methods to know whether the data are credible is fundamental to the job.

Independent agencies such as the Media Rating Council (MRC) and the Alliance for Audited Media (AAM) assess some research vendors' methods (Chapter 1), but the system is imperfect. Submitting to a methodological audit is voluntary for research vendors. Larger national research firms are more likely to seek accreditation or certification than smaller companies. Some audited research firms submit only some research tools or products for assessment but not others. And even the biggest research firms in the industry can have their accreditation suspended by the auditing services, leaving media companies and advertisers wondering what that means for the quality of the data on which their businesses depend (Media Rating Council, 2021, Sept.1).

Research vendors employ different designs, sampling techniques, and methodologies—even when measuring the same things. That can result in wildly different numbers that have real financial consequences for media companies. So it's the analyst's job to question how even accredited vendors' methods affected a specific dataset. What are the strengths and weaknesses of the research design and the methods used to collect the data? What are possible sources of error in the dataset? How well does the dataset represent the population the analyst wants to understand? Finally, can these data be used to answer the questions the analyst is asking?

Even datasets produced by major research vendors using accredited methodologies can have hidden flaws. For example, perhaps some meters collecting viewing data failed during the measurement period, causing audience numbers to plunge. Or maybe the vendor gathered too much data in some sections of the city and not enough in others. That can have a major impact on a station's audience numbers, if it targets its programming to the people living in the less measured neighborhoods. When unusual or extraordinary results show up in data, it's the analyst's job to recognize that and be able to track back through the design and data collection processes to find the problem.

As the importance of data to management decisions increases, so does the range of analysts' responsibilities and their need for research expertise. Media analysts may be asked to design or commission usability testing on a new website, run audience focus groups on a TV series concept, or test the effectiveness of different headlines on a news story. With major media corporations hiring data scientists to manage "big data" research (Chapter 7), media analysts are becoming the interpreters between the data scientists and the executive suite. That means media analysts must speak "research" fluently and understand research methodology.

Fundamental research concepts

Researchers use three different terms, *research methodologies*, *research design*, and *research methods*, to talk about different parts of the research process. Sometimes the three terms are used in confusing ways that intermixes them.

The first term, *research methodologies*, refers to the broad set of assumptions, strategies, techniques, and procedures that surround data collection and other aspects of research. Research methodologies are generally lumped into two types. The first is *empirical*, which depend upon systematic observation and evidence as the basis of knowledge creation. Scientific and social scientific research uses empirical methodologies. Most media analytics work is based in empirical approaches.

The second methodological approach is *humanist*, which depends on personal revelation, interpretation, and insight as the basis of knowledge. Art, music, film, and literary criticism use humanist methodologies. Greenlighting a film script or new TV series based on an executive's "gut instinct" is a media industry example of using humanist methodologies in business decisions.

You will often hear people *incorrectly* use the terms "quantitative" and "qualitative" methodologies as synonyms for "empirical" and "humanist." The terms quantitative and qualitative refer not to methodologies but to the two different types of data. Quantitative data are any numerical data, whether a simple count of something or a statistical analysis. Most data in media analytics is quantitative: ratings, shares, number of tickets sold, total revenue generated, average time audience members spend on a website or reading a particular news story. But quantitative data also includes nonnumerical concepts that are represented by numbers to make them easier to analyze. Gender, for example, might be coded as "Female = 1; Male = 2;" or audience opinions could be converted to a numerical scale such as "1= Strongly agree" and "5 = Strongly disagree."

In contrast, qualitative data are nonnumerical data, such as comments collected during interviews, visual images, scripts, or *emojis*. Qualitative data can be gathered, analyzed, and interpreted using either empirical methodologies or humanist methodologies. When an analyst is using empirical methodologies, qualitative data may be numerically recoded for analysis, such as when counting how many times a particular emoji appeared after a social media *post* or how often an image or theme appeared in scripts during a year.

Qualitative data also can be analyzed using humanist methods. For example, research firms that specialize in spotting emerging trends base their picks on a mix of observation, experience, and opinion. Screenwriters might develop a storyline by interviewing people who have lived a particular experience. In either case, exactly replicating such "findings" would be impossible because the data were gathered through personal interactions and interpretations inseparable from the researcher.

The important point here, however, is that whether the data are quantitative or qualitative, a researcher's choice of empirical or humanist methodology determines what types of research designs and research methods are considered "quality." High-quality empirical research uses very different approaches than does high-quality humanist research. Media analysts must ensure that the research designs and methods used to generate data meet the quality standards for the methodology used.

With all the money at stake, however, most media and advertising executives want evidence, not personal perspectives, to support their business decisions. Thus most media research is based in empirical, social science methodologies. This chapter will focus most of its attention on the standards that define quality empirical research.

Research design

Research design refers to a precise plan for conducting research. A research design includes (1) the specific research questions to be answered, (2) the population to be studied, (3) sampling procedures, (4) the data collection or "research methods" to be used.

The quality of the research design determines the quality of the data generated. Poor research design produces unreliable, invalid data—and bad business decisions. While there is almost always more than one way to design any research project, good research designs include the components listed here. Following these brief descriptions, we will discuss population and sampling more fully.

Comparisons

Comparison is fundamental to good research design and to human understanding. A 2 rating for your station's 5 p.m. newscast may not look good. But if it's higher than your competitors' ratings at that hour or higher than it was the same time last year, the comparison tells you you're actually doing well. Without building in comparisons or control groups into a design, you can't understand what data actually *mean*.

A carefully defined, relevant population

A *population* is the group you want to study. That may be all the people in the city your newspaper serves—or just the subscribers to your publication. It might be all the news stories your TV station produced on a specific topic or all the products advertised around the 5 p.m. newscast last month. A population is comprised of all people or objects that make up whatever you want to understand. It's critical to know exactly what population is relevant to your research question, what the boundaries are that determine whether someone or something is or is not relevant to your question, and where the relevant members of the population can be found. The challenges of defining populations will be discussed throughout this text but particularly in Chapter 13.

Probability sampling/assignment

A *sample* is the subgroup you select from the population from which you gather data. If you gather data from every single person or item in a population, you are conducting a *census*. That's rarely done because collecting data on every member of a population is expensive and nearly impossible. So unless the relevant population is very small and very accessible, or the relevant population is the people using a technology that collects user data, researchers don't use censuses. They use samples.

Randomly or *probabilistically* selecting a sample of cases from your population helps ensure that the cases in your sample reflect all of the characteristics of the population equally well.[1] Random selection and random assignment are the equivalent of rolling dice or flipping a coin. A randomly drawn sample should produce a sample in which all key characteristics of the population such as age, gender, education, income, religion, etc. are represented at the same level they occur in the population.

The goal of random selection is to minimize the likelihood that there is some hidden but systematic factor influencing the results of your data analysis, leading you to wrong conclusions. If, for example, a dataset about general news consumption was created from a sample with twice as many women as men as there were in the population being studied, there would be a high probability of invalid results.

The concepts of population and sampling are two of the most important elements of research design and two of the most important things for a media analyst to understand. Both will be discussed in detail in the next section.

Empirical observation

Empirical observation means the data were generated through observation and measurement, not from the researcher's/vendors' feelings, personal interpretations, and arguments.

Systematization

Data are gathered through some systematic process of measurement that tried to eliminate factors that might affect the data's quality, such as poor sampling or careless data collection methods.

Unit of analysis

The unit of analysis refers to what exactly is being analyzed. For example, are you analyzing teens' video game *usage*, or are you trying to understand teens' *social behavior* around video game usage? In the first example, the unit of analysis would be different measures of game play. In the second example, the unit of analysis would be users' communication or activities surrounding their game play. A project's unit of analysis determines its population and sampling strategy, so most projects have only one unit of analysis.

Variables

A *variable* is something that plays a role in whatever you are trying to understand. The **demographic** characteristics of audience members—age, gender, education—or their **psychographic** characteristics—political affiliation, lifestyle, hobbies—might be variables that influence their video game usage or social behavior around games. What they play, how often they play, how long they play are other variables you might be interested in studying. In good research design, the analyst has thought carefully about what variables might be important to the problems being studied.

There are two types of variables. An *independent variable* is a variable the analyst thinks might be influencing the outcome. A *dependent variable* is the outcome or result that is being studied. In the preceding example, demographic and psychographic characteristics would be independent variables, while the audiences' game usage or social behavior around game play would be dependent variables.

When approaching a dataset, media analysts need to understand what variables are in it and think through what the relationships might be between those variables and the question being analyzed. Equally important is to think about what variables are *not* in the dataset—and that perhaps should be.

Operational definitions

An *operational definition* refers to how each variable is defined for purposes of measurement. In order to measure something accurately, the operational definition of each variable has to be very precise. Said another way, an operational definition is your statement of how you're going to know the thing you're measuring when you see it.

For example, if you are measuring *television viewing*, what counts as "television," and what counts as "viewing?" Is it *viewing* only if someone is sitting with eyes glued to the television, ignoring everything else? Or is it viewing if the television is on in the next room as the family eats dinner and talks? What about if the person is sitting in front of the television—but also using a cell phone at the same time or doing some other activity such as reading or knitting?

Next, is it *television* viewing if the person is streaming the content on demand over a laptop, on a computer monitor, or on a cell phone? Or is it television viewing only if they're watching on an actual television set? If you want to measure only viewing on actual television sets, then what is the difference, if any, between a "smart" television and a computer monitor—and does that difference *really* matter to the question you're trying to answer?

As you can see, developing good operational definitions is not nearly as easy as it looks. A good operational definition is very specific because you can't accurately measure what you can't precisely define. Throughout this text, you will read about how poorly and inconsistently many metrics used by professional media analysts have been operationally defined. That makes it hard for analysts and media executives to really know what the data are telling them. It also makes it nearly impossible to effectively compare many metrics across media platforms and research vendors. It is a huge and ongoing problem in the profession.

Measurement

Operational definitions are related to measurement. The way you measure a variable has to be based on how you operationally define it. But then you also have to figure out how to create measures for that definition that are user-friendly during data collection, while still allowing you to collect useful data on your variable.

For example, if you ask someone to tell you how much money they make each year, they'll probably refuse to answer. It's none of your business. But if you ask them to indicate their annual income by selecting from a list of income *ranges*, they're more likely to do it. But what income ranges do you use? If one range is $0–$1 million, is that a useful measurement of income for the questions you're trying to answer? Are people with annual incomes of $1 million the same in every way important to your research as people who have no income at all? And if $0–$1 million is too wide a range, then how do you break down possible incomes into ranges that provide meaningful *insights* into your question?

Another element of good measurement is mutually exclusive categories. If you offer a choice of "$20,000–$40,000," and "$40,000–$60,000," which category would someone making $40,000 pick? The categories have to be "$20,000–$40,000" and "$40,001–$60,000" to be a good measurement.

Transparency

Is a description available of the research design and methods used to collect the data? Is that description clear, detailed, and transparent enough so that you could use it to repeat the study to see if the findings are *replicable*? Lack of methodological transparency should be a red flag, particularly if the vendor's methods are not reviewed by the MRC, AAM, or other research industry oversight body.

Population

Before we go any farther, let's stop here and drill down on two of the most important elements of research design that a professional media analyst *must* understand: population and sampling.

As mentioned earlier, identifying the population relevant to the question you're trying to answer is one of the first and most important steps in producing quality research. But identifying the relevant population can be hard. In media analytics, it is getting harder all the time thanks to audience fragmentation across distribution platforms.

Let's say you want to understand the size and preferences of the audience for a particular program. How many in the audience are watching a particular program through over-the-air broadcasting? How many through cable subscriptions and on which cable systems in which parts of the country? How many view through satellite TV subscriptions? Among broadcast, cable, and satellite TV viewers, how many of them are time-shifting their viewing with DVRs? And how many are viewing via streaming and on which streaming platforms?

The more fragmented the audience, the harder it is to identify the boundaries of the population. Nor can you assume that the people who view on one platform are the same as those who use a different viewing technology. Just think: Does it seem likely that people who still view only traditional broadcast TV are identical on variables that might matter such as age, gender, education, income, etc. as people who view via streaming?

So let's apply that understanding to a different situation: If a vendor gives you data about audience comments about your new film that are drawn from Twitter, the data tell you nothing except what active Twitter users think about the film. Since only a small percentage of people are active Twitter users, that's a very unrepresentative sample of the general population and your target audience, no matter how well the vendor drew the sample of Tweets. The data would be useful only if active Twitter users were the sole audience that matters to you.

Identifying and reaching the populations relevant to much media and consumer research is becoming harder and more expensive every day. Audience fragmentation across content platforms is one reason. Another is Caller ID and spam blocker technologies, which make it difficult to reach people by phone so you can gather data from them.

A smart analyst would question whether, in the 21st century, people who don't use caller screening technologies and who are willing to pick up the phone and answer personal questions asked by anonymous strangers—are likely to be representative of the general population on any issue of importance? Almost certainly not. Consequently, many researchers now use comprehensive lists of home addresses to define populations for market- or geographically based media and opinion research.

To say that researchers should gather data from a population relevant to their research question may sound obvious—but it's not. Students in "Introduction to Media and Communication" classes in universities around the world are routinely asked to participate in research projects about media use, news consumption, and attitudes toward advertising and public relations messages. The data collected from the students' responses are published in peer-reviewed scientific journals as evidence of how people use or think about media.

Media researchers use students as respondents because the students are available and cheap (even free). They are a *convenience sample*, a sample selected for its convenience for the researchers, not for its relevance to the research question. University students enrolled in a media class are generally younger, more educated, and of higher socioeconomic status than the average person in their countries. They also are more interested in and knowledgeable about media. Therefore, university media and communications students are a completely *unrepresentative* population to use for studying general audiences. In fact, they are probably one of the worst possible populations to study if you really want to understand how the general public thinks about and uses media.

As it becomes ever harder and more expensive to identify and reach the populations media companies and advertisers want to understand, convenience sampling of one kind or another becomes ever more tempting, particularly for research vendors. How the sample was drawn, and from what population, are questions to be asked of every dataset.

Sampling

Once you have identified the right population to study to answer your research question, and assuming a census is not an option, the next step is to draw a sample. There are two types of samples: a random, or "probability," sample and a nonprobability sample.

Probability sampling

In probability samples, every member of the population has at least some chance of being selected. In its simplest form—a simple random sample—every element of the population has an equal chance of being selected. Selection is by chance. Samples drawn randomly, particularly as they increase in size, accurately reflect the distribution of specific characteristics of the population such as age, race, gender, income, religion, political preferences, etc. Probability samples are the ideal way of sampling for two reasons: (1) They allow researchers to calculate the amount of sampling error—that is, the percentage likelihood that the sample doesn't accurately reflect the population. That can't be estimated with nonprobability samples. (2) Because you can calculate the *sampling error*, you can generalize findings to the population, which means you can state that the findings accurately represent the population, give or take the sampling error.

For example, a news media outlet may conduct an election poll and report 53% of voters say they will vote for Candidate A, and 47% of voters say they will vote for Candidate B, with a sampling error estimate of ± 3%. With a sampling error of ±3, you have a *margin of error* on your results of 6%—3% above and below your result. That means if the election were held today, somewhere between 50% and 56% of the voters would be expected to vote for Candidate A and between 44% and 50% of the voters for Candidate B. In fact, the election *might* be a tie, since a 50–50 split is a possibility that falls within the sampling error for that poll. Based on that, a good journalist—or a good media analyst—would say the upcoming election was "too close to call."

But if you used nonprobability sampling, you would be limited to saying, "We talked to X number of people, and the people we interviewed said this . . ." You wouldn't be able to make a prediction about the likely election results because you couldn't estimate how well the sample represented the population. The same thing applies when you're analyzing audience data generated using nonprobability sampling.

Drawing a good sample is not easy. There are multiple, nearly invisible ways samples become biased and nonrepresentative. For example, in most countries, women are much more likely than men to complete surveys or agree to be interviewed. So if you simply mail a survey to a household and take whatever comes back, you're likely to wind up with many more female than male respondents. Similarly, there is seasonal variation in product advertising and in television viewing levels and film ticket sales. The savvy media analyst thinks constantly about what might be influencing the data in ways not immediately obvious but that could lead to false conclusions.

It is not enough, of course, to simply draw a sample. The researcher also must be able to actually collect data from whoever or whatever is sampled. That's getting more difficult. As consumers are inundated by requests to provide online ratings, fill out customer feedback forms, click on social media polls, and participate in other forms of pseudo-research, it's hard to get people in your sample to actually participate in your research. Thus even if you succeed in drawing a representative sample, the data you get may not be representative because of low *response rates* and biased patterns of response, such as underrepresentation of ethnic minorities or, in online research, people who are poor or live in rural areas and don't have internet connections.

Research companies use a number of techniques to solve the challenge of getting people to participate in research. One of them is the use of *panels*, whereby a research firm selects people—usually randomly—from a population and then pays them to participate regularly in the company's research over an extended period of time, usually several years. Recruiting and paying people to be long-term research subjects is obviously expensive and is a technique usually available only to major corporations and large research vendors. Nor does the use of panels entirely solve the problem because individuals and households willing to participate in such projects may or may not be representative of the population as a whole. It's the analyst's job to take a hard look at that question when handed data from panels.

Given how hard and expensive it is to draw a good sample and get a good response rate, sampling is an area where research vendors are likely to cut corners. Media analysts must know enough about good sampling to spot problems.

Sample size

One of the obvious questions media analysts need to answer is, "How big does my probability sample have to be in order for it to be representative?" The answer is: It depends.

At the simplest level, there is a formula to help determine the required size of a probability sample based on the size of the population you want to study. You'll find the formula for calculating sample size and step-by-step instructions for using it in the Discussion Questions and Exercises section of this chapter. The formula calculates the size of the sampling error you'll get for any given sample size given the size of your population. For most public opinion and audience research, the accepted sampling error is ±3 or ±4, depending on the organization (Gallup, 2022).

In addition to producing representative data if used with probabilistic sampling, a ±3 or ±4% sampling error is used at least partly because sample sizes—and therefore research costs—must rise sharply to reduce sampling error below those levels. Additionally, a 6–8 percentage point margin of error is huge when you're trying to make multimillion dollar business decisions or estimate the likely size of a program's audience at a time when live TV ratings are often a 2 or 3. That would mean your margin of error could be as much as four times larger than the rating itself. You can see the problem.

A larger sampling error makes the resulting data less useful; a smaller one makes the research too expensive. So sampling errors of ±3 or ±4 are the widely accepted compromises between research cost and data quality. But even those are problematic in a world where audience fragmentation is shrinking the size of the total population for any single piece of content.

Another key point: The relationship between population size and sample size is inverse. The smaller the population, the larger a percentage of the population you have to sample to achieve a sampling error of ±3. But a sample size of 1,000, if randomly selected and carefully *weighted* to match the population's demographic characteristics, can accurately represent the more than 250 million adults in the United States at a sampling error of ±4 (Gallup, 2022). National polling organizations in the United States historically have used sample sizes between 1,000 and 1,500 to estimate the opinions and preferences of the entire country.

Weighting refers to assigning a value to data points so that their influence on your findings matches the level of the importance of those characteristics in the larger population. For example, if you realized a higher percentage of your audience panel members were urban professional women (UPW) than actually exists in the population, you would reduce the value of each response from a UPW panel member until the combined value of all UPW responses in calculating your final results was the same as the actual percentage of urban professional women in the population.

Other factors also are critical in influencing sample size. The number of variables you can use in an analysis is affected by the number of cases you have in your dataset and therefore sample size. The fewer cases you have, the fewer variables you can use in any single analysis.

Cost is often the biggest factor in determining sample size. As noted, the larger the sample, the more expensive data collection and analysis will be. That may not seem like an issue in large media corporations, but it is. Budgets are always tight. For research vendors, the issue is how much the client will pay for the data. That's a two-edged sword. If the vendor doesn't spend enough to get a representative sample, the data will be garbage, and clients won't buy it. If the vendor gets a great sample but at a cost clients can't afford, the vendor still won't be able to sell the data—and clients won't be able to afford the data they need, a common problem in many countries and for small-market media in most countries.

Clients, of course, always want the best data at the lowest cost. As a result, there is a constant struggle between research vendors and media companies over sample sizes and quality, as well as the cost of data. Negotiating those issues with research vendors is a major part of many media analysts' responsibilities.

Nonprobability sampling

Any sampling method that is not based on random selection is *nonprobability sampling*. Collecting data from an available source that is cheap and easy to access—such as students in an "Introduction to Communication" course or shoppers in a mall—is called a *convenience sample*. But there are other types of nonprobability sampling, such as *purposive sampling*, where you select participants based on certain characteristics of interest, and *quota sampling*, a refined form of purposive sampling where you try to include the same percentage of people with a particular characteristic as there is in the population (Wimmer & Dominick, 2014).

Many types of media analytics research are based on nonprobability sampling. Focus groups and usability testing of new technologies and apps are expensive and labor intensive. Because such research usually includes only a small number of subjects and may involve a major time commitment by participants, it's hard to recruit people. Although researchers may try to find subjects with a range of demographic and psychographic characteristics, the standards for a truly representative probability sample are rarely met. Regardless of the reasons for using them, it is critical to remember that nonprobability samples can never be assumed to be representative of any population. That means the findings from such research can *never* be safely generalized to the population.

This is a major issue for media analysts, particularly as they communicate research results to media executives who, very likely, have no formal training in research methods (Chapter 4). It is easy to say, when reporting the results of a focus group, "The audience thinks . . .", as opposed to heavily qualifying your report by saying, "The seven people in the focus group said . . ." Obviously, the first statement gives more weight and credibility to your work than the second. But such statements encourage your bosses and other listeners to give more weight to your results than any nonprobability sample should have. That can lead to expensively bad business decisions.

Even if *you* are careful and professional in the way you report results from nonprobability samples, your colleagues may hear what they want to hear. In the absence of good data to support important business decisions, executives often see any data—including data of questionable *validity*—as better than no data at all. That belief encourages managers to treat research results from nonprobability samples as if they were fully representative, generalizable, and valid, no matter how limited they actually are. Part of your job as a media analyst is to listen for statements suggesting that's how your clients are thinking, so you can gently point out the need for greater caution.

Censuses

As mentioned earlier, a census refers to collecting data from every member of a population. Thanks to digital technologies, censuses—or, more accurately, near-censuses—of audience data are becoming available. *Return path data* from cable and satellite set-top boxes and on-demand services, websites and mobile apps that track users, and some social media platforms all, ostensibly, provide a census of data on their audiences' behaviors. That seems like a wonderful development for media analysts—but not so fast!

First, almost all "censuses" of audiences are gathered through some form of digital technology. Technologies can and do fail, so what may appear to be a census of audience members may actually have large chunks of missing or inaccurate data. For example, set-top boxes break and stop sending back return path data. Alternatively, they may return inaccurate data, such as when a household turns off the television but leaves on the set-top box. That will return data showing the household was tuned in to Channel X 24 hours a day the entire three months they were on vacation in South America. In addition, even within a single subscribing household, not every television set is connected to cable or satellite, so whatever other viewing (e.g., over-the-air broadcast or wireless streaming) occurs on those other sets does not get measured, unless alternative measurement technologies were used for those sets. Increasing numbers of households don't subscribe to cable or satellite at all—people referred to as "cord-cutters" or "cord-nevers"—so their viewing isn't captured by set-top boxes. Thus no matter how accurately research companies try to capture and merge audience data from across platforms, certain data and certain people just get left out. For a full discussion of the challenges of multiplatform measurement, see Chapter 9.

Second, even when the measurement technology is functioning correctly, the data may be invisibly biased by how the measurement technology is distributed across the population or by who is providing the research vendor with the data. For example, let's say a vendor is selling national-level viewing data based on return path cable and satellite television technology. But there are multiple cable and satellite companies, each serving different areas of the country, and only some of those companies sell their data to the vendor.

That brings two important factors that can bias data into play. People around the world often live in clusters according to socioeconomic characteristics such as income, political affiliation, ethnicity, and religion. So population characteristics are not evenly distributed across any region or country. Second, most companies use a business strategy. They focus on some parts of a market and not others. So a cable company may build systems in certain regions of a country but not others, or it might decide to serve only areas where the population has a certain average income level and leave economically poorer or wealthier areas to competitors.

Because of these two factors, unless the research vendor is getting return path data from 100% of the cable and satellite companies in a country, certain types of audiences are almost sure to be underrepresented and others overrepresented. Then add the fact that we know there are sharp demographic differences between cable/satellite subscribers and nonsubscribers on a number of variables such as age and income (Nielsen, 2019). Put all these factors together, and it quickly becomes clear that even return path and streaming cable and satellite "census" data are not really censuses at all, particularly as these satellite and cable services continue to decline in popularity. They are, in fact, very *un*representative of the actual national viewing audience.

If an analyst's research question is very well-defined and limited completely to the population in the census, then it is safe to treat the data from a census-based methodology as a true census. For example, if you are looking at the online behaviors of people on your news website, your online analytics program can provide you with a true census of those behaviors, subject to the general problems of online measurement discussed later. But in the preceding cable example, you would have to limit your question to "What percentage of people who subscribe to Cable Companies A, B, and C, watched Program X last week," not "What was the national rating for Program X last week?"

Many research vendors try to argue there is a *Law of Large Numbers* that means when you get enough cases, the problems of nonprobability sampling go away. This is untrue. A sample that is not representative of the population you care about is not made more representative by being made bigger. You just wind up with a bigger pile of garbage data on your desktop. Media analysts, then, need to treat most "census" datasets as they do nonprobability samples and talk about the findings they draw from them with the same caution.

The goals of empirical research design

When researchers carefully build the elements just described into their research design, they are more likely to achieve the four primary goals of empirical research that determine whether the data they analyze are high "quality." Those goals are discussed next.

Reliability

In research, *reliability* means that, if the study were repeated with the same population, sampling, and methods, the results would be the same. Reliability is critical because if you get different results each time you analyze the same thing—such as a particular program's ratings—how do you know what's actually going on? If you can't tell what's really going on, how do you make business decisions?

To see the problem of data reliability for yourself, just go to the internet. Many sources publish media industry data, and even a brief search will reveal reliability problems. Different sources produce wildly different measures of the same things: annual industry revenue, audience size, total number of subscribers to different types of media, etc. The fact that numbers are published on the internet does not make them either reliable or valid.

Validity

Validity refers to whether your data and analysis accurately represent reality. There are two types of validity: *validity of measurement* and *validity of inference*. Validity of measurement refers to your level of confidence that the data generated are, in fact, *valid*, that is, they accurately reflect the realities in your population. If data are not reliable (changing with every measurement), they cannot be valid. However, data can be reliable but still not be valid if some form of systematic error was built into the research design.

For example, let's say you want to know what kinds of advertisers buy time around TV news in Canada. If you sampled TV advertisements only from March and April for three years, your data probably would look pretty much the same every year and therefore would be reliable. But it would not be a *valid* reflection of the range of advertisers interested in buying time around TV news because you sampled only three months— and the same three months every year. Different products are advertised at different times of the year. Toy advertisements increase before Christmas. Travel advertising rises before the summer months. An analyst needs to always ask what types of hidden influences might be creating systematic biases in a dataset that invalidate the findings.

Validity of inference refers to whether you're reading your results correctly. The relationship between two variables may be quite strong—highly correlated—so that when one occurs, the other often or always also occurs. But that doesn't mean there is a real—or valid—relationship between the two variables. Researchers often remind each other that "*correlation* is not causation."

Take, for example, the fact that, worldwide, you can reliably predict that as children's shoelaces get longer, their reading ability will improve. Does that mean that if you buy children longer shoelaces, their ability to read will improve automatically? Of course not. The correlation exists because as children get older, their feet get bigger, and their shoelaces get longer. At the same time, they're learning and practicing reading skills. So the relationship between shoelace length and reading ability is highly correlated and highly reliable but not at all valid.

Research turns up many coincidental—but spurious—relationships between variables. The media analyst teases out which relationships are valid and then which of those valid relationships are relevant to your media company's success. That's another question altogether.

Causality

Analysts and media executives want to know what causes things to occur. Why is one video game successful and another a flop? What caused that film to be a box office sensation against all predictions? Why don't young people consume news?

Unfortunately, proving beyond doubt that one thing causes another is very difficult, even in the physical sciences. So the word "cause" should be used cautiously when reporting research findings. Before using it, the analyst must ask: "Do the claims that one variable in the data 'caused' the other meet the basic tests for determining causality?

There are three requirements for causality (Babbie, 1989):

1. The cause has to precede the effect in every case; that is, there has to be a *time-order effect*. If you buy a car, and a month later your new car is featured in a blockbuster film, the movie did not cause you to buy the car. The time-order effect was wrong.
2. There has to be a relationship—a correlation—between the two variables. If TV ratings normally fall in the summer as audiences head outside or travel and then rise again in the autumn, you can't blame timing if your new series premiers in midautumn to bad ratings.
3. If there is a relationship between Variables A and B, there cannot be a third variable that reasonably explains that relationship—as in the example where growing up explains the relationship between the length of children's shoelaces and their reading ability.

Generalizability

Generalizability means the findings apply to everyone in the studied population. You may have collected data on the viewing habits of only 1,000 people, but if you have a good sample, the findings are generalizable to all 80 million people in the country. Whether research results are generalizable is mostly a question of whether they're based on a large and representative probability sample of the population being studied.

Research methods

The third research term mentioned at the beginning of this chapter was *research methods*. Research methods are the specific tools researchers use to collect and analyze data. They are a central element of every research design. The choice of the "right" or "best" method is determined by your research question, your preference for empirical or humanist methodologies, and the time, money, and expertise available.

Research methods include such things as surveys, experiments, *content analysis*, focus groups, field observations, and digital data collection. Each of these methods is complicated and requires in-depth training in order to gather the highest-quality, most trustworthy data. Universities often offer an entire course in each method, but the techniques for using some methods, such as surveys, change constantly in response to shifting technologies and public attitudes toward research. Staying up-to-date with best practices in research methods requires commitment and continuous learning.

Because most media analysts don't do much original data collection, or *primary research*, becoming expert in specific methods may not be necessary. But having at least a basic knowledge of each method is useful when evaluating datasets and commissioning original research from research vendors.

Unfortunately, there is not space enough here to even discuss each available method. However, one method is the foundation of all others, so we'll briefly explore it. But it's important that you seek more information and methods training as you move forward in your career.

Experiments

Experiments are the gold standard for research methods because they contain most, if not all of the elements of excellent research design discussed previously. Because of that, a well-designed experiment is more likely than other methods to generate reliable, valid, and generalizable data and to help researchers identify causes. The downside of experiments is that they generally have to be conducted in laboratories under highly controlled conditions. Most other methods gather data in the field under real-world conditions, making it necessary to compromise on at least some of the research design elements built into experiments, which undercuts data quality.

Because experiments generally produce higher-quality data, they are the primary research method in the physical and medical sciences. They also are increasingly used in research studying consumer preferences, responses to advertising, and the usability of technologies and software. They've been less used in media analytics because of the need to limit the number of variables that might be influencing results, something that's almost impossible to do when collecting real-world data.

Instead, media industries increasingly are turning to controlled "field experiments," such as studying consumer behavior in retail or online environments or in testing the usability of new technologies or software. One of the most frequently used examples of field experiments is *A/B testing*. In A/B testing, content producers create two versions of something, like a headline for a news story. Visitors to the website are randomly served one of the two versions. Editors watch to see which version convinces more people to click on the story, and the weaker version is deleted.

But while such real-time field experiments are easy and valuable, experimental research is not likely to answer the most pressing questions media analysts address, such as what the audience size for last night's newscast was or how much revenue a proposed TV series is likely to produce.

Even though most media analysts are unlikely to find themselves in charge of designing and running experiments, they *should* be checking vendors' research designs against the experimental gold standard as a measure of the dataset's quality. So let's take a quick look at how an experiment works in practice.

The most common type of experiment has three stages. First, you measure your experimental group on the variable that matters to you before you do anything else. For example, how many people prefer Brand X of toothpaste over Brand Y, and how many like using toothpaste at all? Then you introduce the experimental item you want to test, also known as a *stimulus* or *manipulation*. You show them a series of advertisements for all kinds of products including an advertisement for Brand X toothpaste. Third, you measure the group again to see if the item or manipulation caused any change in whatever interests you, such as the subjects' attitudes or buying intention toward Brand X toothpaste.

The third component in experiments is that there are two groups of subjects: One experiences the manipulation, and the second, called the *control group*, doesn't. In our example, the second group would see the same advertisements as the first group but with the advertisement for Brand X toothpaste missing. Then both groups would be given post-experimental tests that included measures of their attitudes and intention to buy Brand X toothpaste. The researcher then compares the groups' before-and-after results for attitudes and intentions to buy Brand X. Finally, the results are compared across the experimental and control groups. This process gives the researcher two sets of comparisons to see whether being exposed to an advertisement for Brand X toothpaste changed people's attitudes toward the product or their intentions to buy it.

The true experiment can determine whether a stimulus or manipulation is *sufficient*—that is, the only thing needed for the effect to happen. But even if it is sufficient, the manipulation may not be *necessary* to cause the effect. You might be able to get the same effect some other way, such as by giving away free samples of Brand X toothpaste. But an experiment can show whether an introduction or manipulation produces a specific effect, which is why experiments are typically used to determine causation.

But even though experiments are the research method against which you should compare all others, you also should study many other methods. Professional media analysts can expect to routinely work with datasets created through surveys, content analysis, focus groups, and various methods of digital data collection. A strong grounding in each of those methods is important, even if becoming expert in each one is not. But the constant evolution of research methods means the professional analyst must be constantly learning. Fortunately, there are major worldwide, national, and regional associations of professional researchers who constantly study and test research methods, working together to understand how to produce the highest-quality research possible. Information about and links to these associations are in the Additional Resources section at the end of this chapter.

Data analysis and interpretation

Media analysts may evaluate the research designs and methods used to generate data, but they spend most of their time on data analysis and interpretation, particularly the latter. In the big data era (Chapter 7), large media firms often hire data scientists to manage and statistically analyze big datasets. But data interpretation, the process of turning data analysis into actionable business insights, remains media analysts' primary responsibility.

What do the data mean? Even more importantly, what do they mean in terms of the company's business goals and problems? Being a good media analyst means understanding not just research methods but also the economics and management of your industry, the market, and the strategic goals of your company. Having a solid grounding in statistical analysis will be helpful for an analyst. Having expert knowledge of the business side of media is *necessary* for an analyst.

Descriptive analysis and inferential analysis

There are two types of analysis when you're dealing with quantitative data: *descriptive analysis* and *inferential analysis*. Descriptive statistics are used to summarize and understand your data. They include things like how respondents' answers are distributed across your variable categories in terms of both raw numbers and percentages. Example: 54% of viewers of Program A were male, 43% were female, and the remainder didn't identify their gender. Descriptive analysis also includes measures of central tendencies in the data, such as *means*, *medians*, and *modes*, as well as minimum and maximum values for variables and the range those values represent.

Inferential statistics are used to make inferences about the entire population on the basis of the sample and can only be used if your sample is a probability sample. Examples of inferential statistics include such things as standard deviations and confidence intervals. When the questions you are trying to answer require you to test hypotheses about the relationships between variables or to use regression analysis to look at the relative importance of multiple variables at once, you are using inferential statistics.

Media analysts spend much of their time focused on descriptive analysis. Because of that, none of the exercises in this book will require the use of inferential statistics. The problems and cases will require you to conduct descriptive analyses of the data provided and think about not just what the numbers are but what they mean to the business of media and the problem described.

Controls in data analysis

One critical issue in data interpretation is controlling your data for things that may be affecting it—and that may affect your understanding of what the data say. This is similar to our earlier discussion of looking for things that may be invisibly influencing your sample.

For example, if you are looking at monetary data over time, such as revenue trends or the total box office revenue brought in by different films, you have to control for inflation in order to make valid comparisons. Every country has a certain level of monetary inflation every year. Inflation is the increase in the average price of goods and services in a country. Inflation means that the actual buying power of a country's basic monetary unit— US $1, for example—is less each year than the year before. In most countries in good economic times, inflation is 1%–2% per year. But the inflation rate changes every year in response to real-world political and economic conditions. In some countries with severe economic problems, it can be much higher—sometimes more than 100% per year.

What that means is that if you don't adjust your monetary data for inflation, your analysis and data interpretation will be wrong. For example, something that cost US $1 in 1970 would cost approximately US $7.71 in 2022. In other words, a film released in 2022 would have to gross US $7.71 million in its first year to equal the box office success of a 1970 film that grossed US $1 million that year.

Adjusting for inflation is country specific and tricky, so not all inflation adjustment charts give exactly the same answers. But you can see why controlling for inflation is important. If you didn't adjust for it, you'd give your boss a very inaccurate picture of how well her remake of a famous film is doing in theaters compared to the 1970 original.

While inflation is one of the more obvious things that can throw off your data analysis and interpretation, it is by no means the only thing. Let's go back to the preceding example. What other controls might you need in order to get an accurate idea of possible changes in audience demand for Hollywood films across the half century? After you adjust the total figures for inflation, you might want to control the results again—this time for the number of films the industry released in 1970 compared to the number of films released in 2022 to see what differences there might be in per-film box office revenue.

If you ask what film was the top-grossing Hollywood film of all time, you would get quite a few different answers, depending on which controls you applied. After narrowing down your list to a few top contenders and adjusting gross revenue for inflation, other things you might want to control include number of years since release; film genre; whether the revenue figures were mostly box office or included secondary markets such as DVD and streaming rights; whether all revenue figures were based on the same measures—just domestic box office, or domestic and international and maybe revenue from *windowing*. Then you might also want to control for population growth by calculating the number of films released per capita or box office revenue per capita, since there are more potential filmgoers today than there were 50 years ago (Chapter 15).

What you see in your data interpretation will depend upon what you look for, and what you look for is achieved by applying different controls. Usually, it takes some thought to identify the variables you need to control in order to get the most accurate answer possible to the question you are asking or the problem you are solving. Critical thinking is the more important thing a media analyst does.

Best practices in data evaluation and analysis

While you've now been introduced to the basic concepts related to research and methods, what are the steps and process you want to follow when first approaching a dataset? The first thing is to stop and ask yourself—or, more specifically, "ask" the dataset—a few questions. Some people refer to this as "interviewing" the data. For instance, what is this dataset capable of telling me? What can it not tell me? What are the relevant and meaningful relationships that could be identified within the dataset?

Then, once you are satisfied the dataset meets quality thresholds and "sniff tests," how do you proceed? Use the steps in Box 3.1 as your guide. Among other things, you will need to "clean" the data before you can analyze them. (Yes, it may be dirty.)

Box 3.1 Best practices for data evaluation and analysis

1. Interview the data:

   a. What is this dataset capable of telling me? What can it not tell me?

      i. Identify the variables that were measured.

         (1) If something wasn't measured that you need, this will not be a helpful dataset for you.
         (2) Is there some other source for the missing data you need?

      ii. Note how the response data were structured and organized for the various questions.

         (1) If the data are not structured or organized in the way you need or in a way that is useful, then this dataset may not be for you.
         (2) If the response data are not structured in the way you need, could you easily transform or convert the data into another form that would be useful for analysis?

      iii. What is the sample population? Who or what is missing?

   b. What relationships seem:

      i. important?
      ii. meaningful or relevant to your industry sector?
      iii. relevant to the bottom line or other strategic goals?

   c. What analytical explorations look interesting and might be worth investigating?

2. Evaluate the dataset:

   a. Validity and trustworthiness

      i. What is the source of the data? What is the origin of the dataset?
      ii. How was the dataset generated? What methods were used (e.g., surveys, automated processes, human vs. nonhuman generated)?
      iii. If a sample was used, how representative is it?
      iv. When was the dataset generated (recency)?
      v. How did the dataset come to be in this format?
      vi. Are the data relevant?

b. Stability

    i. Can you detect irregularities?

    ii. Gaps in data collection (e.g., the source gathered data from November 1–15, then November 17–24, then November 26–30)? If so, is there an explanation for why that makes sense?

c. Data hygiene

    i. How clean are the data (e.g., typos, double entries)?

    ii. Are there any missing data/fields?

    iii. Suspicious-looking data (e.g., survey straight-lining, rapid completion times)?

3. Data cleaning: Look for and fix:

a. typos,

b. misspellings,

c. missing data or data fields,

d. inaccuracies,

e. disparities,

f. contradictions,

g. cases with lack of variation in responses across variables or wildly unrealistic data.

4. Prepare to analyze the data.

a. What do you want to know?

    i. If you don't have specific research questions or goals, you don't know where to start or where to look.

b. How will you know when you get there?

    i. Identify the variables/items in the dataset that will reveal the answers.

    ii. What analyses or statistical tests will you need to perform to generate the answer(s)?

5. Analyze the data and report results:

a. Conduct appropriate analyses and tests.

b. Adhere to statistical principles and accurate interpretation.

c. Draw conclusions based on findings (e.g., do not exaggerate, mislead, or stretch the truth).

Summary and conclusion

Understanding research design, research methods, and basic statistics is a critical skill set for anyone who wants a career in media analytics. Media analytics focuses on human interactions with media, so the field is grounded in social science research methods. With large sums of money hanging in the balance, business executives want assurance that media analysts' findings and recommendations are based on hard evidence, that is, reliable and valid data. That means the quality of the research design and methods used to generate an analyst's findings are all important.

While most of the data an analyst uses will be bought from research firms, it is the analyst's job to understand and to be able to critique the design and methods used to collect those data. Data generated from deeply flawed research designs and methodologies cannot be trusted as the basis of business decisions.

That said, there is no such thing as a perfectly executed research project. All research has limitations. All datasets contain measurement errors. Thus it is the job of media analysts to understand research well enough to judge the quality of the data in front of them.

Learning about research design and methods is a lifelong process—not just because there is so much to learn but also because research professionals constantly develop new methods and test old ones to learn about their flaws and improve them. New technologies also create new methodologies, each with its own opportunities and problems that need to be identified and understood.

If all this talk of research methods, challenges, and lifelong learning sounds overwhelming, never forget that nearly every professional interviewed for this book described her or his job as "fun" and "fascinating." Yes, it's demanding. But who wants a boring career? Media analytics is a career for people who love media, love challenges, and love discovery.

Additional resources

University courses and current textbooks on research design and research methods such as the experimental method, survey research, focus groups, content analysis, and ethnography, among others.

A basic course in statistics is critically important for media analysts. Taking a few more-advanced courses in statistics, data science, or data management will be helpful.

Alliance for Audited Media: https://auditedmedia.com/
American Association for Public Opinion Research: www.aapor.org/
Comscore: www.comscore.com/

94   *Foundations of media analytics*

Media Rating Council: http://mediaratingcouncil.org/
Nielsen: www.nielsen.com/us/en/
World Association for Public Opinion Research: https://wapor.org/

Recommended cases

These cases can be found on the textbook website: www.routledge.com/cw/hollifield

Case 3.1: Understanding Sample Size and Research Costs. Discussion Questions and Exercises 2–5 in this chapter
Case 3.2: Critiquing a Vendor's Research Proposal
Case 3.3: Designing a Content Analysis
Case 3.4: Scraping and Critiquing Data

Case studies, along with accompanying datasets for this chapter, can be found on the text website. We particularly suggest the preceding cases in the order listed. See the companion website and instructor's manual for detailed descriptions of these and other relevant cases.

Discussion questions and exercises

1. The chapter outlines some of the questions media analysts may be asked to answer and the issues they're asked to consider. Look again at some of the questions and discuss them in terms of the research design and methods issues they raise. Pick two or three questions, and discuss how you would design a study to gather the data needed to understand the problem. What population would be important? How would you sample, and what problems might you encounter? What method of data collection would you use? How would you operationally define your most important variables? What measurements would you use? What controls might be important? What problems might threaten the quality of your data? Be realistic in your thinking, and be prepared to communicate your plan to your boss as if you were trying to convince them to fund the needed research.

Box 3.2 Case 3.1: understanding sample size and research costs

Good News! The formula below is not nearly as complicated as it looks. Let's start with the idea that we have 2,000 households in our community, and we want a sample with a sampling error of ±3. If you

---

$$\text{Formula: } 1.96 \sqrt{\frac{pq}{N}} * 1 - \left[\frac{N}{P}\right]$$

Figure 3.1 Formula for calculating sample size

don't remember how to do these types of calculations using algebra, follow these simple steps:

1. Start with "*pq*," which means, of course, *p* multiplied by *q*. *p* stands for population size, or the size of the population from which you will draw the sample. *q* stands for the size of your sample, which we don't know yet. But since this sampling formula assumes you are drawing a probabilistic sample so that every member of the population has a 50–50 chance of being drawn, you replace both *p* and *q* with 0.5. That makes it 0.5*0.5=0.25. So you can start by just replacing *pq* with 0.25.
2. Now we move to N. N stands for the size of the sample you think you will need in order to reach your target sampling error of ±3. So pick a number between 1 and 2,000 that you think will work.
3. 0.25/(by the number you chose) = ?
4. Now find the square root of that answer by hitting the square root symbol ($\sqrt{}$) on your calculator.
5. Multiply that answer by the 1.96 at the left of the equation.[2] The number that results will be your sampling error estimate when you take the ± symbol from the front of the 1.96 and add it to your result.
6. Then round your final answer as needed. So, for example, if your final answer is 3.26, you can round that down to ±3—or you can add a few more cases to your sample size and run the formula again to bring the results closer to 3.0 without rounding.
7. There: You're done.

You've probably noticed that we haven't used the second part of the formula in Figure 3.1 to get this answer. That's because the second half is used to adjust the formula for very small populations, generally a population of 500 or fewer, although there is no firm rule.

8. To use the small population adjustment, first complete Steps 1–7. Run the calculation, and write down the result somewhere, rounded to two decimal places.

9. Then use the second half of the formula by using the same sample size number you used for N in your first calculation and dividing it by the actual number of your small population.
10. Subtract that answer from the number 1.
11. Multiply that result by the final number you wrote down from the first half of the formula.
12. There: You're done.

If you didn't get close enough to your target sampling error of ±3, choose a larger number (or smaller, if you're below ±3) for N, and run the formula again from the beginning.

2. *Exercise: Calculating sample size and estimating research budgets*
   This exercise will have you evaluate sample size and how it affects various decisions and outcomes that a media organization will face. These scenarios are explained next. You will use the formula in Figure 3.1 and Questions a and b to explore the relationships between population size, sample size, and research costs and to gain practice in calculating sample sizes so that you can critique research proposals.
   Calculate the amount of time required, and the cost of each of the following research projects. Note: Use the second part of the formula: (1 – Sample size ÷ Population size), and multiply that with the results of the first part of the formula *only* when you have a very small population, such as a population smaller than 500.

   a. You are the Editor of a newspaper with a circulation 3,051 and are planning a reader survey. What size sample would you need to draw from your readership in order to have the various sampling errors listed next? And if the average cost of the survey was $100 per respondent completion, what would this research project cost you under each scenario?

   ±4 _____   × $100 $_____.
   ±3 _____   × $100 $_____
   ±2 _____   × $100 $_____

   b. If your phone survey takes an average of 15 minutes to conduct, including going through the introductory script with the respondent, and it takes you another five minutes per completed survey to select and dial the number, and finish the paperwork (a total of 20 minutes), and if it takes you an average of five minutes for each call where you have a refusal and your completion rate is one out of three calls, how much *time* will it take for you to complete the survey project if you personally make all the calls? Use the numbers for the sample sizes you calculated for the project in Question a.

±4 _____   (hours/minutes)
±3 _____   (hours/minutes)

3. *Exercise: Calculating a sample size for a small population*
You are the professor of a class with 65 students. How many of those students would you have to survey in order to learn their opinions of the course with a sampling error of ±3?
(Hint: This is where you would use the adjustment for a small population shown in Figure 3.1.)

4. *Exercise: Writing a research question*
Write an audience-related research question you would like to understand. Discuss the question. What do you think would be the most important variables for which you would need data in order to answer your question?

5. *Exercise: Developing a basic research design*
Devise and then write or present to your class a research design for a study to answer the research question you developed in Exercise 4. What methodology would you use? What would your unit of analysis be? What variables would be most important in answering your question (identify no more than three to five)? How would you operationally define those variables? What would your population be? How would you go about sampling that population? What sample size would you need? What methods would you use to gather data?

6. *Exercise: Controlling for invisible influences on results*
Use an online inflation calculator to adjust the following box office figures for inflation to see what their revenues would be in 2020 US $.

Table 3.1 Box Office Revenue for Five Hypothetical Films Released 1940–1987

Film	Year of release	Box office gross in original dollars (US $)
Film A	1941	3.3 million
Film B	1959	15 million
Film C	1935	3.1 million
Film D	1969	57.7 million
Film E	1986	250 million

Notes

1. When a project uses experimental design, instead of sampling from the population, you randomly assign participants to the experimental and control groups and then compare outcomes across the two groups.
2. 1.96 is used to establish the standard confidence interval of 97.5% that is used in statistics.

References

Babbie, E. (1989). *The practice of social research* (5th ed). Wadsworth Publishing Co.
Gallup. (2022). *How does Gallup polling work?* https://news.gallup.com/poll/101872/how-does-gallup-polling-work.aspx
Media Rating Council. (2021, September 1). *MRC statement on pending changes to accreditation statuses of Nielsen Television Services*. [Press release]. http://mediaratingcouncil.org/090121%20MRC%20Public%20Statement%20on%20Nielsen%20TV%20Accreditation%20Statuses.pdf
Nielsen. (2019, January 14). *The Nielsen local watch report: The evolving over-the-air home*. www.nielsen.com/us/en/insights/report/2019/nielsen-local-watch-report-the-evolving-ota-home/#
Wimmer, R. D., & Dominick, J. R. (2014). *Mass media research: An introduction* (10th ed.). Wadsworth Cengage Learning.

4 Communicating insights

You might have the best data output and have worked hours on your analyses, reports, and charts. But guess what? None of it matters if your audience doesn't understand it. "Translation" and "data storytelling" are terms you may have heard, and they refer to just this. Data and analytics are just tools, a means to an end. Findings generated can produce valuable business intelligence that leads to insights. But what is that? And how should it be communicated?

An *insight* can be defined as an understanding of the data findings in a way that is actionable and relevant to the business. How business insights get applied to solve problems—that's what it's all about. As an analyst, your job is to tell people what the data mean, why they should care, and what next steps they might take with the information they have. Essentially, you are telling a story—a data-driven story. That's what communicating insights is all about.

How important are communication skills to the professional analyst? When asked to name the *most* important skill a professional media analyst needed to have, research director after research director said "storytelling" and "communication skills." Having the ability to analyze data is almost useless if you can't effectively communicate what you've learned and why it's important to the people who matter—and be able to do that even if *they* know nothing about research and statistics. Equally importantly, you have to be able to communicate quickly, clearly, and efficiently, whether you're standing in front of a room or responding to an urgent email. Media executives don't have the time or patience to wade through long, complicated explanations.

In this chapter, we'll talk about what effective communication looks like and how to adapt the communications about our findings for different audiences. Certainly, we wouldn't provide the same level of detail or use the same kind of language for a CEO as we would with our fellow analysts or even the general public. We also recognize that we communicate in written, visual, and oral forms. We need to be effective communicators

DOI: 10.4324/9780429506956-6

of data findings across all three modalities—written, visual, and oral—and with different audiences in mind. This begins with practicing effective data storytelling.

Telling a story

Entire courses are devoted to data storytelling and visualization, so important are these skills. The underlying rationale for taking a narrative or storytelling approach with data is that, at the end of the day, most humans do not respond to data and statistics. We respond to stories. So why not communicate in the way we are wired to respond? While we always want to present information that is valid and accurate, the style in which we present our findings can indeed be narrative in nature. That is, there can be a protagonist (the company), a conflict (the company's problem), rising action, climax, and resolution (recommendations to the company). Another element is story structure. Every good story has a clear beginning, a middle, and an end.

Another way to think about storytelling, beyond story structure, is the presence of emotion. Again, most of us do not respond to statistics or data alone. We make decisions and purchases based on how products, services, or ideas make us feel. One Stanford University professor notes that stories are the most meaningful "when they are memorable, impactful and personal" and recommends integrating both statistics and story, saying that "when data and stories are used together, they resonate with audiences on both an intellectual and emotional level" (Jennifer Aaker, as cited in Waisberg, 2014). Professor Aaker notes that we remember stories over statistics, and, while we may think we are making a data-driven decision, we often use logic to later rationalize our decision that was really driven by emotion. In other words, for lasting effect, we need to "persuade the intellectual brain but also resonate with the emotional brain" (Aaker, 2013 @ 4:07). Studies show that we respond to stories because they are more meaningful and that we connect with the storyteller, compared to statistics (Aaker, 2013).

You may be wondering how certain types of workplace storytelling could ever be emotional or even personal. Certainly, the storytelling is different than what you might tell to a friend. But as one industry example, presenting data findings on declining newspaper circulation or monthly magazine subscriptions can feel personal or even emotional—in a corporate or organizational sense—once you connect those findings to the bottom-line implications and make recommendations. Data might suggest you need to halt an underperforming product or service, eliminate staff, or reduce frequency of publication if trends don't change. "Personal" or "emotional" for a company can refer to its bottom line or financial well-being, even to the success or eventual survival of the organization. So we come full circle with the idea of storytelling. It's not about the data; it's about what story the data tell and the implications. Stories are powerful because they are meaningful, and because of this, the most effective storytellers can have tremendous power over their audience (Aaker, 2013).

One of the key strategies for gaining power over your audience or for simply connecting with them is to focus on audience-centered communication. Audience-centered communication means that you, the storyteller, take the time to think about and understand your audience before trying to communicate to them. Who are they? What elements of your story are most likely to interest them, engage them, or be important to them? What types of information or background do they bring to your story? What will you need to tell them in order for them to understand the importance, value, and relevance of what you are telling them? What do they already know, and will they be bored if you repeat it? What style of communication will be most effective with these individuals—businesslike, funny, narrative, something else?

An effective structural way to think about data storytelling may not be in the literary sense but in a journalistic one, following the typical structure of a news story. Skelton (2017) argues that this is a more effective way to think about data storytelling because it removes the idea of the narrative arc with climax and emotion. In a corporate setting, that may feel like a forced and inappropriate story structure. Using the journalistic approach instead focuses on the "lead" or headline of the story you want to tell with your data. The inverted pyramid is the traditional news story structure. The story's lead and most newsworthy information are shared at the top (e.g., who, what, where, when, and how), followed by additional important information and concluding with additional but less important detail, such as general or background information. This structure can also work for data storytelling within an organization, whether it is a media company, retail firm, or governmental organization.

Regardless of what story structure is used, however, we must always keep our audience in mind. It is possible to use the journalistic, inverted pyramid structure but customize the tone and style according to your audience. You may wish to insert some comedic or personal elements, if they would help connect with them and also help tell your data story. For instance, with the example of declining newspaper circulation, a personal or emotional element for the newsroom employee audience might include talking about the paper's historical legacy within the community, how it has helped bring about social change or hold government leaders accountable, and reporters' critical roles in continuing that legacy.

Now that you understand that communicating insights effectively starts with storytelling, what are our other goals, and what types of communications might we use?

Goals for communicating insights

Clarity and understanding. At the most basic level, that's what each of us wants our communications to accomplish for our audience. But how do we get from a bunch of statistical output and Excel spreadsheets to clear, concise communications that mean something to people? It starts by identifying the audience. To whom will you be presenting your information? Who is the audience, and what level of expertise will they have— both in terms of content domain and statistics or metrics? Once you can answer these questions, you'll have a good foundation. You want to match the level of expertise, as well as the information needed, with the type of audience you have and what they need to know, how much detail to provide and what "vocabulary" to use when communicating. For instance, if you are presenting to fellow analysts or data scientists, it's probably okay to use more scientific and statistical language and detail. But your CEO and marketing director probably won't care about those details or how you arrived at your answer to the research objectives— they just want answers, and they want them in bullet points! "Tell us what we need to do, and that's it." Once you identify the audience and their role, you'll have a good idea of the level of depth and detail you need to provide.

That's precisely what many experts say we need to keep in mind when preparing our communications. What is the *reason* for our communication or the action driving it? Put another way, "What do you need your audience to know or do?" (Knaflic, 2015, p. 22). This will help us pinpoint exactly what to say, how to say it, and to whom. Often, Knaflic (2015) states, it helps to identify the decision maker to whom you will be presenting the information. What information, in what form, would best help that person in making their decision or solving the problem? Write with your primary audience in mind, with other audiences in descending order of importance. Knaflic (2015) also states that, if you cannot articulate what your audience needs to know or do, perhaps you don't need to communicate anything— or at least that's not the proper audience for your communication.

Another factor or lens to look through when determining how to prepare your communications, including how much detail to provide, is your own expertise as the analyst. You are the subject-matter expert at this point; you've done all of the in-depth analysis and created the spreadsheets and tables. It can be tempting, Knaflic (2015) notes, to show everyone all your work and the steps that went into your analysis to generate the results, particularly if you are excited about your work! But the truth is that most audiences won't care about all that. This doesn't mean they don't appreciate your hard work—they most certainly do—it's just not relevant to them. By the time it gets to the decision makers, they just need to know what to do and, ideally, how it connects to the bottom line. The three most important questions you are answering in nearly every communication are: (1) What did you find out? (2) Why should the decision makers care? (3) What should they do? You are the expert, so be confident wearing that hat, and give it to them short and sweet.

Next, how are you expected to present your findings? What is the preferred form or *modality* of communication? Sometimes you won't be told, in which case you can use your own judgment. Other times, your supervisor may have stipulated that something should be a written report, an email, or even a live or recorded video presentation with a slide deck. Factors to consider when deciding what form your storytelling should take include not only your audience but the amount of information that needs to be conveyed, the level of detail and complexity, what modality would be the best vehicle for clarity and understanding, and whether visuals or handouts of some sort would be helpful.

Common types of communications

As analysts, much of what we do, as noted, can be described as *data storytelling*. An analyst takes the insights generated and translates them into communications for the appropriate audience, narratives you might call stories. *Forbes Magazine* describes data storytelling as one of the most important and in-demand skills needed by companies today (Dykes, 2016), and it is being taught in academic curricula. Tableau software describes data storytelling as the "new language of corporations" and a top business intelligence trend ("Data storytelling is," 2019). Data storytelling often utilizes data visualizations, as will be discussed later, but, in fact, can be done through written or oral communication or via other types of visualizations as well. Some of the most common types of communications you'll use as an analyst are described here. Be aware that different organizations may have their own internal vocabulary for each of these, so you may see some variation in naming, as well as additional communication forms not listed here.

Memorandum ("memo") or email

This is the shortest type of professional written communication. It is often sent as an email but could also be in hard copy. Its most typical use is to communicate a singular information item, or it has a singular purpose; hence the brevity. Examples of when an analyst might write a memo are to share last night's program *viewership* or the initial results of an advertising campaign, to make known a change in leadership at the company or the acquisition of a new client, or to announce the date and logistics of a product release. The length of a memorandum can vary, and there is no fixed page count; it may be as short as a few sentences or could be a brief report of two or three pages. However, its purpose is to convey smaller amounts of information. Greater quantities of information should be communicated in a report or even a slide deck.

Executive summary

As the name implies, an executive summary is intended to be a short overview of the highlights and findings of a longer report. Its intended audience is the busy executive or manager who may not have time to read the report in its entirety, at least not immediately. It gives a quick summary of what is contained in the report. It can be a section at the beginning of the longer report or a stand-alone document. Executive summaries are usually one page or less, with key findings summarized in bullet points.

Report

This is a written document that can vary in purpose as well as length. Written reports are best utilized to convey in-depth, substantive, or large amounts of information, such as providing detailed insights generated by a custom research project. While some reports are custom, other more routine reports may be produced monthly, quarterly, or yearly to track progress on various **key performance indicators** (**KPIs**) and to provide updates. Many shorter, basic reports can be generated automatically these days via the software or program being utilized. Such automation should be used whenever possible so that an analyst's time can be better spent actively thinking about the more challenging, nonroutine tasks. Slide decks are increasingly taking over the role of written reports, depending on their purpose and the organization.

One sheet

As the name suggests, this is a single page on which a few key data points or statistics are provided, often with supporting visuals such as charts or graphs. Unlike an executive summary that provides a synopsis of a longer report, the one sheet's purpose is usually persuasive, i.e., to try to sell or convince the reader of something, for instance to buy advertising. For a television network or station, this one sheet might display the viewership of key demographics for the previous evening's prime time schedule. One example from Marshall Marketing (see Figure 4.1) shows key data points relevant to mattress firms who may be interested in advertising within a market. It displays a profile of consumers who say they plan to purchase

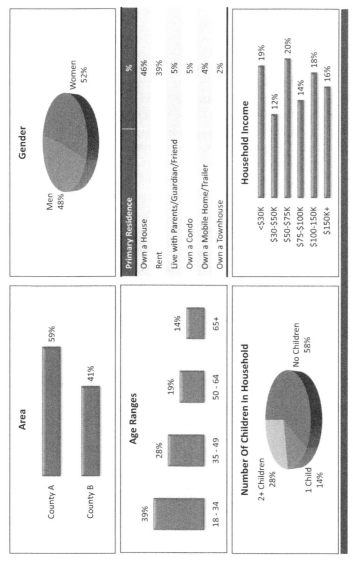

Figure 4.1 One sheet: selling mattresses

Source: Marshall Marketing

a new mattress including breakdowns by geographical location (county), gender, age, and information about residential situation, children, and income level. In some ways, the one sheet is visually similar to a dashboard, but a dashboard is online and interactive, whereas a one sheet is usually a printed copy or single slide of selected information.

Slide deck

This is essentially a PowerPoint presentation (or similar software). Visual slides are created to support a live or recorded audiovisual presentation. Increasingly, slide decks play another role and are being used in lieu of written reports. They often get shared via email or as attachments to emailed memos. Length varies according to purpose. A sample slide deck can be found on the textbook's companion website. It is a pitch presentation that might be used if a local television station wanted to persuade local business owners in the mattress category to buy advertising time on their station. (Due to limited space, see the textbook website for this resource.)

Dashboard

Some of you have seen or perhaps even used these. A *dashboard* is an online, interactive portal or user interface that continually updates various metrics. It is a type of data visualization. Dashboards can be customized to display the metrics, charts, and information you most often use. Examples of platforms with dashboards include Google Analytics, Tableau, Parse.ly, Marshall Marketing, and many proprietary media measurement companies (see Figure 4.2).

Figure 4.2a Dashboard: two views

Source: Parse.ly

Figure 4.2b (Continued)

Visual communications

There's a reason we're familiar with the adage, "A picture is worth a thousand words" (Terrar, 2014). While written communications play an important role in this storytelling, the visuals or data visualizations, when done well, can help your audience understand the story even more clearly. Examples of visualizations can include line graphs, bar charts, pie charts, and other graphics. These can be used in combination with written communications or incorporated within them (such as within a report or a slide deck). Edward Tufte is a well-known scholar in the field of the visual display of information. He has offered what we might describe as the conceptual foundations and best practices for data visualization. At its core, Tufte said, "what is to be sought in designs for the display of information is the clear portrayal of complexity. Not the complication of the simple; rather, the task of the designer is to give visual access to the subtle and the difficult—that is, the revelation of the complex" (2001, p. 191). To simplify what is complex and make comprehensible what is not. That is what data visualizations can do to help your audience hear and see the data story in its clearest possible form. Some basic tenets and best practices follow.

Comparative context

The most helpful visuals provide context. For instance, a line graph may show a sharp increase in sales for a product for the year. The graph seems to suggest strong performance, but was the performance truly "strong?" We cannot know without more information. What if competitors did just as well? (Then the product is performing at market level.) What if that increase in sales is actually a slower rate of increase or represents fewer sales than the company's previous year? (Then it seems that, comparatively speaking, the company is not doing as well as we thought, as last year's performance was even better.) Context matters and is key for the proper interpretation and relevance of the visual.

Data only

This idea is really two ideas. First, don't embellish your data visualizations with superfluous art or aesthetics. It can be distracting and takes away from the story you are trying to tell. The data are the only essential information. Let the data do their job. Second, be sure to remove any redundancies. If the visual is not representing data, remove it. Tufte (2001) uses a term—"chartjunk"—for any extra design, clutter, or information that is decorative or aesthetic and that is not germane or substantive to the data visualization. If there is no value or purpose, get rid of it.

Maximizing the data-to-ink ratio

Related to the data-only idea, the data-to-ink ratio refers to the "portion of ink (i.e. pixels) that makes up data-information on the view" (Sleeper, n.d., para. 1; Tufte, 2001). The idea is that ink or color "fill" should have a specific purpose. Almost always, Tufte (2001) says this purpose is to convey new information; elements like outlining, bolding, gridlines, or "fill" should be used only when they can help a reader more easily understand complicated data. If the data are simple, then the visualization should be presented simply.

Avoid clutter

Somewhat related is the rule of thumb that less is more. You do not want to distract your audience by taking away from the main message. Keep your data visualization as simple as possible. This does not mean boring. It means clear and concise, just as with written communication. If your visualization is cluttered, it introduces cognitive overload, confusion, or both and forces your audience to work to understand the data. You can help your audience by keeping on message and saying it with less. Artists and photographers consciously "frame" their pictures and use light and color to immediately direct the viewer's gaze to the most important thing in their pictures. Data visualizers should use that same principle. Clutter defeats that goal.

White space

Sometimes we are not just avoiding clutter. Rather, we are deliberately utilizing space to help make a point. Knaflic (2015) urges data analysts not to be afraid of white space but rather to leverage its power. It can have the same effect as a dramatic pause in verbal communication. It's like punctuation and can help us make a point. It jumps out at us visually because we are accustomed to space being filled. When a space is not filled and is used effectively, it catches our eye.

Color

While most of us enjoy color in our reading or visuals, Tufte (2001) notes that a gray scale may be one of the best visual communication techniques due to its natural visual hierarchy. As a result, "varying shades of gray show varying quantities better than color" (p. 154), lending a clear visual order for the data measures. As a background color, Knaflic (2015) prefers white above all else, as this keeps the data as the main focus. When another color is used for the background, one's eye tends to be drawn there instead and away from the data story. Contrasting color helps any visual stand out, so black lines or bars on a white background are the easiest to see. Of course, there may be reasons why you want to use color (for instance, the official company logo or a situational reason). One visual help for audiences you may wish to try is color saturation. This is a monochrome idea, but varying shades are used to indicate intensity or quantity as in a heatmap design (Knaflic, 2015). For instance, if the color selected for the visualization was blue, the higher the numbers, the darker the blue, and the lower figures would be represented by lighter blues. When viewed in its entirety, one's eyes are drawn to the darker (higher) or lighter (lower) shades of the table, and we can see at a glance what the data story is.

Easy to understand

This probably seems logical, but Waisberg (2014) notes that a good data visualization should stand on its own. It should not need other narrative support. In addition, interactivity opportunities can add value, enabling curious readers to explore and filter the information they desire by useful *variables*. However, too much interactivity defeats the purpose. A busy visualization becomes too complex and is not user-friendly; our goal should always be clarity.

Graphical integrity

This is something you may not have thought about, but visuals are absolutely capable of distorting the truth and misleading audiences, just as written text can. Of course, this should never be your intent, but there are a few best practices to help guard against this. Tufte says that "a graphic does not distort if the visual representation of the data is consistent with the numerical representation" (2001, p. 55) and is consistent with how people visually perceive relationships. Is the representation drawn to scale? Are graphical elements proportional to the size or percentage of units being represented? Is the increase or decline in sales really as sharp as what is depicted via the slope of the line graph, or is it visually exaggerated? Another guideline has to do with making clear the baseline or bottom of the numerical scale or axis—an absolute reference point—which is usually zero. This can help audiences clearly interpret what may appear to be a major uptick in sales on a line graph, when in fact it may only have been a 2% change. Another best practice includes adjusting for inflation when graphing financial data over time. For more ways to guard against data distortion and protect graphical integrity, check out the cited authors and resources at the end of this chapter.

Presentations

Beyond the importance of a narrative are the basic structure and elements of your message. Good communicators, particularly for presentations, follow a simple three-part structure: (1) Tell people what you're going to tell them. (2) Tell them. And then (3) tell them what you told them. You've probably heard of this triptych before—it's from Aristotle and is more than 2,000 years old (Baldoni, 2012; Miraldi, 2016)! It's a format that's been around for a long time because it works.

Another important structural component—very early in your message delivery—is to tell people why they should care. You might refer to this as the "aha" or the "OK, I get it" element. Good entrepreneurs include this element in their pitch to investors, where it's called "the value proposition." It explains what this new product does for us and why it's important. We break down this triptych a bit.

Aristotle's triptych

First, tell them what you're going to tell them. This is brief and just what it sounds like: give your audience a quick overview of what you're going to talk about. Baldoni (2012) also emphasizes, importantly, that this opener be what your audience needs to hear—what you need them to understand and take away from your time together—and show them that you will be their guide. You can also use this introduction to set the tone for your talk and build excitement for what comes next (Miraldi, 2016). Think of this as an opportunity to hook your audience and lock in their attention. Step two is to "tell them"; this is the meat of the presentation. Here, you can go into all the detail you like. You can build your case, explain a concept or process, present evidence to convince people of your argument, provide all the background and context, and so forth (Baldoni, 2012). For audience analysts, this is where you would present your results and recommendations. It is typically the longest segment of the presentation. As a nod to the ever important aspect of storytelling, Baldoni (2012) reminds us that this section should not just present information and a logical argument but "resonate with the heart" (Baldoni, 2012, para. 5). Emotion and feeling will lead people to conversion and action, not statistics, tables, and graphs alone.

The final step is the recap or conclusion, reminding people what you told them. Briefly summarize and wrap things up, perhaps emphasizing the takeaways you most want them to remember. This final recap also can be where you solidify your audience's trust in what you just told them, along with their confidence in you. They will see your ability to guide them and the project or lead the team in the right direction (Baldoni, 2012).

Why we should care

Good storytellers take the time to learn about and understand their audiences so they can know what parts of the story will matter most to the group they're addressing. Again, this element of your communication conveys the value of your message: the relevance or "aha" factor. In some ways, it's the entire reason you're communicating. Why should people pay attention? What is the big deal about what you are going to say? What is the value proposition? Put another way, what is the problem that your product, analysis, or recommendations are going to solve? *You're going to solve my problem? Now you've got my attention!* Like other aspects of a good presentation, this element should be concise but clear. Once people see the value of what you're going to provide, you'll have their ears for the rest of the presentation! You'll have a captive audience because now they feel you've got something valuable to say, and they don't want to miss the story.

Body language

We've probably all heard this one, but it gets neglected all too often as many presenters fail to leverage one of the best storytelling tools out there! Eye contact, gestures, and posture all make a huge difference in your efficacy as a communicator. Why? Because this is how we emote. Facial expressions, posture, and gesturing help humanize the story we tell in ways that words, tables, and graphs cannot. It is the secret sauce of presenting! It also is an important part of convincing your audience that they can trust what you're telling them. If your body language conveys a lack of self-confidence as you present, your audience will be more likely to doubt what you're telling them. After all, if you're communicating that *you* don't believe in yourself—then why should they? Of course, the wrong body language can do harm, and it takes practice to know what types of body language are most effective and how.

Appropriate body language also depends on culture, and in increasingly global business environments with multicultural workforces, one element of audience-centered communication is to inform yourself about the culture of your audience and the expected verbal and nonverbal courtesies that are appropriate to that audience group. The guidance below is written as it pertains to Western audiences and may not always apply elsewhere. Be sure to research your audience, including their countries and cultures, before presenting to them; you may need to adapt the guidance below so that you do not offend. The better you understand your audience, the more effective you are going to be as a communicator. With practice, body language becomes more natural for presenters and, as a result, will authentically resonate with your audience. We highlight a few critical types of body language here.

Eye contact

No matter the size of your audience, you need to look people in the eye. This personalizes your message and makes people feel that you are connecting directly with them. Now, you may not be able to make eye contact with everyone in your audience, especially if it is a large crowd. But we become better communicators ourselves if we are engaged in a conversation with someone—and that's exactly what you are doing during a presentation. You are not standing in front of a room and speaking into an abyss. You are having a conversation with your audience. And what do we do when we are engaged in a personal conversation? We look people in the eye. You will be perceived as an authentic communicator and someone who personally cares about their audience, and this will give your message credibility.

Best practices for eye contact are not just to look at one person for the entire presentation (that can get awkward fast) but to make eye contact with one person for a few seconds, perhaps as you are making one point, and then move on to another person for a few seconds. That way, you are connecting with different people in the audience but not "staying" on one person for too long and risking creepiness. Of course, not all presentations are live and in-person. If you are giving a video presentation and you cannot "see" your audience, be sure you are looking directly into the camera. Then your audience on the other end will feel that you are looking and conversing directly with them.

Facial expression and vocal intonations

Related to eye contact, our facial expressions help us emote. These can include raised eyebrows, widening of our eyes, winking, smiling, frowning, squinting, or any number of things that we may do with our face and not even realize it sometimes! Indeed, we use our face to communicate in tandem with our words to the extent that it's almost subconscious and we don't actively think about it (e.g., I should now raise my eyebrows)— we just do it naturally. But presenters who think deliberately about facial expression and how to most effectively use expression to deliver their message will be one step ahead, with stronger audience response to follow. Don't be afraid to emote—it speaks volumes, even when it's not through our words.

A related consideration is your vocal tone and speed. Speaking too quickly makes you hard to follow and understand and makes you sound nervous. Speaking with a high-pitched tone also communicates stress and nervousness. Before starting to speak, consciously relax your throat muscles and try to speak in your deeper registers at a measured pace to communicate that you're relaxed and confident, so your audience can be, also.

Gestures

We probably all know individuals who talk with their hands. This is a type of gesturing, and, when used properly, it can help us accentuate important points and say things that our voices cannot. There are numerous forms of gesturing, from the waving of our hands or arms to indicate expanse or excitement, to pointing a finger, to giving a thumbs up, to endless other gestures. Use gesturing to enhance your communications, but don't overdo it—then it can become a distraction. It's worth mentioning that some gesturing may occur as a result of being nervous in front of people—like shifting our weight to one side or fidgeting with our hair or a pen. Try to avoid this. One way to know if you're gesturing in an unintended and distracting way is to present in front of others and let them honestly critique you. Most of the time, we don't even realize we're doing this! Nervous gesturing can take away from our storytelling, so we want to try to avoid it. Gestures can also have different meanings in different cultures, so, again, be sure to research cultural etiquette.

Posture

You are always sending a message with your posture, and this includes when you are giving a presentation. By standing up straight and holding your head high (but not holding your nose in the air), you will be perceived as confident and alert by your audience. Slumping or slouching is

unprofessional and can also be interpreted as a lack of interest or enthusi-
asm. Try to strike a balance by having a relaxed posture but avoid looking
stiff. Consider doing practice presentations while watching yourself in the
mirror, or video record yourself presenting so you can see for yourself what
your posture, body language, gestures, and vocal intonations communicate
to your audiences.

Practice

Speaking of practicing, no matter how many times you've presented in your
life, you should always practice a presentation in advance. The reasons are
many. First, you need to find out how long the presentation is. If it was to
be 15 minutes, and you're going on 20 with half of the presentation to go,
you're in trouble. Practice helps you know whether you need to cut or add
material. Do not try to squeeze in additional material by talking faster. As
you practice, you may also realize you omitted crucial information and you
can then add it, or you may realize that you really don't need certain details
and can leave them out. You may also decide to change the order of some
slides for better storytelling and flow. You might notice where you should
pause or add a transition (vocal or visual, if using slides).

Practice also helps us become more familiar with the content itself, and
as a result, we become more confident, rely less on notes, and look at our
audience instead. If you have others you can use as a practice audience
(like roommates), this is even better, as they will notice things that you may
not (e.g., posture issues, fidgeting, whether you are speaking too softly or
too fast). Finally, each person is unique in terms of how many times they
need to practice their presentation to feel comfortable, so there is no magic
number as to when a presentation is "ready." But you might consider three
times for the following reasons. The first practice is a stop-and-go practice,
in which you identify material that was left out or should be removed and
notice whether order changes are needed as you get to know the material,
stumble, and so forth. This first run takes the longest to get through. Once
you've made edits as needed, the second practice serves as the first "real"
practice. Here, you will get a truer sense of the length and will become
more comfortable with the content. A third practice will take you further
toward knowing the material and the flow, and it will enable you to make
more eye contact with your audience and rely less on notes. It is usually a
good indicator of final length.

Finally, expect that when you actually deliver the presentation, it will
take longer than it did when you practiced it. There may be interruptions
from the audience, or you may find yourself ad-libbing about something in
the room so as to better connect with the audience. A good rule of thumb
is that, when you are practicing, your presentation should consistently end

a minute short of your planned or allotted time. In most instances, that will bring you in right on time in the actual presentation. But even if not, running short is better than running out of time or boring an audience by talking too long.

The slide deck and visual aids

In a live or video presentation, as the term "visual aids" suggests, these are intended to aid or support the presenter—you—and not be the focus. Less is more, and clutter distracts. Under almost all circumstances, your Power-Point or slide deck should not contain full sentences but instead focus on bullet points or even just images (no words). Images could be relevant photos, charts, graphs, or other data visualizations. Avoid tables during a live presentation, however, as there's probably a better way to communicate your point (Knaflic, 2015). Never read your slides. You are the presenter—the expert in the room—and people want to hear from you. As with other forms of communication, the length and nature of the presentation will be driven by various factors, including the objectives of the presentation, the amount of material that needs to be covered, and the audience.

Sample presentation: Marshall Marketing

For an example of an effective slide deck that tells a story using data, refer to the slide deck from Marshall Marketing on the companion website. This 22-slide presentation file is longer than some, but it is shorter than what is often used by the company when it presents the results of survey research to clients. This particular example was prepared for a local TV station client who would like the advertising business of mattress retailers within the market. You will notice how the presentation starts quite broadly about the topic. Then, over the course of the presentation, it becomes much more specific about the nature and type of person who is considering a new mattress purchase, finally pointing out the most effective media buys for reaching those persons in that market. Data visualizations help to effectively tell this story with little supporting text. Each slide tells a different story (or a few) without clutter, extraneous design, or distraction. Color and chart formats are used to draw the audience's attention to certain highlights or points. One of this chapter's recommended cases further demonstrates how this slide deck is utilized.

Adapting your message to your audience

Who is your target audience? This is the most important question of all because if you don't get that right, none of your communications will resonate. Sometimes you just have one audience for whom you are preparing a report or presentation. However, sometimes you will prepare for multiple audiences at once or at different times of the week or month. Each audience has different needs and levels of familiarity with your topic, and this variation demands different versions of our communication deliverable. If it's for a lay audience, you cannot assume a high level of *domain*, or subject, expertise. You will need to keep things fairly conversational; save the statistics and inside jargon for others. Also, you probably want to keep it brief to hold everyone's attention. Interestingly, brief is also a good approach for top-level executives like a CEO, CFO, or CMO. Certainly they have expertise (though maybe not statistical or analytical expertise like you do), but they are busy people. They do not have time for all the beautiful details. Just tell them what they need to know—clearly and concisely—so that they know how the findings apply to the business, its bottom line, and how to employ any recommendations (e.g., "Here are the four takeaways, and here is how you can apply these insights to the business tomorrow"). Save the statistics and analysis for your research director or analyst team, as they are the only ones who will likely appreciate or need them. For a helpful breakdown of matching level of detail to audience type, Stikeleather (2013, para. 4) offered these categorizations for effective data storytelling:

- Novice: First exposure to the subject, but doesn't want oversimplification
- Generalist: Aware of the topic, but looking for an overview understanding and major themes
- Managerial: In-depth, actionable understanding of intricacies and interrelationships with access to detail
- Expert: More exploration and discovery and less storytelling with great detail
- Executive: Only has time to glean the significance and conclusions of weighted probabilities

Source: Harvard Business Review

Summary and conclusion

If you remember nothing else from this textbook, let it be this: The most important part of being an analyst is communicating well. Strong data storytelling skills will make you a valued member of your organization. Being able to translate data findings and insights into recommendations that your supervisors can use is what this analytical work is all about! Effective, clear communication is dependent on a number of factors: knowing your audience so that you can adapt your message accordingly, knowing the best type of communication to achieve your purpose, and choosing the best modality and method for conveying the message. The best analysts spend time and effort in becoming better communicators. This includes written, oral, and visual communications, along with learning which visual aids and data visualizations can best help you tell your story. Most people are not born knowing how to be effective communicators, so be patient with yourself, be willing to put in the work, and get ready to be an influencer in your workplace—because at the end of the day, that is what you are trying to do! You are communicating insights in a clear and persuasive way to help others make good decisions.

Additional resources

Dashboards

Additional dashboard examples from Parse.ly: www.parse.ly/overview. This URL typically shows a sample dashboard featuring sample digital publisher metrics. If not accessible at this specific URL, look for the "Demo" button to access one or tour Parse.ly's website.

Data visualization

Evergreen Data and Data Visualization Checklist by Stephanie Evergreen and Ann K. Emery: https://stephanieevergreen.com/data-visualization-checklist/

The Extreme Presentation™ Method: Chart Chooser, Slider Chooser: https://extremepresentation.typepad.com/

Flowing Data blog: https://flowingdata.com/

Knaflic, C. N. (2015). *Storytelling with data*. Hoboken, NJ: Wiley.

Kosara, R. (2016, Apr. 24). Spreadsheet thinking vs. database thinking. Eager Eyes: https://eagereyes.org/basics/spreadsheet-thinking-vs-database-thinking

Mackinlay, J., Kosara, R., & Wallace, M. (n.d.) *Data storytelling: Using visualization to share the human impact of numbers*: www.tableau.com/sites/default/files/media/whitepaper_datastorytelling.pdf

Skelton, C. (2017, Mar. 30). A different way to think about "data storytelling": www.chadskelton.com/2017/03/a-different-way-to-think-about-data.html

Storytelling with Data blog: www.storytellingwithdata.com/

Tableau software for creating data visualizations: www.tableau.com (Note that a free version exists called Tableau Public, but this may have some limitations compared to other versions.)

Tufte, E. (2001). *The visual display of quantitative information* (2nd ed.). Cheshire, CT: Graphics Press.

Yau, N. (2013). *Data points: Visualization that means something.* Indianapolis: John Wiley & Sons, Inc.

The Guardian Datablog:

www.theguardian.com/news/datablog+technology/data-visualisation

www.theguardian.com/data

The Financial Times Visual Vocabulary: http://ft-interactive.github.io/visual-vocabulary/

https://datastori.es/71-tapestry-conference-review-with-robert-kosara/

Additional communications skills

LinkedIn Learning (formerly Lynda.com). Offers videos on various communication skill topics and tips, such as presentations and writing effective business reports.

Potent Presentations. American Evaluation Association: www.eval.org/Education-Programs/Potent-Presentations (various resources)

Steiner-Williams, J. (n.d.) *Writing a business report.* (3-part video series available on LinkedIn Learning).

Sample industry report: IAB CCPA Benchmark Survey. www.iab.com/wp-content/uploads/2020/11/IAB_CCPA_Benchmark_Survey_Summary_2020-11.pdf

Recommended cases

These cases can be found on the textbook website: www.routledge.com/cw/hollifield

Case 4.1 (5.4): Equipping Mattress Advertisers
Case 4.2: Writing a Professional Memo

Case studies, along with accompanying datasets for this chapter, can be found on the text website. We particularly suggest the preceding cases in the order listed. See the companion website and instructor's manual for detailed descriptions of these and other relevant cases.

Discussion questions and exercises

1. What was the worst presentation you ever listened to? Why was it so bad? What best practices discussed in this chapter would have made the presentation more effective?

2. Is there a particularly memorable data visualization you've seen recently that you thought was effective? (You may wish to do a quick web search to find one.) What made it effective?

3. *Exercise: Writing a persuasive email*
   Take a look again at Figure 4.1, the one sheet describing the consumers in a metropolitan area who are planning to purchase a mattress. Assume you are part of the local TV station's advertising sales team. How would you write a persuasive email utilizing this information in order to try to get a local mattress retailer to purchase advertising time on your channel? Remember to keep things clear and concise.

4. *Exercise: Persuasive presenting*
   Referring again to the one sheet in Figure 4.1, develop a two- to three-minute presentation (PPT slides are best as a visual aid) using the information provided. Assume you are a sales associate at the local TV station and you will be presenting or "pitching" this idea to a local mattress retailer. Once you've prepared your slide deck, practice your oral presentation three times, time yourself and edit as necessary, and then present it to the class or to a classmate. For the most effective outcomes, be sure to review what you've learned in this chapter about effective visuals and effective oral communication and presenting as you prepare.

5. *Exercise: Creating a line graph*
   Line graphs are a great way to visually tell a data story over time. It is probably the easiest tool for conducting a longitudinal or "trend" analysis, which simply means analyzing performance of some metric over time. As analysts, we can save ourselves a lot of time in data analysis and writing reports by creating line graphs first, as we can literally "see" the story we need to convey. In this exercise, you will be creating a line graph based on local TV station ratings and household television usage (HUT), which could then be used for comparative trend analysis.
   Using the data shown here, create a line graph in Excel using the data from all columns: ratings data from all three TV stations for the time period, along with the HUT levels. The dataset represents the average ratings for the 6 a.m. news hour for each of the three TV stations in the market for each year in the seven-year period from 2017 to 2023. It also includes the average HUTS at 6 a.m. in the city for the same period. HUTS stands for Households Using Television and refers to the percentage of all households in the city that have the TV turned on at 6 a.m. For both HUTS and ratings, 1 point equals 1% of all television households (TVH) in this market. An Excel sheet of this data can be found on the companion website; however, you can quickly enter the data into Excel yourself and create the graph in a just a few minutes. To create a graph fast (using Excel features at time of press), enter the following data into an Excel sheet in rows and columns with labels as shown. Then drag your mouse over the entire area to select it. While it

is still highlighted, in the toolbar above, click "Insert" and then look for "Recommended Charts." You will see various styles. Look for line graph there or under "All Charts" and select "Line Graph." You should have a total of four lines depicted in the finished graph. Line graphs are best for longitudinal analysis as they help us best see trends over time.

	Year						
Station	*2017*	*2018*	*2019*	*2020*	*2021*	*2022*	*2023*
AAAA	2.5	2.1	2.1	3.2	2.8	2.5	2.1
BBBB	6.8	7.4	6.8	8.5	8	6.8	6.6
CCCC	4.8	4.9	5.1	6	6.2	6	5.8
HUT	28	26	25	35	30	28	26

Once your graph is complete, you may also wish to then conduct a trend analysis (optional but helpful for Case 4.2, if you are assigned to do that). Be sure to examine individual lines over time but also compare between stations over time.

References

Aaker, J. [Future of StoryTelling]. (2013, September 14). *Persuasion and the power of story.* [Video]. Vimeo. https://vimeo.com/80004187?gclid=Cj0KCQjwspK UBhCvARIsAB2IYuuU-Dw4Liv6rI5GOTHHpU6xdrixws6dqawR44PeE0ITY TkYggeNPMAaAn_gEALw_wcB

Baldoni, J. (2012, May 4). Give a great speech: 3 tips from Aristotle. *Inc.* www.inc. com/john-baldoni/deliver-a-great-speech-aristotle-three-tips.html

Data storytelling is the new language of corporations. (2019). *Tableau.* www. tableau.com/reports/business-intelligence-trends/data-storytelling

Dykes, B. (2016, March 31). Data storytelling: The essential data science skill everyone needs. *Forbes.* www.forbes.com/sites/brentdykes/2016/03/31/data-storytelling-the-essential-data-science-skill-everyone-needs/#33f06b452ad4

Knaflic, C. N. (2015). *Storytelling with data: A data visualization guide for business professionals.* Wiley.

Miraldi, S. (2016, January 13). The best advice for presenting is actually 2,400 years old. [Article]. *LinkedIn Pulse.* www.linkedin.com/pulse/best-advice-presenting-actually-2400-years-old-scott-miraldi

Skelton, C. (2017, Mar. 30). *A different way to think about 'data storytelling'.* www.chadskelton.com/2017/03/a-different-way-to-think-about-data.html

Sleeper, R. (n.d.). Data-ink ratio animation and how to apply it in Tableau. *PlayfairData.* https://playfairdata.com/data-ink-ratio-animation-and-how-to-apply-it-in-tableau/

Stikeleather, J. (2013, April 24). How to tell a story with data. *Harvard Business Review.* https://hbr.org/2013/04/how-to-tell-a-story-with-data

Terrar, D. (2014, December 24). The myth and reality of "a picture is worth a thousand words?" *Medium*. https://medium.com/@dt/the-myth-and-reality-of-a-picture-is-worth-a-thousand-words-a4ea985f8932

Tufte, E. R. (2001). *The visual display of quantitative information* (2nd ed.). Graphics Press.

Waisberg, D. (2014, March). Tell a meaningful story with data. *Think with Google*. www.thinkwithgoogle.com/marketing-strategies/data-and-measurement/tell-meaningful-stories-with-data/

Part 2

Media analytics and the business of media

Advertising and consumers

5 Advertising analytics

In the beginning, advertising was the raison d'être for media analytics.

The price advertisers pay for advertising space and time is determined primarily by the size of the audience the media company promises will see the ad. The profession of media analytics was born because advertisers got tired of taking publishers' word on circulation sizes, and in 1914 a group of North American advertising agencies, advertisers, and publishers got together to standardize the process of measuring newspaper and magazine audiences (Bennett, 1965). They created the Audit Bureau of Circulations (ABC), an independent cooperative tasked with developing uniform procedures for measuring circulation and verifying publishers' claims about circulation size.

Voila! A new profession was created: media analyst/audience researcher. Media analytics became *the* thing underpinning the commercial media industry. As new forms of media emerged—radio, television, digital—one of the most urgent tasks was to develop methods to measure the new medium's audiences that advertisers would agree to trust. Today, billions of dollars change hands between advertisers and media companies around the world each year based on audience analytics.

These days, analytics are used to support decisions across almost all areas of the media business: new product development, content design and targeting, content marketing, talent and human resource decisions, and strategic business planning, to name just a few. But advertising remains one of, if not the most important, applications of media analytics. Media analysts who work for small and medium-sized media companies, such as individual television and radio stations, probably spend most of their time supporting the advertising department's efforts to sell time and schedule spots for advertisers. In large media companies, teams of analysts work exclusively with the advertising department—and often with just one product category or *vertical* within that unit, such as luxury goods, transportation, or health and beauty products.

DOI: 10.4324/9780429506956-8

Thus, understanding advertising and marketing metrics is a fundamental job requirement for anyone aspiring to a career in media analytics. This chapter will lay out the basic concepts that underlie advertisers' priorities and decisions.

Advertising fundamentals

Let's start with the most basic point: Advertisers are companies that *buy* advertising time and space from media companies. Media companies are companies that *sell* advertising time and space to people who want to market something.

Let's say that another way: Advertisers are companies that sell products or services, such as restaurants, grocery stores, car dealers, or hospitals. They buy advertising to make potential customers aware that their product or service exists and to try to convince the audience to buy it. The advertiser wants to place the ads around whatever media content is most likely to attract the people most likely to buy the product or service being advertised.

On the other side of the transaction, media companies sell time (broadcasting and cable) or space (publications and digital platforms) to advertisers. For commercial, for-profit media companies, selling advertising historically has been where they make most of their money.[1] For that reason, it is fair to say that commercial media companies' primary business is selling advertising—not the creation and distribution of content—and their most important customers are their advertisers, not their audiences.

In this understanding of the commercial media industry, media companies are not in the business of creating content; they are in the business of creating audiences. Audience members are not people; they are a commodity that is being collected and packaged by media companies so that their attention can be sold to advertisers. The content media companies create and distribute is simply the bait used to attract specific audience groups advertisers want to reach. Different types of content—drama, comedy, news, music, special interests—make it easy to collect audience members with similar traits into packages that are easily measured and sold.

In the 21st century, there has been an explosion of media platforms and content choices. Many of these new media platforms depend on advertising for all or a major part of their business models. This has created two major problems for media companies and advertisers:

1. Audiences have fragmented across the new platforms—resulting in smaller total audiences for individual media outlets such as television and radio stations and networks and for individual pieces of content such as TV programs. Thus it's harder for media companies to attract

large enough audiences to interest advertisers. At the same time, the fragmentation has made it harder for advertisers to reach as many people as they once could without having to spend more money buying more ads across more media outlets and content placements.

2. The competition between media companies to sell advertising has increased dramatically. Advertisers now have many choices of where to place ads. But as advertisers fragment their *ad spends* across more and more platforms, each media company's share of the advertising market is shrinking. Thus media outlets are having a harder time generating enough revenue to pay for quality content—or even to just to stay in business. Small and local media organizations have been particularly hard hit. Consequently, media across all sectors are shifting their business models to focus more on subscription revenue.

A third player in the transactions between advertisers and media companies are advertising agencies. Advertising agencies usually work for the advertiser, or brand, designing the advertisements and advising on the best placement to reach the client's target audience. Ad agencies are important players because of their influence over ad spend and placement decisions. The large agencies also wield enormous influence when it comes to demanding changes in the research industry's audience measurement methodologies and metrics.

All of this buying and selling between media companies, advertisers, and advertising agencies depends on data—data about audience size, audience characteristics, and audience behavior. Media analysts call those crucially important data "media math."

For a professional media analyst, being fluent in media math is a required skill set. Fortunately, it's pretty simple. "Media math" refers to understanding the set of simple formulas that are used to calculate the most important and widely used media metrics. Most of those metrics have to do with advertising. The metrics are designed to help advertisers quickly gauge whether they have achieved their goal with an advertising campaign.

Advertisers' goals and "media math"

So what are advertisers' goals? The specifics may vary, depending on the advertiser and the campaign, but the fundamental goals are always pretty much the same:

1. Advertisers want *audience size*. They want to reach as many people as possible, for every advertising dollar spent.
2. Advertisers want *audience quality*. They want to reach audiences made up of the people most likely to buy whatever they're advertising. If

the advertiser is doing *brand awareness* messaging, the goal is to reach whatever group the advertiser wants to influence—potential future buyers of the product, even if an immediate sale is not likely; likely voters, policy makers, regulators, etc.

3. Advertisers want as high a *return on advertising spend* (*ROAS*)—or as much "bang for the buck"—as they can get for each dollar spent, which means reaching as many high-quality audience members as possible at as low a per-person cost as possible.

Box 5.1 outlines the most important metrics advertisers use to track how well they are achieving these goals. The list is not comprehensive because new metrics are developed all the time. Specific metrics also fall in and out of popularity as goals, technologies, and audience behaviors change. But these are the fundamental advertising metrics. Most have been in use for a long time and are likely to continue to be used for the foreseeable future.

Audience size

The foundational metric for advertisers is, of course, audience size. How many people will an advertisement reach, if an advertiser pays to place it around a particular piece of content on a particular platform on a particular day and time?

While that sounds simple, in fact, it's not. Accurately measuring audience size always has been difficult and expensive to do (Chapter 3). But since the 1990s, it's become even harder to achieve as audiences fragment across more and more media platforms. Fragmentation makes it almost impossible to get a large-enough sample of viewers for any single media channel or piece of content, such as a program or article, to accurately measure audience size (Chapter 3). Accurately measuring circulation size for publications, ratings, and shares for broadcasters and cable companies, as well as the unique views and impressions on digital platforms, is both complex and controversial. Those metrics are discussed in detail in Chapters 8–12. Then there is the challenge of measuring a media outlet's total audience across its different distribution platforms and across time (Chapters 3, 9).

Even getting agreement among media organizations, measurement companies, and advertisers on who should be counted as part of the measured audience can be difficult. For example, some publications have both *paid circulation* and nonpaid circulation, and advertisers question whether both should be counted in circulation size. Other chapters in this text address such issues within the contexts of the media industry sectors where they are most important. Similarly, advertisers argue that audience size metrics measure the size of the audience that consumed the media content, not necessarily the size of the audience that paid attention to the ads.

Then there is the difference between duplicated and **unduplicated reach** (or **audience**), or on digital platforms: unique visitors. Advertisers run ads multiple times in the same program to increase the impact of their message and in similar programs that draw a similar audience. That means they often are advertising to the same individuals multiple times. One question is always how much of the audience size measured was measuring the same people twice and how much represented unduplicated reach to a greater percentage of the total possible audience?

Audience size is a contentious issue between advertisers and media companies because the prices advertisers pay for advertising space and time usually are based on size. For most media, advertising prices are calculated on the basis of **CPMs**, which stands for "*cost per thousand.*"[2] An advertising price quote usually refers to the price for every 1,000 *impressions*—that is, individuals or households—who are expected to see the ad.

There is another aspect of measuring audience size that also is important to advertisers, and that is measuring the total *weight* of an advertising campaign—that is, the total size of the audience reached through a particular advertising campaign across all of the different times and places that the ads in the campaign ran. Built into measures of weight are metrics related to the likelihood that an advertisement was effective in influencing people.

Box 5.1 Key advertising metrics, their definitions, and formulas

Term	Definition/notes	Formula
Metrics for an advertising campaign's "weight"		
Frequency	The number of times a consumer is exposed to advertisements for a product. Frequency is positively related to their likelihood of buying it	
Recency	Average length of time between exposure to an ad and the consumer's buying decision. Media that reach customers while they're going to a store or in a store have a recency advantage.	

(Continued)

(Continued)

Term	Definition/notes	Formula
Gross rating points (GRP)	Measure of "weight" of an advertising schedule or campaign. Sum of all rating points generated in an advertiser's campaign.	(Number of ads × Average rating). The same as (reach × frequency) expressed in rating points.
Impressions/gross impressions (GI or IMP)	Impression is a metric of reach that has varying definitions. Generally, an impression is counted when an audience member is exposed to a piece of content. Similar to GRP, but with rating points translated to actual number of audience members in the market. *Gross impressions* is a measure of the total "weight" of a media campaign, usually expressed in thousands.	GI: The average number of people (or TVHs) reached by an ad multiplied by the number of ads run. Calculated for each daypart or platform where average audience sizes differed and then summed across the total schedule.
Watch time	Usually the total amount of time people spent watching a video or video ad. Measured in seconds for individual videos. A metric of viewer retention and engagement as compared to a *view*, which may be measured even if a video is only played for a few seconds.	
Average watch time	Average amount of time viewers spent with a video ad. Measures effectiveness of ad in getting audience engagement	(Watch time/Total impressions)
Share of voice (SOV)	Measures the visibility of a brand or product amid all the relevant advertising competing for consumers' attention; percentage of all relevant advertising during a time period that belonged to the advertiser's campaign.	(Number of ads for a product or brand/Total number of ads for similar products or brands of interest to the advertiser)

Term	Definition/notes	Formula
Metrics for audience "quality"		
Demographics	Personal characteristics that generally are not changeable. Gender, age, race, income are the most important to advertisers. Demographics of interest vary by advertiser and product. Advertisers pay higher CPMs for more desirable demographics	Total number of audience members with a particular characteristic and total number with combinations of desirable characteristics (Age + Gender, etc.)
Psychographics	Changeable characteristics related to lifestyles and preferences. Living environment, lifestyle, hobbies, political party, religiosity, etc. Microformatted media content often attracts audiences based upon psychographic characteristics (radio station music formats; news networks' political slant; interest-based TV networks, such as science, cooking, or travel channels).	Total number of audience members with a particular psychographic profile and total number with combinations of targeted psychographics
Geography	Physical location of a consumer relative to the point-of-purchase of a product. Consumers will travel longer distances to purchase high-cost durable goods than for low-cost consumable goods. If an advertiser pays to reach customers who can't or won't travel to a product's point of sale, it's wastage	The overlap between the geographic distribution of the advertising and the geographic distribution of likely customers for that product or store.
Affordability	Match between product's price point, product availability, and audience's income. Low-cost, widely available goods match well with mass media advertising; luxury goods or expensive products with narrow appeal are better placed in special-interest media	Overlap between the audience's average income and the average income of buyers of the product.

(*Continued*)

(Continued)

Term	Definition/notes	Formula
Behavioral targeting	Uses an individual's previous buying behaviors to predict future product purchases and prepurchasing ("funnel") behaviors. Allows advertisers to serve individual consumers advertisements when they start prepurchase behaviors; maximizes the "recency" effect.	Based on big data analysis of multiple purchases and other interactions to develop predictive model for different types of consumers.
Metrics for an advertising campaign's effectiveness		
Conversion rate	Measurement of desired outcome; evidence that consumers exposed to the ad or message took the desired action.	Outcomes divided by unique visitors to the content/ page where product was advertised.
Effective reach	Measures number of people reached and influenced by an ad.	
Effective frequency	Measures number of times average consumer must be exposed to an ad before conversion occurs. Advertisers use metric to decide how many ads they must buy in a campaign to achieve sales targets without overbuying.	Marketers use 3 as the estimate for effective frequency, but that number is largely untested.[a]
Metrics for measuring and comparing the cost of advertising		
Cost per thousand (CPM)	Price advertiser pays to buy an ad per 1,000 impressions.	(Total price of an advertisement/ Total predicted impressions)
Cost per click (CPC)	Payment based on evidence that the advertisement actually was viewed because someone clicked on it. Vulnerable to ad fraud.	Usually recorded as maximum cost advertiser is charged for a click.
Cost per conversion (also CPC or CPCon)	Estimates the cost to the advertiser of each conversion achieved.	Cost of the ad campaign divided by the number of conversions attributed to the campaign.

Term	Definition/notes	Formula
Metric for measuring the value of the advertising spend to the advertiser		
Return on advertising spend (ROAS)	Value of conversions generated—such as total revenue from sales of the advertised product—per dollar spent on the advertising campaign.	(Total revenue from sales/Total campaign cost)

ᵃ Bendle et al., 2016
Sources: Bendle et al., 2016; Muhammad, 2020

Frequency measures how many times an individual was exposed to the same ad. A single exposure to an ad is unlikely to be enough to influence someone to buy a product, so often you will see the same ad run multiple times within a single program or publication, which means the advertiser is paying multiple times to reach the same people with the same message—called *duplication*. Research has shown most people have to be exposed to a message multiple times before they are influenced by it, although the exact frequency of exposure required is uncertain and almost certainly varies by individual and circumstance (Bendle et al., 2016). The *total weight* of an advertising campaign is a measure of the average size of the audience in a given program or publication multiplied by the frequency or the number of times the ad ran in that program or publication.

Recency is another time-related audience metric. What is the likely time-lapse between exposure to an ad and the point at which the audience member makes a buying decision about that product? The advertiser wants to deliver the ad to a potential buyer as close in time to the buying decision as possible. Grocery stores have historically placed most of their ads and coupons in daily newspapers' Wednesday editions to give families time to review them and clip coupons before Saturday—the weekday most US families shop for groceries. Radio stations sold their ability to deliver ads even as customers were driving to stores as an advantage of advertising on radio as opposed to in publications or on TV. Now apps and search engines offer advertisers an even greater recency advantage by following potential buyers right into the store on their smartphone screens or by delivering an ad to their phone or computer screen as they search for a product they intend to buy online.

Probably the most widely used measures of total campaign weight are *gross rating points* (*GRP*) and *gross impressions* (*GI*). GRP is calculated as the average rating of programming on a television or audio station or network during a particular daypart, multiplied by the number of times an advertiser's ad ran during that daypart, summed across all the dayparts in which the ad ran for the length of the campaign. The final number is the total weight of the campaign expressed in television or radio rating points.

Gross impressions is a similar calculation but translated into an actual number of television households (TVH), viewers, or Persons Using Radio (PUR) in the market where the ad campaign ran. In television and radio calculations, each rating point represents 1% of the TVH, PUR or other universe of interest (e.g., Women 18–34), in the market. The total size of the universe is multiplied by the percentage of the audience reached by the content as represented by the rating. Unlike GRP, which is a metric specific to radio and television, GI is used to measure the weight for advertising campaigns across all media, using circulation size for publications and views on digital platforms, instead of ratings.

In the digital video world, the weight of a video advertising campaign is measured by *watch time*—the total number of seconds an ad was rolled by viewers across the campaign—and *average watch time*—which is calculated as watch time divided by the number of *views*. Average watch time is an indirect measure of *engagement*, telling the advertisers the average amount of time each viewer spent watching that ad before either clicking onto something else or hitting the "Skip Ad" button.

Finally, *share of voice* (SOV) measures the percentage of advertising for a particular product an advertiser is generating. Said another way, it measures how likely an advertiser's campaign is to rise above the advertising clutter competing for an audience member's attention. SOV is usually measured as a percentage of total advertising for a particular product that a specific brand had placed, or the percentage of all advertising that was bought by companies in a product category during a specified period of time. For example, what percentage of all beer advertising during a sports season was for Beer Brand X? Advertisers may also want to know what their share was of all the advertising put before a particular audience, such as the audience for a major televised sporting event.

All of these measures of audience size and market share are important to advertisers and will continue to be. But as audiences fragment across more and more platforms, competition for audience attention rises, and advertisers have to buy time and space across more platforms in order to get the same number of impressions they used to reach on one. As a result, other considerations are creeping into advertisers' calculations of what they want. As Steve Walsh, Chief Revenue Officer of Consumer Orbit, explained: "A television station or network may boast in their sales pitches about having the '#1 News' at a given time in terms of overall HH or demographic audience size," Walsh said.

But to an advertiser or an agency, that messaging is growing less relevant than understanding the *density*, or percentage, of that overall audience, which represents the actual shopping or product search behaviors the client is trying to reach. *That* determines the relative Cost Per Thousand (CPM) or Cost Per (Rating) Point (CPP) for reaching that highly targeted audience in a given program.

In other words, while audience size is and will continue to be important to advertisers, it's no longer the most important factor in buying decisions.

Audience quality

So, yes, size matters—but only if all the people an advertiser is being charged to reach are likely customers for the product being advertised. The higher the percentage of people in the audience who actually are potential customers for an advertiser's product, the higher the *audience quality* for that advertiser. Thus, from the advertiser's viewpoint, not all audiences and not all media outlets are created equal. The effectiveness of an advertising campaign depends on delivering ads to a large audience that is also a quality audience. But the "quality" of an audience differs for each advertiser and sometimes for each product.

In the last half of the 20th century, advertisers started demanding more precise audience information so they could target ad spends more narrowly. Initially, at least, they focused primarily on *demographics*. Demographics are the characteristics about a person that the person generally cannot change: gender, age, race, education, and income being the main ones. Advertisers historically have viewed gender and age as the most important demographics for identifying quality audiences. The majority of consumer products advertisers target women between the ages of 18 and 49 because in most countries, women tend to make most family buying decisions, and people between the ages of 18 and 49 spend a higher percentage of their total income on consumer goods, particularly in households with children. Within that target group, 18- to 34-year-olds are particularly attractive because they're still establishing personal brand preferences and are more likely than older audiences to be swayed by advertising. Income also is important because marketers want to pay only for audiences who can afford to buy the product being advertised.

Once you get past these basic advertising "truths," the idea of audience quality becomes even more complicated. Advertisers might be willing to pay a higher CPM to reach a target audience that is harder to reach through traditional media, such as young men. Scarcity makes those audiences more valuable to marketers. Conversely, advertisers may demand a lower CPM for older audiences, even though they tend to be wealthier, because they are easier to reach through media but are less susceptible to advertising because they already have established brand preferences.

Children and teens are very valuable advertising targets for some advertisers, despite having no independent income. In the United States and some other countries, children and teenagers control a surprising amount of purchasing power, and they have been shown to powerfully influence their parents' buying decisions on products ranging from groceries to cars. Additionally, for some types of media, such as video games, children and teens are a primary target for in-game advertising and product sales.

In addition to demographic factors, increasing numbers of advertisers use *psychographics* to define audience quality. Psychographics are personal characteristics that are more changeable than demographic characteristics. Psychographics include such things as living environment—for example, apartment, city-center urban, suburban or rural—lifestyle, hobbies, and political views. Psychographics are particularly important in media that use *lifestyle* or *microformats*, to attract audiences. For instance, people who watch a cooking channel are more likely to buy cooking-related equipment or high-end groceries than people who watch a children's cartoon network. Those lifestyle differences represent potential product sales. Psychographically based content preferences allow advertisers to more precisely target likely buyers, increasing their ROAS.

Digital distribution allows media companies to develop even more refined psychographic profiles of individual audience members. Every "like," "love," or "angry" emoji someone hits on social media is cataloged against the content to which they responded, allowing media companies to develop a detailed profile of each user's preferences and emotional triggers (Chapter 13). Such data helps advertisers understand how individual psychographics relate to consumers' product and brand preferences and *consideration sets*, the set of brands a consumer considers at least briefly as they make a buying decision. Advertisers can then target their advertising more narrowly—increasing their campaign ROAS—and develop messages more likely to effectively influence people. Character traits, purchase intentions, media habits, and a host of other data points derived from the trail of online bread crumbs we leave behind us as we surf the internet have been added to the elements some advertisers use to define as "quality."

Digital measurement has enabled another new approach to identifying quality audiences: *behavioral targeting*. Behavioral targeting uses a person's previous web browsing and other shopping behaviors and activities to identify not only their psychographic profile and likely future product purchases, but also to understand the series of online activities they usually engage in immediately before buying something (Chapter 6). That *funnel* of pre-purchase activity can then be programmed into an *algorithm* that automatically serves up ads to persons when their online activity matches prepurchase behaviors. This improves the recency factor—helping the advertiser time ad delivery to someone with purchase intention, state of mind, and opportunity.

While behavioral targeting remains a key goal for advertisers, privacy regulations passed by the European Union and the US state of California in recent years are making it a harder strategy for advertisers to use. The regulations limit companies' ability to track individuals' online activities across multiple platforms and apps. Those protections make it difficult for data aggregators to develop accurate behavioral profiles to sell to media companies and advertisers. Difficult or not, the value of such behavioral data to marketers is so high, you can be sure marketers will continue pursuing behavioral data.

Two other factors, geography and product price point, also are critical considerations in determining audience quality. Advertisers only want to pay to reach audiences who can actually buy from them both in terms of geography and affordability. In a world where online shopping seems ubiquitous, geography, in particular, would not seem to be a major consideration any longer. But for many local advertisers—and local media companies—it is.

As discussed in Chapter 2, a local small business owner would probably get a much higher ROAS from advertising in the local daily or weekly newspaper, on local billboards, or through a geographically targetable direct mail, email, or social media campaign than from advertising on TV.[3] Similarly, a company that manufactures luxury goods such as yachts or custom jewelry also would be wasting money to advertise on TV. Most of the audiences they would pay to reach couldn't afford the advertised products. Thus such advertisers are more likely to buy space in lifestyle-specific consumer magazines (Chapter 11) or social media, which can more specifically target who sees the ad (Chapter 13).

But while advertisers might value specific media platforms differently, thanks to granular data on consumer behavior, they're increasingly in agreement about what makes audiences valuable, and it has less to do with demographics. Steve Walsh, Chief Revenue Officer for Consumer Orbit, says:

> An example of the declining relevance of age/sex demographics is the way Automotive advertisers target their campaigns. Traditionally, Men 25–54 had been the go-to age/sex targeting demographic. But what that fails to take into account is the fact that many people (including Women) older than 54 buy and lease new vehicles day in and day out and, in fact, for many people 55+ it is a time of their lives when their disposable income is at its peak. So it's not just that they might want a new car, they can afford to buy one. So now, the real target for reaching potential auto purchasers is redefined to, a) how long have they owned

a car, or b) is their auto lease up within the next 6 months, or c) do they tend to buy a new car every 4 years, or d) do they almost always purchase a Honda vehicle—but the last car they bought 3.5 years ago was a Nissan, or e) their household income is $125k+;—or the advertiser is thinking in some combination of all of those types of targets.

So important to advertisers are audience quality and reducing wastage that finding ways to deliver advertisements to the exact individuals and households most likely to buy a particular product has become a major battleground between media companies and media industry sectors. Social media platforms track individual users' online behaviors and develop detailed profiles of their interests and likely purchasing behaviors (Chapter 13). Social media platform technologies then can deliver specific advertisements to specific users—the individuals whose digital data suggests they are most likely to be interested in and able to buy a particular product. That advantage has helped social media companies capture a steadily increasing share of the global advertising market, leaving legacy media scrambling to develop similar capabilities.

In response, US cable companies are starting to offer advertisers *addressability*, the ability to deliver an advertisement to specific households based upon data-derived profiles of those households. The cable company can address specific advertisements to some households—but not others—based upon the IP addresses used to deliver *video on demand* (*VOD*) and streaming services. Although still only a small percentage of television advertising, addressability might mean that one household is watching an advertisement for pet products during the middle of a major sporting event—because consumer data indicated the people in that home were pet owners—while the home next door is served soft drink ads or fitness club memberships.

In summary, then, a large number of *variables* affect how advertisers define "quality" in an audience and therefore how much they will pay to reach those audience members. Those variables include first and foremost the advertiser's own industry and product. Based on that, the audiences' characteristics begin to matter (gender, age, income, education, race/ethnicity, living environment, lifestyle, hobbies and other psychographic traits) and their media use (frequency of use, type of content consumed, platform used for content consumption, level of interactivity, the ease or difficulty the advertiser faces in reaching a particular type of audience), and the timing of the ad delivery to coincide with the recipient's interest or opportunity to buy.

As you can see, understanding what advertisers want is complicated. It also is dynamic. How advertisers and advertising agencies in a country or a particular market define "quality" in audiences today may be very different tomorrow. Advertiser preferences are subject to fads and fashions. Part of media analysts' job is to help their employers keep up with current trends in media buying—and to measure the actual effectiveness of the client's proposed strategy.

Return on advertising spend (ROAS)

A famous saying among advertisers and marketers widely attributed to John Wanamaker, a 19th century American businessman, is, "Half the money I spend on advertising is wasted; the trouble is I don't know which half." Indeed, many experts think 50% is a low estimate.

Maximizing the return on investment from each ad spend is a key goal for advertisers. But, as our discussion of the vagaries of audience quality demonstrates, accurately measuring advertising ROAS is extremely difficult and, in fact, probably impossible. Marketing managers around the world must prove to their bosses that they're good at their jobs, however. Being "good at their job" means generating maximum additional sales at a minimum marketing cost. Proving to your boss that you're accomplishing that means using advertising metrics—and lots of them.

Numerous metrics have been developed to gauge the effectiveness of advertising spends. Not surprisingly, measuring advertising campaign effectiveness starts with measuring audience size and campaign weight. Factored into those analyses is the "quality" of the audience that was reached. Then the advertiser drills down on campaign results. Among the metrics used for that are:

1. *Conversion rate.* Used on digital platforms, conversion rate is the percentage of people who saw the ad and then bought the product or performed the desired activity within a particular time period.
2. *Effective reach* is a measure of how many of the audience members reached through the campaign were actually influenced to buy the product, vote for the candidate, or change their opinion of the brand. In other words, how many *conversions* were there? Any audience members an advertiser paid to reach who were not "quality" audience members— that is, they were never likely to be converted—represents money wasted.
3. *Effective frequency* measures how many times the average audience member saw the ad before the conversion occurred. Any frequency for which an advertiser paid that was higher than the average effective frequency also was wastage.

A key component in understanding ROAS is on the other side of the ledger: the cost of the campaign. The industry uses a number of different metrics to make it easier for advertisers to compare the relative costs of placing the same ads on different platforms and, within a platform, different channels, publications, or websites. These platforms include:

4. *Cost per thousand* (**CPM**). How much did the ad campaign cost the advertiser for every thousand people/households reached with each ad? CPM is the primary cost measure used, and gives advertisers a fairly straightforward price comparison across different ad-placement options.
5. *Cost per click* (**CPC**). This measure is specific to digital platforms and combines cost data with one of the more frequently used measures of engagement—the act of clicking on an ad.
6. *Cost per conversion* (**CPC or CPCon**). CPC is a measure that combines cost data with effectiveness measures—specifically, conversion data. How many conversions can be attributed to the ad campaign, divided by the total cost of the ad campaign? The more duplication and noneffective frequency there is in a campaign, the higher will be the cost per conversion rate.

The ultimate metric for measuring the value of the advertising expenditure to the advertiser is, of course, Return on Advertising Spend (ROAS) itself. The formula for that is simply the total amount of revenue (or votes, or actions) attributed to the campaign divided by the total campaign cost.

As always, the challenge of calculating ROAS is to get an accurate estimate of the actual amount of revenue or positive change a campaign generated. How possible is it to determine how much, if at all, any single individual's personal decision to buy or not to buy something or to vote or not vote for a candidate was influenced by an advertisement they saw? The fact that someone was exposed to an advertisement and later bought that product is not proof their purchase was influenced by the ad. Similarly, not buying a product or buying a competing brand of a product seen advertised does not mean that someone was *not* influenced by the ad. Advertisers also have to be concerned—but rarely can measure—whether their advertisement had a positive influence on someone's perception of their brand—or the exact opposite—a negative one. But even though accurately measuring ROAS is probably impossible, media analysts—whether working for advertisers or media companies—can expect to spend a lot of their time trying.

It's important to remember that the metrics used to measure the effectiveness of marketing campaigns change over time and are subject to changes in popularity among marketing professionals. So the media analyst should expect to work with many different such measures over the course of a career. A single metric that will provide a reliable and valid measure of advertising ROAS remains a Holy Grail to advertising agencies and marketing managers, but it is unlikely ever to be achieved. For one thing, the *reliability* and *validity* of ROAS measures are wholly dependent on the reliability and validity of measures of audience size—which, as discussed throughout this book, are and will remain problematic. It also depends on the definition used for audience quality relative to the product being marketed—and the ability to discern what percentage of the measured audience were quality audience for the purposes of a specific advertiser.

The buying and selling of advertising

Media analysts play a central role in the buying and selling of audiences, so it's important to understand some of the key concepts in those transactions. There are three stages of audience measurement (Napoli, 2003): the *predicted audience*, the *measured audience*, and the *actual audience*.

The audience that advertisers buy and media companies sell is the predicted audience—the size and demographic makeup of an audience that is predicted for a piece of content before it is aired or published. A large proportion of advertising time and space is sold before a television program airs or a publication is printed. Indeed, the number of pages that are printed in a newspaper or magazine edition is determined not by the amount of copy the publication wants to produce or the amount of news that occurred but by the amount of advertising the media outlet managed to sell into that edition. In television and radio, the commodity being sold is time, not space, so the number of advertising minutes available in a half-hour of programming doesn't change as much from episode to episode. What does change, however, is the price advertisers pay to get one of the available advertising spots. The larger and higher-quality the audience being drawn to a particular TV series, the more advertisers will want to buy time in and around episodes. Because the supply of time available for advertising can't be increased, the price or CPMs for spots in the series will rise.

The problem, of course, is that historically, advertising has had to be planned, produced, bought, and scheduled *before* a publication was printed, a digital page was published, or a TV program aired. That means the advertising CPMs for content have been negotiated between media companies and advertisers based upon the size and quality of the audience a media company *predicted* would consume the content. In the US television industry, for example, most advertising inventory for the fall network television season that begins in September historically has been sold during what the industry calls *upfronts* several months before, usually May or June. Advertisers who buy ads in fall programs during upfront pay lower CPMs than if they wait until September or later to buy time. But particularly for a new series or for a syndicated series new to a particular network, the audience estimates on which CPMs during upfronts are based are nothing but predictions.

In recent years, the advent of *programmatic buying* and *real time bidding* (*RTB*) technologies have reduced advertisers' dependence on long-term forecasts about audience size and characteristics as the basis of ad pricing and placements. We'll discuss that more shortly. But despite the development of those technologies, other key processes in media management still rely heavily on such projections. Decisions about what films, programs, or video game concepts to greenlight and produce or which syndicated program rights to buy are made by entertainment companies based on analysts' projections of the audience size and the revenue the concept is likely to produce. The size of production budgets that are approved and the prices networks and streaming companies agree to pay for program rights are all based on such predictions.

Thus a major part of media analysts' jobs is predicting audience size and composition—often *years* before the content is actually created or the rights bought. Each media firm has its own formula for predicting audience size and demographics in advance, but most include consideration of the audience size and characteristics that similar programs or concepts attracted in the past. In television, the audience prediction process includes data not just on how similar content performed but also on how different release dates and scheduling might affect ratings and demographics. Analysts also run prediction models that include the potential boosts from the *inheritance effect*s a program might get with different lead-in programs, as well as current trends in audience behavior. One network analyst said that given the complexities, they consider themselves lucky if their prediction gets within 10% of the show's actual performance when it airs.

But the pressure on analysts to get those predictions right is enormous. The media company, in particular, stands to lose if the measured audience is off by more than the range agreed on in the advertising contract. If the measured audience is significantly smaller than the predicted audience, the advertiser is entitled to *make-goods*. The media company either refunds some of the money paid for the spots or, more commonly, has to give the advertiser additional advertising placements to make up for the original audience deficit. In either case, the media company loses revenue.

The reverse, however, is not true. If the advertiser agrees to pay a particular price for a spot and the audience is much larger or higher quality than the contract specified, the advertiser gets all the benefit at no additional charge. That means the media company lost revenue it should have earned from its success.

The second stage of audience measurement, the measured audience, is the size and composition of the audience for a piece of content that is measured and reported by the media company or measurement firms. Accurately measuring audiences is extremely difficult and always a source of contention between media companies, measurement companies, and advertisers. At best, even on digital platforms, the measured audience is an estimate, especially given widespread digital ad fraud today.

The third stage of measurement, the actual audience, is the number and demographic profile of the people who actually consumed a piece of content. In truth, it is impossible to ever know accurately the size of the actual audience or who was in it. Moreover, as audiences have fragmented across more and more channels of content, the ability to draw large enough samples to even accurately estimate the actual audience has largely disappeared. Sampling errors for each individual piece of content are now often larger than the measurement itself—meaning that the gap between measured audiences and actual audiences is probably growing (Chapter 3).

Programmatic ad buying

In the traditional buying and selling of advertising, advertisers or their agencies negotiated advertising placements with media companies, negotiating the price and placement of advertising on the basis of audience metrics. The process involved a lot of human interaction and negotiation. But in recent years, technology has started transforming some aspects of the ad buying/selling process.

Programmatic ad buying uses software and algorithms to automatically search data on media audiences and prices for different content and then almost instantly place the ads (Rogers, 2017). Humans are largely removed from the process of negotiating ad prices and handling the placement paperwork (Marshall, 2014). Initially used mostly for digital ad purchases, proponents argue it is more efficient and less expensive than traditional media buying approaches. But it is not foolproof.[4] The algorithms won't work without high-quality, granular audience data and skilled data analysis on the part of both buyers and sellers. Advertisers have to know what audiences they need to target. That requires detailed analysis of their existing customer base, their desired customer base, and general consumer behavior (Chapter 6). Media companies need to have detailed, accurate audience data on the different types of content around which they are trying to sell ads. Getting granular high-quality television audience data always has been a challenge. But it is particularly difficult in small television and radio markets and for stations and networks that have small audiences. Audience fragmentation has greatly increased those problems in recent years.

Real-time bidding is a form of programmatic buying that all but eliminates the use of predicted audiences because ad buying and placement are done in real time. Advertisers preset the parameters for the audiences they want and prices they're willing to pay, and then computers bid in real time for current advertising availabilities (aka "avails") that match those parameters, much as is done in stock markets. When an advertiser wins a bidding war for a placement, their ad is instantly and automatically inserted into the target site. Because everything is done in real time, RTB is used mostly with online content.

Because programmatic buying depends on having detailed audience and consumer data, skilled analysts, and sophisticated technology, it will mostly benefit large media companies. The shift to programmatic buying makes it harder for smaller media firms and those in smaller markets to attract the regionally targeted advertising from national companies that used to be an important part of local media revenue. Thus programmatic advertising works against the survival of small market local media. It is likely, however, to increase the demand for skilled media analysts.

Key challenges for the advertising analyst

Ad fraud

Technology is not only changing the processes of buying and selling advertising and increasing the challenges of measuring audiences, it also is introducing new challenges media analysts are required to understand and address. One of these is ad fraud.

Estimates vary on how much ad fraud costs advertisers and media companies globally, but several experts place the number at around US $15–$16 billion annually between 2017 and 2021 (Alliance for Audited Media, 2018; Statista.com, 2021). But the problem is growing rapidly, and, in addition to its financial impact, it is eroding trust among both advertisers and media firms in the ad buying and selling process.

Ad fraud has three different sources: media companies, advertisers and their agents, and third parties who are trying to steal from both. Most digital ad fraud occurs through one of two ways: (1) buying fake digital traffic and (2) setting up fake media sites.

In the digital advertising world, higher traffic means more money for media houses and advertising agencies. Not surprisingly, a growth industry in manufacturing fake digital traffic has sprung up to supply the need. Most fake traffic is created by sending automated digital "bots" or automated software to ping a particular site or ad so that the server counts it as human traffic. Some "traffic" companies hire humans to drive up traffic at client sites through targeted "visits."

Media companies have an obvious incentive to drive up traffic numbers. So too do advertising agencies, who are paid a percentage of the value of their client's campaign. Finally, marketing directors who need to prove to their boss that they're good at their jobs have an incentive to ignore signs of fraud in the audience numbers their campaigns generate. The loser in this game is the company paying for the advertising.

Domain spoofing

A second and even more costly type of ad fraud comes from *domain spoofing*. Domain spoofing is done several ways, including setting up fake websites that look almost exactly like a media company's real website or ad buying portal. The fake site then competes for advertising with pirated content and audience data from the real media company. Most of the ads domain spoofing steals are being placed through programmatic buying, so no humans are involved to check the legitimacy of the site where the ad winds up. The fraudulent company gets paid by the advertiser, and the media producer loses critical revenue. In an era of audience and advertising fragmentation, when total revenue for many media companies is falling, advertising fraud threatens the very survival of some media firms, particularly smaller ones. The advertiser also loses because their message never reaches the audience they paid to reach.

While buying fake traffic and domain spoofing are among the most common forms of ad fraud, there are other methods (Fou, 2020; Vrountas, 2020). *Ad stacking* refers to loading ads on digital pages one on top of another, so audiences see only the top one. But the site traffic is recorded for all of them, and the advertisers are charged accordingly. *Pixel stuffing* reduces an ad to a few pixels in size, too small for audiences to see. But all visitors to the site are recorded as having viewed the ad. Another common form of ad fraud comes from apps containing malware that roll video ads continuously in the background on users' devices, invisible to the user but recorded as "views" that are charged back to the marketer.

Media analysts often are tasked with detecting the clues that ad fraud is being committed. If traffic levels on a site surge suddenly just before the end of the month or the fiscal period, that suggests someone is paying a traffic supplier to top-up audience numbers before account balances are calculated. If long-time advertisers suddenly disappear or audience numbers drop sharply without obvious explanations, it suggests domain spoofing is happening. With so much money on the table, media analysts can expect ad fraud tracking to be one of their major responsibilities.

Ad blocking

Another challenge facing digital marketers and, by extension, advertising analysts is ad blocking—the use of software to stop ads from appearing unbidden on users' screens. For media companies and marketers, the spread of ad blocking software is a significant threat to revenue. Media executives argue that people consuming the content they produce have an obligation to pay for it, even if only with their time and attention. As with ad fraud, the media analyst's primary role is to detect when ad blocking is occurring and to try to accurately calculate its impact on the audience metrics being generated.

Advertising metrics and their larger impacts

Client and partner relationships

Media analysts who work with advertising metrics play a central role in determining the financial success or failure of all the companies in the transaction—advertiser, advertising agency, media firm, or the research companies providing data to all of the others. Because of this central role, the analyst needs expert skills not only in data analysis and interpretation but also in communication, negotiation, interpersonal relations, and client management.

When money is at stake, tension and conflict between the competing interests are nearly inevitable. But more than corporate success is involved. The personal reputations and professional success of the various company representatives also can be affected. Advertising agencies and marketing managers need to be able to prove to their clients and employers that their marketing strategies and ad placement decisions were smart and effective, not dumb and expensive failures. Similarly, the media companies need to demonstrate that buying time and space around their content is an effective way to reach an advertiser's target customers.

Thus, whether working on the agency/advertiser side or for the media house, a media analyst is expected to be expert at finding the good news in even the most dismal results—or, to use a popular expression, at "putting lipstick on a pig."

As one analyst explained it, the marketing manager who hired your advertising agency or media house needs to look successful to their own employer. If you find a way to help that person look good even with bad results, they'll probably continue to bring their company's business to your company.

This is not to say that an analyst should lie about what the data show. To do so would be professionally unethical at best and, at worst, could damage your professional reputation and credibility, as well as that of your employer. Instead, the skill almost universally mentioned by analytics professionals is the ability to "spin" results to put them into a favorable light from the advertiser's perspective. Often that means identifying some unique benefit that was delivered to the advertiser, no matter how small the audience segment that received it. "Your message was delivered to a larger share of the wealthiest 1% of the metro population than any brand competitor"—without mentioning that the majority of that demographic was over age 50 and therefore unlikely to be influenced by the message. "Your message received active 'engagement' from 40% of those who viewed it on social media"—without mentioning that most of that engagement was in the form of "angry" *emojis* and negative comments. Chapter 4 discusses ways to effectively communicate analytics results to different audiences.

Societal impacts

It also is important for media analysts to keep in mind that how advertisers value different audience segments has real effects on society. So too does every method used to measure audiences.

No method or technology used for collecting audience data is entirely benign. Some segment of society will be undercounted in any given method. Sometimes it's because a group, such as older people, is not as comfortable using the technologies that collect audience data. It might be that one demographic group or another is more concerned about privacy and potential surveillance, so few will participate in audience research. People living in rural areas may be underrepresented in audience samples for lack of internet connections. Lower-income people are often undersampled in audience research because advertisers aren't interested in reaching them.

But if advertisers don't value particular groups in society, media companies will produce less content for and about those groups. Research has found that news media rarely cover groups and communities they aren't monetizing through subscriptions or advertising (Gans, 2004; Squires, 1993; Vu, 2014), while entertainment media have been pilloried for ignoring and misrepresenting different groups (Why is Hollywood, 2020). Other studies have shown that when media ignore or misrepresent groups, policy makers are less aware of or more able to ignore those groups' needs (Cook et al., 1983).

History teaches that that has real consequences. In 1968, the report of the President's National Advisory Report on Civil Disorders, known as the Kerner Commission Report, found that the lack of media coverage about the needs of America's poor and minority communities was an important factor in the civil unrest that tore apart American cities during the "Long, Hot Summer" of 1967 (National Advisory Report on Civil Disorders, 1968).

While most of the focus on such research has been on news media, advertisers' preferences also strongly influence entertainment media. The format a radio station owner uses to program a radio station—country, rap, rock, classical, news talk—is determined by the revenue potential of that format in that market. The revenue potential is determined by how large the potential audience for that type of music is in a given community and how appealing that audience is to the advertisers available in that community. Decisions about which TV programs a network will produce or distribute are made the same way. People in demographic groups that don't interest advertisers are likely to have a harder time finding content that appeals to their tastes or needs.

As Chapter 1 discusses, the practice of media analytics should never be divorced from a constant and conscious consideration of the ethical implications of media management decisions. Media analysts specializing in advertising research will be on the front lines of the evolving privacy and access issues created by data analytics. Advertising plays a critically important role in both media and society, providing much of the revenue that makes news and entertainment content possible and fueling the 21st century global economy. But as ethical professionals, media analysts must remain aware of the negative effects the advertising business model has on equal access to information across society and the even more troubling implications of personal data-driven marketing (Chapters 6, 7).

Summary and conclusion

The field of media analytics got its start because advertisers needed better data to make buying decisions. While today media analysts work on media management issues far beyond just measuring audiences for advertisers, advertising analytics is still the core function of the profession. Understanding what advertisers want from buying advertising, knowing basic "media math," and keeping up with the evolving metrics used to measure audiences and the success of advertising campaigns are all fundamental job requirements for media analysts. To this day, most media analytics jobs touch, at least in some way, on advertising.

In the 21st century, advertising analytics have become increasingly challenging as audiences fragment across platforms and the internet creates a nearly unlimited supply of advertising time and space for advertisers to buy. Those developments have increased the competition among media companies for advertising clients and revenue and have made it increasingly important for platforms to be able to demonstrate that their content delivers a solid ROAS to advertisers.

While digital technologies help advertisers more *effectively* target "quality" audience members, those same technologies make it harder to *efficiently* find and reach large numbers of quality customers because potential buyers are now scattered across so many different content platforms. At the same time, digital technologies are increasing advertisers' advertising wastage by enabling ad blocking and ad fraud.

All of these trends increase the importance of having skilled media analysts employed throughout the industry, working for media companies, consumer products manufacturers and retailers, advertising agencies, and syndicated research firms. But as the pressure to attract and serve advertisers grows in media companies, it's important for analysts to remain keenly aware of and committed to protecting individuals' personal privacy rights and ensuring that they themselves behave ethically in their use of personal data. Similarly, as advisers to media executives and advertisers, media analysts are in a key position to raise questions about the potential impact advertising and content decisions may have on society in the 21st century.

Additional resources

For more information on Real Time Bidding: www.smaato.com/real-time-bidding/ and https://clearcode.cc/blog/programmatic-advertising/

Muhammad, F. (2020, July 10). *25 advertising metrics all digital marketers need to be tracking.* Instapage. Online. https://instapage.com/blog/key-advertising-metrics#:~:text=19.,or%20100%25%20of%20your%20video

YouTube. (2020). *About video metrics and reporting.* Online. https://support.google.com/youtube/answer/2375431?hl=en

Recommended cases

These cases can be found on the textbook website: www.routledge.com/cw/hollifield

Case 5.1 (6.2): Converting Local Radio Listeners into Car Buyers
Case 5.2 (6.1, 12.4): Shopping for Cars
Case 5.3 (11.3): Analyzing the Automotive Vertical for a Local Newspaper
Case 5.4 (4.1): Equipping Mattress Advertisers

Case studies, along with accompanying datasets for this chapter, can be found on the text website. We particularly suggest the preceding cases in the order listed. See the companion website and instructor's manual for detailed descriptions of these and other relevant cases.

Discussion questions and exercises

1. The chapter outlines many of the questions analysts working on advertising analytics are asked to answer and the issues they're asked to consider. Let's look again at some of these questions and discuss them. Use your university's student newspaper, radio station, or other type of student media as the context you use to think about these questions (or hypothetically, if your university does not have student media). Use the university community as the primary audience for a hypothetical news or entertainment channel. Would all members of the university community—administrators, faculty and staff, as well as students—be part of the audience for your medium or just one or two of those groups?

   With that context in mind, discuss the following questions:

   a. What local businesses might find the university media product you're thinking of to be a good advertising vehicle? Why?
   b. Approximately what size and demographics could your media platform deliver to those businesses?

c. What variables would you use to determine whether the university community would be a quality audience for the specific potential advertisers you are considering?
d. Given the size of your university and the percentage of the university population you can realistically expect to regularly consume your content, what would a reasonable CPM be that your target advertisers would likely accept?
e. What might the media organization do to maximize the effectiveness and efficiency of using your university media as a vehicle for their advertising?
f. What metrics would you use to measure the success or failure of their campaign through your media?
g. What variables might you consider? What other issues and topics have come to mind as you've discussed these?

Write a list of the variables *you* would use to try to answer these questions and discuss why you would pick those. How would you combine variables to get *insights* into the question? What controls would you use, and where might you get the data for your variables? Be realistic as you think about the questions. Approach it as if your boss just gave you this assignment.

2. The chapter discusses how advertisers value different audience segments and how that affects the content that media companies produce. What are your thoughts about these issues? How do you see these issues affecting media in your community or country?

3. *Exercise: Practicing media math*
A city has 2.3 million TVH and 2,473,320 adults between the ages of 18–49.

a. If a TV program has a rating of 2 in the 18–49 demographic, how many 18–49 viewers were watching last night?
b. If the CPM for the 18–49 demographic in that market is $21.11 for a local 60 second spot, how much would a local advertiser pay to run one 60 second advertisement in that show?
c. If the percentage of Households Using Television (HUTS) at 8 p.m. last night was 35%, and a program airing at 8 p.m. had a share of 6 in that market, how many TVH in that market were viewing the program?

4. *Exercise: Calculating GI*

Refer to Table 5.1. Calculate the GI for each daypart, given the number of advertisements the client wants to run and the total weight of this proposed campaign.

Table 5.1 Calculating Gross Impressions for a Proposed Advertising Buy

Daypart	Average impressions	No. of ads	GI
6–10 a.m.	7,420	12	
10–3 p.m.	2,473	6	
3–7 p.m.	42,046	10	
TOTAL			

Table 5.2 Calculating Gross Rating Points for a Proposed Advertising Buy

Daypart	Average rating	No. of ads	GRP
6–10 a.m.	0.3	12	
10–3 p.m.	0.1	6	
8–11 p.m.	1.7	10	
TOTAL			

5. *Exercise: Calculating GRP*
   Refer to Table 5.2. Calculate the GRP for each daypart, given the number of advertisements the client wants to run and the total weight of this proposed campaign.

Notes

1. Even in countries with public service broadcasters and government-owned media, advertising is an important source of revenue for media firms, while nonprofit media such as the United States' Public Broadcasting System and "community" radio often seek "sponsorships" from local businesses. The media company thanks its sponsors by name, another type of marketing.
2. The "M' comes from the Latin word for "thousand," which is *mille*.
3. Another illustration is advertising by what are called *business-to-business (B2B)* companies (Chapters 2, 11).
4. In fact, leaving such transactions to computers and algorithms has resulted in some poor ad selections/placements for brands, raising concerns about "brand safety" with programmatic advertising.

References

Alliance for Audited Media. (2018, May 17). *Three truths that help confront the digital ad fraud crisis.* [White paper]. https://blog.auditedmedia.com/newsviews/3-truths-confront-digital-ad-fraud-crisis

Bendle, N. T., Farris, P. W., Pfeifer, P. E., & Reibstein, D. J. (2016). *Marketing metrics: The manager's guide to measuring marketing performance* (3rd ed.). Pearson Education Inc.

Bennett, C. O. (1965). *Facts without opinion: First fifty years of the Audit Bureau of Circulations*. Audit Bureau of Circulations.

Cook, F. L., Tyler T. R., Goetz, E. G., Gordon, M. T., Protess, D., Leff, D. R., & Molotch, H. L. (1983). Media and agenda setting: Effects on the public interest group leaders, policy makers and policy. *Public Opinion Quarterly*, 47(1), 16–35.

Fou, A. (2020, December 11). 2020 Ad fraud year-in-review. *Forbes*. www.forbes.com/sites/augustinefou/2020/12/11/2020-ad-fraud-year-in-review/?sh=1a078c041762

Gans, H. J. (2004). *Deciding what's news: A study of CBS Evening News, NBC Nightly News, Newsweek and Time*. Northwestern University Press.

Marshall, J. (2014, February 20). WTF is programmatic advertising? *Digiday*. https://digiday.com/media/what-is-programmatic-advertising/

Muhammad, F. (2020, July 10). 25 advertising metrics all digital marketers need to be tracking. *Instapage*. https://instapage.com/blog/key-advertising-metrics#:~:text=19.,or%20100%25%20of%20your%20video

Napoli, P. M. (2003). *Audience economics: Media institutions and the audience marketplace*. Columbia University Press.

National Advisory Commission on Civil Disorders. (1968). Report of the National Advisory Commission on Civil Disorders. *US G.P.O.* www.eisenhowerfoundation.org/docs/kerner.pdf

Rogers, C. (2017, March 27). What is programmatic advertising? A beginner's guide. *Marketing Week*. www.marketingweek.com/programmatic-advertising/

Squires, J. D. (1993). *Read all about it: The corporate takeover of America's newspapers*. Times Books.

Statista Research Department. (2021, January 14). Estimated cost of digital ad fraud in the United States from 2011 to 2021. *Statista*. www.statista.com/statistics/778733/digital-ad-fraud-cost-us/

Vrountas, T. (2020, April 3). The 8 most common ad fraud methods & how to avoid them in your campaigns. [Blog]. *Instapage*. https://instapage.com/blog/ad-fraud

Vu, H. T. (2014). The online audience as gatekeeper: The influence of reader metrics on news editorial selection. *Journalism*, 15(8), 1094–1110. https://doi:10.1177/1464884913504259

Why is Hollywood still so White, and why responding to the protests isn't enough. (2020, June 4). *Vanity Fair*. www.vanityfair.com/hollywood/2020/06/little-gold-men-podcast-franklin-leonard-tananarive-due

6 Consumer behavior and marketing

Some would argue that all media behavior is consumer behavior, so why have a separate chapter about it? It's true that audiences are consumers. They consume media as well as many other products and services, and advertisers and brands want to reach them. Because advertisers rely on media vehicles to place their messages, the examination and understanding of audiences as consumers are central. In this chapter we dive deeply into this aspect to better understand how analytics can help brands reach consumers and build a relationship with them. It's a relationship that has significantly evolved in large part due to technology, which has dramatically expanded businesses' opportunities to engage with consumers. Digital technology, in particular, has transformed the brand–consumer relationship because it delivers so much of the content we consume and links us with the products we buy, making our behaviors easily trackable. Once collected and analyzed, the data provide valuable feedback to brands about our consumer preferences and behaviors, which brands can use to entice us or serve us better. To fully understand how consumer data is being used to create relationships with brands, let's first take a look at the industry itself.

The consumer data industry

We are now in what many are calling the data economy. While data has often been considered a type of currency, with media analytics, data is becoming the coin of exchange for almost every business sector today due to both accessibility, how much data can be gathered about us from digital sources, and the value that can be extracted from the data when properly analyzed and strategically applied. Among the biggest players in today's data industry and economy are companies known as data brokers.

DOI: 10.4324/9780429506956-9

Data brokers

Data brokers are "corporations that buy and collect information about major life events, hobbies, interests, income, behavior, and whatever else they can find, harvest information from store loyalty card programs, credit card data, or publicly available information, which can include Department of Motor Vehicle data or voting records. They then bundle and sell this information, largely for marketing purposes" (Angela, 2019). Data brokers are also known as data providers, data suppliers, or information brokers and can possess up to 1,500 pieces of information per individual (Wlosik, 2022). Data brokers in this burgeoning audience data industry cover the full range of sectors within the consumer and analytics industry. Some are firms you've never heard of and are quite specialized, while others are much larger and well-known, such as Acxiom and Experian, the latter of which is also a major credit reporting agency. To give you an idea of the capabilities and volume of data collected on consumers, as of 2018 Acxiom was able to provide up to 10,000 unique attributes on 2.5 billion different consumers around the globe (Melendez & Pasternack, 2019). Through analysis and segmentation of these attributes, data brokers can identify and "create" audiences. This makes them a central player in today's advertising and marketing technology sector, which involves sophisticated processes and systems including demand-side, supply-side, and data management platforms (Wlosik, 2022, see Figure 6.1).

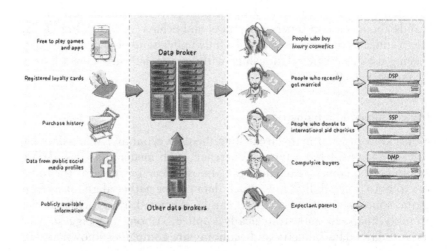

Figure 6.1 How data brokers work

Source: What Is a Data Broker and How Does It Work? Clearcode, www.clearcode.cc/

Other data companies provide something akin to "secret consumer scores" that rate consumers on things like risk, trustworthiness, or whether they have been "high-maintenance" as consumers, and these scores can affect things like how long we wait on hold over the phone, whether we are allowed to make returns at a retail store, or what level of service we receive (Hill, 2019). According to Hill (2019), such companies have years of data on each of us that include everything from the dates, times, and details of our takeout food orders, to personal messages we typed to Airbnb hosts, dates we returned merchandise to stores, or entries we made on a blog a decade ago. The personal nature of much of this data can feel unsettling. Most people have no idea that this level of data exists on each of them. As you can imagine, the depth of information that data brokers have on consumers is concerning to many and raises questions about privacy. We will return to this topic, but for now let's take a look at how this consumer data is utilized by brands to develop relationships with us.

The evolving consumer–brand relationship

While consumers are now more trackable due to digital technology and tools, the interactive nature of digital technology has enabled a two-way relationship between consumers and brands. Consumers can readily *post* feedback about products and services on websites, engage in social media conversation, and the like. This has given consumers more agency, or power, with brands than ever before. Some brands have embraced this new reality by viewing consumers as being in a relationship with the brand. Because brands cannot control consumers' communications, it makes sense to invite them into the branding process as a co-creator, and in fact, the term *co-creation* refers to this process in which "brands and consumers work together to create better ideas, products and services" (Alida, 2016). The toy company LEGO has practiced this collaboration particularly well. By asking their customers for ideas for the next LEGO model, they save time and money on market research and end up pleasing their customers, who not only feel included in the process but then remain loyal (Alida, 2016; Ideas4all Innovation, n.d.). Co-creation can also mean observing how consumers use or perceive a given product, even if this varies from the brand's original intent. If consumers are using it differently, the brand perception can be recrafted with an updated brand identity. In some cases, co-creating meaning with a brand means engaging consumers in marketing campaigns and allowing them to help create content around the brand.

Consumers exercise influence with brands in other ways as well, and that is through pressure or negative comments posted on social media or online product reviews. Because companies do not want negative feedback or negative public perception, they are quick not only to respond to comments but also to address problems that consumers make known. Many brands have social media managers dedicated to *social media listening*, so that they can stay on top of consumer conversation, respond quickly and professionally, and ideally maintain a positive public image. Similarly, negative product reviews can alert a company to product flaws that can then be fixed. In all cases, consumers leverage today's two-way communication to wield power in the consumer–brand relationship. While this is mainly positive for consumers because it holds companies more accountable and makes them more responsive to consumer needs, some consumers abuse online communication privileges and deliberately post negative comments (sometimes with no basis) with the hopes of receiving free merchandise or services from the brand.

Consumer journey and the marketing funnel

Our online behavior can resemble travel. Perhaps that's why the term *consumer journey* is commonly used to describe how someone encounters and navigates a website and moves toward some type of conversion decision. This concept can also be referred to as the customer or audience journey. Specifically defined, the consumer journey is "how a user engages with your website. It is a walk in the user's shoes, so to speak—from their online search for your product type, brand or category, all the way through your landing pages, shopping carts, checkout process and payment partners" (Glaze, n.d., para. 4). Observing the consumer journey can help a product or service provider better understand the process by which someone first encounters their brand, considers it, engages with it, and potentially makes other decisions about it. Understanding this journey can provide *insight* on how brands can better serve their consumers or potential consumers from making the website experience as seamless as possible and creating awareness, to learning what most interests them, to understanding what makes them ultimately purchase an item.

Because most companies hope that consumers ultimately purchase their product or service, online and mobile marketing efforts are geared toward positively influencing consumers about the brand at each opportunity or "touchpoint." Different websites visited by the consumer represent advertising or marketing opportunities for the brand, but it may not be until the seventh or eighth touchpoint that a conversion is made.

A *conversion* is simply the desired outcome or behavior that the brand wants a consumer to make. Often this is a product purchase, but it could also be a subscription or membership sign-up, video view, petition signature or a request for more information. Collectively, the online metrics used to understand the consumer journey and touchpoints are referred to as *clickstream data*. This includes many metrics such as websites visited, pages viewed, and so forth, which reflect the nature of the consumer's online navigation and behavior.

The *marketing funnel* is a more concrete way to think about the consumer journey. While there are many versions of the marketing funnel with various stages, the simplest funnel model is typically described in four stages also known as AIDA, an acronym for awareness, interest (i.e., consideration), desire, and action (i.e., conversion or purchase). This four-stage process of consumer thinking and action is referred to as a funnel due to its shape when seen in diagram form (see Figure 6.2); there are more consumers at the top of the funnel during the awareness stage, and the number of consumers gradually decreases as they move through the funnel to the conversion stage.

Awareness of a product or business is a broad idea and must occur before any interest in the product can develop, including media products. Once there is consumer interest or curiosity in a product or service, a consumer is more likely to do research to learn more. The business hopes that a desire for the product results (particularly due to their marketing efforts), and, ultimately, it hopes that a conversion or purchase is made. Marketing funnels are not an exclusively online concept, but the availability of clickstream data certainly makes it easier to target consumers at each of

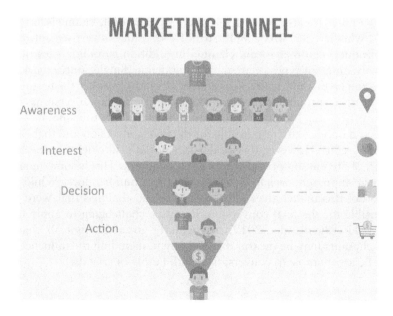

Figure 6.2 AIDA marketing funnel

Source: Shutterstock

the funnel stages, as well as measure the response levels to a company's marketing efforts at each stage. As an example, useful "top of the funnel" metrics that help measure brand awareness can include *brand recall*, *branded search*, and increased *web traffic*, while "mid-funnel" metrics include things that indicate audience education or engagement like *cost-per-new-visitor* to the site or *page-view lift*.

Finally, "bottom-of-the funnel" key performance indicators (KPIs) are focused on measuring outcomes and actions such as *total leads*, *cost-per-lead*, *sales revenue*, or other conversions or calls to action (Davis, 2021; Moothart, 2017). As many may know, online marketing has historically depended on cookies, i.e., the files or data from browsers embedded into websites to record settings and user activity, but new regulations are now pushing the industry to methods that better preserve consumer privacy.

Attribution

Broadly speaking, *attribution* is a method of determining **return on investment (ROI)** for a brand's marketing and then allocating marketing expenditures or "marketing spend" based on attribution results. In the online space, this return could come from a single source or multiple sources. What was the site or touchpoint credited with the final conversion? Was it the first click? The last click? While a consumer journey may have occurred entirely online, it's also possible that there were multiple channels as touchpoints, whether that was a billboard, TV or radio advertisement, direct mail product, or other media channel in addition to online sites or ads. There are different types of attribution modeling. Single-source marketing attribution credits one source—assigning all credit to either the first touchpoint or the last touchpoint—for making the consumer conversion. Multi-source attribution, by contrast, recognizes that multiple touchpoints—both online and offline—are responsible for the final conversion and that each is assigned credit.[1] However, this model does not take into account the actual portion of attribution provided by each touchpoint. This is something that the third approach, weighted multisource attribution, does. While difficult to do, this model gives more weight to the channels that were most responsible for the final conversion. It can be challenging to apply in the real world (Rheinlander, 2019), particularly given that not all channels or touchpoints may be measurable or known, including the influence that might be attributable to conversation with family or friends.

Microtargeting

One result of the digital footprints we leave along our online consumer journey is a unique level of granular and precise information (or data) about our behavior and preferences that marketers may leverage for microtargeting. *Microtargeting* "is a marketing strategy that uses consumer data and demographics to create audience subsets/segments. It's possible to predict the buying behavior of these like-minded individuals, and to influence that behavior through hyper-targeted advertising" (MNI Targeted Media, n.d.). It has also become a popular strategy for political campaigns to target voters. By examining the demographic and psychographic traits of consumers who already have purchased a certain product or service, this tactic can provide clues as to potential new, "look-alike" customers to target because they have similar interests, preferences, income levels, location, and so forth. *Big data* can provide a treasure trove of information to mine to identify like-minded individuals as prospects (anonymously). By layering similar characteristics that were shared by customers who had already purchased a product in that category, it is possible to identify potential new customers for microtargeting (MNI Targeted Media, n.d.)

A related concept, *advertising addressability*, refers to the ability to target messages directly to a specific household or individual using *personally identifiable information* (*PII*). This can take place if a marketer already has that information (due to a preexisting relationship) or via anonymized data in the case of a marketer who has the information about that individual's preferences and behaviors from other sources and is able to digitally address personalized advertising via the IP (internet protocol) address. Addressable advertising enables efficiency for a brand because there is no "waste" with the message going to a broader audience that may or may not be interested in the advertised product. Addressability benefits the targeted consumer because the product is likely something wanted or needed; it is more relevant for that consumer. Much of television advertising addressability is enabled by set-top box (cable box) data. It is anonymized data, but a "data matching" process is typically used after data collection in which the viewer data can be reconciled with detailed data broker information about the household (Angela, 2019). One data broker, LiveRamp, says it assigns anonymous identifiers and applies other privacy-protecting policies and practices, in order to match the households with the rich information in other big datasets. The result, according to a LiveRamp executive, is that the company can locate "yogurt-loving moms," "customers who bought a car six months ago," "Ford owners [who] watched NFL games over the last two seasons," "tech enthusiasts with $100K investable assets," "consumers who have sailed three or more times in the last three years," "auto intenders with a minimum income of $75,000 and at least one child in the home," among other valuable niche segments (Angela, 2019). This is really a form of microtargeting as described previously, and the result is that households on the same street may see different advertisements while watching the same television program because the advertisements are customized for the individual household.

Cookies

Microtargeting does not happen automatically. As previously noted, it usually needs a network IP address and browsing history. This can be gathered with the help of *cookies*, which are text files that are embedded into your browser when you visit a website and track your user preferences and behavior, as well as IP address. Cookies can be first-party or third-party. First-party cookies are those used by the website we are visiting in order to better understand our online navigation and movement, the functionality of features, and our usage while there in order to enhance our user experience and improve the performance of the site itself. Third-party cookies are "outsider" tracking tools used for advertising and marketing purposes and can follow us even after we leave a given site, usually in order to serve us personalized ads as we browse elsewhere (Stewart, 2019). Cookies have been critical to the digital advertising industry in its pursuit of the microtargeting of consumers, addressable advertising, and particularly *programmatic advertising*. A 2020 study found that 99% of cookies were used for user tracking and targeted advertising purposes (Urban et al., 2020).

As of 2022, industry efforts were underway to migrate away from cookies. Due to increasing scrutiny of consumer privacy and mandates by new laws such as the **General Data Protection Regulation (GDPR)** in the European Union and the *California Consumer Privacy Act (CCPA)* in the United States, personal information cannot be gathered without consumer consent, and third-party cookies indeed collect data that can be considered personal information. That's why, when viewing a website, you now see messages appear stating that the site uses cookies. In order for cookies to collect data, websites under these new regulations must now receive your consent to track you. As another outcome of these new regulations, Google announced that its Chrome browser would likely cease using third-party cookies by sometime in 2024 (although the company had pushed the cutoff date back multiple times at this writing), and other browsers such as Apple's Safari and Mozilla's Firefox have made similar announcements (Bohn, 2021; Lawler, 2022). This means a replacement method will be needed in order to measure and track consumer behavior online.

The most likely alternatives to cookies seem to be device-centric and/or browser-centric solutions that would keep consumer data within the specific browser like a walled garden. Such solutions would then constitute first-party tracking and not third-party. In addition, some proposals include the ability to target groups of consumers using anonymized data, so that similar interest groups can be targeted (based on browsing behavior) but without individually identifying users. This is often made easier by partnering with data aggregation companies, also known as data brokers or data partners (e.g., Acxiom, Experian), that collect massive amounts of consumer information from a variety of sources (e.g., home ownership and address, vehicle registration information, voter registration records, age and gender information, household income, credit card purchases). This external data about a household can then be matched with an organization's first-party data. The data are anonymized and aggregated into what are commonly referred to as "big data" sets (Chapter 7), which can then be used to identify relevant segments an advertiser may wish to target. As of this writing, the industry alternatives to third-party cookies were still a work in progress.

Cookies do not function in the same way on mobile platforms. Specifically, they do not work across mobile environments, something that's essential for tracking and optimizing digital campaigns (IAB, 2013). Also, within an app, the cookie is stored within a webview, not a browser, so that the cookie information cannot be shared with other apps or the web browser within the phone (Tamte-Horan, 2019). Because of the limitations of cookies, various identifiers are used instead, including the "Client/ Device Generated Identifier, Statistical ID, HTML5 Cookie Tracking, and Universal Login Tracking" (Tamte-Horan, 2019) or Mobile Ad Identifiers (MAIDs). These other identification strategies are used for mobile sites and apps to understand our behaviors and preferences as identified by our device. Many in the industry believe that a similar "identification matching" or *identity resolution* system—in which first-party data are linked with external third-party data to help match individuals or households—is the best option for a post-cookie online environment, and many companies now exist to provide such services (e.g., Acxiom, Experian).

In addition to this, there are alternative ways for measuring consumers for personalization purposes. For instance, consumers who already have accounts with certain online services can be contacted directly by that service for survey purposes. Statistical modeling is another possible approach, similar to how it is also used in television measurement (Luján, 2019). *Software development kits* (*SDKs*) also can be used to track the consumer journey on mobile devices because user consent must be gained at the time of app installation or purchase. However, any alternative personalization methods must ensure they are compliant with emerging privacy regulations.

Online/mobile search

Online and mobile search via internet browsers may represent one of the biggest opportunities in analytics in terms of understanding consumer needs, wants, and desires. The reason? People are literally asking questions of Google, Firefox, Safari, and other browsers! These questions are not always in the form of a direct question, such as, "How do I know if I have pneumonia?" although they can be. Most often, consumer questions come in the form of keywords entered into the browser search box, such as "symptoms of pneumonia," "cough," "fever," and so forth. The previous example was quite informational in nature and concerns physical well-being, and, of course, it's important to be able to analyze and understand audience need for health information. But brands and marketers want to be able to turn such queries into revenue opportunities by making sure their product and brand appear as a search result; in the previous example, this might be a cough medicine. Search engine optimization and search marketing can help achieve such outcomes.

Search engine optimization (*SEO*) is the practice of making website content more discoverable and likely to appear as a top search result by a search engine. This happens by making content more relevant in terms of quantity and quality. Brands can accomplish this by inserting *keywords* into their web content that are commonly used in consumer searches. Strategists should consider words and phrases that are narrowly focused to what their brand and website do and what might be desired by a consumer. They should also make sure the website content that is delivered as a result of a search request is robust and of high quality.

Language is a critical area for companies to understand. Many countries around the world are multilingual, and consumers in a single city may be entering search terms using a variety of languages, combinations of languages (like Spanglish), misspellings of words in those languages, and country-specific spellings of words in the same language (e.g., British and American English). All of these possibilities must be considered by brands that want to attract consumers through search marketing. Such terms and combination of terms (in multiple languages and combinations) must be considered and included in analyses. This is also where *machine learning* and *algorithms* can be efficient and useful. Search engines can "learn" what words or combinations of words, and in which languages or combinations of language and slang—including misspellings—are used to achieve certain search objectives. Over time and multiple iterations, the browser comes to deliver the desired search results to consumers, in the appropriate language and with the appropriate context.

Voice search

Historically, we've always searched for information (from the phone book to our social networks); over time we've simply changed the way we search. Voice is the latest iteration of search and another way that analytics can be used to engage consumers with brands and provide search marketing opportunities.

Here, too, ethics are paramount. Personal conversations may be overheard by smart speakers, and that information is then stored on a server. Geolocation and mobility metrics, combined with voice search requests, could provide an intimate window into people's lives and lifestyles. When they go to the gym and what they need before, during, and after the gym could be revealed via search metrics, for example. Do they request a certain playlist, do they search for a juice bar or restaurant afterward? If so, there may be excellent microtargeting and promotional opportunities for the juice bar nearest their gym, based on this data. If and when they have a medical question, what do they ask, what level of detail do they provide to the voice assistant, and what private details do they share? Geolocation data combined with voice search requests for the nearest medical clinic could provide efficiency benefits to someone, particularly during a time-sensitive health crisis, but what potential ethical issues arise from the voice assistant having data about such a request, particularly if geolocation data also indicates which clinic someone visited and when? As of 2022, there were no reliable voice analytics measurement providers, but that is likely to change as time progresses.[2]

Language-related analytics

Search-related behaviors can also provide valuable clues about who lives in an area, in what ways they prefer to be communicated with, and what culturally relevant opportunities might exist to establish relationships with them, according to one online search industry executive. This, in turn, can lead to brand success. For instance, "Do Hindi audiences in the US respond better to *in-language*[3] or English with a cultural nod?" "Do people who have their browsers set to Spanish have a higher conversion on Spanish or English ads?" These are some potential questions that could lead to insights and bottom-line brand success. If there are regional accents, local slang words, or sayings, a brand can tailor its creative content and strategy in those ways as well, not to mention localized culture. For instance, a campaign could be culturally more Cuban in Miami, more Mexican in Texas, and so forth in order to better align with regional cultural identities.

Integrating search and mobile

In an acknowledgment of just how central mobile phones have become to the consumer shopping experience, more retailers are looking for ways to integrate the platform into the consumer experience. In addition to understanding how mobile phones are used in-store to compare brands, price shop, or check product availability at various locations, some creative strategies use location and in-store analytics to optimize their advertising.

One search industry executive gave the example of being able to track people who go into physical stores and make some assumptions about advertising efficacy. If a company has its data loaded into the search firm's tool, the executive explained, "we're able to sort of calculate roughly how much time people spent in your store based on if they saw your ad or not. You didn't even have to click, you just got served the ad, but they later end up going to the store." While not perfect science, they said it's a way for a client to combine the power and analytics of mobile's geolocation capability along with advertising analytics to better understand how much foot traffic their online ads are generating.

As a second example, the company explained how online analytics can help a retailer such as a local car dealership know they're getting what is referred to as *qualified traffic*—not people who are just browsing or who admire cars but people who are really in the market for one and most likely to buy. Analysts can look at the number of car company manufacturers' sites visited that month and see whether a consumer is looking at Kelly Blue Book and local dealers, data that suggests someone is seriously considering a vehicle purchase. Then, by identifying those types of online consumers, specific advertising can be targeted to them, whether it is by make of car, in-language advertising that may be effective (like Spanish or Mandarin), or other strategies. It's a more efficient approach because the individual has been identified, through analytics, as a more motivated and likely purchaser. The executive also noted that digital and TV advertising together are a powerful and effective combination.

More geolocation opportunities

Because of the unique nature of mobile devices and how they can be combined with *geolocation data,* there are some special opportunities not only to create features and services that benefit consumers but to learn more about consumers' preferences and patterns in order to grow or expand the business. One such example is targeted mobile advertising using *geofencing* technology. Geofencing tracks consumers' movements and allows a business to serve up targeted content such as ads or coupons when a user gets within a certain distance of the business (Sullivan, 2016). Consumers must opt in, and media buyers determine the proximity radius, but if a chain of coffee shops, for instance, wanted to utilize geofencing, whenever an opt-in customer came within the radius, a mobile ad would be pushed to their device. *Beacons* are another type of proximity technology for mobile phones. Often used in retail outlets, they are installed throughout the store, including on merchandise and mannequins, and, using Bluetooth or short-wave radio technology, they can sense customer interaction, browsing, and buying patterns. As a result, they help increase consumer engagement and sales (Martin, 2015).

Another example comes from the Disney theme parks. They've used a combination of website, mobile app, and radio-frequency-enabled wrist bands to gather personal data in order to customize a guest's experience (providing guests with information such as average wait time or walking time to attractions based on their current location) or to personalize and recommend future experiences. A marketing industry professional explained that this may end up delighting customers further and result in greater loyalty and future park visits. But the information gathered from either the mobile app or wrist band as guests wander through the park also provides valuable feedback to the theme park about traffic patterns, wait times at rides and attractions at various times of day, frequency of visits to attractions, visits to eateries and gift shops and how much is spent, even the most common resting places between attractions. All of this consumption data, in the aggregate, can provide valuable information to the company about how better to optimize the experience for guests, where efficiencies might be gained, and to highlight potential opportunities (Marr, 2017, 2019).

Another example of the benefit of mobile app data is the restaurant sector. While many people still enjoy dining out, takeout and delivery options have become increasingly popular in recent years, particularly since the advent of food takeout and delivery service apps. One search industry professional noted that some restaurants with takeout apps quickly realized that they were making more money from takeout than from their brick and mortar stores. For small businesses in large cities with high rent prices (like New York), they said, it made sense for such businesses to not pay for a property with lots of seating but focus instead on takeout and delivery service. Likewise, a business may opt to be only "e-delivery" with no dining room at all. Many restaurants have also rolled out QR, or *quick response codes*. In addition to enabling contactless ordering, QR codes provide all kinds of customer information, from behaviors and preferences to past food purchases and amount spent (Lucas, 2021).

Artificial intelligence

When you hear the term *artificial intelligence* (*AI*), you might think of machine learning, self-driving cars, robots, chatbots, or voice assistants like Alexa. But it is quite a broad concept and is defined as "a system's ability to interpret external data correctly, to learn from such data, and to use those learnings to achieve specific goals and tasks through flexible adaptation" (Kaplan & Haenlein, 2019, p. 17). Due to its wide array of applications, AI is being adopted across many industries for a variety of purposes. For our discipline, artificial intelligence is becoming one of the most efficient ways to conduct audience and consumer research because it saves time. It can help identify insights within minutes rather than days or weeks, which means those insights can be applied sooner to business operations. You might be surprised to hear that AI isn't really new. "Established as an academic discipline in the 1950s, AI remained an area of relative scientific obscurity and limited practical interest for over half a century. Today, due to the rise of big data and improvements in computing power, it has entered the business environment and public conversation" (Haenlein & Kaplan, 2019, p. 5). Artificial intelligence is entering a golden age due to greater data access than ever before.

One type of AI that comes to mind for many is *machine learning*. However, AI is much "broader than machine learning since it also covers a system's ability to perceive data (e.g., natural language processing or voice/image recognition) or to control, move, and manipulate objects based on learned information be it a robot or another connected device" (Kaplan & Haenlein, 2019, p. 17). With machine learning, Amazon, Netflix, Spotify, and Google's algorithms all "learn" about your preferences, habits, and routines and become trained so that results become more refined. The more data and information you feed the algorithms, the better they get at predicting what you might want, even before you finish typing—or maybe before you even go to the website. On web portals, we can be "fed" stories that are customized to our preferences based on our prior clicks. For instance, Microsoft "uses reinforcement learning to select headlines on MSN.com by rewarding the system with a higher score when more visitors click on a given link" (Kaplan & Haenlein, 2019, p. 19). AI can also help monitor how long we look at certain articles, where we stop scrolling, when we slow down to view an image, and what captures our interest even without our clicking on it and respond accordingly by providing similar content the next time.

Machine learning also can be used to mine big consumer datasets, including text and social media. Queries can reveal relationships between *variables* that we did not previously know existed. In many ways, this approach to consumer intelligence has the potential to replace traditional survey research, as vast amounts of data now can be collected about actual consumer behavior online rather than surveying consumers about their purchase intent or questions about a limited number of survey topics.

Another type of AI relevant to the consumer realm has to do with emotional intelligence and facial recognition. A company founded by MIT, Affectiva, "uses advanced vision systems to recognize emotions like joy, surprise, and anger at the same level (and frequently better) as humans. Companies can use such systems to recognize emotions during customer interactions or while recruiting new employees" (Kaplan & Haenlein, 2019, p. 18). AI also can be used to identify thousands of "psychotypes" of consumers and create customized messaging based on individual preferences for sales and marketing purposes (pp. 19–20). Such "emotion detection" could also be used to predict a consumer's mood state and identify what type of product or service they might be willing to purchase or what type of promotion might be most effective. While this is all quite impressive and presents numerous new opportunities, it raises some ethical concerns.

Ethics, privacy, and regulation

As previously noted, AI's ability to quickly identify consumer profiles and preferences is both fascinating and efficient. But these profiles and preferences are not always accurate, and sometimes—because they rely on external, historical information—such outcomes can even be discriminatory. Algorithms are only as good as the information fed to them, which can result in *algorithmic bias*. What if the data are wrong or unfair? Machine learning might be fueled by historical data that was less representative or inclusive of the population you are trying to serve today. As a result, the algorithms could be lacking and even prejudiced. Even if the data you are using to train the algorithm are historically accurate, we live in an imperfect world, and historically, not everyone has been treated well or fairly. So does it really make sense to build models or algorithms based on unfair data? Is it ethical to make consumer targeting decisions based on that historical data (algorithmic bias)?[4]

Another ethical question has to do with how we use technology. Do your goals ethically justify how you're planning to use the data? What is your intent? The tracking technology may be capable of extracting certain data or doing something really impressive (that may push the boundaries of consumer privacy and identification, for instance), but maybe it's not something you should ever do. What information is essential to serving the consumer, and what has the consumer consented to? Once the essential data is gathered to meet these objectives, you do not need to collect additional data about the consumer.

Consumer data and privacy regulation

Ethical concerns related to consumer privacy are on the rise as access to consumer data is greater than ever, along with the amount of digital data being collected. While data brokers operate legal businesses, some consumers are rightly concerned about the threat of so much personal information being in the hands of others. Along with this, consumers are increasingly aware of their rights in this area, as new laws governing consumer privacy and data have taken hold in many places around the world, with the European Union's General Data Protection Regulation (GDPR) serving as a blueprint for many others. Companies are now having to reassess their digital relationship with consumers and must learn how to be compliant with these new regulations.

In effect since 2018, the European Union's ***General Data Protection Regulation* (*GDPR*)** may be the strongest set of consumer privacy regulations to date. It is:

> designed to give individuals more control over how their data are collected, used, and protected online. It also binds organizations to strict new rules about using and securing the personal data they collect from people, including the mandatory use of technical safeguards like encryption and higher legal thresholds to justify data collection. Organizations that don't comply will face heavy penalties of up to 4 percent of their global annual revenue or €20 million, whichever is higher,
>
> (Wolford, n.d., para. 3)

Not only is this a strict regulation with steep consequences for non-compliance, it's 11 chapters long and covers both data protection regulations and consumer privacy rights. The regulations apply to any business that processes the personal data of EU residents, regardless of where the company is located, so the GDPR has already had wide-ranging impact across the globe with businesses in many countries making their websites and data collection procedures GDPR-compliant. Dozens of countries have followed suit by developing their own regulations, many of which are modeled after the GDPR. The main provisions of the GDPR include elements such as data privacy and security, as well as consumers' rights over their data. Information about the GDPR and other privacy and data regulations can be found in the Additional Resources at the end of the chapter.

Summary and conclusion

As with many of the other topics discussed in this text, technology has been a primary driver in the evolution of consumer behavior and measurement. Sophisticated tools now enable us to understand consumer behavior and preferences with greater specificity than ever before, as well as enable more customizable ways of personally marketing to consumers. With these tools come new ethical questions as well as regulations. Understanding and honoring both will be critical to maintaining consumers' trust, the foundation for any healthy relationship.

Additional resources

Martech: https://martech.org/
Acxiom: www.acxiom.com/
Live Ramp: https://liveramp.com/
Clearcode: https://clearcode.cc/resources/
General Data and Protection Regulation (GDPR): https://gdpr.eu/

Articles on privacy

www.pewresearch.org/internet/2019/11/15/americans-and-privacy-
   concerned-confused-and-feeling-lack-of-control-over-their-personal-
   information/
www.ftc.gov/business-guidance/privacy-security/consumer-privacy

Marketing and consumer professional associations

American Marketing Association: www.ama.org/
Consumer Brands Association: https://consumerbrandsassociation.org/
Hispanic Marketing Council: https://hispanicmarketingcouncil.org/
Federation of African American Advertisers + Marketers: www.thefaaam.
   org/
Asian American Advertising Federation: www.3af.org/
African-American Marketing Association: www.aa-ma.org/
Black Marketers Association of America: https://blackmarketers.org/

Recommended cases

**These cases can be found on the textbook website:
www.routledge.com/cw/hollifield**

Case 6.1 (5.2, 12.4): Shopping for Cars
Case 6.2 (5.1): Converting Local Radio Listeners into Car Buyers
Case 6.3: Understanding Radio Listener Profiles
Case 6.4: Funnel Analysis
Case 6.5: Google Merchandise Store I

Case studies, along with accompanying datasets for this chapter, can be found on the text website. We particularly suggest the preceding cases in the order listed. See the companion website and instructor's manual for detailed descriptions of these and other relevant cases.

Discussion questions and exercises

1. What is the difference between consumer targeting and consumer tracking?
2. If a consumer has consented, should companies gather whatever information and amount of behavioral data that they like? Or should they just collect what they need to serve the consumer effectively? Other approaches? Explain and defend your answer.
3. What all should be involved in the process of consumer consent? What does a reasonable consent policy or document look like? How long should it be? How should it be worded? As a consumer, how do you feel about various companies' consent policies? (See also Question 7.)
4. What do you think about what you've read about the data broker industry? If the consumer information is readily available, either via public records, or internet-based consumer transactions or conversation, does this make it ethical to collect? To aggregate and sell or share with others? Explain and defend your answer.
5. What do you think about the consumer data protection and privacy regulations as mandated by the EU's General Data Protection Regulation (GDPR)? Are they too stringent? About right? Other? Answer each of these questions first (a) from the perspective of a business that needs to be compliant with GDPR and then (b) as a consumer whose rights are protected by GDPR. Why do you feel the way you do in each situation? For reference, see https://gdpr.eu/. For a summary, you may wish to start with the Overview section.
6. Research the current consumer privacy regulations where you live. Make note of the basic principles for data protection as well as consumer rights, as well as what is required for corporate compliance. Then select another country (or state or province), and do the same research. How do the regulations compare? Which set of regulations is more pro-consumer and protective of consumer rights? What is similar and what is different between the two places' regulations? Has one set of regulations been recently updated compared to the other? What would you recommend to one or both countries (or states or provinces) for strengthening their regulations?
7. Read the following opinion piece from *The New York Times*: Litman-Navarro, K. We read 150 privacy policies. They were an incomprehensible disaster. *New York Times.* www.nytimes.com/interactive/2019/06/12/opinion/facebook-google-privacy-policies.html (Subscription may be required but this resource is often available via your university library.) After reading this article, based on what you've read and your own experiences as a consumer, write a user-friendly Privacy Agreement for a mobile app or a website. Keep in mind what

important elements such an agreement would need to include, as well as what kind of language and style would make it user-friendly for the average consumer.

8. *Exercise: Google Merchandise Store*

Just as it sounds, Google has an online store where fans can purchase branded merchandise: www.googlemerchandisestore.com/. For this exercise, we will be exploring the store's web analytics. In your search browser window, search for "Google Merchandise Store analytics." A page should appear that is a Google Analytics demo account for this store's analytics: https://analytics.google.com/analytics/web/demoAccount. Click on "access Demo Account" with a Google account, and choose the "Flood-It!" version URL option. If you do not have a Google account, you can create one in order to freely access these data. Follow these steps, and then answer the questions.

a. If not already there, navigate to the Home page (see icons/navigation on the left side). What do you notice for the seven-day time period displayed? Are there particular days with a high volume of users? Lower numbers of users? How about compared to the previous seven-day period (if displayed)? Any ideas for possible explanations for what you see?

b. Repeat the preceding process in Question 8a but with the other metrics listed (e.g., new users, average engagement time, average revenue).

c. Now, using the left side navigation icons, select "Reports." A left-side menu called "Reports Snapshot" should appear. Scroll down to "User → Demographics," and click on that. Then click "Demographics Overview." You should see some charts about users by country, age, and gender for the store, as well as some interest areas (psychographics) and other categories. What stories do these data and charts say about who shops at the Google Merchandise Store?

d. Look at the chart labeled "Users by Gender." What do you observe, and what story does this graph of gender tell? Does anything interesting jump out? If so, do you have thoughts as to why this might be?

e. Now look at the table on "Users by Age." What do you observe, and what story does this graph of age breakdown tell? Does anything interesting jump out by age group? Is any age group a lot higher or lower than others on any of these variables? If so, do you have thoughts as to why this might be?

f. Repeat this exercise for the charts "Users by Language" and "Users by City." How might Google strategically use or apply this information to enhance online store sales or other objectives?

g. Using the left-side navigation once again, select "User→Tech" and then "Tech Overview." A new set of tables will appear. How should Google Merchandise Store strategically use the information found here?

Notes

1. Determining return-on-investment (ROI) and attribution across both online and offline platforms requires what is known as *omnichannel measurement*. While a full treatment of how omnichannel measurement functions is beyond the scope of this chapter, it integrates both online and offline attribution sources using person-level data. It can be complex and typically involves big data and tools such as machine learning (Marketing Evolution, n.d.).
2. However, there have been various reports of voice assistants collecting voice data from people's homes without the trigger word (e.g., "Alexa"), recordings being stored indefinitely, and employees listening in on what often are personal, intimate conversations, raising many consumer privacy concerns (Fowler, 2019). Stored content is what trains the artificial intelligence (AI) of a voice assistant device.
3. In-language advertising is the practice of using the target audience's preferred or dominant language when communicating with them, such as in an advertising or promotional campaign.
4. For more information on examples of algorithmic bias and other ethical issues that arise with the implementation of artificial intelligence (AI) tools, as well as prevention strategies, see the Additional Resources section at the end of the chapter.

References

Alida. (2016, August 5). *5 examples of brands driving customer-centric innovation.* www.alida.com/the-alida-journal/5-examples-how-brands-are-using-co-creation

Angela, M. (2019, December 11). Personalized ads are coming to television. *The Startup.* https://medium.com/swlh/personalized-ads-are-coming-to-television-c10ad7d62514

Bohn, D. (2021, June 24). Google delays blocking third-party cookies in Chrome until 2023. *The Verge.* www.theverge.com/2021/6/24/22547339/google-chrome-cookiepocalypse-delayed-2023

Davis, S. (2021, June 1). Key KPIs for full-funnel programmatic advertising. *ROI Revolution.* https://roirevolution.com/blog/key-kpis-for-full-funnel-programmatic-advertising/

Fowler, G. A. (2019, May 6). Alexa has been eavesdropping on you this whole time. *The Washington Post.* www.washingtonpost.com/technology/2019/05/06/alexa-has-been-eavesdropping-you-this-whole-time/

Glaze, M. (n.d.) What is the customer or consumer journey? 3 phases to know. *The Future of Customer and Engagement and Experience.* www.the-future-of-commerce.com/2016/09/26/definition-consumer-journey/

Haenlein, M., & Kaplan, A. (2019). A brief history of artificial intelligence: On the past, present, and future of artificial intelligence. *California Management Review*, 61(4), 5–14. https://doi:10.1177/0008125619864925

Hill, K. (2019, November 4). I got access to my secret consumer score: Now you can get yours, too. *The New York Times*. www.nytimes.com/2019/11/04/business/secret-consumer-score-access.html

IAB. (2013, November). *Cookies on mobile 101: Understanding the limitations of cookie-based tracking for mobile advertising.* www.iab.com/wp-content/uploads/2015/07/CookiesOnMobile101Final.pdf

Ideas4all Innovation. (n.d.). *Some examples of co-creation that bring brand and consumer together.* www.ideas4allinnovation.com/innovators/examples-cocreation-consumers/

Kaplan, A., & Haenlein, M. (2019). Siri, Siri, in my hand: Who's the fairest in the land? On the interpretations, illustrations, and implications of artificial intelligence. *Business Horizons*, 62(1), 15–25.

Lawler, R. (2022, July 27). Google delays blocking third-party cookies again, now targeting late 2024. *The Verge*. www.theverge.com/2022/7/27/23280905/google-chrome-cookies-privacy-sandbox-advertising

Lucas, A. (2021, August 21). QR codes have replaced restaurant menus: Industry experts say it isn't a fad. *CNBC*. www.cnbc.com/2021/08/21/qr-codes-have-replaced-restaurant-menus-industry-experts-say-it-isnt-a-fad.html

Luján, J. A. (2019, November 28). A web after cookies and its impact on marketing measurement. [Article]. *We Are Marketing*. www.wearemarketing.com/blog/cookie-authentication-vs-token-authentication.html

Marketing Evolution. (n.d.). *What is omnichannel marketing? Definition, tips, and examples.* www.marketingevolution.com/knowledge-center/topic/marketing-essentials/omnichannel

Marr, B. (2017, August 24). Disney uses big data, IoT and machine learning to boost customer experience. *Forbes*. www.forbes.com/sites/bernardmarr/2017/08/24/disney-uses-big-data-iot-and-machine-learning-to-boost-customer-experience/#5f72c12b3387

Marr, B. (2019). *Artificial intelligence in practice: How 50 successful companies used artificial intelligence to solve problems.* Wiley.

Martin, C. (2015, August 28). 46% of retailers move to beacons; 71% learning buying patterns. *MediaPost*. www.mediapost.com/publications/article/257146/46-of-retailers-move-to-beacons-71-learning-buy.html

Melendez, S., & Pasternack, A. (2019, March 2). Here are the data brokers quietly buying and selling your personal information. *Fast Company*. www.fastcompany.com/90310803/here-are-the-data-brokers-quietly-buying-and-selling-your-personal-information

MNI Targeted Media. (n.d.). *What is micro-targeting and how does it affect advertising?* [Blog]. www.mni.com/blog/advertmarket/what-is-micro-targeting/article_a12cbac0-137c-11e9-84d4-73b6685fa60c.html

Moothart, R. (2017, February 23). PPC, KPIs, and the marketing funnel. *Hero Blog*. www.ppchero.com/ppc-kpis-and-the-marketing-funnel/

Rheinlander, S. (2019, April 19). Everything you wanted to know about marketing attribution models (but were afraid to ask). [Blog post]. *The 360 Blog*. www.salesforce.com/blog/2017/11/what-is-marketing-attribution-model.html

Stewart, E. (2019, December 10). Why every website wants you to accept its cookies. *Vox*. www.vox.com/recode/2019/12/10/18656519/what-are-cookies-website-tracking-gdpr-privacy

Sullivan, L. (2016, August 10). MediaMath integrates proximity to create geo-location targeted ads. *MediaPost*. www.mediapost.com/publications/article/282186/mediamath-integrates-proximity-to-create-geo-locat.html

Tamte-Horan, K. (2019, June 3). Do cookies work on mobile phones? [Blog]. *Vici*. www.vicimediainc.com/do-cookies-work-on-mobile-phones/

Urban, T., Degeling, M., Holz, T., & Pohlmann, N. (2020). *Beyond the front page: Measuring third party dynamics in the field*. Proceedings of the Web Conference 2020 (WWW '20), April 20–24, Taipei, Taiwan. https://doi.org/10.1145/3366423.3380203

Wlosik, M. (2022, June 7). What is a data broker and how does it work? *Clearcode*. https://clearcode.cc/blog/what-is-data-broker/

Wolford, B. (n.d.). Does the GDPR apply to companies outside of the EU? *GDPREU*. https://gdpr.eu/companies-outside-of-europe/

7 Big data

Contrary to all the hype, big data is not a new phenomenon.[1] It's been with us a long time. What *is* relatively new is how accessible data has become, the sheer amount that exists, how quickly data is generated, and how diverse and complex it can be. Depending on the source, these qualities often get summarized as the "three Vs" (Council for Research Excellence, 2014)—volume, velocity, and variety—or the "five Vs"—volume, velocity, variety, veracity, and value (Hadi et al., 2015; Marr, 2014). Sometimes complexity ("C") is added to this list, depending on the source. We'll look at each of these big data traits in a moment. But to define big data exactly can be a bit of a challenge. Why? Well, there is no one exact point at which a dataset automatically becomes "big" or receives the official designation of "big data." It's not based on a particular number of rows, columns, or file sizes (although it's worth mentioning that, if Excel—which can support a million rows of data—can run the analysis, this is still not considered "big data"). So when we refer to big data, we mean *really* big. Most would concur that petabytes[2] are in the land of big data. But experts agree it's still a somewhat nebulous concept.

The nature of big data

In sum, *big data* can be defined as "any source of information that is too large to process using one's current computing environment" (Buskirk, 2020, para. 1), cannot be analyzed using a standard database or processing software, cannot be managed by a single file server due to the dataset's size and or variety, or cannot be analyzed using traditional statistical methods. Some of these factors can differ by organization—certain companies' internal systems can handle larger data files than others—so there is not even uniformity based on those standards grounds. Suffice it to say that data comes to us in various file sizes, shapes, speeds, and formats, and we need to know how to approach data and assess its quality and usability, regardless of how big or small that dataset is, before deciding to use it and analyze it.

DOI: 10.4324/9780429506956-10

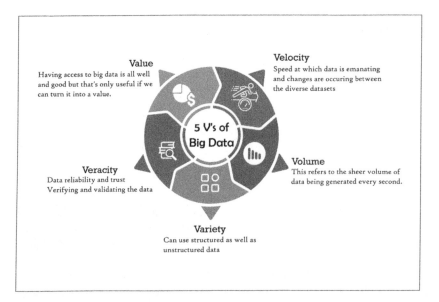

Figure 7.1 Diagram showing the Five Vs of big data

Source: Shutterstock

Big data is almost always "found data" (Connelly et al., 2016), i.e., data that has been generated for some primary purpose other than research (e.g., video surveillance streams, GPS tracking data, banking transactions, etc.). While big data offers promise and exciting opportunities for researchers, analysts, and the companies they serve, bigger is not necessarily better, and data is only as useful as the people who know how to ask the right questions of that dataset. A great dataset can come in almost any size or shape, and that is what we hope you take away from this chapter. Now, let's learn more about big data and how to make it work for us! To get started, let's return to the nature of big data to better understand it. We begin with the five Vs or key characteristics of big data (see Figure 7.1).

Volume

Volume refers to the amount or quantity of data. With greater storage capacity, file sizes can now reach gargantuan proportions compared to years past. Think of the many mobile storage drives you've used over the years. It may be hard to believe, but there was a time when one gigabyte (GB) of memory on a mobile drive was a really big deal! Today we enjoy storage capacity in a single thumb drive that many people in years past would never have imagined, even on the hard drive of a desktop computer.

The nature of big data is such that its sheer volume is beyond what most of us can comprehend. Here are some examples of what big data—by volume—might look like: a dataset containing every single credit card transaction in the United States on a given day, a dataset containing video files of every single television program that aired on every cable network for the past ten years, a dataset containing all social media posts ever made during a US presidential election campaign cycle, or a dataset containing all search activities performed by Google users within a given month. Data is being generated constantly, 24 hours a day, seven days per week. Whether it's internet search activity or credit card transactions, as just noted, much of this data is being gathered in real time. Because there's no "off" switch for many of the processes being used to gather the data, the volume of data only continues to grow, and big data only gets bigger. Datasets of this size are almost impossible to imagine, and yet the capacity to collect and store this data now exists.

Velocity

Related to the concept of volume is the velocity, or speed, at which big data is being created. As processing speeds continue to increase along with internet speeds (with much big data being digital and created or stored online or in the cloud), big data is coming at us more quickly than other types of data, in large part because of the automated processes behind digital data collection. For many data systems, the data generation and flow are constant, so the data spigot is never really turned off. This also can present a bit of a challenge, as with more rapid data generation comes the need to analyze or process some things faster to maximize the data's capabilities. Hadi et al. (2015) give the examples of "analyz[ing] 500 million daily call detail records in real-time to predict customer churn faster" or "scrutiniz[ing] 5 million trade events created each day to identify potential fraud" (p. 21).

Variety

Big data can be either structured or unstructured. What does this mean? Structured data is typically organized in the format of rows and columns, as you might see in an Excel spreadsheet or a database. There is a "structure" to it that is predictable and that makes it relatively straightforward to analyze using common software programs. Unstructured data is not formatted this way and now makes up more than 80% of big data (Marr, 2014). In fact, unstructured data can come in a variety of forms: video or audio streams and files, photographs, graphics, text documents or files, social media posts, and the like. Often, this unstructured data is recoded into structured data for easier analysis but not always. A helpful analogy provided by Hadi et al. (2015) explains that "structured data is like a data warehouse, in which data is tagged and sortable, while unstructured data is random and difficult to analyze" (p. 17). As Christine Pierce of Nielsen's Data Science Division[3] explains, big data was never designed or created for measurement, and that's one of the challenges. More on this topic later. But this rich variation in the format of the data is what we mean by the "variety" of big data today.

Value

This characteristic of big data has to do with its worth as a result of what can be done with the data and *insights* generated (Gillis, 2021). Put another way, it's "the added-value that the collected data can bring to the intended process, activity or predictive analysis/hypothesis" (Hadi et al., 2015, p. 21) and is what excites businesses most about big data. Of course, this value is relative and depends on what the data represents and what it is capable of addressing, as well as its breadth and depth. So this value is also somewhat related to volume and velocity, according to Hadi et al. (2015). But have no doubt, the "value" of big data has to do with what it can do for a company's bottom line, either directly or indirectly. New consumer preferences can be discovered and monetized to generate new revenue, but profit may also be gained from new efficiencies revealed by big data analyses. For instance, a firm can lower its inventory costs by analyzing individual consumer preferences and behavior, ridding itself of low-demand items and making smarter inventory decisions (American Association for Public Opinion Research, 2015). Of course, expense is associated with extracting insights from big data, and this must be factored into any analysis decision. The costs of big data initiatives can include everything from the infrastructure, systems, and software required to the personnel, time, and expertise required for each analysis.

Veracity

Veracity refers to the extent to which we trust a data source (Hadi et al., 2015) or, as Marr (2014) puts it, how "messy" or "trustworthy" is the data? Accuracy and quality are less controllable with big data, and these accuracy and quality issues can include anything from typos to colloquialisms in speech (such as what might be found in social media posts) as well as abbreviations (Marr, 2014) or the invisible technological flaws in the way the data was collected, as discussed in Chapter 3. By its very nature, big data has veracity challenges because of how it is often produced. *Reliability*, bias, and "noise" are commonly confronted issues because big data are "not generated from instruments and methods designed to produce valid and reliable data amenable to scientific analysis" but are instead more of a byproduct, "sometimes called data exhaust, from processes whose primary purposes do not always align with those of data analysts" (American Association of Public Opinion Research, 2015, "The Big Data Process and Data Quality Challenges," para. 3).

These limitations represent a growing area of concern for many business leaders and analysts, as well as big data providers who are trying to capture businesses as clients, because "one in three business leaders do not trust the information used to reach decisions" (Hadi et al., 2015, p. 21), even as the number and variety of big data sources continue to proliferate.

Complexity

The complexity of big data is related to its variety (and may be why this trait is not used in all descriptions of big data). Data complexity can include "complex types, complex structures, and complex patterns," along with variation in quality and complex interrelationships within the data, which can all lead to computational complexity for analysis (Jin et al., 2015, p. 62).

Pros of big data

There are enormous potential benefits to using big data, which is why companies are so excited about it and are hiring audience analysts and data scientists to make sense of these data sources. Among the benefits of big data are its granularity and richness, stability, accessibility, volume, speed, and continuity, and the data's potential to reveal actual consumer behavior, rather than intent or self-reported behavior. The development of predictive tools and use of data fusion and linkage also are priorities for many in the industry. Big data capabilities can lead to benefits such as greater efficiencies and optimization for a company and may help identify new consumer trends and preferences before they are recognized by the larger marketplace. As stated by Hadi et al. (2015), big data "has the potential to generate more revenue, while reducing risk and predicting future outcomes with greater confidence at low cost" (p. 16). Let's examine some of these pros or benefits.

Granularity

This refers to the granular, specific level of detail that is possible when collecting and analyzing large datasets. There is a richness of information about individuals and their behaviors that we are able to achieve with big data and a micro level of detail that may not be possible to capture using other methods or data sources. This *granularity* is what aids *microtargeting* of consumers because there is such a level of precision and minute detail about individual preferences (Council for Research Excellence, 2014). As an example, by tracking a consumer's music preferences (e.g., her playlist) online, a streaming service may be able to provide more customized, satisfying recommendations for her in the future. Similarly, by tracking the frequency of certain online purchases (e.g., dog food), a retailer can anticipate when the next purchase will occur, offer incentives or coupons for that brand, and suggest related pet products that may interest her. Each new online purchase helps build and hone an increasingly granular consumer profile.

Stability

This refers to consistency over time. Because big data is continuously gathered, the flow of data is constant and is never "turned off." As a result, there are fewer deviations or fluctuations in the data patterns than if the data were gathered at several individual points in time, particularly if that data were gathered via sampling methodology versus census (all data units or cases). An example of *stability* in action can be seen in the media measurement industry with the adoption of set-top (cable or satellite) boxes, which gather what's known as *return path data*. These set-top boxes are always "on" unless the homeowner turns it off for some reason. Because of this, viewing or tuning information is constantly being gathered, instead of being gathered from a nationally selected sample of households for just one week during a ratings collection period, as was done before set-top boxes were developed.

While tuning information gathered from separate ratings periods might reveal major deviations in the numbers of persons viewing or even in the number of persons in the sample from each period, the return path data is more "stable" in that it is constantly being gathered. There are no breaks in the data collection, which could reveal dramatic drops or increases. To be sure, differences are detected over time as tuning behavior changes, but the constant flow ensures that stability is provided minute by minute, day by day. Return path data gathered via cable set-top boxes does have its own challenges and quality control issues to consider; however, these are addressed in Chapter 9.

Accessibility

Largely due to the digitalization of data and of society in general, data is more accessible than ever, both to the public and to companies. We can access data from computer desktops via portals, through our mobile phones and in any number of ways. Data is stored on servers and with just a few clicks and maybe a password, if it's proprietary data, we can look right at it and begin analyzing. Faster processing speeds also aid data accessibility.

Ability to reveal actual consumer behavior

Much of consumer and audience research has been limited to what people say they'd buy or plan to buy (purchase intent) or self-reporting in surveys on what they've purchased in the past. Such approaches are subject to consumers' memory loss, potential bias, untruthfulness, and more. With consumer behavior data, we get an unfiltered record of what truly occurred. For instance, credit card transaction data tell us exactly what was purchased and when and how much was paid. We know exactly what types of restaurants were frequented and when and what the orders and total bill amounts were. We can know exactly what types of products were purchased online with which account and when, and sometimes how many other web pages were viewed before the purchase was made. Actual behavioral data are not only rich with truth but provide many clues about our behaviors leading up to the purchase and the conditions surrounding that purchase. The behaviors leading up to an action or purchase decision are called the *funnel*, and understanding the funnel the average consumer uses before deciding to purchase a particular product is a major goal of big data analysis.[4] Eventually, trends and patterns reveal themselves. Predictive models can then be developed by brands based on this behavioral data. Such models can help managers strategically craft messaging, informing them about what types of promotions may make the most sense and when, what times of year to launch certain campaigns, and so forth.

Going one step further, companies also are using big data to understand the funnel that individual customers use before making the decision to buy a particular product. The goal of this individual-level analysis is to understand when to push a message to a specific person and what message to use with that individual so as to subtly influence that person to buy. For example, a sports marketing company may know from big data that when Harold Smith checks his mobile weather app on Wednesday night, there is an increased likelihood that he will buy tickets to a sports event on the weekend (Chapter 15). The marketing company then programs an *algorithm* so that if Harold checks his weather app on a Wednesday or Thursday, he'll automatically be a fed an advertisement for tickets to the marketing company's client sports team.

Knowing actual consumer behavior and being able to predict future behavior within a "continuously flowing" large dataset enable companies not only to pivot or adapt their sales or promotional strategies but to do so quickly based on what the data may be saying in real time.

Data linkage and predictive modeling

As previously noted, after so many consumers and transactions, patterns and trends become distinguishable. Datasets can be categorized as containing first-party, second-party, or third-party data. *First-party data* refers to the owned, proprietary data a company has on its own customers. If one company strategically partners with another to access that company's consumer data through agreement, then *second-party data* is created with *data linkage* or *data integration*. This creates more detailed consumer profiles that can lead to additional competitive advantage beyond the original first-party data. Finally, *third-party data* refers to data that is commercially or even publicly available for purchase (Ahuja, 2015). This data can be linked or integrated with first-party or second-party data to learn even more about individual consumers, their behaviors, purchasing patterns, and preferences. Predictive models can be built using all of this foundational data to better understand what similar consumers—those with similar psychographic or consumer behavioral profiles—are likely to do in the future (Ahuja, 2015) or even what they might do next online after visiting a particular website. Product development and strategic messaging strategies can be crafted based on this information to anticipate consumer needs and wants, better serve those consumers, and, ideally, financially reward those brands or companies. These new opportunities generated by the harvesting of first-, second-, and/or third-party data linkage have collectively been referred to as the "data economy" (Ahuja, 2015). One risk of linking data records and creating new *variables* from those records is the introduction of error, so it's important that integrations occur with careful oversight. Even so, experts warn that "using Big Data in statistically valid ways is increasingly challenging, yet exceedingly important for quality inference" (American Association of Public Opinion Research, 2015, "The Big Data Process and Data Quality Challenges," para. 2).

Ability to identify patterns and trends

Due to their sheer size, big datasets supply us with the opportunity to identify trends and patterns that we may not have previously identified or considered, or they may help us identify relationships that were not previously visible. In a smaller dataset, such trends or patterns may not emerge. As an example, a data analyst at The Weather Company noted that one of the findings generated by their IBM Watson platform was that, whenever it was windy outside, juice sales spiked (Fernando, 2016). This is not necessarily an intuitive finding, but it emerged from their big data nonetheless. Consider the many opportunities that present themselves just with that simple, previously unidentified relationship: juice brands now have another occasion and new opportunity for messaging, stores that sell juice may reach out with customized messaging on windy days to remind customers of their juice offerings, geolocation offers the opportunity for stores to send juice messaging and store promotions to those who are nearby, and the list goes on.

Cons of big data

Perhaps one of the most common myths surrounding datasets is that "bigger is better." Even with smaller datasets, including those gathered using traditional methods (e.g., from a survey), many inexperienced analysts and scholars assume that the larger the sample, the better. In reality, if a sample is not representative of the population it was intended to query, then size is irrelevant, and a large sample is just as meaningless as a small sample (Wimmer & Dominick, 2000).[5] With big datasets, sampling issues become even thornier: Sampling error cannot be calculated because the complete sampling frame is unknown. That is, there is no way to know what the full population or final number of cases would be from the entire population under study, particularly for data that is being continuously generated in real time.

Dirty data

A similar issue pertains to big data when the dataset is not clean; it contains what many refer to as "dirty data." Examples of dirty data may be typographical errors that were entered into various data cells, missing data, and data that came from nonhuman sources including fraudulent data entry or bots. While some dirty data can be "cleaned" such as by fixing typographical errors, this is most possible when you were the one who created the dataset and are familiar with the data, and the dataset is relatively small. However, if it is a big dataset and you are unfamiliar with the source that generated the data, if you do not know the range of data values or how such values were determined or do not know anything about the mechanisms or instrumentation used in the data collection, cleaning dirty data so that you are working with valid data becomes an almost impossible task.

Fraud

As alluded to previously, fraud is prevalent in big data, as it is often generated automatically, digitally, and by a third party. So many unknowns can be a recipe for disaster. Extreme care is required when considering using any big dataset, so much so that the Media Rating Council devised a list of procedural guidelines one should follow to determine whether to use a dataset, depending on whether the dataset originates from one or multiple sources. These guidelines were incorporated into a valuable report on big data by the Council for Research Excellence. Because many of these guidelines go beyond the scope of this text, you may wish to review this on your own at the link under Additional Resources.

Many types of digital advertising fraud exist (Chapter 5), from the basic to the sophisticated. While space does not permit an exhaustive discussion, a few are important to mention in order to illustrate how ad fraud impacts big data.

Bots have become one of the primary sources of digital fraud. They are a source that creates serious issues in big datasets because so much of the big data is generated online. Essentially, bots are not robots so much as they are software programs designed to create clicks and traffic to a website. Bot activity often can be found in online advertising and social media postings, and such bots were created for the sole purpose of generating revenue or influence for the bot creator. This can occur in various ways. For example, in ***domain spoofing***, a fake website is created to mimic a well-known brand such as The New York Times or ESPN, with the goal of tricking ad buyers of programmatic advertising to mistakenly place their ads on—and pay—the fake website instead of the real one (Davies, 2019). Other forms of fraud include ***ad stacking, pixel stuffing***, and ***ad injection***, just to name a few (Joseph, 2022). Ad stacking is when multiple ads are stacked on top of one another in the same content space so that audiences only see the top one, even while the system records audience impressions for each ad in the entire stack. Pixel stuffing is reducing ads to single pixel size wherever they're placed, and ad injection refers to scammers selling ads that are then placed in a publisher's content without the publisher's permission of the publisher being paid.

In addition to stealing revenue from both publishers and advertisers, ad fraud messes up the analytics. These forms of ad fraud create false data in big datasets that say audiences viewed advertisements that they never actually saw. That distorts analyses examining the relationship between audience exposure to advertising, in general, with subsequent audience behaviors. As a result, firms don't get an accurate picture of an ad's or campaign's performance, which makes it difficult or impossible for brands to understand how people are responding to their marketing campaigns. Finally, it distorts attempts by analysts to model and predict future consumer behavior. All of these effects cause real and substantial financial losses to both brands and media companies.

Dr. Augustine Fou, an expert in ad fraud, has described it as a sophisticated cybercrime, which nets more than US $300 billion worldwide (Fou,

2021; PRNewswire, 2018). Some industry experts have described the fraud-chasing endeavor as a game of whack-a-mole, in that as soon as we find a solution to one area of fraud, another pops up that is even more sophisticated, and we need to find another solution for that. Due to the prevalence of fraud, more diligence and care must be exercised when considering a big dataset, although we should exercise this same caution and ask similar questions with any dataset.

Who uses big data and for what purposes?

Due to the unprecedented access to digital data sources today, using big data is within reach for most companies. Some big data is autogenerated within an organization or industry, while other data must be purchased from a third party. The primary purpose for mining big data is business intelligence. Insights that can shed new light on consumer behavior or preferences are golden opportunities for new product development and offerings, and occasions for promotion or sales such as insights that reveal certain behaviors are more common at certain times of year, specific times of day, and the like. Insights identified through big data can provide a competitive edge, supplying business intelligence that one's competitors don't possess. As noted by Thomas Davenport, the "point is not to be dazzled by big data, but rather to analyze it—convert it to insights, innovations, and business value" (Davenport, 2014, p. 2). Examples of such business value noted by industry executives include "uncovering valuable ad exposure and sales conversion that was not possible before," "integrating datasets that will bring TV/digital/syndicated and proprietary resource[s] together for [a] holistic consumer view for more effective targeting," "rebuilding predictive models of campaign performance every day for thousands of advertising campaigns based on billions of ad impressions," and "understanding customer experiences, what customer touchpoints are most optimal, building on marketing-mix model work" (Council for Research Excellence, 2014, p. 32).

While there are some known reasons for using a particular dataset—especially if the dataset has been used before and the analyst knows what types of questions can be answered with it—one of the key terms that comes up with big data is "opportunity." This refers to the unknown relationships and insights that can emerge from querying a large dataset. Some refer to this as "interviewing the data." Trends, patterns, and relationships often surface in a large dataset that may previously have gone undetected. Such insights or relationships may not be intuitive, but, as a warning, they also might not be meaningful. A role of the analyst is to determine whether, in fact, they are. The best way to know this is to be well versed in the industry sector covered by the dataset, to know the business drivers, logical variables, and their relationships, and so on.

Formats of big data

As noted earlier in this chapter, big data may be structured or unstructured. Unstructured data often gets recoded and reshaped into a structured format for analysis. This structure of data formats is not the only type of variety. The sources of big data are just as varied, and they don't have to be generated online. Shopping and retail data, cash register transaction data, biometric data generated from wristband devices, financial data, surveillance video feeds, GPS data from mobile phones, and social media content are all examples of the variety of data that may exist in a big data format.

Approaches and processes for analyzing big datasets

Data management is central to a successful data analysis program. This entails not only having the proper internal systems, software, and servers to store, protect, process, and analyze the data but also having qualified, trained personnel to oversee these systems and a data-friendly infrastructure at your company. Indeed, big data initiatives often involve a multidisciplinary team including a "domain expert, a researcher, a computer scientist, and a system administrator" (American Association for Public Opinion Research, 2015, para. 5). Other personnel essential to a successful big data environment in the media and consumer space include data scientists, who are people trained in analyzing large, unstructured datasets and who possess an advanced statistical background; consumer or audience analysts, who work with smaller or standard-sized datasets; and someone who serves as the "internal champion" for your organization's data initiatives. This internal champion or "chief data officer" leads the way for the rest, reminding the organization's members that data is a priority and constantly advocating for data needs. He or she educates everyone on what the company's data-centric approach looks like and answers any questions or concerns about the organization's data strategy or priorities.

Communication is critical within any organization hoping to have successful data initiatives. Not everyone is going to agree with having a data-driven approach to everything within an organization—particularly if they feel is it connected to their employee performance and compensation—so it is important to establish open communication channels early on. Communication about the role of data in an organization should include having honest conversations about data and how it will be used within the organization and perhaps externally, making sure everyone is on board with the "data approach" and mission. Often, people are concerned out of a fear of the unknown. If they do not understand or have questions surrounding data collection and usage, these uncertainty gaps become filled with fear or a sentiment that is, by default, "anti-data." Organizations have the opportunity to avoid this completely by having the "data conversation."

Once data is in hand, though, an entirely different conversation needs to occur. More specifically, a series of critical questions must be asked, whether big data or not. Is this data trustworthy? How do we know? Is the data from a reputable source? What were the methods and procedures used to generate the data? If it was from a consumer survey, what were those questions? Are we able to review the question wording to feel secure that the survey was conducted scientifically using proper protocols? Finally, can we be certain the dataset is free of fraud? Have we scanned the dataset for telltale signs? Certain information should be verifiable and known. Does it surprise you to learn how many preliminary steps must be taken before you can even begin to analyze data? These preliminary steps are essential, and you must not omit them. If you do, you will pay a steep price, because research is a "garbage in, garbage out process" (Chapter 3). If you move forward with using datasets that fail the aforementioned "sniff tests" and/ or do not follow proper procedures, the recommendations you make to your boss based on these data will be—you guessed it— "garbage." So let's learn about one of the very first steps of data evaluation and management: data cleaning.

Data cleaning

As alluded to earlier, data can be dirty. In fact, even legitimately gathered datasets developed by qualified social scientists who are experts in study design are imperfect. Data cleaning is a basic, preliminary step in data analysis, and no analysis should be conducted without assessing the nature and trustworthiness of the data and cleaning it. So what does data cleaning look like? Here are examples of "dirty data" that may need to be addressed:

- Missing data
- Misspellings and typos
- Inconsistencies, contradictions, or data/responses that do not change over time[6]
- Data entry errors

"Cleaning" the data refers to taking the necessary steps to correct these issues, which may mean fixing errors in data entry or misspellings when the intended data point is clear. For missing data, are entire data fields missing? Or just a few instances of nonresponse? Is there a way to correct for the missing data and still use it for analysis? After assessing how much missing data you have, can you trust the data's integrity?[7]

Prior to cleaning the data, if the dataset was produced by an outside source or third party, you must assess its quality. Again, there is a set of questions one should ask about every dataset—big or small—before deciding to use it, as well as a process to follow. Christine Pierce, SVP of Data Science at Nielsen, says to first consider the source. "What is the origin of the data? How was it collected? How did it come to be in this format?" Once those questions can be answered, she says, the next question becomes "Who is excluded from this dataset?" Pierce gave the example of set-top box data from a satellite television provider. While this return path data may represent all viewing occurring in that satellite TV company's subscribing homes and such a dataset may indeed be large with several million households represented, many homes across the United States do not have satellite television and would be excluded. Moreover, she noted that satellite television is not a popular choice in urban environments due to signal reception challenges. Such a sample would naturally exclude many urban dwellers. These two issues combined illustrate the dangers of big datasets: They may look appealing as a valuable source for mining consumer preferences but are often not representative of the overall population. This leads to the next logical question, Pierce says, which is, "What are the potential sources of bias?" This can be a result of not only who's excluded but who or what cases might be duplicated within a dataset. (For a deeper discussion of issues of population, sampling, and the representativeness of data, review Chapter 3.)

Do you have the right data?

Part of assessing a dataset should also include asking what the dataset is capable of addressing. If you have particular research questions, how do you know whether that dataset even contains data that can answer those questions? Did it even query in the same subject area? What are its limitations? Big data—any data—is only useful if it is the right data. Know your research question and/or objective, and then determine whether that dataset can actually address it. If not, you've got the wrong dataset, and you can stop before you waste your time.

Filtering for fraud, bots, and invalid traffic

An analyst's guiding set of questions for approaching online datasets should also include scanning for fraudulent activity/data and *invalid traffic*. As digital platforms continue to be a primary collection and delivery method for data, fraud will continue to be a problem. While systems and personnel are getting better at detecting fraud, the fraudsters also are getting better at their game. Some common fraud can be detected by various "blacklists" of known invalid traffic via IP addresses. But this is only the beginning of the detection and filtering process. One's data team must also analyze traffic patterns and other invalid traffic identification techniques.

So how can an analyst begin to identify possible fraud in a dataset? As general guidance, scrutinize anything that looks suspicious or abnormal. Here are a few specific signs of likely web fraud: low CPM for ad buyers; extremely high website click rates (greater than what a human is capable of) or high ad click-through rates (which tend to be low); heavy website traffic and high numbers of clicks occurring in the middle of the night when most people are sleeping (Fou, 2021); repetitive response patterns in an online survey, e.g., all 7s or some other number; spending two minutes or less completing an entire online survey; and irregular patterns of web traffic at certain times of day. But fraudsters are getting better all the time, and the more sophisticated tactics are harder to identify than typical blunt tactics, says Christine Pierce of Nielsen's Data Science division. "They'll try to make it look like a human and so they know all the tricks," noting some of the general filtrations analysts would look for as signs of fraud, such as the frequency by which a device is coming to a site. For instance, if the frequency is 100 times per second, the company knows (and the fraudster knows) it is impossible for a human to do that, so the fraudster would adapt the frequency of the fraudulent visitation to a human level. Data measurement companies need to counteract such sophisticated approaches, which requires putting their engineers on the task to create sophisticated detection software "to filter out that more sophisticated invalid traffic," Pierce says. Identifying fraudulent data also requires having personnel and internal systems in place to assess the quality of the data. Fraud and bot detection software programs do exist and are getting better all the time, but it is always a game of catch-up.

Ad fraud detection services can help filter some of the more sophisticated bot traffic, but there is no way to catch all of it. The Media Rating Council has developed guidelines and accreditation processes on General Invalid Traffic Detection and Filtration (Media Rating Council, 2015) and related matters.

Ethical considerations

While ethical considerations are paramount to any data usage, they become even more so given the passive nature of many data collection methods today. Cookies and online tracking tools are regularly gathering *internet protocol* (*IP*) addresses and, potentially, *personally identifiable information* (*PII*). While consumers can opt out of such tracking, many do not, finding the process too complicated, burdensome, or time-consuming, even if they'd rather not be tracked. The European Union, as of this writing, has much stronger privacy regulations concerning the gathering and protection of consumer data than the United States and elsewhere. Its **General Data Protection Regulation (GDPR)** went into effect in 2018.

Online data collection often automatically picks up identifying information. In addition to the IP address, an online retailer might have personal information stored for each customer's account, including credit card information, residential address, demographic profile, session information from each time we visit the website, and the like. This information can be used in combination with third-party data sources to provide a very specific profile of who we are as consumers and private citizens. While this seems creepy to many, much of this other data is culled from publicly available sources like tax and property records, Department of Motor Vehicle (DMV) records, and information available just by conducting a basic online search. For those on social media, this provides another treasure trove of information that can help marketers get to know you better. And let's face it, some people share huge amounts of highly personal information on their social media pages. This fusion of multiple datasets can be integrated to connect the dots to develop a detailed profile about a consumer. Such practices and the availability of third-party datasets to integrate are big business. Imagine having this granularity of data on all adult consumers in the United States who have a credit card. Such customized business intelligence on consumers can convert to major competitive advantages for a brand. Big data is big business, but this comes with big ethical strings attached. Just because we can legally gather all of this information, combine it, and use it for microtargeting and other purposes, does that mean we should? Some organizations and countries have started having "the conversation" about what is ethical and appropriate, while others have not. The ethics surrounding big data will continue to be a relevant conversation for years to come.

Best practices and applications

Let's assume that you know your data has been ethically gathered. What next? What is the best way to approach a dataset to which you've been given access? George Ivie, Executive Director of the Media Rating Council (MRC), provided the following guidance (Council for Research Excellence, 2014, p. 6):

- Inspect the underlying representativeness of the sample.
- Ensure consistency of reported metrics over time.

  - Are there major fluctuations? Or is the data fairly stable?

- Understand how the data collection process might have impacted the accuracy of the reported data.

  - What was the instrumentation or mechanism used to gather the data?

- Look for full disclosure of methods by the data provider to integrate/fuse datasets.

  - A trustworthy source should provide details of the methodology it used to produce the dataset. If the source is unwilling to provide this information, you do not want to use that dataset.

In addition, Ivie stated[8] the following factors should be assessed for single-source data:

- **Underlying data values**. The valid values for each field and business rules surrounding each field within the datasets should be known. These field definitions should be tested for *validity* prior to using the dataset. It helps to understand the processing used to derive the dataset.
- **Time period**. The exact time period that the data reflect should be known (e.g., July 1, 2023–June 30, 2024).
- **Representation**. Assess what members of the population are included or absent (e.g., credit card versus cash customers).
- **Consistency**. Data should be consistent over time and monitored for anomalies to ensure that the relationships remain true. Changes to the underlying fields or business rules for the dataset should be captured and noted on a timely basis.

Using big data in the consumer/audience analytics realm

We've alluded to some examples and useful applications in the consumer industry already, but let's talk more about what types of big data can be useful and why they might be valuable. Let's first examine media measurement. We've talked about *viewership* and tuning information. Return path data using set-top (cable) boxes provides a record of people's viewing preferences in those households. Rather than guessing at which new programs should be developed for the coming season, the television studios—if they have the ability to utilize set-top box data—would have an exact record of what genres of shows were viewed, which shows, and how often, all of which can be an indication of the intensity of that preference, e.g., a "favorite" show. Demographic data are not typically available from return path data sources however, so it would be unknown who in the household preferred which programs.

Using another media example, online news sources can mine vast quantities of reader behavior information over a period of time to learn what types of stories are most popular, how deeply people read into the stories, which types of stories are read in their entirety, which stories tend to get shared most on social media, what time of day the website receives the most traffic and at what times of year, which pages receive the most traffic, etc. These data points, taken in aggregate, can paint a detailed picture of that online news provider's readership and online behavior patterns, which can inform future strategy and news content decisions. Similarly, radio stations, including online stations and streaming platforms, can use listenership data to inform their music selection and playlist, refine their sound, develop podcasts, and even help determine an optimal advertising load and schedule.

In the consumer realm, preferences—and quite nuanced preferences at that—can be easily identified with large datasets. A log of one consumer's online behavior provides digital breadcrumbs that reveal which sites were visited, in which order, how much time was spent on each site and its internal pages, which ads were clicked on, if any, what purchases were made and in what amounts, and even what styles or colors of items were preferred. Many retail sites also keep track of what items you place into your shopping cart but don't purchase! (Don't be surprised if you get ads or coupons for that product encouraging you to buy it later.) Of course, there are many other applications and uses of big data in all types of industries from finance to health care; however, our conversation in this text focuses on the media audience and consumer realms.

Tools for analyzing big data

While the actual process of big data analysis is beyond the scope of the current text, stand-alone courses devoted to this topic are recommended and worthwhile. Programming languages such as R and Python are common to such courses in teaching students how to write code and query large datasets. Becoming proficient in one of these programming languages for data mining requires time, typically more than one course. However, becoming conversant is a great start and can be beneficial when working with data scientists and computer scientists. Many big data teams also use a tool called Hadoop, which can be explained as "a set of open source programs and procedures—meaning essentially they are free for anyone to use or modify, with a few exceptions—which anyone can use as the 'backbone' of their big data operations" (Marr, n.d., para. 1). Hadoop is made up of four modules—Distributed File System, MapReduce, Hadoop Common, and YARN—each of which carries out a particular task involved in big data analytics. It is widely used by Fortune 500 companies and, because of its flexible, open-source nature, can be easily adapted and customized as needed (Marr, n.d.). The field of big data "product solutions," programs, data mining tools and software is growing daily. Some are sophisticated and require the skills of data scientists and engineers, while others are tailored to other types of analysts with more simplified interfaces and dashboards. Of course, the best guidance is to do your research on the available tools and match them with your understanding of your team's or company's needs, goals, capabilities, and budget.

Summary and conclusion

Big data lures analysts to endless opportunities for uncovering audience insights and preferences, as well as information that could lead to stronger financial performance for a company. But it does so while waving a flag of caution. Big data initiatives and analysis demand both a critical eye and proper organizational support to be successful. Big data requires a team of trained personnel, an organizational infrastructure and commitment of resources, as well as a commitment to best practices in data evaluation, cleaning, and analysis. Such practices can not only help filter out data fraud but also ensure the data are valid and can yield the opportunities you are seeking. For those willing to devote the time and the organizational, financial, and human resources toward big data, the rewards can indeed be great.

Additional resources

Data Science Association: www.datascienceassn.org/
INFORMS: www.informs.org/Get-Involved/Welcome-to-Our-Data-Science-
    Community
Digital Analytics Association: www.digitalanalyticsassociation.org/
"Big Data: A Report on Algorithmic Systems, Opportunity, and Civil Rights"
    Executive Office of the President (May 2016): https://obamawhitehouse.
    archives.gov/sites/default/files/microsites/ostp/2016_0504_data_
    discrimination.pdf
Women in Analytics: www.womeninanalytics.com/
PyLadies: https://pyladies.com/

Recommended cases

There are no cases for this chapter on the text website because working with big datasets requires special tools and extensive training in data management. We suggest working through the following discussion questions and exercises.

Discussion questions and exercises

1. What is valuable about big data? What potential and capabilities does it offer that make companies and their analysts so excited? Why is so much attention and emphasis being placed in this area?

2. This chapter mentions many of the sources of data that are used to build big datasets. But there are others: Personal data from health-related apps and smart devices you might use to track your sleep, your heart rate, or menstrual cycle often wind up in big datasets. Connected cars can track your movements, your entertainment preferences, your contacts, and communications while driving. Your car also may be measuring and sharing changes in your weight over time, and/or your driving behaviors—speed, braking, acceleration, tailgating, or lane stability, which could be shared with your insurance company. Stores are tracking your purchases and often actively analyze them to identify whether you are developing a new medical problem that could give them new marketing opportunities.

   When you think about these things, how do you feel about them? What regulations, if any, do you think should be put on big data collection and use? Should consumers have the right to review, challenge, or delete personal data collected on them, just as they have the right to review and challenge information about their credit and financial records?
   Now how does your personal reaction differ from the reaction you had as a future media analyst as you read about all the insights and benefits big datasets can give you?

3. While there are many positives surrounding the potential uses and applications of big data, you also read about the negatives or cautionary notes related to this type of data, beyond those discussed in Question 2. Do these "cons" outweigh the "pros" in your mind? Why or why not? Do you think some companies would be turned off by these negatives? In your opinion, what kinds of companies might not pursue big data initiatives, and why not? Which companies would be more likely to, and why?

4. *Exercise: Big data*

   Your online retail consulting company has acquired a digitally generated dataset that is several petabytes in size. The dataset is a record of a major e-commerce website's consumer traffic and transactions for the past year, which was provided to you by the e-commerce company that is your client. It is a structured dataset (rows and columns) that contains fields including:

   - IP address
   - Time and date stamp of when each user arrived on the site,

- Referral page (where they came from),
- Total time spent on the site per session,
- Which page URLs (e.g., product pages) were visited within the site and for how long,
- Whether a purchase was made on the site and, if so, the product number(s) and price(s),
- Total transaction/purchase amount,
- Date and time of purchase,
- Items added to and deleted from shopping cart,
- Whether a discount code was applied and for how much,
- Consumer's name and shipping address,
- Consumer's email address,
- Credit card information (encrypted),
- Order confirmation number,
- URLs of the web pages visited directly before and after the product purchase(s).

   a. What questions would you pose to evaluate this dataset's quality and to determine whether to use it?
   b. What steps would you go through in order to assess its quality and appropriateness for analysis?
   c. What red flags would you look for?
   d. Let's assume you ultimately decided to use this dataset. What are some possible insights that might be revealed from its analysis? What opportunities might this dataset uncover for the e-commerce company? What types of questions might you ask of this dataset, and which analyses would be appropriate in order to answer those questions? What kind of business intelligence might you be able to be generate from this dataset that could be converted into a competitive advantage, additional sales, or other? Think strategically and long-term, as well as short-term.

Notes

1. The term "data" has historically been a plural noun of the singular form of the Latin word "datum." In recent years, however, the terms "data" and "big data" have evolved, now increasingly used and accepted as an "uncountable" noun (e.g., water, information), particularly when referring to the singular phenomenon of data or big data. We do so here and elsewhere in the text where appropriate, also giving the term a singular verb ("is"). We may utilize "data" in its plural form when referring to specific data (e.g., when conducting a specific analysis) and give it a plural verb in such instances, although many people now treat data as a singular form in this case as well.
2. One petabyte of data could be generated by taking 4,000 digital photos every day of your life, according to one source. For an explanation of data file sizes, including petabytes, see www.makeuseof.com/tag/

memory-sizes-gigabytes-terabytes-petabytes/. See also www.lifewire.com/
terabytes-gigabytes-amp-petabytes-how-big-are-they-4125169
3. Title at the time of interview (now Senior Vice President, US Media Operations
at Nielsen).
4. For a more thorough discussion about the marketing funnel, see Chapter 6.
5. See Chapter 3 for a more detailed discussion of sampling issues.
6. Examples of this might result from a set-top box being left on, a web page being
left open, or a respondent giving the same answer to all questions on a survey.
7. We recommend a full course on research methods to best prepare you for making
such decisions. We only offer an introduction here to some common scenarios.
8. See "A Primer for Defining and Implementing Big Data in the Marketing and
Advertising Industry." www.researchexcellence.com/files/pdf/2015-02/id114_
big_data_primer_10_23_14.pdf. Adapted and used with permission.

References

Ahuja, A. (2015, December 29). How marketers can navigate the new data economy. *AdAge.* https://adage.com/article/digitalnext/marketers-navigate-data-economy/301892
American Association for Public Opinion Research. (2015, February 12). *AAPOR report: Big data.* www.aapor.org/Education-Resources/Reports/Big-Data.aspx
Buskirk, T. (2020). Big data. In P. Atkinson, S. Delamont, A. Cernat, J. Sakshaug, & A. Williams (Eds.), *Big data and data science.* SAGE Publications. https://dx.doi.org/10.4135/9781526421036943171
Connelly, R., Playford, C., Gayle, V., & Dibben, C. (2016). The role of administrative data in the big data revolution in social science research. *Social Science Research, 59*, 1–12. https://doi.org/10.1016/j.ssresearch.2016.04.015
Council for Research Excellence. (2014, October 23). *Big data: A primer for defining and implementing big data in the marketing and advertising industry.* www.researchexcellence.com/files/pdf/2015-02/id114_big_data_primer_10_23_14.pdf
Davenport, T. (2014). *Big data at work: Dispelling the myths, uncovering the opportunities.* Harvard Business Press.
Davies, J. (2019, January 30). Ghost sites, domain spoofing, fake apps: A guide to knowing your ad fraud. *Digiday.* https://digiday.com/media/ghost-sites-domain-spoofing-fake-apps-guide-knowing-ad-fraud/
Fernando, N. (2016, April 14). How data has taken Weather Company's advertising, audience strategy by storm. *International News Media Association.* www.inma.org/blogs/conference/post.cfm/how-data-has-taken-weather-company-s-advertising-audience-strategy-by-storm
Fou, A. (2021, December 10). How to spot ad fraud, and how to combat it. *WARC.* www.warc.com/newsandopinion/opinion/how-to-spot-ad-fraud-and-how-to-combat-it/en-gb/4430
Gillis, A. (2021, March). 5V's of big data. *TechTarget.* www.techtarget.com/searchdatamanagement/definition/5-Vs-of-big-data
Hadi, H. J., Shnain, A. H., Hadishaheed, S., & Ahmad, A. H. (2015). Big data and 5 Vs characteristics. *International Journal of Advances in Electronics and Computer Science, 2*(1), 16–23.

Jin, X., Wah, B., Cheng, X., & Wang, Y. (2015). Significance and challenges of big data research. *Big Data Research*, 2(2), 59–64. https://doi.org/10.1016/j.bdr.2015.01.006

Joseph, A. (2022, February 1). Ad fraud: What it is, the different types and how to prevent it. *Edgemesh*. https://edgemesh.com/blog/the-complete-guide-to-ad-fraud

The link between digital ad fraud and cybercrime. (2018, July 2). *PRNewswire*. www.prnewswire.com/news-releases/the-link-between-digital-ad-fraud-and-cybercrime-300675144.html

Marr, B. (2014, March 6). Big data: The 5 Vs everyone must know. *LinkedIn Pulse*. www.linkedin.com/pulse/20140306073407-64875646-big-data-the-5-vs-everyone-must-know

Marr, B. (n.d.). What is Hadoop? *Bernard Marr & Co*. www.bernardmarr.com/default.asp?contentID=1080

Media Rating Council. (2015, October 15). *Invalid traffic detection and filtration guidelines addendum*. http://mediaratingcouncil.org/101515_IVT%20Addendum%20FINAL%20(Version%201.0).pdf

Wimmer, R., & Dominick, J. (2000). *Mass media research: An introduction*. Wadsworth.

Part 3

Media analytics across industry sectors

8 Foundations of audiovisual measurement

A prologue for Chapters 9 and 10

Radio and television are our earliest forms of broadcast media and represent what we refer to today as "legacy" media. They are analog technologies rather than digital.[1] As the first broadcasting media, there had been no previous way to measure these kinds of audiences. Print had been measured via newsstand sales and circulation, and film by the number of tickets sold, things that broadcast did not have in common.

While radio and television are different media platforms, they have much in common when it comes to audience measurement technologies, methodologies, key concepts, and metrics used. So we preface our video and audio chapters with this common discussion, including how the industry has evolved from an analog to a digital one and how measurement has evolved as a result. The individual video and audio chapters will then provide greater detail on those sectors. We begin with what could be described as "first-generation" measurement methods and metrics.

First-generation or legacy methods

Because it is impractical to survey every television viewer or radio listener about their viewing and listening habits, legacy methods sample these audiences instead (see Chapter 3). Once a *sample* is selected, the participating household or individual is equipped with the relevant measurement technology, usually a meter of some kind (see Chapters 9 and 10 for details). These measurement tools gather the audience consumption data, which is then processed by the measurement company (e.g., Nielsen) to produce the audience metrics used by the industry. When we are discussing legacy media, we are primarily talking about *linear media*, that is, content that is delivered according to a specific programming schedule. *Nonlinear media*, by contrast, do not follow a set schedule and tend to be accessed on demand.

DOI: 10.4324/9780429506956-12

First-generation metrics

While numerous types of metrics exist for analyzing radio and television audiences, we limit our discussion here to those most commonly used. Be sure to read the individual chapters that follow for more nuanced discussion. We should note that you sometimes will see the term *ratings* or *ratings data* used in a collective sense to refer to all kinds of metrics including rating, share, number of viewers, and the like. In fact, rating means something quite specific as well.

The context for traditional broadcast metrics begins with understanding Universe Estimates for a particular market, whether it is national or local. *Universe Estimates* represent the total number of persons or households for the measurement area and are the basis for calculating things like rating and share. Television and radio measurement differ in one regard here in that television measurement occurs at the household and individual (or person) levels, with estimates created for both, while radio measurement occurs only at the individual level. In television, *TV households (TVH)* provide the foundation for calculating audience estimates in the United States. Nielsen's national definition for TVH is the number of households with at least one operable TV that can receive audio and video signals via over-the-air, cable, satellite, or the internet (Nielsen, 2020). While radio is not measured at the household level, the geographic market population is known. Once the overall Universe Estimates are known, viewer or listener estimates for individual programs or time periods can be calculated, as well as estimates for specific *audience universes*, the viewer/listener demographic segments such as Adults 18+, Women 18–29, or Men 55+.

Households Using Television (HUT) is just what it sounds like. It's the number of TV homes whose television screens are in use at a given time and is the basis for calculating household share. Similarly, *Persons Using Television* (PUT) is the same concept applied to the individual level rather than households. In radio, we use the term *Persons Using Radio* (PUR), as radio is a more personal medium and, as noted, is typically not consumed by a household but rather in vehicles or by an individual outside the home. HUT and PUT can vary seasonally; it is common, for instance, for TV viewing levels to drop over the summer months as people spend more time outdoors and traveling rather than watching TV. This, of course, affects ratings and shares.

Rating

Rating is probably the most commonly used metric globally in the television and radio industries. It is the percentage of the audience tuned into a particular program out of the total potential audience in the geographic area being measured. Said simply, a rating measures how many households or audience members you succeeded in getting to tune in to your show out of everyone in a market who owned the necessary equipment and *could* have been part of the audience.

We drop the percentage and typically just say the number. So a "4" rating means that 4% of the potential audience in the area was tuned into the program or station. Ratings—and any of the other metrics we discuss—can be national or local, and they can refer to household *viewership* or specific audience universes as noted earlier. For instance, a rating of 7 for Women 18–49 means that 7% of all women aged 18–49 in the geographic market being measured were tuned into the program. Because ratings are percentages and because the base number used to calculate the percentage is the number of television households or persons in whatever market is being measured, this translates to different numbers of viewers in different markets; a 7 rating in New York City represents many more viewers or listeners than a 7 rating in Casper, Wyoming. This is because the base number used to calculate the percentage refers to the number of TV households (TVH), the number of individuals with access to a TV screen, or the number of persons with access to radio (depending on what type of rating is being calculated), and these base numbers will vary by market.[2]

Share

A *share* is similar to a rating except that it measures the percentage of the audience tuned into a program out of the total audience whose TV sets or radios were in use at the time, rather than all of the potential TV or radio audience. In other words, it measures the percentage of the available viewing audience that was tuned into a show at a given time—or how successful a program was in attracting audiences from among those who were actually watching or listening at the time the program ran. Like ratings, shares can be local or national, and they can represent household or individual viewing or listening. Also like ratings, the actual number of households (or individual audience members) that a share number represents depends on the number of television or radio households (or persons) in the market being measured. Ratings and shares are used to track individual program performance over time but, even more importantly, are used to compare performance with respect to the competition.

Other foundational metrics

Time spent listening (TSL) is typically used in reference to radio or audio but also used with television or video. It is essentially a measure of audience loyalty and is expressed in average number of hours and minutes per day, week, or other time period that the average viewer or listener spends consuming content from a particular station.

Reach is the total number of unique audience members who saw or heard certain media content at least once within a given time period. It is also referred to as *unduplicated audience* or cume. *Cume* is short for *cumulative audience* and is more commonly used by the radio industry but is also used in television. Cume or reach can be expressed daily, weekly, or in some other time increment. In calculating cume or reach, each individual audience member or household is counted only once, no matter how many times they tuned in during the measurement period.

As you might guess, *frequency* refers to the number of times an audience member is exposed to a piece of content within a given time period. You will often see the term expressed as *average frequency*, which averages the frequency of individual exposure across an entire audience. This term is often used in the context of advertising (Chapter 5).

This serves as an introduction to some of the key concepts driving legacy media measurement. However, be sure to carefully review the tables and figures in the next chapter for more on these and other definitions and examples.

The digital revolution and measurement

The legacy measurement terms discussed so far are still used in many places and are still important to know. But with the advent of digital technology, approaches to measurement are changing, and with them the measurement *currency* on which the audiovisual industries focus. The radio and television industries have digitized, and audiences now consume digital audiovisual content over the air, through cable and satellite, and via online, on-demand streaming across multiple devices. In the face of these changes, the traditional legacy measurement tools and concepts were no longer sufficient. You will notice, also, that digital technology rendered the broadcasting sector's terminology insufficient. Hence this becomes a discussion of video and audio media, not television and radio.

One major difference with digital or nonlinear media is that sampling is no longer necessary for audience measurement because almost everything is easily trackable. Mouse clicks, video views, downloads, and the playing of audio files are all potentially knowable because a "data trail" of these actions is left behind. When we are able to measure every case in a population, we refer to this as a *census*, which is better than a sample—assuming it's a true census (Chapter 3). Assuming all audience activity on a digital media platform can be tracked and counted, these data then become the basis for digital audience measurement and metrics, and the sample-based *panel* approach is no longer needed or relevant. Online video and audio consumption are measured using a *census-level* approach.

Next-generation or digital metrics

Along with legacy media metrics, the video and audio sectors use numerous digital metrics. While each sector will be covered in detail in their respective chapters along with sector-specific terminology and nuances, the measurement concept unifying the digital environment is one of impressions. Stated generally, *impressions* are the total number of times a piece of content appears in front of an audience, whether that content is text on a website, an advertisement, a video stream, or an audio file. The idea is that content was displayed or delivered and the audience had an opportunity to consume it.

While the term's origins are in the online and digital environment, impressions are increasingly being used in the audiovisual media sector as audio and video content has gone digital, but they are also starting to be used with linear media as a "next-generation" yet foundational metric. Impressions are simply another metric of reach. More specifically, impressions are becoming a preferred cross-platform metric for buying and selling advertising and also help advertisers to know how their brand or campaign is performing across media platforms.

Because the digital experience is trackable and census-level, audience measurement in the digital environment renders much more *granular* information, providing a finer level of detail and specificity. In addition to each website click or play of a video or audio file, second-by-second measurement of these files is also possible. Analysts can learn how long someone listened, whether they watched a video in its entirety, or, if they didn't, when they stopped watching or listening. This has enormous implications and opportunity for advertisers, of course, as they try to develop the most engaging creative content, but also for producers and distributors of other scripted content.

Gross rating points (GRP)

One other key metric central to both legacy and digital media has to do with the monetization of that content, in other words, advertising. *Gross rating points* (*GRP*) refers to the sum of all rating points for all programs within a given advertising schedule, with one rating point equaling 1% of the total broadcast audience (Video Advertising Bureau, n.d.). This metric helps advertisers measure the "weight" of an ad campaign and understand the overall performance or impact of their content within a market (see also Chapter 5). Gross rating points (GRP) and gross impressions (GI or IMP) are two metrics often used for this purpose and can be calculated in a few different ways:

GRP = (Reach)(Frequency)
GRP = (Rating)(Number of Spots)
GRP = Impressions/Universe Estimate

Measuring the total audience

Because audiences are still consuming both legacy and digital media and likely will for some time, both types of media still need to be measured. What is the best way to do this in such a hybrid environment? One approach is to continue to measure and report on all media platforms separately, whether legacy or digital. In fact, most media managers want to know how each media platform individually performs so that they can strategically respond to audiences who consume content on those platforms. But media companies also want to measure their entire audience, regardless of media platform or technology. This measurement approach is referred to as *total audience measurement*, and companies like Nielsen and Comscore have been working for years to refine this process in the United States. Other companies are doing the same elsewhere around the world. The challenge is that you cannot just merge or combine data from linear and digital sources; they were gathered using two different approaches (sample- and census-level) that result in different outcomes, and merging them would cause *validity* and usability issues.

In a sense, it would be like trying to make an apple pie, but with the requirement that you had to use both apples and grass. (Yes, exactly.) It would no longer be an apple pie. In fact, it would not even be a fruit pie or anything that people would recognize as pie.

The good news is that measurement firms such as Nielsen and Comscore have been diligently working on a total audience measurement or cross-media solution. A single metric that represents all audience consumption across all media platforms would enable content providers to have a total accounting of all of their media content consumption, which would also aid in selling advertising across media platforms and monitoring overall brand performance across these platforms.

So while well-known metrics such as ratings and shares are still important and relevant to the audiovisual industries, they are no longer the whole picture or sufficient. Many new metrics are available for measuring various qualities or aspects of an audience, particularly in the digital space, and their use depends on one's goal or objective. Beyond linear legacy media, there are dozens of new metrics for digital audio and video.

Regardless of media platform, most content providers still want to know three basic things about their audience with regard to a specific piece of content or their media platform as a whole: *how many* people consumed it (reach), *how often* they consumed it (frequency), and *how long* they consumed it (duration). Beyond these three key measurements, there may be other metrics of interest. Which metric you use depends on what you want to know, which should always be related to a specific goal or objective for your organization. Do you want to know whether someone watched the program or video in its entirety? Do you want to know whether they watched the first five minutes? Do you want to know what time of day they streamed a particular video or podcast and whether it led to them stream another? Beyond these metrics, which typically would be reported quantitatively, you may want some qualitative understanding of the audience's experience, such as their engagement level or appreciation for the content and to understand why they enjoyed or did not enjoy certain aspects of the content. Sometimes even these qualities are operationalized quantitatively. You may have multiple objectives and therefore will need to use multiple metrics. Of course, regardless of which metrics are used, they should be valid ones, produced by a reputable measurement firm and ideally accredited by an independent body such as the Media Rating Council (Chapter 1).

Audience measurement firms

As you will see throughout this text, many companies measure media. The newer digital platforms, not surprisingly, have more audience measurement providers, and these providers vary around the world. Companies like Nielsen, Comscore, Ipsos, GfK, and Kantar are international and serve media clients in many different countries. Other measurement firms, like OzTAM in Australia, serve just one country. Similarly, some companies provide services for one or more media sectors, cross-media measurement services, or digital measurement services but not legacy measurement services. Individual companies' services can also be of a limited scope within some countries, even if they are capable of offering more.

Syndicated audience research

Companies such as these just mentioned are known as *syndicated research* firms. As an example, clients purchase subscriptions or pay fees to receive regular syndicated reports about the overall media markets in which the clients compete, helping them to not only track their own ratings performance but also keep tabs on their competition. Such reports typically come out on a regular basis (daily, monthly, quarterly, etc.) and enable comparisons, e.g., by all measured TV stations and networks, times of day, channels tuned, and specific viewer breakdowns by age, gender, and race. All of these traits and more can be analyzed by the subscribing client to identify the strengths and weaknesses in their platforms' performance in order to strategize and, hopefully, optimize future performance. The product being sold by syndicated media measurement firms is information or, put another way, competitive intelligence. This differs from other measurement tools, such as Google Analytics, which is a service for individual performance monitoring. Unlike syndicated media measurement firms, Google does not report on or publish the metrics of all websites for everyone to see.

Nielsen and Comscore

Nielsen and Comscore are two of the biggest names in syndicated media measurement in the United States. While they do compete in some areas of media measurement (e.g., cross-media measurement, video), they are very different companies in both origin and focus. At this writing, Nielsen is still considered the currency for television or video advertising in the United States, as the industry continues to rely heavily on Nielsen ratings for its advertising transactions. As a company, it has been measuring media since the 1930s, and, while it got its start measuring linear analog media and continues to do so, it has expanded its capabilities into the digital and cross-media realms.

Comscore, on the other hand, is a younger company. Launched in 1999, it is a "digital first" enterprise that is best known in the United States for online and mobile measurement but has expanded into the linear TV measurement sector. More recently, it has created some competition for Nielsen in local TV measurement, in large part because of its census-level approach using cable and satellite set-top box **return path data** (**RPD**). Nielsen's approach to measurement, in contrast, primarily uses household samples and panels. Interestingly, due to industry trends and opportunities in statistical modeling, Nielsen also now utilizes the RPD approach to supplement its panel data. Both companies continue to innovate and strive toward providing the industry a cross-platform measurement solution, which will be discussed in the next chapter.

Summary and conclusion

This foundational introduction was intended to provide an overview of some of the key concepts shared by the video and audio industries when it comes to measurement. The next two chapters will take you more in depth and also outline the differences between the sectors. You may wish to refer back to this foundational chapter as you go along.

Finally, the United States historically has been, in many respects, the audiovisual media sector's measurement laboratory for other nations. This is because the US broadcast system—unlike many other countries—is almost entirely commercial and privately owned and the comparative size and affluence of the US viewing population has meant vast amounts of money changing hands on the basis of these audience measurements, particularly in the video sector. The United States will be a primary orientation of the next two chapters and will guide the description of video and audio consumption platforms that follows. However, there are many global similarities and applications to these video and audio industry and measurement basics.

Notes

1. Analog signals are electrical, continuous, and transmitted via waves. Radio and television signals transmit information via these waves through specific frequencies within the electromagnetic spectrum. Digital broadcast signals, by contrast, are not continuous but rather are transmitted as pulses through the electromagnetic spectrum because digital information is encoded via 0s and 1s, also known as binary code. When not being broadcast through the electromagnetic spectrum, digital signals are sent through cables with electrical or light pulses.
2. Examples of how ratings, shares, and other metrics are applied nationally and locally can be found in the Chapter 9.

References

Nielsen. (2020, August). *Nielsen estimates 121 million TV homes in the U.S. for the 2020–2021 TV season.* www.nielsen.com/insights/2020/nielsen-estimates-121-million-tv-homes-in-the-u-s-for-the-2020-2021-tv-season/
Video Advertising Bureau. (n.d.). *Media math.* https://thevab.com/storage/app/media/Toolkit/mediaterminologyformulas.pdf

9 Video analytics

What is television? It's not as straightforward a question as it was 30 years ago, and the primary reason is that less and less viewing actually occurs on a television set today. The term "video consumption" is a more precise description and encompasses the many devices and methods of viewing, whether this viewing occurs on an actual television set (viewed live, streamed through a gaming console, or time shifted via DVR), a tablet, mobile phone, or other type of screen. In terms of content distribution services, traditional broadcast and cable television networks and local broadcasters have been joined by endless internet streaming services such as Hulu, Amazon, and Netflix, as well as dMVPDs (digital multichannel video programming distributors) such as SlingTV, Roku, YouTubeTV, AppleTV, and Google TV. Each passing year ushers in new providers, as well as new technologies and platforms upon which we can consume content. As an example, according to a Nielsen executive, "even though Hulu and Netflix started out as websites and apps, 90% of it is being watched through the TV now" (Rini, personal communication, 2017).[1]

Complicating the discussion of video measurement even more is that there is now so much video available that has nothing to do with what was formerly known as the television industry. Retailers offer video tutorials and branded content to help generate sales. Podcasters create video links in their audio content to showcase sponsors' products. Children create their own YouTube channels and TikTok videos to share their hobbies or skills with friends and relatives, only to find their efforts morphing into successful commercial ventures or "influencer" businesses.

Audiences are in the driver's seat, and the measurement industry is trying to follow them across the various devices, locations, times of day, and delivery platforms where they consume. This phenomenon is known as *audience fragmentation* because the audience that was once so easily aggregated into a single time and space is now fragmented across time and space and must be reassembled for comprehensive measurement. And that's just the beginning! Today, measurement of newer forms of video on different

DOI: 10.4324/9780429506956-13

devices increasingly overlaps with what might still be called "television" measurement. So what do we mean by television, now video, and how are those audiences measured? Let's first become familiar with the many video consumption platforms used today, followed by the tools and methods used to measure them.

Video consumption platforms

Over-the-air (OTA) broadcast TV

Broadcast television is the earliest and simplest form of video delivery and is still popular around the world today. This television signal is delivered through a particular frequency range through the electromagnetic spectrum. Because the spectrum is a scarce resource, not everyone who would like to be a television broadcaster can be one, so a license must be acquired. In the United States and some other countries, the government's condition for awarding broadcast licenses is that the broadcaster must, at least nominally, act in the public interest. Digital antennae are capable of delivering multiple over-the-air (OTA) channels into homes.

Cable, satellite, and telco (MVPD)

Cable and satellite television service came about in the 1960s and 1970s (NCTA, n.d.; Tech-FAQ, n.d.). Both are video services provided by what are known as multichannel video programming distributors (MVPDs). These are companies that provide hundreds of channels through a subscription service to people's homes via cable or satellite dish. Examples are Comcast (one of the largest cable companies in the United States) and Dish (satellite service). Cable and satellite services can provide video on demand services. They can also deliver local broadcast channels to households. Another type of MVPD comes in the form of "telcos," short for telecommunications companies. They are comparable to cable or satellite, but the video content is delivered through a telco provider. AT&T is an example of such a service. Telco video providers continue to evolve toward more software and cloud-based streaming services.

Streaming video

The emergence of reliable broadband technology ushered in a new form of video content delivery: streaming. Streaming video services are a general category including any video delivered over the internet, or *"over-the-top"* (*OTT*).[2] As of 2021, Nielsen estimated that about 25% of viewing occurred via streaming among streaming-capable households (Nielsen,

2021a). Examples include Hulu, Pluto, Netflix, Amazon Prime Video, Disney+, Peacock, and Tubi, many of which are viewed today through Connected TV (CTV) apps. Within this streaming category are various business models (subscription or advertising based, for example) as well as streaming models. While many streaming services are on demand, a rapidly growing service as of 2022 was *FAST*, which stands for Free Ad-Supported TV. Rather than on demand, FAST services stream live, linear programming through an app (Boyle, 2022). Pluto is an example of a FAST service. Other streaming services within this emerging area are hybrid, offering both on-demand and live content in some form.

Video on demand (VOD)

Video on demand (VOD) is just what it sounds like—video that can be accessed and consumed at a time and place (and device) that is convenient and preferred by the consumer. With VOD, the audience does not need to be in front of a screen at a certain time. As just alluded to, cable and satellite MVPDs typically provide VOD services. These can be in the form of films, special sporting events (such as boxing matches), or TV programs. VOD can be provided for free along with a consumer's MVPD subscription, or there may be a fee for each VOD selection. VOD also can be delivered over-the-top via internet streaming (rather than via cable or satellite), and as noted, includes internet-only services such as YouTube. VOD can be free, or there may be a charge.

These VOD versions have distinctive names. Subscription video on demand (SVOD), as the name suggests, requires a paid subscription to access video content. Examples of SVOD include Netflix, Amazon Prime Video, and Disney+. Subscription fees are typically charged monthly.

Advertising-based video on demand (AVOD) is available to viewers for free, or rather the model relies on advertising for revenue (whereas SVOD contains no advertising). Examples of AVOD include YouTube, Peacock, Crackle, and Tubi. AVOD is similar to a FAST service (ad-supported and free to viewers) but is on demand with multiple options available to viewers at any given time, whereas FAST is linear-streamed programming.

Yet another form of VOD is known as TVOD or transactional video on demand. This is essentially pay-per-view, where a consumer pays a fee not for access to an entire library of content but just for a single video event or program (Elmokadem, 2019). iTunes is one example of TVOD (Kaysen, 2015). Of course, hybrids of these services are also possible. For instance, Hulu has two tiers of service (at this writing), and both require monthly subscriptions. However, Hulu's least expensive subscription tier also has some advertising, whereas the higher tier is ad-free (Lopez, 2019). Other hybrid types can include advertising as well as TVOD options, and SVOD/TVOD combinations.

Digital MVPD

With the evolution of digital technology and the cloud, content libraries can now be stored more efficiently. While many consumers still want access to multiple video channels, not everyone wants the hundreds of channels supplied by traditional cable and satellite packages. The digital or virtual MVPD, also referred to as dMVPD or vMVPD and sometimes also referred to as "skinny bundle," was the solution for many households. Examples of dMVPDs are SlingTV, Roku, YouTubeTV, AppleTV, and Google TV. It is perhaps the closest the video programming industry has come to à la carte service.

As you can see, while it has taken time, video content platforms and distribution services have gradually adapted to consumer demand for autonomy, in terms of both the type and the amount of content received, as well as the technology platforms on which the audience wants it delivered. However, this fragmentation across media platforms, devices, and time (live versus on demand) has made measurement of the video industry a more complicated endeavor than during any other time in history. As such, several measurement technologies—old and new—are used to accommodate the various platforms.

Measurement technologies

Diary

While the *diary* has been retired from television audience measurement in the United States, we include it here because it is still used for audio measurement in some US markets and may be used elsewhere around the world for video and audio. The most primitive form of data collection, the diary is a written log of sorts, where selected audience members record their consumption behaviors such as the program name, channel, and time of day that it was consumed, in the diary columns provided.

Set-top meter

Not to be confused with cable/satellite set-top boxes, *set-top meters* sit atop a television set (or nearby) in a home and record what is being watched or at least what channel the television set is tuned to and for how long. It does not record "who" is watching, which is its primary limitation. It is a passive form of measurement because it does not require anything of the viewer (other than permission to have the meter installed and to be a participating Nielsen household). One of the most common set-top meters in use is the Global Television Audience Meter (GTAM) (Ramaswamy, 2017).

People Meter

People Meters (see Figure 9.1) are the next step up from set-top meters in terms of sophistication. In this case, the meter not only tells us what is being watched but who is watching. This is used in conjunction with a set-top meter (like GTAM) and is usually accompanied by a hand-held remote with several buttons on it; each member of the household is assigned their own button. When individuals enter the room to watch television, they push their buttons or enter their codes to indicate they are watching TV. Prior to data collection, the Nielsen field representative would know what age and gender each button or code corresponds to, and this information then gets recorded when that person's designated button is pushed (or their code entered), giving a particular program credit for having that (anonymized) individual in the audience. Of course, this system is not foolproof. People can forget to push their button or enter their code, or they can accidentally push the wrong button or enter the wrong code.

Viewers' tuning choices are identified in People Meters using watermarking technology. **Watermarks** are codes, or hidden data embedded by Nielsen clients within the audio signal, that can be masked using

Figure 9.1 Nielsen People Meter

Source: Credit: Dr. Amy Jo Coffey

psychoacoustic masking of neighboring audio frequencies so that they are inaudible (Ramaswamy, 2008). A second method used by Nielsen to identify content involves audio fingerprints or "signatures." The company holds a vast reference library of all such signatures for broadcast content in each market, so that content recognition and matching may be used if needed (Ramaswamy, 2017).

Portable People Meter

This small meter is not placed on a television set but rather is carried by an individual person, like a pager. It is a version of the original *Portable People Meter* (**PPM**) device created by Arbitron (Jacobs, 2017), the audio measurement company acquired by Nielsen in 2013. Because it can measure almost any type of signal, it is being used to measure not only audio but also video signals, both at the local and national levels. Its most valuable contribution to measurement may be that it measures out-of-home media consumption. It captures exposure to any signal (the strongest in range), not just active viewing, wherever it occurs. Stop and consider for a moment the vast number of viewing or exposure opportunities that might occur out-of-home: restaurants and sports bars, fitness centers, airports and other mass transit areas, and retail centers, just to name a few. Given the amount of viewing that occurs out-of-home due to our mobile lifestyles, the acquisition of the Portable People Meter technology has enabled a more complete and valuable accounting of *viewership* for Nielsen clients. Nielsen has now incorporated the PPM into local video measurement, and this singular device can be used within the same household to measure both audio and video, enabling helpful cross-media comparisons (Inside Radio, 2017).

The Portable People Meter also uses a watermark, as previously described. The meter "listens" for these watermarks and matches the content to the viewer carrying the meter. Interestingly, this technology is already what is being used as the primary audience measurement tool in many countries around the world rather than set-top meters. While it might seem logical to just universally adopt this for all video measurement across the United States and other countries that still use intrusive set-top meters, one Nielsen executive notes that the set-top meters provide valuable information that Portable People Meters don't, including identifying the type of device from which people are viewing content (i.e., how the content gets to the TV set, whether by gaming console, vMVPD, AppleTV, a smart TV, etc.). Set-top meters also provide data on many other in-home characteristics that are gathered using the traditional metering approach such as income level, geographic area, ownership of vehicles, and other consumer information that can be valuable information to clients.

Out with the old, in with the new

The adoption of new metering technologies and the retirement of older, less accurate data-gathering tools are viewed as essential best practices by measurement executives. The Nielsen diary was discontinued for video measurement in 2018 after many years of discussion (diaries are still used for some audio measurement, however). While some TV station news directors valued the comments written into diaries by viewing households, the primitive nature of handwritten records and the active role required by household members caused many *validity* issues, including respondent error due to lack of memory, inaccurate records of viewership due to poor recall, or intentionally misreporting what was viewed due to social desirability bias. In addition, handwriting could often be challenging to decipher. Local markets that had previously relied on diary measurement now rely on a combination of Code Readers (discussed later in the chapter) to capture over-the-air (OTA) viewing, as well as return path data generated by MVPD cable and satellite set-top boxes (STB) with whom Nielsen has data agreements, similar to Comscore's approach.

As the previous sentence implies, not all cable and satellite companies share their set-top box data, so this approach is not an option in all local markets and cannot be used to capture viewing comprehensively on a national level. However, return path data is a passive approach requiring nothing of the viewing household. It also captures all viewing, no matter how small the viewership level, so long as each television set has a cable or satellite set-top box (STB). Set-top boxes only provide tuning information, however, and do not indicate who is watching (demographics), as a People Meter does. Demographic and psychographic information about a household must be obtained either from the measurement firm's sample panel or another data source.

While Comscore was the first US measurement firm known to use STB return path data, it does not utilize household panels as part of its local TV measurement approach. One media industry expert described the difference as Nielsen being able to provide viewing estimates at the household, person, and demographic level but Comscore only being able to provide viewership about households *with* certain demographics represented in them (LaSardo, 2020). Measurement is calculated differently on other levels as well.

In addition to these approaches and tools, new metering technologies offer even more accuracy for the future of video measurement. The *Code Reader* was introduced by Nielsen in 2015 (Guinness, 2019). As the name suggests, it uses inaudible audio signatures, or codes, to identify programs when they air. It tends to be used in small markets and captures over-the-air (OTA) viewing in markets that are now utilizing return path data

(RPD) from set-top boxes (STB). It serves as a supplement to RPD because the STBs cannot measure OTA viewing (Guinness, 2019). This combination of Code Reader and STB measurement is referred to as Return Path Data Plus (RPD+). Introduced in 2018, it is considered the replacement for diary measurement. This innovation has also enabled Nielsen to provide 12 surveys or "sweeps" per year in those markets instead of four (Lasardo, 2019).

The *Nano Meter*, as the name might suggest, is small. Used in Code Reader markets (as just mentioned), it is similar to a set-top meter but captures internet-connected viewing as well as linear viewing on the TV set. It uses audio signatures to detect such viewing through content recognition (Inside Radio, 2017) and will also have better capability compared to other meters to determine whether the TV set is on or off (Guinness, 2019). Nano Meters may eventually replace Code Readers (Lasardo, 2019).

Streaming meters, as you might guess, measure internet streaming in homes by using the same Nielsen panel for linear television viewing. These meters capture viewing via smart TVs, gaming consoles, and connected devices (informitv, 2021). The streaming meter is a component of the nano infrastructure but also "tells us from where streaming content originates, and also allows us to say how much time was spent overall on Netflix vs. Hulu, etc.," according to a Nielsen executive. It is the foundation of the Streaming Platform Ratings service, and the data can be directly compared and reported along with linear viewing.

Because Nielsen also measures the viewership occurring via virtual MVPDs (multichannel video programming distributors) such as SlingTV, it is working with these types of companies to install streaming meters on their players. Such cooperation enables Nielsen to measure every view that occurs via these platforms or apps, whether through a laptop, mobile phone, tablet, or any other device. It uses a similar metering technology to measure viewing from Hulu and YouTubeTV. The technology also enables Nielsen to see how consumption varies across such apps and platforms and the audience's movement between them, including SVOD, AVOD, and MVPDs (Jagwani, 2021).

Finally, while not new per se, *software development kits* ("*SDKs*") are used by Nielsen on participant devices to capture digital (mobile and computer) consumption, including video consumption, and to ensure it is properly identified and credited. According to the Senior Vice President of Product for Nielsen, SDK installation participation has been increasingly successful because "the MVPDs, the cable companies, are starting to partner with us, primarily because the networks are writing it in the contracts now that you need to implement Nielsen's SDK as part of their deal," he said (K. Rini, personal communication, August 16, 2017).

Status of the video measurement industry

The evolution of audience measurement is important for many reasons, but the economic implications are central to why the media industry places such emphasis on measurement approaches, technologies, and innovations. That, in turn, has a direct impact on measurement outcomes and revenue. Measurement technologies and methodologies are not benign and, in fact, are typically developed in a way to serve the media industry and its objectives, something Napoli (2010) has referred to as the "institutionally effective audience." While the industry depends upon audiences as part of its business model, the economic value of such audiences can have downstream effects, such as affecting which audience sectors are served by entertainment and news content providers. Those effects have real consequences for democracies and societies as a whole. Therefore, careful scrutiny of audience measurement practices, technologies, and their evolution is a critical topic for the video industry and mass communication professionals.

Linear television measurement

In order to understand the types of measurement now being conducted, it is best to understand some terminology used to compare the types of video content delivery. While briefly mentioned in the previous chapter, *linear television* refers to video content that is provided according to a specified schedule or time slot, whether distributed via broadcast, cable, satellite, or the internet (Figas & Sweeney, 2022). Linear television includes live viewing as well as time-shifted viewing (referring to content that is recorded and consumed later using a digital video recorder). It may be viewed using a virtual MVPD such as SlingTV or Roku or using a TV-connected device such as a gaming console, media streaming player, or smart TV.

For measurement purposes, this also means the content contains a linear advertising load. Nielsen is the firm best known for video measurement in the United States (and many other countries) and has historically been considered the currency of record within the United States, so this company's video ratings tend to be used to negotiate advertising rates. However, Comscore video measurement also has been widely adopted, particularly at the local level.

In 2022, the US video industry began shifting to an *impressions*-based currency for advertising purposes, even for linear programming, to better enable cross-platform buying and selling for brands (Gilberti, 2022; Inside Radio, 2021; Nielsen, 2021b). However, ratings and shares will remain important metrics for other reasons, such as media planning and station performance. The shift to impressions is just one example of how metrics are always in flux and is something analysts will need to monitor throughout their careers. We will describe current video metrics from both Comscore and Nielsen, beginning with Nielsen. Keep in mind that while one company or another may have coined a term, many of these terms today are used by a variety of measurement firms across the industry and around the world and are now considered general measurement vocabulary.

Nielsen linear metrics

Ratings and *shares* (Box 9.1, Figures 9.2 and 9.3) may be the most commonly used television measurement terms. Simply put, a rating is a percentage or ratio. It expresses the estimated percentage of viewers or households, with access to a viewing screen, who watched a particular program (or other piece of content) at a given time or within a given time period.

Box 9.1 Nielsen video measurement terms and definitions

Term	Definition
TV households (TVH)	Total universe of eligible homes in the US used for video measurement purposes, calculated annually by Nielsen. Can be calculated at the national or local level and serves as the basis for other audience estimates. To qualify as a TV household, the home must have at least one TV set or screen that is able to receive audio and video signals via broadcast, cable, satellite, or the internet.
Universe estimates (UE)	Provides the total number of households or persons in a given population. Nielsen produces UEs for total US as well as for each of the **Designated Market Areas (DMAs)**. UEs are the basis for the calculation of all audience estimates. Without an accurate understanding of the entire universe, it is impossible to understand what percentage of that universe viewed an ad or piece of content.
Households using television (HUT/PUT)	The percentage of all television households in a geography with one or more sets in use during a specific time period. The sum of the average ratings for a given time period is sometimes higher than the HUT number because of households viewing multiple programs at the same time. If a household is watching two programs, it is counted toward each program rating but only once toward a HUT number. PUTs stands for Persons Using Television, so the percentage in that case refers to persons rather than household.

(Continued)

(Continued)

Term	Definition
Average audience ratings	The percentage of people who tuned into an average minute of a program. This metric is used in national TV ratings to buy and sell advertising during a given program. This can also be reported as projections rather than as a percentage that displays the number of people who were exposed to the content in an average minute.
Share	Shows the percentage of people exposed to programming among those using television at a particular moment in time.
Impressions	The number of times ads appear in front of viewers or, more generally, the act of seeing content and advertising.
Reach	Tells you the number of unique, or different, people who were exposed to a piece of content or ad.
Frequency	Indicates the number of times each unique person was exposed to a piece of content or ad.
Time spent	These figures show long each unique person viewed a piece of content.
Average quarter hour ratings (AQH)	Show the percentage of people who tuned into any five minutes within an average quarter hour (15 minutes) of the program. This metric is used in local TV ratings, rather than average audience, to buy and sell local advertising during a given program. This can also be reported in projections or in estimated viewer numbers, rather than as a percentage that displays the number of people who were exposed to the content in an average quarter hour.
Average commercial minute ratings	Show the percentage of people who tuned into an average minute of a commercial airing within a program. This metric is used in national TV ratings. This can also be reported in projections, or estimated viewer numbers, rather than a percentage which displays the number of people who were exposed to an average minute of the commercial airing within a program.
Gross rating points (GRP)	These provide an understanding of the total size of your audience. Also referred to as the sum of all ratings for all the content in a schedule. GRP can also be calculated by Reach × Frequency. Used in advertising, it measures the overall "weight" of a campaign.

Source: Nielsen (various)

PROGRAM A:

Demo Group	Playback Period	How Many			How Often	Ratings			How Long
		Projections (000)	Share	Reach (%)	Frequency	Average Audience (%)	Average Commercial Minute	GRPs	Time Spent
P2+	Live + SD	9,527	11.20	29	2.09	3.22	3	47.8	23

HOW TO READ:

- Demographic Group = P2+: This report shows how all people who are 2 years or older interacted with Program A

- Playback Period = Live + SD: The metrics shown here capture all viewing from the time the program aired live and the rest of that day (same day)

- Projections = 9,527,000: 9,527,000 persons 2 years or older tuned into an average minute of the program

- Share (%) = 11.20%: 11% of persons 2 years or older who were watching TV at the time tuned into the program

- Reach (%) = 29%: 29% of persons 2 years or older tuned into the program

- Frequency = 2.09: On average, people 2 years or older viewed this program 2 times

- Average Minute Audience (%) = 3.2%: 3.2% of people 2 years or older tuned into an average minute of the program

- Average Commercial Minute = 3%: 3% of people 2 years or older tuned into an average minute of the commercials shown during this program

- GRPs = 47.8: The TV program delivered 47.8 GRPs to people age 2 and older

- Time Spent = 23: On average, people 2 years or older spent 23 minutes viewing this program

Figure 9.2 Interpreting national television ratings
Source: Credit: Nielsen

Ratings can be expressed at the national or local level, and they can be specific to any number of "universes," or viewer group types. Some common age demographics (**universes**) may be Adults 18+, Adults 18–34, Adults 18–49, Adults 55+, and so on. Gender is also often part of these ratings breakdowns, for example, a "3" rating for Women 25–54 or Men 18–34.

LOCAL TELEVISION RATINGS

PROGRAM Z:

			How Many			Ratings	How Often	How Long
Demo Group	Playback Period	DMA	Projections (000)	Reach (%)	Share	Average Quarter Hour (%)	Frequency	Time Spent
P2+	Live + SD	Boston (Manchester)	8,208	34.5%	8%	1.40	2.97	47

HOW TO READ:

- Demographic Group = P2+: This report shows how all people who are 2 years or older interacted with this program

- Playback Period = Live + SD: The metrics shown here capture all viewing from the time the program aired live and the rest of that day (same day)

- DMA = Boston (Manchester): This report shows the viewing which occurred in Boston (Manchester) [as opposed to the entire country]

- Projections = 8,208,000: 8,208,000 persons 2 years or older tuned into the program in Boston (Manchester)

- Reach (%) = 34.5%: 34.5% of persons 2 years or older tuned into the program in Boston (Manchester)

- Share (%) = 8%: 8% of Persons 2 years or older tuned into TV at the time watched this program in Boston (Manchester)

- Average Quarter Hour =1.40: 1.40% of people 2 years or older tuned into an average quarter hour of the program

- Frequency = 2.97: On average, people 2 years or older viewed this program 3 times in Boston (Manchester)

- Time Spent = : On average, people 2 years or older spent 47 minutes viewing this program in Boston (Manchester)

Figure 9.3 Interpreting local television ratings

Source: Credit: Nielsen

When the rating is listed for one of these universes (taking the last one as an example), it means that 3% of Men aged 18–34, who had access to a viewing screen in that market, were watching that program. Results for these demographic segments are audience estimates. At the national level,

Nielsen uses *average audience ratings* and *average commercial minute ratings*, while *average quarter hour (AQH) ratings* are used in local markets. Definitions and examples for these and other terms can be found in Boxes 9.1 and 9.2 and Figures 9.2 and 9.3.

However, the most common program rating (unless otherwise stated) for television is the household rating. This rating refers to the percentage of TV households that were tuned in to a particular program, out of all TV households in the geographic market, whether national or local and regardless of whether those households were watching video—or were even home—at the time. But individual demographic ratings can also be calculated and expressed as previously noted.

Shares are a similar metric to ratings and are often reported together with ratings (the rating is typically listed first, followed by the share). The difference lies in what group of viewers is measured. Rather than examining "all TV households" as the denominator, a share is the percentage of households (or viewers or listeners) who were tuned in to a particular program out of all those whose TV sets or screens (or radios or audio receivers) were actually *in use* at the time (see Box 9.1). In other words, share represents the percentage of the *available* audience who consumed the content.

Live viewing metrics are available as well as time-shifted metrics (Box 9.2). As audiences now watch more time-shifted content, many television networks have abandoned the usage of just Live or Live-plus-Same-Day ratings because the delayed viewership is more representative of actual viewing and "when" audiences consume is becoming less important (Maglio, 2021). Similarly, just as program ratings report the estimated viewership of a program, commercial ratings also exist to report the estimated viewership of a video advertisement (Boxes 9.1 and 9.2, Figures 9.2 and 9.3). Ratings and shares are also used to measure audio consumption (Chapter 10). As this discussion shows, the measurements used by the industry are constantly evolving as audience preferences and behaviors evolve.

Box 9.2 Common Nielsen video measurement currencies in the United States

---

Linear metrics

LIVE	Measurement of live linear video consumption.
LIVE + SD	Measurement of live linear video consumption in addition to time-shifted consumption within the same day.

(Continued)

(Continued)

LIVE + 3-DAY	Measurement of live linear video consumption in addition to content that was time-shifted and consumed up to three days later.
LIVE + 7-DAY	Measurement of live linear video consumption in addition to content that was time-shifted and consumed up to seven days later.
C3	Measurement of live linear video commercial viewing and their time-shifted viewing up to three days later. Expressed as average commercial minute rating.
C7	Measurement of live linear video commercial viewing and their time-shifted viewing up to seven days later. Expressed as average commercial minute rating.

Digital metrics

Digital in TV ratings	Measurement of linear TV with the linear ad load that is viewed through mobile and PC devices. This viewing is included in the C3 and C7 ratings currency.
Digital content ratings	Comprehensive measurement of content consumed across all major digital platforms, both video and static (e.g., computer, tablet, mobile, video, static web pages, and gaming consoles). Program-level and episode-level ratings (for video) as well as static content ratings (for web pages and app sections). Unlike Digital in TV ratings, Digital Content Ratings includes digital content whose ad loads do not match the linear load, as well as digital content with no ads.
Streaming platform ratings	Comprehensive measurement of streaming activity across connected-TV (CTV) video apps including SVOD and AVOD services, dMVPDs, gaming and social sites. Gathered as part of the national panel.
Streaming content ratings	Measurement of nonlinear streaming content through the TV at the program/episode level.

Sources: Jagwani, 2021; K. Rini, personal communication, June 17, 2022; Nielsen, n.d., a, n.d., b, 2017a, 2021a.

Time-shifted metrics

The digital video recorder (DVR) has had a revolutionary effect upon television viewing. It has enabled viewers to become not only their own schedulers but their own programmers. Gone are the days when one had to be in front of the TV set at an appointed time. Now, with current storage capacities of DVRs enabling entire seasons of programs to be saved, viewers are

watching more of what they want to watch (being their own program-
mers) and, in some cases, watching programs up to a month after they air.
Examples of time-shifted program metrics include *Live-Plus-Same Day*,
Live-Plus-3, and Live-Plus-7, and time-shifted commercial ratings C3 and
C7 are commonly used in advertising deals (see Box 9.2). Nielsen can currently measure linear telecast-based content viewed up to 35 days later.[3]
One Nielsen executive notes this can actually be a good thing, especially
for advertisers, because "the more time shifting and the further you get
out, the audience gets younger, more upscale, more affluent . . . you're not
just recapturing the viewing, you're recapturing your most important viewers" (B. Fuhrer, personal communication, 2017), adding that binge viewing
regularly occurs with a DVR and is not just an SVOD behavior.

It is important for sales personnel to understand their audiences' time-
shifting behaviors, particularly for specific programs. Some programs are
more time-shifted than others. For instance, it's not uncommon for certain prime time programs to have up to half of their audiences watching
the show on the DVR or through VOD, with a few programs even having higher delayed viewing rates than live viewing (Fitzgerald, 2018). It is
important to negotiate the purchase of advertising time on the metric most
appropriate to the audience's behavior, which is also the most advantageous
to the network or station. For instance, if a drama has a high proportion
of its audience consuming in a time-shifted manner, then a C3 or C7 metric
(Box 9.2) is the best currency for negotiating ad rates because it takes into
account all of the delayed (time-shifted) viewing of ads up to three or seven
days after the program's airing, respectively. However, if that same show's
ad buy is negotiated on just live same-day viewing—leaving out the thousands or even millions of viewers who watched the show days later on their
DVR—that network or station also leaves thousands of dollars on the table
because they don't receive "credit" for all of those time-shifting viewers.

Comscore linear metrics

Comscore is a cross-platform media measurement company that also
measures linear television. Some clients view Comscore as a competitor
to Nielsen, while others view Comscore data as supplemental or comple-
mentary to Nielsen ratings. For its video measurement, Comscore relies on
return path data from set-top boxes from local cable or satellite providers
(MVPDs). Return path data (RPD) is also often referred to as census-level
viewing data, as it is gathered from all TV sets that have a set-top box in
the MVPD's market and not a sampling of those homes. A passive measurement approach, the set-top box (STB) records all tuning information,
second by second, regardless of whether there is anyone actually watching.
We'll discuss more later on the pros and cons of using STB data.

Using this data, Comscore can provide viewing information, including TV viewership data, for local broadcast programming as well as for cable networks. Comscore linear TV measurement products at the time of this writing included *StationView Essentials* (local TV measurement), *TV Essentials* (national TV measurement), and *OnDemand Essentials* (video on demand measurement).

Digital video measurement

Digital video is nonlinear and refers to video on demand, which is not contingent on a particular delivery schedule. Think of digital video measurement as a subset of all digital measurement. Within this type of video measurement are SVOD viewing and set-top box VOD viewing.

As noted elsewhere, digital measurement relies on a census-based approach. Because each click and view can be potentially tracked, everything can be counted (a census) so no sampling of the population is needed. Thus, in digital measurement, instead of ratings and shares, we use terms such as *viewership*—the total number of persons who viewed a piece of video content—and **impressions**, which, broadly speaking, is the total number of times a piece of content appears in front of an audience. Nielsen's own definition of impressions is similar, described as "the actual number of times ads appear in front of viewers" (Gilberti, 2022, para. 14) or, more generally, "the act of seeing content and advertising" (para. 3). Both Nielsen and Comscore measure digital video. We'll discuss those metrics in detail shortly. See also Box 9.2. Other video measurement services have emerged in recent years, but these two have remained the most dominant in the United States.

The following examples illustrate how changes in the technologies audiences use to consume video and audio content force measurement companies to constantly develop new approaches to audience measurement. And by extension, that means that professional media analysts must be constantly scrambling to keep up with learning the new measurements coming into the marketplace.

Nielsen digital metrics

Nielsen's Digital Content Ratings is a comprehensive metric that encompasses any type of content consumption on a digital platform. It could be video, audio, website, mobile app, or other form of media. In order for all of this digital measurement to work, however, Nielsen needs to get permission from the content providers to install their software development kits (SDKs) into the various websites or mobile apps to be measured. Thus industry cooperation is more critical than ever for comprehensive, accurate measurement. Some executives at Nielsen have referred to measurement today as a "team sport."

Digital in TV Ratings measure traditional linear video content (e.g., broadcast and cable network programs) with the linear ad load that is viewed through mobile and PC devices (K. Rini, personal communication, 2022).

Comscore digital metrics

Comscore also provides digital measurement including video that is consumed on tablets, phones, and desktop computers. Its *Media Metrix Multi-platform* product provides person-level measurement of digital content in any form across all types of screens and devices (Comscore, n.d., a). Another product, *Video Metrix Multi-platform*, measures video consumption specifically on platforms including smartphones, tablets, desktop computers, and other OTT devices (Comscore, n.d., b). Consumption level is expressed as minutes spent on video. Another platform-specific measurement product is Comscore's *Mobile Metrix*, which, as one might guess, focuses on mobile platform consumption specifically—tablet and smartphones—that occurs within apps and browsers (Comscore, n.d., c).

Measuring streaming video

Both Comscore and Nielsen measure video streaming consumption, both advertising-supported video on demand (AVOD) and subscription-supported (SVOD). Comscore accomplishes this with its CTV Intelligence tool, which is generated from the company's Total Home Panel (Comscore, n.d., d). Nielsen uses its streaming meter to capture viewing from several connected-TV (CTV) app services, social and gaming sites, and dMVPD services. SVOD is measured using an audio fingerprinting technique, which does not require embedding audio codes, and a streaming meter, which measures how much time a household spends streaming out of all viewing and then how much of that streaming comes from each SVOD service. The company's Streaming Content Ratings, as they are now known, are provided on an "average audience-per-minute" basis, just like national television measurement, so they are comparable for strategic analysis (Nielsen, 2017b, 2021a; Poggi, 2017; K. Rini, personal communication, 2022).

Because Netflix, Amazon, and the growing field of SVOD providers are largely subscription-based and not advertising-supported, they receive their revenue up front, and ratings are not required for their business model. Thus companies such as Netflix and Amazon typically do not release their viewership figures publicly. However, many in the television industry want this information, particularly content providers who negotiate with Netflix in order to know how much they should charge in licensing fees for Netflix to use their content. This has made the development and release of SVOD metrics particularly important.

Best practices for measuring video consumption

Hybrid approach

Most measurement firm and media company executives agree that a hybrid approach that incorporates both linear and digital is a necessary best practice for video measurement today. It's the approach that best reflects the reality of video consumption and helps aggregate an audience that has become increasingly fragmented across multiple platforms. While each measurement approach has its strengths and weaknesses, legacy measurement practices that use representative sampling to build household and individual panels will remain important, as linear television consumption is not going away anytime soon.

That said, census-level measurement for digital (nonlinear) video consumption is also essential, as it is the easiest way to capture that type of audience behavior. Because all digital nonlinear viewer behavior can be tracked (with permission or consent), there is a possible record of everything. There are pros and cons to this type of census-based measurement, which will be discussed later.

Media executives say a responsible integration of linear and digital video measurement approaches is the key to success. But while integrating linear and digital media is critical, it's a complex process, and not all countries and media providers measure the same way. For example, due to the country's unique characteristics, OzTAM—Australia's primary national TV measurement firm—with its partners devised a "Total TV" reporting standard called Virtual Australia (VOZ). VOZ captures the TV viewing that takes place on all screens in the country (D. Peiffer, personal communication, January 27, 2020).[4]

Total audience measurement/cross-platform measurement

As noted previously, this combined data approach is called **total audience measurement (TAM)**. The industry is moving rapidly toward TAM because of the need for comprehensive, comparable measures of video consumption across all delivery platforms, whether linear or digital.

When we refer to total audience measurement, we're really talking about cross-platform or cross-media measurement, assuming this measurement is comprehensive.[5] The idea is that total audience consumption across all devices and platforms be represented by a single metric that could serve as its currency. That has been the industry's Holy Grail for years, and media measurement firms have been trying to deliver it. The metrics being developed for TAM or cross-platform measurement are changing rapidly. So what's the current state of play?

At this writing, Comscore and Nielsen have been competing hard in the United States on this front. Comscore announced new cross-platform advances in October 2020 that built upon its impressions-based model and the ability to measure the deduplicated performance of specific advertisements and individual web traffic or viewership information, rather than traditional age- and gender-based ratings (Comscore, 2020).

In December 2020, Nielsen announced an initiative similar to OzTAM's in deduplicated cross-media measurement called Nielsen ONE. It would provide single, standardized, impressions-based currency for buying and selling advertising across the industry (Nielsen, 2021c). The Nielsen ONE reach and frequency metrics would provide a demographic profile of individual users and capture their media consumption by individual platform on a subminute basis—whether linear, digital, or streaming. It would also provide greater granularity and precision than are provided by existing Nielsen currencies. The process would enable advertisers to more seamlessly buy audiences across platforms and monitor total brand performance.

Some details about the process remained undetermined at the time of this writing, such as setting a standard rule as to what would be counted as an "impression." The new Nielsen ONE metric was scheduled to launch in late 2022 with older metrics possibly retired by 2024 (Ha, 2020).

Not to be outdone, Comscore countered by announcing its planned Comscore Everywhere service, also scheduled for rollout in 2022 (Schiff, 2022). The Comscore–Nielsen competition is just an example of how dynamic video measurement is currently and how much it is being driven by competition between syndicated research firms. While this example is from the United States, video measurement is in similar flux around the world.

Thus, while traditional legacy video metrics like ratings and shares are still important, they are no longer the whole picture, particularly in a cross-platform video environment. As one broadcast network vice president explained, the metric to be used depends on the context and financial strategy outcome you are hoping to evaluate. While total audience measurement remains a goal, it is not viewed by the industry as a replacement for individual sector or device metrics. Analysts and firms still want to know how their content performs individually on specific platforms, as this helps in their future planning and strategy development.

Total cross-media audience measurement, then, is supplementary measurement that can provide firms a more comprehensive view of how a particular piece of content performs across all media platforms, devices, and time periods. While we've been referring to total audience as it pertains to video, this concept can apply to content of any kind in terms of aggregating the fragmented audience in order to comprehensively measure it.

Psychographics, not (just) demographics

While demographics are still relevant to media companies that want to know who watches their content and to the advertisers who want to reach specific audiences consuming this content, the reality is that *psychographics*—interests, hobbies, beliefs, and behaviors—are a much better predictor of consumer behavior and product purchases. This has been understood by the industry for some time, but demographic data were simply easier to attain and had become an accepted way of segmenting and buying audiences. In the digital interactive world where consumers readily share their hobbies, consumer preferences, and interests on social media and elsewhere, these digital profiles are ripe for harvest and more easily accessible for marketers. Psychographic or *behavioral segmentation* is now a reality and can be used in combination with viewership data to target audiences with precision.

Devices and behavioral segmentation

Because behavioral targeting is now possible, what is valued in video measurement is changing, according to Steve Walsh, Chief Revenue Officer, Consumer Orbit. The new metrics are now:

> moving alongside and in fact replacing the traditional demographic metrics of "how many Adults 25–54 am I reaching?" to "how many consumers who have viewed a competitor's video content, or shopped in a competitor's store, am I reaching?," "on what devices am I reaching them and what do people who view this content on that device, what else do they view on different devices?"

While demographics are still relevant in some situations, equally if not more important are things like auto purchase information, voter registration, and credit card purchases, he says, and television stations and networks need to understand how their viewers differ across platforms. For instance, how are the households or persons who watch the 6 p.m. news on linear television different from those who consume the station's news products online or through the station's app? Walsh went on to explain that demographics are an outdated metric for effective and efficient advertising because, with the prevalence of large third-party datasets and methodologies today, it is possible to know actual consumer behaviors. By combining actual consumer media exposure with actual purchase and online search behaviors, a highly granular understanding of the consumer can be revealed, which makes for greater media planning precision. In sum, he says:

> It's not so much about being #1 or #2 or #6 anymore (in traditional demographic ratings—also known as the "body count"), but rather demonstrating how your programming and inventory deliver the right consumers for advertisers to target . . . across your linear, CTV and digital platform. You've got to train your salespeople to sell not just the size of your audience, but its value and its relevance to the advertiser that you're standing in front of on a Tuesday morning in a pitch meeting, and that involves utilizing quantitative and qualitative data to understand and compellingly communicate the relationships between media exposure and consumer purchase activity and how media content delivers consumers—not just demographic surrogates—effectively and efficiently.

Put another way, it's about delivering the *right* content to the *right* consumers on the *right* device at the *right* time.

Video measurement considerations, tools, and practices

Panels vs. set-top box "census" approaches

Both census data and panel data are valued for different reasons, and there are pros and cons to both when measuring media audiences. Many industry experts explain that **census-level** data are valuable for the volume or scale they can provide, as well as the **stability** and **granularity** of the data. However, they lack identifying information about the consumers connected to that data. Therefore, the value is limited in terms of how an analyst can use that information to better serve the consumer, when the analyst knows nothing about them. Conversely, *panel data* serves as a "truth set" because the dataset contains identifying information about the consumers who consumed on those devices or within a given household. This information also tends to be representative of the **population** due to the random sampling techniques used to create the **panel** (see Chapter 3); so it is more accurate than census-based data from that standpoint.

Census-level data in video measurement is also referred to as **return path data** (**RPD**). As defined by Comscore, RPD is "any user activity gathered from a digital device defined by a start time and a duration returned to the platform provider" (Boehme, 2017, p. 14). Some device such as a mobile phone or tablet is "pinged" or receives a signal that a user is on the website or app or has started a video stream. This information is "returned" as a view or at least indicates that something was clicked. However, that doesn't necessarily mean the entire video was viewed or that an entire page of content was read, and it certainly doesn't provide any information about the user who clicked it. It just registers the device. By contrast, with sample-based panel data, the "who" information is there. Companies like Nielsen have the demographic information connected to the content consumption. Because of this, the industry often refers to the sample-based panel data as the "truth set." In contrast, census data does not know "who" consumed "what," only the "what."

Set-top boxes (return path data): pros and cons

There are pros and cons to utilizing set-top boxes (STB) and their census data for video measurement. First, the pros. Due to the scale and continuous nature of the data collection compared to the panel approach, there are fewer instances of "zero cells" or insufficient data to calculate viewership (Vinson, 2021a). This data stability and granularity have enabled new and smaller audience television networks to see the directionality of their viewership (whether the numbers are trending up or down) in order to simply know whether the network's audience is growing or not, even when the numbers are quite low. Second, this approach is less intrusive than the Nielsen "panel family" approach, as the household already has the necessary equipment in place (if they are a cable or satellite TV subscriber), and the set-top box passively collects the tuning data.

Despite these upsides, there are validity issues with using set-top boxes. First, not every TV viewing household subscribes to cable or satellite, so many homes do not have set-top boxes. Moreover, the number of cable and satellite homes has been declining due to cord cutting. Thus the viewership from set-top boxes is neither exhaustive nor representative of all television viewership. In addition to this, households with Pay TV services do not necessarily have set-top boxes on every television set or screen within the household, so some viewership even within these households does not get measured. A third shortcoming with set-top box use is that, if the box is left on but the TV is off (as is often the case), the box gathers tuning information even when no one is watching. Thus, the "viewing" information being gathered is actually false, being credited as viewing when none has occurred. In addition, not all set-top boxes are enabled to deliver return path data. It is also worth noting that not all cable and satellite MVPDs share their RPD with companies like Comscore or Nielsen, which means that entire markets or partial markets of data are missing from the "census," which affects how truly representative the data are for a given area. Finally, set-top box data do not tell us who is watching, only "what" is being watched or, more specifically, what station the set is tuned to and for how long (B. Fuhrer, personal communication, 2017).

Research firms that collect STB data use various methods to validate it and correct potential issues. Projections are carefully calculated using many pieces of household-level, market-level, and other data traits. STB data companies also point to the stability and volume of return path data as benefits over the panel or sample-based approaches, which have their own challenges, including the active role required of participants, declining participation rates, and the statistical and reporting fluctuations that can result (Vinson, 2021b).

Amid the debate and due to the upsides such as stability and granularity, some local TV stations have begun using Comscore's (set-top box) TV data as currency rather than Nielsen data (Alsop, 2018), and some clients use both Nielsen and Comscore data to negotiate advertising deals. Despite the shortcomings and due to the benefits, Nielsen also began using STB data in a controlled and limited hybrid fashion in some markets. But because using STB data alone can be problematic, Nielsen uses viewer assignment modeling based on its panel methodology, which utilizes representative random sampling as a "truth set" in conjunction with the STB data.

Viewer assignment modeling

Viewer assignment modeling is a relatively new innovation by Nielsen (and perhaps other measurement firms) to statistically calibrate the return path data (RPD) provided by set-top boxes. Because set-top box data provides information about what was watched but not who watched it, Nielsen extrapolates viewers' demographics in those markets by using demographic data from distant Local People Meter markets (Buckman, 2015). Essentially, Nielsen takes the demographic data from its national panel and matches it to households where return path data are gathered. If a home is "very similar in composition, location, program availability, all those types of metrics," then it can also statistically estimate the viewing that TV sets tune to, as well as the type of people viewing, and ascribe those characteristics to that return path data home, according to a Nielsen executive.

"Simply put, it's a probability technique to determine who is most likely watching TV in the [household] based on regional people meter data. Set Meters, Code Readers, and RPD homes are only capable of reporting [household] data viewership. Nielsen knows who is in their sample panel and takes a best guess on who is watching" (Lasardo, 2019, para. 8).

Viewer assignment modeling is particularly useful in the smaller markets, where data can sometimes be inconsistent due to the small samples.

The RPD provides much needed stability and consistency in such cases, where there otherwise could be wild fluctuations from day to day or from one data gathering period to another. A Nielsen executive explained that this approach helps avoid "zero cells" in some smaller samples. He quotes clients in these smaller markets who explain that, "Look, I can sell low numbers, but I can't sell a zero!"

Data fusion and integration opportunities

With the generation of large quantities of digital data, third-party data has become its own industry. Large consumer datasets can be combined and fused with video viewership data to identify new *insights* about consumer preferences and purchasing patterns. Often called "big data" (Chapter 7), *data fusion* and *data integration* provide opportunities for new consumer intelligence and enable more advanced targeting of consumers based on demographics, psychographics, and purchasing habits. Many third-party data services, sometimes known as *data brokers*, exist today with companies such as Axciom and Experian among them. By matching third-party household-level data with that household's media consumption data, a granular profile of a household, individual consumer, or even a device can be constructed.

Summary and conclusion

The future of video measurement is one of uncertainty as well as promise and excitement. In a technology-driven industry, measurement processes will never truly be "finished" but will be ever evolving. In addition, as you may have surmised by now, there is no perfect measurement system or approach. Firms do their best to minimize error and maximize validity to deliver trustworthy metrics and reports to their clients and in a timely way. But the economic stakes are as high as ever, even as viewing consumption patterns have fragmented; some would argue the economics have become more important due to this fragmentation.

Both census data and panel data are valued by the industry for different reasons, and there are pros and cons to both. Many video industry experts explained that census data are valuable for the volume or scale they can provide, as well as the stability and granularity of the data. However, censuses typically lack information about the consumers connected to that data and must be supplemented by third-party data. Therefore, the value is more limited in terms of how an analyst can use that information. Conversely, panel data serves as a "truth set" because it contains demographic and sometimes psychographic information about the consumers who viewed on those devices or within a given household. This information also tends to be representative of the population due to the random sampling techniques used and so is more accurate than census-based data from that standpoint.[6] Nevertheless, there seems to be a recognition by the video industry that both linear and digital measurement approaches will coexist for some time because this is reflective of today's audience viewing habits. However, there is a concomitant desire to ensure that all platforms are measured and that comprehensive deduplicated measurement of the fragmented audience can be accurately established. Thus a comprehensive cross-media measurement currency remains both a challenge and sought-after opportunity.

Video sector measurement is in a season of transition that may not see stability for some time. This certainly suggests job security for those in the video analytics profession but also guarantees no shortage of measurement challenges and problems to solve, as the industry strives to maintain currencies that serve industry constituencies, as well as develop new ones that are appropriate to the video consumption platforms and devices enjoyed by today's audiences.

Additional resources

Nielsen: https://global.nielsen.com/
Comscore: www.comscore.com/
OzTAM: https://oztam.com.au/Default.aspx
VOZ reports: https://virtualoz.com.au/market-reports/

Recommended cases

These cases can be found on the textbook website: www.routledge.com/cw/hollifield

Case 9.1: TV Viewing Down Under
Case 9.2: Viewing Behavior during a Pandemic
Case 9.3 (14.5): News Viewership and Voters

Case studies, along with accompanying datasets for this chapter, can be found on the text website. We particularly suggest the preceding cases in the order listed. See the companion website and instructor's manual for detailed descriptions of these and other relevant cases.

Discussion questions and exercises

1. Why is accurate video measurement so important for video content providers such as broadcasters, cable networks, and video streaming

services? Are the reasons the same? Different? How would each type of video content company strategically use video viewership data?

2. Given the rapid pace of technological change and constant emergence of new video consumption platforms, does the idea of total audience measurement seem a possibility to you? Do you view this as the best measurement solution? Why or why not?

3. Do you think the video measurement industry is best served by a single agreed-upon currency for advertising transactions? Or do you think it's helpful to have more options? Why or why not?

4. Do some internet research to see if you can locate the pricing for some syndicated television or video analytics in your country. Compare and discuss with what some of your peers found. Do these prices surprise you? As a manager for a video or television enterprise, how would these prices affect how you feel about (a) the return on investment these metrics must provide to you, (b) paying and budgeting for an annual subscription to these metrics, (c) the metrics' accuracy and, related to this, whether they were accredited by a third-party agency such as the Media Rating Council?

5. Do some internet research to identify two or three video analytics providers in other countries. Examples in the United States could include Nielsen, Comscore, Kantar, iSpotTV, or others that might emerge. Take some time to analyze and contrast the various metrics and products offered in the other countries. How do they compare? Are the products nearly identical, or do they differ in some ways? If so, how do they differ? Does one company's product seem more valid or reliable to you? More practical or user-friendly? If so, which company and why?

6. *Exercise: Cable news audiences*
   Examine the audience viewership data in Table 9.1, "Midsize Market USA, Cable Networks 6 p.m.–12 Midnight." Focus on the viewership data for News Network A, News Network B, and News Network C. Then answer the questions.

   a. How do the audiences of News Network A, News Network B, and News Network C compare (from 6 p.m.–midnight) in terms of the following demographic factors for this midsize market?

      i. Household income
      ii. Age/generation
      iii. Gender

   b. Build an audience profile of each of these three cable news networks based on this (limited) data. How might each network leverage their consumer profile in terms of (i) content development and offerings and (ii) advertisers?

Table 9.1 Midsize Market USA

Cable Networks 6 p.m.–12 Midnight
In the past 7 days, which of the following cable networks did you watch between 6 p.m. and 12 midnight?

	Total adults	Men	Women	Millennials (1982–2004)	Generation X (1965–1981)	Baby boomers (1946–1964)	$30–$50K	$50–$75K	$75K+
	n=800	n=382	n=418	n=240	n=219	n=237	n=184	n=148	n=216
Sports Network 1	7%	11%	3%	6%	8%	8%	4%	11%	11%
News Network A	4%	5%	3%	2%	2%	7%	3%	4%	7%
Home and Family	4%	2%	6%	2%	5%	5%	4%	4%	8%
Dramas for Everyone	4%	3%	4%	5%	4%	3%	4%	4%	2%
Nature Channel	3%	3%	3%	0%	5%	5%	2%	3%	2%
Movie Channel A	3%	4%	2%	2%	4%	3%	2%	3%	4%
Romance Movie Network	3%	1%	4%	3%	3%	3%	3%	3%	3%
Sports Network 2	3%	5%	1%	2%	5%	3%	1%	3%	4%
Culinary TV	3%	1%	5%	2%	4%	3%	3%	3%	5%
Sitcom and Rerun Network	3%	2%	4%	3%	4%	3%	3%	3%	4%
Action Movies and Shows	3%	3%	2%	1%	3%	3%	3%	3%	2%
News Network B	3%	4%	1%	1%	1%	3%	0%	1%	7%
Documentary TV	2%	3%	2%	1%	3%	4%	3%	1%	4%
Superheroes & Fantasy	2%	4%	0%	2%	3%	3%	3%	3%	1%
Movie Channel B	2%	2%	2%	1%	3%	3%	2%	1%	5%
Love Stories and Tearjerkers	2%	1%	3%	1%	2%	3%	1%	3%	2%
News Network C	2%	2%	2%	0%	0%	4%	2%	2%	4%
None	68%	69%	67%	75%	64%	65%	71%	67%	63%

Source: Marshall Marketing. Adapted with permission.

    c. Conduct some of your own original research using US Census Bureau data, selecting other metropolitan areas and comparing some of the variables you've examined in Question 1. (Visit www.census.gov. The American Community Survey data is a good place to start.) What are some likely explanations for your findings?

7. *Exercise: Cable TV and gender*
Examine the audience viewership data in Table 9.1, "Midsize Market USA, Cable Networks 6 p.m.–12 Midnight." Then answer the following questions.

    a. Which gender (proportionally) is more likely to be a viewer of Sports Network 1?
    b. Which network(s) tend to have a more female skew?

Conduct an analysis to identify the biggest "gender gap" networks in terms of networks. How might you leverage and optimize these gaps for these networks?

Notes

1. This type of viewing is enabled by "connected TV" (CTV), referring to an internet-connected device that permits video streaming, including smart TVs.
2. Over-the-top (OTT) content delivery is so named because the distribution bypasses or goes "over the top" of traditional delivery systems, e.g., not delivered through a cable box.
3. It is worth noting that linear content measurement is based on time of program transmission. However, Nielsen can measure most streaming content indefinitely, as it is an episode-based measurement, which is tied to when something was viewed, not broadcasted by a TV network.
4. Current VOZ market reports can be accessed at https://virtualoz.com.au/market-reports/
5. We will use the terms interchangeably in this chapter. Be aware that not all cross-platform measurement may be comprehensive.
6. Refer to Chapter 3 to learn how nonrepresentative sampling can affect TV viewership data.

References

Alsop, P. (2018, February 13). *Spot TV advertisers: Understanding Nielsen's measurement updates.* www.mediaaudit.com/post/spot-tv-advertisers-understanding-nielsens-measurement-updates

Boehme, J. (2017). The data dig: Going deep with advanced consumer metrics. [PowerPoint slides]. *Comscore.* www.cynopsis.com/wp-content/uploads/2017/01/Jeff-Boehme-comScore.pdf

Boyle, A. (2022, May 16). AdExplainer: The difference between AVOD and FAST. *AdExchange.* www.adexchanger.com/adexplainer/adexplainer-the-difference-between-avod-and-fast

Buckman, A. (2015, September 2). *Nielsen's code reader getting mixed reviews*. https://tvnewscheck.com/article/88118/nielsens-code-reader-getting-mixed-reviews/

Comscore. (2020, October 26). *Comscore announces advancements in cross-screen media measurement* [Press release]. www.comscore.com/Insights/Press-Releases/2020/10/Comscore-Announces-Advancements-in-Cross-Screen-Media-Measurement

Comscore. (n.d., a). *Get a complete unduplicated view of how digital audiences consume content across devices*. www.comscore.com/Products/Digital/Multi-Platform-Content-Measurement

Comscore (n.d., b). *Get a complete, unduplicated view of how digital audiences consume video across devices*. www.comscore.com/Products/Digital/Multi-Platform-Video-Measurement

Comscore. (n.d., c). *Understand total mobile audience behavior across browsers and apps*. www.comscore.com/Products/Digital/Mobile-Measurement

Comscore. (n.d., d). *Leverage precise CTV streaming insights from TV-connected devices to capitalize on media trends*. www.comscore.com/Products/CTV/Streaming-Insights

Elmokadem, P. (2019). Pricing. *uScreen*. www.uscreen.tv/video-business-school/svod-tvod-avod-monetization-models/

Figas, N., & Sweeney, M. (2022, August 9). The difference between traditional, linear, Connected TV, OTT, and Advanced TV advertising [infographic]. *Clearcode*. https://clearcode.cc/blog/tv-advertising-explained/

Fitzgerald, T. (2018, November 27). These five TV shows draw the biggest DVR audiences on broadcast. *Forbes*. www.forbes.com/sites/tonifitzgerald/2018/11/27/these-five-tv-shows-draw-the-biggest-dvr-audiences-on-broadcast/#51b4b69396cb

Gilberti, K. (2022, February 8). Impressions 2.0: The great equalizer. *Nielsen*. www.nielsen.com/us/en/insights/article/2022/impressions-2-0-the-great-equalizer/

Guinness, S. (2019, August 28). Understanding changes Nielsen is making in local audience measurement. *Katz Media Group*. https://blog.katzmedia.com/on-measurement/understanding-nielsen-changes

Ha, A. (2020, December. 8). Nielsen plans to combine traditional and digital TV ratings. *TechCrunch*. https://techcrunch.com/2020/12/08/nielsen-one/

informitv. (2021, April 22). Nielsen introduces streaming video ratings. *Informitv*. https://informitv.com/2021/04/22/nielsen-introduces-streaming-video-ratings/

Inside Radio. (2017, May 22). Nielsen looks to change game with next-gen PPM. *Inside Radio*. www.insideradio.com/free/nielsen-looks-to-change-game-with-next-gen-ppm/article_3fda7168-3ecb-11e7-a71b-7bfb87282ad0.html

Inside Radio. (2021, September 23). TV is leading the move to impressions: Radio may be next. *Inside Radio*. www.insideradio.com/free/tv-is-leading-the-move-to-impressions-radio-may-be-next/article_aa09d8f2-1c35-11ec-ac75-6fb81e1849fc.html

Jacobs, F. (2017, February. 22). PPM turns 10: Celebration or regret? *Jacobs Media Strategies*. https://jacobsmedia.com/ppm-radio-ratings/

Jagwani, A. (2021, May 26). *Making it count: Nielsen starts measuring streaming viewing. Extreme Reach*. https://ps.extremereach.com/blog/making-it-count-nielsen-starts-measuring-streaming-viewing/

Kaysen, M. (2015, August 24). Understand the "SVOD," "TVOD," and "AVOD" terms and business models of streaming services like Netflix. *LinkedIn*. www.linkedin.com/pulse/understand-svod-tvod-avod-terms-business-models-streaming-mads-kaysen

Lasardo, M. (2019, February 27). Nielsen TV measurement: Simplified. *Katz Media Group*. https://blog.katzmedia.com/on-measurement/nielsen-measurement-simplified

Lasardo, M. (2020, January 6). Spot the differences: Nielsen and Comscore. *Katz Media Group*. https://blog.katzmedia.com/on-measurement/nielsen-comscore-spot-the-differences-series1

Lopez, M. (2019, April 2). What the Hell is a vMPVD? The modern streaming market explained. *The Wrap*. www.thewrap.com/vmvpd-svod-avod-tvod-streaming-market-explained/

Maglio, T. (2021, February 17). NBC joins FOX and ABC in ditching Nielsen's Live + Same Day TV ratings. *The Wrap*. www.thewrap.com/nbc-tv-ratings-live-same-day-stop-abc-fox/

Napoli, P. M. (2010). *Audience evolution: New technologies and the transformation of media audiences*. Columbia University Press.

NCTA. (n.d.). *Cable's story*. NCTA. www.ncta.com/cables-story

Nielsen (2017a, February). Nielsen announces MRC accreditation of Digital in TV Ratings. *Nielsen*. www.nielsen.com/us/en/press-releases/2017/nielsen-announces-mrc-accreditation-of-digital-in-tv-ratings/

Nielsen. (2017b, October 18). New Nielsen service shines a light on subscription-based streaming content consumption. *Nielsen*. https://ir.nielsen.com/news-events/press-releases/news-details/2017/New-Nielsen-Service-Shines-A-Light-On-Subscription-Based-Streaming-Content-Consumption/default.aspx

Nielsen. (2021a, April 22). *Nielsen doubles down on streaming, adds viewership by platform and advanced audience demographics* [Press release]. www.nielsen.com/us/en/press-releases/2021/nielsen-doubles-down-on-streaming-adds-viewership-by-platform-and-advanced-audience-demographics/

Nielsen. (2021b, September 21). *Nielsen announces 'impressions-first initiative' and the integration of broadband-only homes into local measurement in January 2022*. https://global.nielsen.com/news-center/2021/nielsen-announces-impressions-first-initiative-and-the-integration-of-broadband-only-homes-into-local-measurement-in-january-2022/

Nielsen. (2021c). *Nielsen ONE: Single cross-media currency*. www.nielsen.com/us/en/solutions/measurement/nielsen-one/

Nielsen. (n.d., a). Top 10: Discover what Americans are watching and playing. *Nielsen*. www.nielsen.com/top-ten/

Nielsen. (n.d., b). Digital Content Ratings. *Nielsen*. https://markets.nielsen.com/us/en/solutions/capabilities/digital-content-ratings/

Poggi, J. (2017, October 18). Nielsen says it can now measure Netflix streaming. *AdAge*. http://adage.com/article/media/nielsen-measures-netflix-streaming-real-time/310928/

Ramaswamy, A. (2008, December 30). Solving the content identification problem for digital TV. *SPIE*. https://spie.org/news/1344-solving-the-content-identification-problem-for-digital-tv?SSO=1

Ramaswamy, A. (2017). The big picture: Technology to meet the challenges of media fragmentation. *Nielsen Journal of Measurement, 1*(3), 1–8. www.nielsen. com/wp-content/uploads/sites/3/2019/04/the-big-picture-technology-to-meet-the-challenges-of-media-fragmentation.pdf

Schiff, A. (2022, January 5). Watchout, Nielsen ONE, Comscore is busily building a unified cross-platform measurement offering of its own. *AdExchange.* www. adexchanger.com/platforms/watch-out-nielsen-one-comscore-is-busily-building-a-unified-cross-platform-measurement-offering-of-its-own/

Tech-FAQ. (n.d.). *The history of satellite television.* www.tech-faq.com/history-of-satellite-television.html

Vinson, M. (2021a, April 26). Relative errors in television audience measurement: The future is now. [Blog]. *Comscore.* www.comscore.com/Insights/Blog/Relative-Errors-in-Television-Audience-Measurement-The-Future-is-Now

Vinson, M. (2021b, October 14). Media currencies: The past, present, and future. [Blog]. *Comscore.* www.comscore.com/Insights/Blog/Media-Currencies-The-Past-Present-and-Future

10 Audio analytics

As with the television industry, the radio industry has experienced disruptive change since the advent of broadband technology. "Audio" is now a more descriptive and inclusive term for the content we listen to on the various platforms and formats available, including streaming radio stations, streaming music services (such as Spotify, Pandora, and Apple Music), podcasting and other on-demand audio, as well as satellite and terrestrial radio. Add to these options new devices—like smart speakers—through which we can now enjoy audio content. Opportunities abound for consumers and content providers alike.

Despite many changes,[1] the audio medium continues to be a popular one for audiences. Even traditional AM/FM radio continues to reach more than 90% of the US population every week (The Nielsen Company, 2019). High penetration levels but also the intimacy and personalized nature of audio media may be what keep the trend lines increasing across all platforms. According to the 2019 Infinite Dial Report by Edison Research and Triton Digital, online audio listening in the United States continues to rise, with an estimated 60% of persons 12+ listening weekly (Edison Research & Triton Digital, 2019a). As of 2021, podcasts are being listened to by an estimated 41% of the US population aged 12+ each month (Triton Digital, 2021). And while younger listeners have certainly demonstrated their preferences for streaming and podcast listening options, terrestrial radio is not dead to them. Nielsen data show millennials were responsible for a surge in listening within the news radio format, with steady increases between 2015 and 2017 (Nielsen, 2017). The 2016 US election was one reason for such interest in news radio, but the younger demographics showed stronger growth than other segments.

Audio consumption and measurement today

Despite all of the technological change and new media platforms that have followed the development of radio, the audio industry has managed to

DOI: 10.4324/9780429506956-14

evolve alongside these new platforms. Audio remains alive and well, with US consumers listening to audio an average of four hours daily (Edison Research & Triton Digital, 2018). Eighty-one percent of US adults still tune in to AM/FM radio when in their car, despite the many other audio options available (Edison Research & Triton Digital, 2019a). After terrestrial radio, we tend to consume streamed audio and owned music, followed by services such as YouTube, satellite radio, TV music channels, and podcasts (Inside Radio, 2020b; see Figure 10.1). AM/FM radio listening is increasingly occurring through other means such as streaming,[2] which now makes up 12% of all AM/FM listening in the United States (Edison Research, 2021).

Online radio listening is at its highest level in recent years in the United States, with 169 million persons 12+ listening for an average of 16 hours and 43 minutes per week (Edison Research & Triton Digital, 2019a). Despite the many platforms and mobile devices available for consuming audio, most of us still turn to traditional AM/FM as our top choice for in-car listening, and, according to an Ipsos In-Car Audio Study (2015), 99% of us wouldn't change anything about how we operate the radio when in the car. Some mobile phones now come with a built-in FM tuner chip that can be activated with an app and that enables listening without the need of wi-fi or cell data service. Other FM listening apps are available with wi-fi or cell data service, including iHeartRadio ("You can use your smartphone," 2020). This has become an especially popular way to listen among

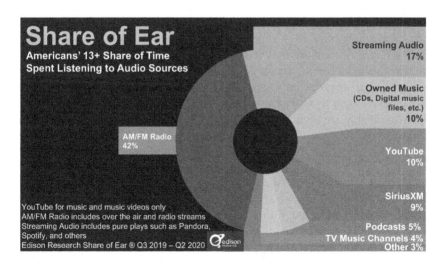

Figure 10.1 Share of Ear 2020

Source: Credit: Edison Research

smart speaker owners, with AM/FM radio listening making up nearly a quarter of all smart speaker listening time (Inside Radio, 2020a). Finally, other commercial audio networks exist to capture listeners during other parts of their day, providing background music when shopping in stores or when filling up with gas at the pump.

Now to the challenges of audio measurement today. How does the industry begin to measure all audio consumption in an equitable, accurate way, regardless of platform? What challenges do the issues associated with multiplatform audio measurement pose for the ability of producers to monetize audio content, including broadcasting, streaming, and podcasts? What constitutes "listening?" In the case of downloaded podcasts, how can companies know the content was in fact consumed? And was it consumed in its entirety? What are the implications of these measurement issues for the future of audio industry segments?

Total audience measurement

As noted elsewhere in this text, media content companies want *total audience measurement*. They want all of their listeners to count. They want to be able to receive credit for all listeners on all platforms—regardless of how segmented these platforms might be, now that digital platforms make *census-level* measurement possible. They want linear and nonlinear listening platforms aggregated to provide the whole picture with an entire accounting of their listenership. Total audience initiatives try to combine all streams, signals (HD and analog) and listening, no matter the platform, and integrate them into a single number that clients can look to in order to see that all listeners have been represented. Industry executives acknowledge that each type of measurement has its strengths and weaknesses but that the industry feels the tension, resistance, as well as the push and pull of linear and nonlinear approaches, depending on their companies' tradition. But overall, they seem to understand the need to integrate both approaches to better understand audiences across a given media entity's various platforms.

Integration of sample-based panels and census-based big data

Just because there are more data sources that can be measured does not mean they are all valid or clean sources. All data sources and methods have limitations, and these extend to the digital realm. With the availability of large datasets, *return path data* (such as the tuning data gathered via cable television set-top boxes), server, app-based measures such as those used in podcasting, and other external digitally generated sources come new limitations and issues that must be addressed. While the equivalent of set-top boxes does not yet exist in the audio realm except in a limited way through proprietary app-based audio players, the same concerns of census-based data sources do exist. Caution must be exercised when using all data and, even more so, when aggregating or integrating data from different sources.

Among the biggest observed shifts in audio measurement in recent years has been the move by some audience research companies from sample-based measurement panels (typically used for measurement of traditional or "legacy" broadcast listening) to census-based, or "counting," measurement (used within the digital realm because everything can be tracked). According to Larry Rosin, Cofounder and President of Edison Research, this may also be the most controversial change in audience measurement. Rosin notes the "push and pull" tension this has caused within the industry but says that each method has its advantages and can also maintain its position in certain ways. While more organizations are now "on board" or open to a census approach to measurement, Rosin says this change is happening slowly, and there is resistance because so much is at stake, particularly in terms of impact on advertising revenue (Chapters 2, 5). "It's the fear of change itself and what will be the impact of change," he says. When measurement technologies change, even as they may improve accuracy, some content providers are going to go up in ratings, while others will go down.

Trends in passive measurement

Digital measurement solutions, by their very nature, are more passive methods of data collection. *Cookies* and other digital tracking technologies record every mouse click, page view, and more, with no effort needed on the part of the digital content consumer. Whether listening to music online, scanning news content, or purchasing products from an online vendor, consumers' behaviors are tracked and noted passively, with nothing required of the consumer—except perhaps agreeing to a website's privacy policy or use of cookies, which, of course, most of us never read. Nevertheless, this passive approach to audience measurement results in higher accuracy than approaches that ask consumers to assist with the data collection or the recording of their media usage, for instance documenting listening habits in a weekly radio diary, pushing a button on a *People Meter* each time they enter a room to view TV, etc.

However, passive measurement is not exclusive to the digital realm. Arbitron, the company that dominated the audio measurement space prior to its acquisition by Nielsen in 2013, successfully developed its *Portable People Meter* (**PPM**) device several years ago. This device relied on a type of inaudible embedded coding technology called *psychoacoustic masking* as part of a signal encoding process (Buzzard, 2012; "Encoding for Ratings in the PPM World," 2007), so that all broadcast signals that had Arbitron's client identification codes embedded were able to be detected by the meter.

This process was not restricted to audio signals, and Nielsen is now using this device or a version of it (sometimes also referred to as the Personal People Meter) to measure video and out-of-home signals (Chapter 9). Passive measurement is a goal for measurement companies because, with the human element removed, it typically results in more accurate, higher quality data.

Measuring terrestrial radio

Let's take a closer look now at some common audio measurement approaches used today. Like other media platforms, the audio industry has had to evolve with new technologies and user habits, and the same is true for its measurement. As with video measurement, both panel measurement and census-based measurement are used, depending on what type of listening is being measured. Traditional or "terrestrial" radio (in which the radio signals are broadcast over the airwaves) is measured using a panel-based sample. Audio streams of terrestrial radio stations can also be measured this way (by utilizing the Portable People Meter worn by panelists), through a census-based approach or a combination of the two. Both approaches will be described here, but we begin with some terminology and tools for terrestrial, or broadcast, radio measurement.

Process and metrics

The process of measuring broadcast audio or radio audiences is similar to that for broadcast television audiences. The metrics and terminology used are also similar, so we refer readers to Chapters 8 and 9 for more detailed explanations, where these were first introduced. That being said, some metrics are used more frequently in radio listening compared to television viewing. *Cume* (short for cumulative listening), represents the number of unique (unduplicated) listeners within a given time period. While this metric certainly exists on the broadcast television side, it tends to be more used by broadcast radio. Similarly, *time spent listening (TSL)* is a valued metric for radio stations. It is essentially a measure of listener loyalty and represents the average number of hours or minutes listened to by the audience within a given time period. In addition, the geographic market area utilized for local radio measurement is much smaller than that for television and is known as the Metro Survey Area or Metropolitan Statistical Area (MSA, or *metro*), which stands for the US government's defined metropolitan areas.

Diaries

Diaries are the oldest data collection instrument for radio measurement. Most would agree it is also the form of measurement most subject to error, due to the level of active participation required of panelists. Participants are given paper booklets and asked to write down what they listen to during each quarter hour, including the station frequency and call letters. While diaries were retired by Nielsen for video audience data collection, they are still viewed to be a useful and practical solution for radio listening measurement, due to the different ways audiences consume radio compared to TV ("Why the ratings diary still works for radio," 2018). At this writing, these listener logs were still being used in more than 200 markets in the United States.

Nielsen Audio launched its "Continuous Diary Measurement" service in July 2019 in markets that were previously measured just four times yearly. The idea was that continuous diary measurement, monthly reporting, and three-month rolling averages within that reporting would not only provide greater stability in the ratings numbers and reduce the fluctuations that many stations observed when diaries were only administered a few times per year but that they would provide greater leverage for stations when negotiating advertising rates ("What continuous measurement means," 2019). Previously, small and midsize radio markets had to rely on delayed and less frequent reporting, which made it difficult to compete against advertisers like Facebook and Google, which provide immediate and real-time numbers. In addition, industry experts say, continuous measurement should allow a station to know much sooner whether a format change—such as a station converting from country music to a Top 40 format—has been effective rather than having to wait several months for ratings results ("What continuous measurement means," 2019). As of 2022, continuous diary measurement was being used in 44 US markets (Inside Radio, 2022).

Portable People Meter

As alluded to earlier, the Portable People Meter (PPM) was developed by Arbitron but is now used by Nielsen to measure local radio markets as well as television (Figure 10.2). It's a more sophisticated and accurate method for measuring listening habits than diaries. The PPM is a small wearable device that measures individual (not household) audio signal exposure, which includes passive listening, such as music one might be exposed to while walking through a shopping center, as well as active listening, such as that in the car or home. The PPM works by reading an inaudible embedded code that is carried within the content's audio signal. Nielsen clients place it there using an encoding device so that, whenever that signal is detected by the PPM, it will be counted as listening for that station. As also discussed in Chapter 9, the value of the PPM—along with its passive measurement approach—is that it works for both audio and video measurement, including cable, satellite, and digital. It is not just a measurement

Figure 10.2 Portable People Meter
Source: Credit: Dr. Amy Jo Coffey

solution for out-of-home listening and viewing (e.g., that which occurs in bars, airports, restaurants, etc.) but also a single-source solution for cross-platform measurement, something the industry has been seeking for years. Analysts and advertisers will be able to observe consumers' audio and video consumption habits together and extract valuable *insights* about their behaviors, which can provide valuable information for advertisers' cross-platform media campaigns. The new version of the PPM would have a companion mobile app that users would download to their smartphones and that would, with their cooperation, upload their media usage data to Nielsen.

Measuring streaming audio

Streaming audio refers to audio content delivered over the internet and can include music, news and information, and entertainment, including podcasts. Podcasts can be described as a type of streaming audio, which can be enjoyed live or downloaded as audio on demand. It is a digital audio file or series of files on some topic, like episodes of a program. Essentially, podcasting is a form of streaming audio, but not all streaming audio is a podcast. Streaming music services such as Pandora, Spotify, Apple Music, and others are yet another segment of the on-demand audio industry. Most streaming services collect their own listenership data from their servers and track their measurement this way. However, advertisers value third-party, independent measurement. Independent companies that measure streaming audio content, including podcasts, include Triton Digital, Edison Research, and Podtrac, among others. Triton Digital's Webcast Metrics platform, which is 100% census-based, has emerged as a popular independent metrics provider for measuring digital audio publishers and networks (online streaming audio) in the US digital audio industry. The company provides monthly rankings data through its monthly Rankers reports globally and for specific regions. Triton Digital's Webcast Metrics provides information such as *average active sessions, session starts, total listening hours*, and *cume*. Valid measurement for inclusion in audience reporting requires a listening duration of at least one minute (Triton Digital, 2022).

Webcast Metrics utilizes two methods of data collection to measure audio streams: (1) the raw log files of a network's streaming traffic, also known as a Content Delivery Network (CDN), or (2) a client-side approach referred to as *"listener tracking" (LT)* or the *"ping"* method, which gathers the data directly from the web-based player or mobile device (Triton Digital, 2022).[3] Nielsen Audio also measures listenership of on-demand audio, including podcasts, as well as the streamed signals of a terrestrial radio station known as a "stream." All are measured using a *software development kit (SDK)* within an app or player during listening (Nielsen, n.d.). This digital audio measurement may also include demographic data from Nielsen panels or from third-party data providers (Nielsen, n.d.). As noted by one audio industry executive, while Nielsen holds the technology necessary to produce a podcast listenership *currency* rating, as of this writing there was not yet sufficient participation from the industry side, to create a valid currency (Inside Radio, 2019a). As will be discussed later, the difficulty in measuring podcasts has to do with downloads, which do not necessarily result in actual listening.

Streaming audio is a component for most audio companies today, whether it be a terrestrial radio station that also streams its signals online or a pure-play streaming site like Pandora or Spotify. Some streaming audio services are advertising-supported, others are subscription-based, while still others are a hybrid model (e.g., freemium models, where the basic listening plan is free but contains advertising spots, while the premium version costs money but is ad-free). Many streaming companies subscribe to measurement firm services, such as those provided by Triton Digital ("Spotify does it again," 2018) and Nielsen. Companies such as Spotify and Pandora use digital ratings produced by Triton Digital to monitor their audience levels and growth. In addition, Nielsen also provides measurement of listenership on streaming services as well as advertising efficacy (Flynn, 2018).

Podcasting measurement

Increasing numbers of people are familiar with podcasting. More than half of US persons aged 12+ are estimated to have listened to a podcast at some point, and another 32% have listened to one in the past month (Edison

Research & Triton Digital, 2019b). A majority of this listening is happening on a smartphone or other mobile device (rather than a computer) and, perhaps surprising to many, the home is the most common location for listening to these podcasts. Ninety-three percent of listeners reported listening to the podcast episode in its entirety or "most" of the podcast (Edison Research & Triton Digital, 2019a). In terms of podcast publishers, NPR (formerly known as National Public Radio) is the industry leader, with eight of the top 20 podcasts in terms of rankings (National Public Media, 2017).

The current challenge for podcasters and marketers is that there is no official measurement currency for podcasts, such as a rating. Certainly there are tools that can measure the number of downloads or even live streams. However, podcasting, or any on-demand audio, presents a unique challenge because of the fact that it may get downloaded but not necessarily consumed at the same time. On-demand audio also can be circulated and shared with others. Thus measuring the actual podcasting audience is less of an exact science.

Metrics in development

But as podcasts grow in popularity with audiences, commercial media companies and advertisers are increasingly interested in monetization. Thus there is growing demand for detailed data regarding audience consumption and behavior. Metrics seem to be in development. Edison's Podcast Metrics offers a Top 50 quantitative ranking of podcasts based on actual listening behavior, along with demographic, psychographic, and consumer behavior data, informed via interviewing methods (Edison Research, 2022). Nielsen offered a qualitative measurement designed for advertisers (Inside Radio, 2019b). Another company, Podtrac, releases rankings of podcast publishers with audience consumption and behavior information and offers monthly audience estimates for listenership based on downloads and streams. The company claims to measure 90% of the United States' top podcast publishers (Podtrac, 2016). As a reminder, however, downloads are not a proxy for actual listenership. Podcast downloads may never be listened to, they might be partially listened to, or the files may be shared with others, resulting in potentially additional unknown listenership.

Podtrac uses a technologically based measurement approach, requiring podcasters to embed its proprietary measurement prefix in the podcast's URL (Podtrac, 2016). The embedded code allows Podtrac to log requests for the file from users. The requests are then cleaned to eliminate nonlistener requests such as those generated by bots, click fraud, or multiple requests from the same listener. This method generates data about the date and time of the file download, the country from which the download request originated, the type of device used to make the request, and the IP address that initiated the request. Podtrac then adjusts the data using a proprietary algorithm to account for multiple downloads through a single IP address, such as might occur because of an organizational firewall, and multiple downloads from a single user who puts the episode on multiple mobile devices.

Based on the data gathered using these methods, Podtrac then releases a number of metrics on podcasting, including unique downloads per individual podcast episode on a daily, weekly, monthly, or quarterly basis; global unique audience by show and publisher; show-level statistics; and publisher rankings (Podtrac, 2016).

Podtrac's white paper on its podcasting analytics methodology notes that, as with all research, its methods have numerous limitations (Podtrac, 2016). For example, IP addresses may not relate to the actual location of the individual downloading a file, which can skew data about the location of listeners. Only podcast publishers who embed Podtrac's measurement prefix into their podcast's URLs are included in the measurement, which means that the company's data are incomplete and it is not possible to know what proportion of the podcasting market is unmeasured. Play data on podcast episodes are largely unavailable because most commercial *podcatcher* software does not measure plays because of privacy concerns. Questions of whether listening occurs at the time of download or later and whether listeners *binge listen* are also unmeasured outside of focus groups. Podtrac's data also do not provide insights on listener demographics and psychographics.

Nielsen uses streaming measurement technology via a software development kit (SDK), which tracks actual listening and gathers general demographic data on podcast listeners through its Nielsen Scarborough subsidiary (Carman, 2019; Jacobs, 2016). In a new data gathering initiative, Nielsen Scarborough will be utilizing phone surveys to learn more about podcasting listeners and their consumption habits, including genre preferences and how long they listen (Carman, 2019).

In the absence of a podcasting currency, advertisers and other stakeholders have been patient, says Larry Rosin of Edison Research. He noted that podcasting is new and exciting and that, because advertisers are enamored with it, "they've been willing to accept certain general information and buy on that." But he added, while advertisers will tolerate this for a while, over time, "the big media buyers demand more precise information" and the industry will need to commit to some agreed-upon system. "It's not even so much that it has to be a perfect system—it's just important that it be agreed to and that everyone get on the same measurement system," Rosin says.

Voice assistants and smart speakers

One of the most recent audio consumption devices is the smart speaker, powered by a voice assistant platform (e.g., Amazon Alexa, Google

Assistant, Apple Siri, Microsoft Cortana, etc.), with one study reporting 21% of US homes having at least one smart speaker ("Exclusive," 2019) and another reporting consumer ownership at 36% (Abramovich, 2019). It has become an increasingly popular way for audiences to listen to their favorite music. Nearly half of online radio streaming still occurs on mobile devices, but streaming music on laptops and desktops has decreased. For some audio streaming companies like iHeartMedia, smart speaker listening has surpassed web listening. But thanks to the evolution of natural language processing, consumers are finding voice activation increasingly useful for their everyday lives, with top actions such as setting alarms, checking the weather and news, and getting directions and information already creating trend patterns (Abramovich, 2019). Consumers still tend to use the voice assistant on their mobile phones most, but the smart speaker comes in second.

New media devices need measurement, and smart (voice-activated) speakers are no exception. Sessions are measured, but so are actions such as *utterances* and responses. Brands considering developing a voice app should consider measuring the utterance or intent (what the consumer is asking for), the length of session, frequency of use, and *conversions* (Besik, 2019). Experts also caution that measurement of voice assistance should not occur within singular platforms or devices; in fact, the technology may have indirect benefits on other brand channels, as voice assistance and search can happen on home devices, smartphones, or other mobile devices where consumers may use the voice search feature. They use the example of shoppers' usage of smartphones and how they often pull it out to aid their experience while in-store (e.g., price comparisons, product availability by location), and how retailers initially failed to see "the impact of helping shoppers close the deal elsewhere" (Besik, 2019, para. 7), including with a competitor and/or placing an online order at home. Voice search is already being used by shoppers in ways similar to regular online search, using natural spoken language.

Digital Audio Standards

One existing challenge to both equitable measurement and monetization surrounds something the Media Rating Council (MRC) refers to as *Digital Audio Standards*. The US independent accreditation and auditing organization issued new digital measurement standards for video (Phase 1), which it hopes will serve as a framework of best practices for digital measurement, including audio, as the industry moves forward in the cross-media audience environment. A planned Phase II will further address the electronic measurement of "radio and digital audio combinations and comparisons" (Media Rating Council, 2019, p. 5).

As audio measurement standards evolve along with the technology platforms used for listenership, MRC executive director George Ivie noted that a primary concern held by the terrestrial radio broadcasters is maintaining trended, customary metrics such as the AQH (average quarter hour or 15-minute) rating. In order for a station to qualify for measurement inclusion for an AQH and receive listener credit, there is a so-called *five-minute qualifier rule*, meaning that if an audience member listened for at least five minutes, their data were included in the measurement sample with credit for that entire quarter hour (15 minutes). With digital audio services such as Pandora and Spotify, however, there is no such thing—or even a need—for a five-minute qualifier. Digital measurement, when properly instrumented, can track every second, every minute, or any denomination. This places the legacy (audio) broadcaster and digital camps at odds, Ivie says, because the MRC is essentially creating new metrics for the newer services. "The digital streaming services don't like it," Ivie says, "because I'm not allowing them comparable metrics with the legacy metrics of the broadcasters." And the broadcasters "don't like it because they're afraid it's going to erode their usage of AQH in their legacy media, which can be as much as 8–10% inflated" (due to the five-minute qualifier). In sum, Digital Audio Standards would not only level the playing field and make the existing competition even more visible, but it likely will eventually result in a drop in ratings for legacy audio, revealing listenership levels without the five-minute rule.

Definitional issues

As in the television or video industry, audio broadcasting has become a multiplatform environment, and definitional issues make measuring specific categories or platforms a unique challenge. As an example, we now speak of the audio industry rather than radio because audio better captures the many ways that a traditional radio broadcaster might disseminate its signals (terrestrial over-the-air signal, HD signals, online streams, podcasts or on-demand audio files), not to mention other audio content providers such as satellite radio and streaming services including Pandora, Spotify, iHeartMedia, iTunes, and the like. Due to their multiplatform offerings, many traditional broadcasters today can be considered digital publishers, just as any pure play site may be. It is increasingly unlikely that a radio broadcaster only provides an over-the-air signal. "Our definition of what radio means has to expand," says Futuri Media's Daniel Anstandig. "It's much more sophisticated and complex now."

One additional definitional issue that affects measurement is the definition of a podcast. Because many podcasts are downloadable on-demand files or streams, some industry authorities use the term *on-demand audio* instead of podcast. However, many say podcasting is just one segment within the larger on-demand audio market. Because of this evolving definition of what the podcasting market really comprises, podcast measurement is still in its early stages. To be precise, "there is no podcasting currency," states Larry Rosin of Edison Research, saying that it really comes down to "did people hear the commercials?"

Summary and conclusion

Audio consumption behavior continues to thrive despite the technological evolution of this media sector. As with the video measurement industry, audio measurement is in flux. Traditional measurement approaches and tools are no longer sufficient as the audio industry also strives for total audience measurement, which requires the integration of sample panel-based and census-based systems. As the challenges noted here illustrate, this is a complex undertaking with many stakeholders. We can expect the evolution of audio consumption and measurement to continue as the adoption of new audio technology grows.

Additional resources

Nielsen Audio: https://global.nielsen.com/solutions/audience-measurement/audio/
Triton Digital: www.tritondigital.com/
Podtrac: https://analytics.podtrac.com/
Edison Research: www.edisonresearch.com/
Historical overview of broadcast industry measurement (and other topics):
Webster, J., Phalen, P., & Lichty, L. (2014). *Ratings analysis: Audience measurement and analytics* (4th ed.). Routledge.

Recommended cases

These cases can be found on the textbook website:
www.routledge.com/cw/hollifield

Case 10.1: Analyzing Radio Ratings
Case 10.2 (14.4): Evaluating a News Podcast Launch
Case 10.3: Local Radio Opportunities
Case 10.4 (2.4): Calculating the Revenue Potential of a News Podcast

Case studies, along with accompanying datasets for this chapter, can be found on the text website. We particularly suggest the preceding cases in the order listed. See the companion website and instructor's manual for detailed descriptions of these and other relevant cases.

Discussion questions and exercises

1. Why do you think broadcast radio stations have continued to survive all of the audio marketplace changes over the years? What is your prognosis for the future?
2. What are some of the current challenges surrounding measurement in the audio environment, and why?
3. Who are all of the stakeholders involved in the quest for total audience measurement in the audio industry today? What interest does each stakeholder have, and why? How does their interest relate to their own financial success?
4. Related to Question 3, audio industry leaders don't all agree on changes to measurement processes and standards, even when the changes might result in greater measurement accuracy. Why is this? What's at stake for terrestrial stations if the traditional system of AQH measurement goes away? (If this system has disappeared by the time you read this, what were the consequences and for whom? What other areas of contention do you anticipate within the audio industry in the future?)
5. If you were to enter the audio media marketplace right now as a young entrepreneur, what sector would you choose, and why?

6. *Exercise: Radio station ratings*
   Refer to Table 10.1, along with the line graph based upon the data (Figure 10.3). They display estimates of audience share for Radioville, USA, radio stations (hypothetical city and data). Take a few minutes to examine the trends and patterns, along with the information in the table. Then, answer the questions that follow.

   a. Which station has the highest AQH share overall for the time period (August previous year–July current year)? Which station has the second highest? Do the first- and second-place stations ever change places?
   b. What format are these top stations? Why do think that might be?
   c. Which stations seem to be in closest competition with one another? Why did you draw the conclusion you did? Explain in detail.
   d. Are there any interesting patterns you see in the graph? What might some potential explanations be for these patterns?
   e. Look specifically at stations that share the same format. How do their audience share data and trend lines compare? What might some potential explanations be for the patterns you see? What might some stations of the same format do to compete with one another

Table 10.1 Radio Station Share Estimates for Radioville*

Station	Format	July (Yr 2)	June (Yr 2)	May (Yr 2)	Apr. (Yr 2)	Mar. (Yr 2)	Feb. (Yr 2)	Jan. (Yr 2)	Dec. (Yr 1)	Nov. (Yr 1)	Oct. (Yr 1)	Sept. (Yr 1)	Aug. (Yr 1)
AAAA-FM	News Talk Information	4.3	4.2	4.4	4.4	4.5	4.6	4.6	4.4	4.6	3.7	4.7	3.5
BBBB-AM	News Talk Information	3.5	3	3.2	3.3	3.5	3.5	3.4	3.2	3.3	3.3	3.3	3.3
CCCC-FM	Sports Talk	2.9	3	3.1	3.2	3.4	3.5	3.8	3.9	4	3.8	3.6	3.2
DDDD-FM	Pop Contemporary Hits	4.4	4.5	4.5	4.6	4.7	4.7	4.6	4.5	4.6	4.7	4.8	4.7
EEEE-FM	Country	4.9	4.9	4.9	4.8	4.8	4.7	4.7	4.5	4.6	4.7	4.6	4.7
FFFF-FM	Country	5.2	5.1	5.3	5.4	5.4	5.5	5.3	5.1	5.4	5.5	5.5	5.4

*Hypothetical stations and data. AQH share for all persons aged 12+ (total day averages).

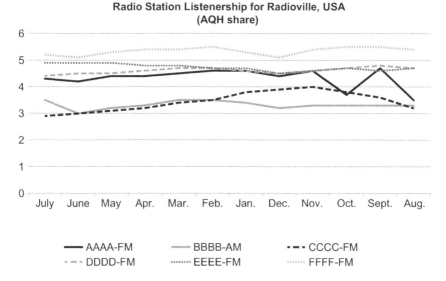

Figure 10.3 Radio station listenership for Radioville, USA

and sway listeners to their station and away from their competitors'? You may wish to do some research on your own or discuss with classmates.

f. While these are hypothetical data representing a fictional metropolitan area in the United States, see if you can do some research for your own home market. Radio listenership data may be available online or through other sources. What can you learn about audience listening habits, trends, and patterns where you live?

7. *Exercise: Developing a new audio metric for the industry*
You have been hired by a start-up media measurement company that wants to try to establish a new industry metric that would provide total audience measurement for the audio sector. The goal is to include all listening audiences, whether terrestrial radio stations or streaming services, live listening and on-demand, including podcasts. How would you do this? Based on your reading of this chapter, what would you need to consider? What steps would you follow to undertake this process? What standards would you follow or establish? Create a one-page outline explaining the issues and standards that must be taken into consideration, as well as the process you would follow to try to develop this new total audio audience metric that could be used by the entire industry.

Notes

1. For a detailed history about audio measurement and other topics, see the Additional Resources section of the textbook website.
2. As a reminder, streaming refers to content distributed over the internet, also known as over-the-top (OTT).
3. A detailed description of this methodology can be found at https://userguides. tritondigital.com/mea/domwcm/index.html

References

Abramovich, G. (2019, February 26). Voice ads are more engaging than other formats, consumers say. *Adobe Blog.* https://blog.adobe.com/en/publish/2019/02/19/adobe-voice-report-feb19

Besik, H. (2019, May 14). 91% of brands are investing in voice: How to make it work. *Adobe Blog.* https://theblog.adobe.com/91-of-brands-are-investing-in-voice-how-to-make-it-work/

Buzzard, K. (2012). *Tracking the audience: The ratings industry from analog to digital.* Routledge.

Carman, A. (2019, July 11). Podcasters need listening data, so Nielsen is going to call people's homes to ask for it. *The Verge.* www.theverge.com/2019/7/11/20689096/podcast-nielsen-scarborough-listener-data

Edison Research. (2021, August 24). *Streaming now accounts for 12% of AM/FM listening in the U.S.* [Blog]. www.edisonresearch.com/streaming-now-accounts-for-12-of-am-fm-radio-listening-in-the-u-s/

Edison Research. (2022, May 10). *The top 50 most listened to podcasts in the U.S. Q1 2022.* www.edisonresearch.com/the-top-50-most-listened-to-podcasts-in-the-u-s-q1-2022/

Edison Research, & Triton Digital. (2018). *The podcast consumer 2018.* https://info.tritondigital.com/hubfs/The_Podcast_Consumer_%202018.pdf

Edison Research, & Triton Digital. (2019a). *The infinite dial 2019.* www.edisonresearch.com/wp-content/uploads/2019/03/Infinite-Dial-2019-PDF-1.pdf

Edison Research & Triton Digital. (2019b). *The podcast consumer 2019.* www.edisonresearch.com/wp-content/uploads/2019/04/Edison-Research-Podcast-Consumer-2019.pdf

Encoding for ratings in the PPM world. (2007, March 13). *Radioworld.* www.radioworld.com/columns-and-views/encoding-for-ratings-in-the-ppm-world

Exclusive: New data shows radio listening on smart speakers has doubled. (2019, March 4). *Inside Radio.* www.insideradio.com/new-data-shows-radio-listening-on-smart-speakers-has-doubled/article_00f00dea-3e4d-11e9-9e94-07916bec3a60.html

Flynn, K. (2018, September 11). 'The industry is demanding it:' Spotify adopts Nielsen Brand Effect for verification on ad platform. *Digiday.* https://digiday.com/marketing/industry-demanding-spotify-adopts-nielsen-brand-effect-verification-ad-platform/

Inside Radio. (2019a, April 30). Edison moves podcasting a step closer to quarterly ratings. *Inside Radio.* www.insideradio.com/free/edison-moves-podcasting-

a-step-closer-to-quarterly-ratings/article_232294b2-6b13-11e9-997c-8760b78
60878.html

Inside Radio. (2019b, July 10). Nielsen launches qualitative podcast measurement service. *Inside Radio.* www.insideradio.com/nielsen-launches-qualitative-podcast-measurement-service/article_7651340a-a2da-11e9-bdc6-334f326b2b11.html

Inside Radio. (2020a, January 24). AM/FM's share of smart speaker audio listening climbs to 24%. *Inside Radio.* www.insideradio.com/am-fm-s-share-of-smart-speaker-audio-listening-climbs-to-24/article_e6d923b0-3e8c-11ea-90a8-13730caaa9ba.html

Inside Radio. (2020b, August 31). AM/FM radio still has biggest 'share of ear,' according to Edison data. *Inside Radio.* www.insideradio.com/free/am-fm-radio-still-has-biggest-share-of-ear-according-to-edison-data/article_9e09f674-e8ea-11ea-8219-27b9a71011b4.html

Inside Radio. (2022, August 23). Office listening trended higher during second quarter in CDM markets. *Inside Radio.* www.insideradio.com/free/office-listening-trended-higher-during-second-quarter-in-cdm-markets/article_6b24f748-22a6-11ed-84d0-573ffb6f7837.html

Ipsos. (2015). *Ipsos in-car audio study.* www.rab.com/whyRadio/iHeartIpsosInCarStudy.pdf

Jacobs, F. (2016, February 12). Rob Kass: 5 things every radio professional should know about Nielsen's SDK. *Jacobs Media Strategies.* https://jacobsmedia.com/rob-kass-5-things-every-radio-professional-should-know-about-nielsens-sdk/

Media Rating Council. (2019, September). *MRC cross-media audience measurement standards (Phase I Video).* www.mediaratingcouncil.org/MRC%20Cross-Media%20Audience%20Measurement%20Standards%20(Phase%20I%20Video)%20Final.pdf

National Public Media. (2017). *NPR podcasts: On-demand listening, unparalleled engagement.* https://careersdocbox.com/73047080-Career_Advice/Npr-podcasts-on-demand-listening-unparalleled-engagement.html

Nielsen. (2017). *Young listeners are driving the surge in news radio listening.* www.nielsen.com/insights/2017/young-listeners-are-driving-the-surge-in-news-radio-listening/

Nielsen. (n.d.). *Nielsen audio.* www.nielsen.com/us/en/solutions/capabilities/audio/

The Nielsen Company. (June 2019). *Audio today 2019: How America listens.* https://worldradiohistory.com/Archive-Arbitron/Archive-Arbitron-Radio-Today/Audio-Today-2019.pdf

Podtrac. (2016, May 24). *Podtrac releases the podcast industry's first rankings* [Press release]. http://analytics.podtrac.com/press/podtrac-launches-the-first-podcast-industry-rankings

Spotify does it again, topping Pandora in Triton ratings. (2018, September 17). *Inside Radio.* www.insideradio.com/free/spotify-does-it-again-topping-pandora-in-triton-ratings/article_fc260d4e-ba4b-11e8-b336-83c7fb8dd2e4.html

Triton Digital. (2021). *The podcast data kit.* https://info.tritondigital.com/hubfs/Podcast_DataKit%202021_US.pdf

Triton Digital. (2022). *DOM: Webcast metrics & webcast metrics local.* https://userguides.tritondigital.com/mea/domwcm/index.html

What continuous measurement means for diary markets. (2019, February 11). *Inside Radio.* www.insideradio.com/free/what-continuous-measurement-means-for-diary-markets/article_8b984838-2dca-11e9-92e3-e716d9dd1002.html

Why the ratings diary still works for radio. (2018, December 10). *Inside Radio.* www.insideradio.com/free/why-the-ratings-diary-still-works-for-radio/article_9152c034-fc4a-11e8-b59f-b78c9eb36dda.html

You can use your smartphone to listen to FM radio even when offline. (2020, February 6). *Tampa Bay Newswire.* www.tampabaynewswire.com/2020/02/06/you-can-use-your-smartphone-to-listen-to-fm-radio-even-while-offline-83939

11 Publishing analytics

Media analytics were born in the publications industries, and those sectors still invest heavily in audience and advertising research. At the end of the 19th century, the mass production of goods made it necessary for manufacturers to advertise their goods widely. Advertising agencies sprang up to create marketing messages for those manufacturers, and publications—which until then had mostly depended for revenue on direct sales to readers—became the vehicle for delivering manufacturers' advertising to consumers. At that point, of course, broadcasting didn't exist, and film was, at best, in its infancy. So publications were the only vehicle available to widely distribute advertising.

To advertisers and their advertising agencies, the value of placing an ad in a particular publication was determined by the size of the publication's audience (Chapter 5). But circulation numbers were proprietary business information, and publishers were generally unwilling to share that business intelligence (Bennett, 1965). Additionally, some publications inflated their circulation numbers. Poor record keeping by publications and the lack of common definitions, terms, and measurement practices across the industry created confusion and distrust among advertisers, agencies, and publishers. With no agreed-upon standards for measuring circulation and no means of verifying publishers' claims about circulation size, the market for buying and selling advertising was chaotic.

In 1914, a group of advertisers, advertising agencies, and publishers in the United States and Canada banded together to create a nonprofit, membership-based cooperative to provide reliable measurements of publications' circulations (Bennett, 1965). The organization, an effort at industry self-regulation, was named the Audit Bureau of Circulations (ABC). Publishers that joined the ABC gained a competitive advantage by being able to offer advertisers reliable circulation data as the basis of their advertising prices.

In 2012, ABC changed its name to the Alliance for Audited Media (AAM). The goal of the rebranding was to reflect the changed nature of

DOI: 10.4324/9780429506956-15

ABC member organizations, most of which were now multiplatform content companies. AAM continues to provide verified circulation audits, digital and cross media audience audits, digital platform certifications, analysis of third-party web metrics, and verification services designed to identify ad fraud and other technology-enabled distortions that have become common in global advertising markets.

While ABC's—now AAM's—original mission was providing trusted circulation data, the scope of research employed by publishers has expanded dramatically. Publishers now use media analytics to pursue much deeper understandings of their audiences and advertisers.

The state of publishing industries

In the 21st century, many people, particularly younger people, have viewed traditional print media—magazines, books, journals, and newspapers—as media dinosaurs, destined for extinction in the digital age. Indeed, print media have been hit harder by digital disruption than other media sectors. The high costs of paper, ink, and four-color high-speed printing presses make the per-unit production costs of print products much higher than for other media, while the physical nature of books, newspapers, and periodicals creates high storage and distribution costs. Thus publishing companies tend to have smaller profit margins to cushion them during periods of market turmoil.

Nevertheless, those who predicted publications would disappear entirely were wrong. If it happens, it won't be soon. Industry data make that clear.

In 2021, book publishing globally was estimated to be a more than a US $109 billion industry, with almost 41,000 publishing firms operating worldwide, employing nearly 300,000 people (IBISWorld, 2021). In the United States, the book industry generated nearly $26 billion in revenue in 2020, with 77% of US adults reporting in 2021 that they had read at least one book in the previous year and 18% reporting they had read 20 or more (Watson, 2021b).

In 2022, 7,416 consumer magazines were being published in the United States in both print and digital formats, a new high for the industry (Watson, 2021a). The estimated number of consumer magazine readers was 220 million, a number that had been stable for more than five years (Watson, 2022b). There remained more print consumer magazines circulating than digital editions, but the number of digital titles was growing, as was the revenue those titles generated (Watson, 2022a).

Academic and professional journals publish peer-reviewed scientific and academic research to a global audience. According to the International Association of Scientific, Technical and Medical Publishers (STM), in 2018, approximately 33,100 active English-language peer-reviewed journals were being published globally, with another 9,400 published in languages other than English (Johnson et al., 2018).[1] The industry employed more than 100,000 people worldwide, with English-language STM journals alone generating more than $10 billion in 2017.

In contrast to the book and periodical publishing industries, the newspaper sector of publications is unquestionably declining. In the United States, more than 1,800 local daily and weekly newspapers have closed since 2004 (Abernathy, 2022; Levin, 2019). Advertising revenue in local newspapers also has fallen sharply, and 2020 was the first year that total circulation revenue surpassed total advertising revenue for local newspapers (Matsa & Worden, 2022). At the same time, newspaper readers continue to shift their consumption from print to digital editions.

The handful of large national newspapers in the United States have fared better than smaller local and regional papers, with some indications that digital subscriptions at the major newspapers are growing steadily (Pew Research Center, 2021). However, total employment in the newspaper sector continues to decline (Walker & Matsa, 2021), and the newspaper industry's struggles in the United States are mirrored elsewhere around the world.

One trend that appears clear in the publishing industries is a slow migration among readers from paper to digital editions. Many print media companies have pivoted to include digital and multimedia content among their products and now offer content through multiple formats, including print. But experience has shown some content—particularly material heavily dependent on photographs and graphics—is less user-friendly in digital formats, leading readers to reject digital versions. Furthermore, frequent changes in digital hardware, software, and search engines can quickly render digital content from past years inaccessible. High-value content that an individual or society wishes to keep long-term is more safely stored in print. Finally, publications always have been a mobile medium—and one that is both electricity- and battery-free—something no other medium can boast. These factors continue to create consumer demand—and media analytics jobs—in the traditional publications industries.

Even so, the publishing industries have probably changed more dramatically in the past generation than at any time since the printing press was invented 600 years ago. Publishers must rethink their relationships with audiences and advertisers in the digital age and innovate new ways to provide value to those stakeholders.

Media analysts stand at the heart of those efforts. It is through research that the publishing industries that have provided the world's news, information, education, and entertainment for centuries are finding their paths into the future.

Publishing industry metrics

In publishing industries, the metric that matters most is *circulation*. "Circulation" is the general term for the number of people who read each edition of the publication. In the days when publications were distributed only on paper, calculating circulation should have been easy. Just count the number of copies of an edition that were printed and subtract the number that were still unsold when the next edition went to press. Voila! The difference would be your circulation, right?

But, of course, it was never that easy, and it's gotten much harder now that most publications also have growing digital readership. The AAM is the oversight body that defines the metrics used to measure circulation and confirms that member publications are using those metrics correctly. Measuring circulation for publications—and for so many different *types* of publications, serving so many different types of audiences across multiple platforms—is extremely complex. Consequently, the AAM has developed *pages* of definitions of the metrics required to measure audience size for each type of publication it audits. While there is some overlap on key terms, there are many critical differences because of the different marketing and distribution strategies different types of publications use to reach their target audiences. See Box 11.1. It would be impossible to cover all of the important terms here. But to provide examples, just a few of the key metrics are included, with their definitions abbreviated and paraphrased.

Box 11.1 Examples of circulation metrics for publishing industries

Term	Definition/notes	Publishing sector
Paid circulation	Size of the audience paying to acquire a publication. Generally defined as copies of a publication sold through subscriptions and single-copy sales for a price of at least US 1 cent and not for purposes of resale.	News media, consumer magazines
Qualified nonpaid circulation	Copies of a publication distributed to consumers without charge such as copies requested for distribution in business lobbies or given to students for educational use, but in compliance with AAM rules.	News media, consumer magazines

Term	Definition/notes	Publishing sector
Total average circulation—print and digital	The size of a publication's total qualified paid and nonpaid audience across all platforms.	News media
Analyzed nonpaid bulk circulation	Copies delivered in bulk to specific locations for redistribution to unknown readers.	Consumer magazines
Verified subscriptions	Subscription copies the publisher designates to be read in public places or intended for individual use by recipients who are likely to be very interested in the content, with or without payment.	Consumer magazines
Print/digital unduplicated circulation	When a reader gets both the print and digital editions of a publication, it is reported in this category and not in either print or digital.	B2B publications
Qualified paid association circulation	When readers get the publication as part of membership in professional associations/organizations, regardless of whether the subscription is deductible from members' dues, but at least US 1 cent of the dues must go to the publication and members must be told of the value of the publication.	B2B publications

Source: Alliance for Audited Media (2022); definitions edited for length and clarity for nonspecialists; used only as examples

Box 11.1 shows just a few examples of the metrics AAM has had to develop in order to help publishers accurately and consistently measure circulation across a wide range of publications, platforms, and business and distribution models. They are paraphrased here to show how complicated accurately measuring circulation is in the digital age and across so many different kinds of publications. But without such detailed definitions, advertisers would have no better idea of what circulation numbers represent in terms of the size of the audiences actually reached than was possible in 1913, before the ABC was established and the media analytics industry was born.

Publishing sectors

The book industry

The book industry is the oldest form of printed media still in use today, long predating the invention of the printing press. Revenue in the book industry comes almost entirely from direct sales, with advertising playing almost no role in book publishers' revenue models. As with other traditional publications, the industry has been revolutionized by the digital age, with books now being produced in multiple formats. Print, digital text for consumption on e-readers and other digital devices, and audio books are among the primary distribution formats today.

In developed countries such as those found in North America and Western Europe, demand for books remains strong as measured by the number of books sold, but the industry is considered largely mature. Industry analysts believe the global market for books will continue to grow for the foreseeable future as literacy rates rise in less developed countries. But again, the shift from print to less expensive digital formats will undercut revenue growth.

Book publishing has been somewhat slower than other sectors to embrace media analytics as a management tool for a number of reasons. Book publishing is an old and deeply traditional industry. Book industry professionals value the creative aspects of their medium and respect the ability of talented editors to "know" through instinct and experience what will succeed with readers. Because creativity is, by definition, not predictable and because what succeeds in cultural industries is always subject to the trends and tastes of the moment, traditionalists argue media analytics has little to contribute to book publishing. Finally, as one of the few media sectors that does not depend on advertising for revenue, the industry has never faced demands from advertisers for verifiable audience numbers.

Nevertheless, as long-term revenue growth slows and reading formats change, large publishing houses are increasingly turning to data analytics to improve company performance. Thus there are growing career opportunities for book-loving media analysts.

The structure of the book publishing industry

The first step to landing a job in any industry is to understand that industry. The book publishing industry is divided into industry sectors based on the types of books a company publishes, with most publishing companies specializing in a content category. More than half of all books sold in the English language are what are known as "trade publishing" books, which are produced for the general public. These include nonfiction and fiction books in a wide range of popular reading genres. Generally, most of the books found in bookstores fall into the trade publishing category.

Within the trade publishing categories are numerous subcategories. Fiction is subdivided into categories such as romance, crime/mystery, classic literature, and science fiction/fantasy, among others. Nonfiction trade publishing is subdivided into categories such as history, current affairs, politics, self-help, health and wellness, etc. All of those categories are then further subdivided into more specific groupings for industry tracking purposes. Because the trade publishing category is so large, some trade publishers may focus on specific content sectors within the broader trade publishing category.

In addition to trade publishing, another book publishing category is the "children and young adult" sector, which focuses on age-appropriate content for younger readers. There also is professional, technical and scholarly publishing, which focuses on books related to business, professional and industry subjects, and educational publishing, which provides textbooks, scholarly books, and other resources to students and teachers across all educational levels. Those are just of the few of the publishing categories used by the industry.

Understanding book audiences

After thousands of years in which book production involved putting ink on paper, digital technologies have revolutionized the industry. Today, one of the most important questions analysts and publishers ask is what format readers are most likely to use to read specific types of books. Print, e-books, and audiobooks are the industry's three primary distribution platforms. Analysts carefully track which formats are growing or shrinking in popularity as reading platforms—and for what types of books.

Questions focus not just on the book format but also on the reader's technology of choice for accessing that format. When consuming books in print, do audiences buy more hardbacks or paperbacks? With digital text, are readers more likely to use e-readers, tablets, laptops, or desktop computers for reading? With audiobooks, are more people listening on their phones, on their tablets, on MP3 players, smart speakers, or some other audio technology? And where do most users listen to audiobooks? In their cars? At home? While out of house? If they're listening to books, are they doing something else at the same time? Driving? Exercising? Walking the dog? Cooking? The questions of when, where, and how readers consume different types of books are key to understanding trends in reader preferences and the reader experience.

Analysts also closely study audience characteristics. Who reads books? What genders, ages, ethnicities, educational levels, and income levels read what types of books on what platforms? What motivates people to read books, particularly given that, on average, an individual book carries a higher time cost of consumption (Chapter 2) than individual pieces of content in any other medium? What are the reading trends related to specific types of audiences?

Another key metric for the book industry, particularly in trade publishing, is the relative success of specific authors. Each author's global sales are carefully tracked by country and by other key *variables*. Book publishers also track how book sales are affected by changing patterns of audience demand and consumption of other types of media content. For example, a slow decline in reader demand for novels and short stories through the second decade of the 21st century, even as total book readership was otherwise growing, may reflect the impact of streaming services (Perry, 2019).

Because book publishers depend on direct sales, and printed books still outsell digital formats (Faverio & Perrin, 2022), book analysts track where readers buy books and how points of purchase may change over time. Important sales outlets for book publishers include large chain bookstores, independent bookstores, supermarkets, airports, big box stores, department stores, convenience stores, general merchandise stores, online sellers, and libraries. Particularly for professional, technical and scholarly, and educational publishing companies, book sales to university and public libraries are a critical metric. Similarly, because media content is rarely consumed by any consumer more than once (Priest, 1994), the sale of used books is a significant source of competition for book publishers, particularly textbook publishers.

Marketing is another key area for analysts. Understanding the effectiveness of different marketing approaches and the timing of marketing efforts is critical since publishers live on direct sales.

An analyst for a trade publisher might look at how different advertisements for an upcoming new work of fiction affected its preorders and sales over the first months after release and how that compared to the effectiveness of advertising for a new nonfiction release. Another question would be how much reviews of a book drove sales—and whether it mattered who reviewed the book, where the reviews appeared, or whether particular reviews were positive or negative. How long after a book's release do sales peak, and is that projected sales timeline different for different genres or with different marketing and promotion techniques? How do book tours and authors' media appearances affect sales? How does a book's cover art affect sales?

In contrast, an analyst for an educational publisher might look at how and when the publisher releases a new catalog of its books affects sales of the titles included in that catalog—and the sales of the titles that were not included. How does a book's cover art, description, or endorsements in the catalog relate to sales? Above all, what can a publisher do to improve the discoverability of specific titles by potential buyers?

Analysts in the book industry also study production processes in the search for greater efficiency and cost control. Efficiency questions include such things as whether the amount of time and effort invested in the production process affects sales. If a publisher spends more time and money perfecting the copyediting of a book, does that investment pay for itself? Or would it be more profitable to release a less perfectly edited title? Is the company producing the right number of print copies, or are unsold printed copies taking up warehouse space and for how long? Increasingly, analysts also are being asked to engage questions about how publishers can operate in a more environmentally sound manner and reduce a publishing company's carbon footprint.

In the end, analysts in the book industry focus on trying to help editors figure out what questions they need to be asking as they select books for production and work with authors, production staff, and marketing staff. They're always trying to predict what is likely to happen in terms of topics, technology trends, and changes in readers' tastes. Although the book industry is rarely seen as a major player in the media analytics game, there are careers to be had in what remains a growth media industry globally.

The newspaper industry

The newspaper industry is another major sector of the publishing industries, one that has existed in various forms since the printing press was invented. Globally, there is a great deal of variation in how the newspaper industry is structured. In some countries, newspapers are national news organs in both focus and distribution. In other countries, most newspapers are national, supplemented by a few smaller newspapers that cover specific regions. In some geographically large countries, including the United States, newspapers are primarily local news providers, with a handful of big city newspapers covering both local and regional news, daily newspapers in most small and midsize cities, weekly newspapers serving small towns and rural counties, and only two or three entirely "national" newspapers.

There is also variety in newspaper industry revenue models globally. In the United States and many other Western countries, newspapers are an entirely commercial for-profit industry that receives no public subsidies. Traditionally, the US industry received approximately 60% of its revenues from advertising and 40% from subscriptions and single-copy sales, although those percentages began shifting in the first years of the 21st century because of digital disruption. In some countries, such as China, most general-interest newspapers are government controlled and partially subsidized, while still expected to sell subscriptions and advertising. Finally, other countries, such as Egypt, have hybrid newspaper ecosystems. Some newspapers receive government subsidies, while others operate as privately owned, commercial businesses.

There also are many different types of newspapers. In some countries, there are niche newspapers that cover only business or entertainment in a community or that report stories for a particular ethnic or cultural community. Then there are hyperlocal newspapers that report for only specific sections or neighborhoods in a community. Hyperlocal newspapers often are *free circulation*, with 100% of their revenue coming from small local advertisers, who can't afford to buy ads in larger circulation daily newspapers or on radio or TV. In return, the papers are distributed free to 100% of the residents in the paper's target geographic area, giving advertisers broad reach to their most likely customers.

A large percentage, perhaps the majority, of newspapers today also are multiplatform, producing news both in traditional ink-on-paper formats as well as online. Printing and distributing paper copies of newspapers is considerably more expensive than producing digital content. But many newspapers' most loyal subscribers still prefer to receive paper copies, particularly in countries with limited internet infrastructure or high data costs. Perhaps even more importantly, unlimited digital advertising space drives down online advertising prices, while digital platforms such as Google and Facebook capture much of the revenue from the advertising that appears online around newspaper content. Thus print copies of newspapers remain a critical source of revenue for newspaper organizations.

Nevertheless, the newspaper industry is the media sector that probably has been most disrupted by digital technologies. Newspaper failures are creating *news deserts*, that is, communities and regions with no independent journalism to serve as watchdogs on local government and business and to keep residents informed about local issues and concerns (Abernathy, 2022; Levin, 2019). This is a major problem for societies because high-quality journalism is a necessary condition for governments and businesses to be transparent and uncorrupted, for government systems to be democratic and inclusive, for human rights to be protected, and for businesses and consumers to have access to the information they need to support economic development (Cauhapé-Cazaux & Kalathil, 2015; Hollifield et al., 2005; Islam, 2002; Priest, 1994). Nor does the prevalence of online information sources fill the local information deserts historically filled by newspapers. A 2010 study found 95% of the news stories that moved online in a major US city were reported and written by traditional news media—with the majority of them coming from the local daily newspaper (Pew Research Center, 2010). Historically, newspapers have had more resources than broadcasters to devote to the in-depth investigative reporting that has major societal impact.

Although some argue that the newspaper industry eventually will disappear, in fact there are some positive signs for the sector. Major newspapers are seeing subscription numbers growing as they establish digital paywalls and create user-friendly digital apps. The key to newspaper survival will be a deep understanding of readers' and advertisers' needs and behaviors. Consequently, newspapers are turning now, more than ever, to research and media analytics.

The questions driving researchers and analysts in the newspaper industry fall under the category of "News Analytics." Chapter 14 in this text focuses entirely on those issues.

The periodicals industries

Periodical publishing is a multifaceted industry with at least two distinct sectors where media analysts play important roles: magazines and academic/professional journals. While different, both sectors produce fact- or information-based publications traditionally distributed in print on a regular but less than daily basis.

Periodicals have been tremendously influential throughout their history. They shape cultural trends in fashion, art, music, cuisine, and myriad other aspects of lifestyle and culture, and they drive progress in business, industry, science, medicine, the social sciences, and the humanities. A truly global media industry, many periodical titles are distributed worldwide. Let's look at each sector and its use of analytics.

Consumer magazines

The magazine industry has a long history. It emerged in the United States at least as early as the mid-1700s (Noam, 2009) and probably even earlier elsewhere. Thousands of popular magazine titles are published across an enormous range of topics and interests. A *lifestyle medium*, consumer magazines typically offer audiences highly specialized, in-depth niche content tailored to specific interests—news, sports, fashion, travel, cuisine, or specific hobbies.

Historically, the magazine industry has been fairly competitive because the entry costs of starting a publication are relatively low (Noam, 2009). Nevertheless, a few large media corporations own many, perhaps most, of the best known global magazine titles, and it is those companies that are investing most heavily in media analytics.

As with other media, magazines have been hard hit by digital competition. Consumer magazines started losing audience and advertising market share decades before the internet, when television captured much of the market for visually engaging entertainment, but the digital age has put additional stress on the sector in the United States. Historically, consumer magazines brought in as much as two-thirds of their revenue from advertising. Magazines appeal to advertisers because the narrow content focus of most titles attracts predictable and valuable audiences. For sellers of specialized products with narrow consumer appeal—specialized chef's tools, horses, or yachts, for example—magazines offer a much more efficient "buy" than other media (Chapter 5).

While magazines still attract high-quality niche audiences, the digital age has created significant competition for those readers. Special-interest digital websites, how-to videos on YouTube, and long-form content on other platforms have siphoned off many subscribers, particularly from the print versions of publications. Falling readership numbers have undercut the appeal of magazines as an advertising platform. Today, circulation accounts for at least half of the industry's revenue (Watson, 2019), with more publications moving toward circulation-based or circulation-only business models.

In the face of these challenges, the consumer magazine industry has been reinventing itself, and analytics have played a major role in the process. Publishers have shut down some titles, merged others; radically redesigned a few, digitized others either wholly or partly, and kept some focused entirely on print. The industry also is producing more *special interest publications (SIP)*. SIPS are produced less frequently—quarterly, biannually, annually, or around a special topic or event, and many are subscription only. Publishers are aggressively seeking opportunities to develop new products based on brand extensions of their leading titles, such as apps, a wine club or online recipe service for subscribers of cooking or wine magazines, a television series based on a magazine, or vice versa, and even branded consumer products and service companies such as real estate agencies or home remodeling franchises.

In all of these processes, major magazine publishers have turned to data and analytics. In the magazine world, the dynamics of content management, subscription marketing, and advertising all impact one another. It's the media analyst's job to untangle those dynamics and understand how all three factors affect the success of each title.

Satisfaction is the audience metric that matters, according to media industry executives, although there is no formal metric or data point that defines it. Still, the questions are: What drives the reader to run to the mailbox to pick up a magazine? How engaged are readers with the magazine, and what is it about the content that engages them? How much do the readers of a particular title want a 'lean back' experience as opposed to one that requires activity? Publishing companies also monitor reader reactions to story selection and framing, art, design, advertising, subscription price, and delivery.

To answer such questions, magazine analysts create multiple *panels* of readers who have opted in to contribute to ongoing readership research. The panels are surveyed often, sometimes on a monthly basis, with different panels asked to evaluate different aspects of the *user experience* (*UX*). One question is how often did panel members actually read the publication after receiving it? Was it only one out of the last four issues or all four? How much and what features or advertisements in each issue did they read? Panel members are asked to rate their enjoyment of articles, with the scores correlated to the articles' content categories and reader *demographics*. An editor may want to know what type of language or word choices will offend her readers in a given title.

Cover testing is a critically important and regular element of content research, since cover art has a major impact on magazines' newsstand sales and readers' perceptions of what a magazine offers. Magazines do *A/B testing* of different covers on their websites (Chapter 3). They also float different cover concepts before focus groups in different cities and regularly survey readers to get reactions to different covers. Should the concept be clean, or should it be cluttered? Should it feature art or photographs? Should there be three muffins on the plate or five? What colors work best with the title's readership or the issue's theme? If it's a holiday-themed issue, how do you make your cover stand out among all the other covers featuring Christmas decorations or national themes? What cover will work best, if most single-copy sales take place in a grocery store checkout line, as compared to an airport newsstand? So important are covers in attracting readership that according to one industry executive, some editors have research on cover concepts underway almost continuously.

Distribution format also is a question for analysts but surprisingly less so than for other media industry sectors. With the introduction of digital tablets around 2010, the magazine industry eagerly embraced digital editions and began developing interactive content. Digital, interactive content seemed perfect for visually rich, long-form magazine content. But those innovations largely flopped with readers. Only a small percentage of magazine subscriptions in the United States are for digital content. As one industry executive noted, while much of the industry's current focus is on growth opportunities in the digital world, "[print] magazines are where we make our money."

While most titles have related websites, currently the website usually exists to support the magazine, not the other way around. The industry is investing more in video content that readers can link to through QR codes printed in magazine copies. The videos often are designed to amplify the print copy, such as by demonstrating how to make something featured in the magazine. For potential subscribers who find the video first, the videos direct viewers back to the magazine titles.

While some experts believe such brand extensions will evolve into stand-alone products, the long-term value of these digital innovations to the magazine industry is yet to be determined. Such decisions will be driven by the media analysts studying how readers are using the industry's digital add-ons and whether that content is producing a large enough return to make the investment worthwhile.

As consumer magazine companies try to figure out the future of digital brand extensions, they raise new questions for media analysts. For example, from where do viewers of travel-magazine-related videos come? Is it from the QR code in the magazine? From an email or a travel newsletter? From a search on the web or directly from the video platform? From a *post* on social media? If from social media, from which social platform? And once they find the video, how do the people who find it through those various *referrals* behave? What is readers' *average watch time* for videos? What about for the embedded video ads? What is the *conversion rate* for the advertised travel products? And do the different visitors who come to the video through different types of referrals systematically differ from one another in terms of behavior? At this point, with so much of the industry's focus still on print copies of magazines, these questions are still a small—but increasingly important—area of focus.

For media analysts, the lack of digital subscriptions in the magazine industry also means a lack of granular digital data about reader behavior. Thus magazine industry analysts must rely on more traditional readership research methods such as reader panels, focus groups, and national media-use survey data generated by commercial research firms. As is true for many media industry sectors, tracking audience size and reader behavior across platforms remains a challenge.

A critical question constantly monitored by industry analysts are readers' *intentions to renew* their subscriptions. Readers' satisfaction scores for a title are monitored in case they start trending down, what one industry executive called "disaster management." Analysts want to know what changes in a magazine or problems with its delivery might make a subscriber decide to cancel, and what content will convince them to renew. Analysts constantly scan readers' behaviors and attitudes toward the magazines to which they subscribe, trying to identify reliable predictors of a pending subscription cancellation.

And on the flip side, magazine editors and analysts struggle to figure out how to get nonsubscribers to open a title for the first time to see what it might have to offer. Potential readers can't be convinced to become subscribers if they've never even looked into a particular magazine. Analysts are tasked with thinking creatively about this, including about how new and younger readers might be led to a title through digital brand extensions or title-related events such as online cooking classes or concerts.

Marketing is a key area of consumer magazine management for media analysts. Direct mail marketing is still considered the most efficient way to market magazines to potential readers. Analysts evaluate the financial efficiency of direct mail campaigns by measuring response rates. They look at factors that might affect those rates such as differences in messaging between campaigns and the timing of mailings to different reader demographics or different geographic areas. They also look at how direct mail compares to subscription card inserts placed inside magazines in attracting new subscriptions.

Social media also is a key element in magazine marketing, with increasing focus put on *social media listening* (Chapter 13). What are people saying about a magazine title—or the specific stories published in the last issue? How much are those stories being *shared*, by whom, and on which social media platforms? How much *click-through* is happening? Is greater sharing related to subsequent increases in subscriptions or advertising? Or is sharing of a title's content on social media costing the publisher money because it is simply giving the publication's product away for free?

Analysts tasked with listening to social media are expected to feed their findings back to magazine editors—and not just what they're hearing about the magazine. Being on the leading edge of trends is critical to the success of magazine content, so spotting hot topics, emerging celebrities, fads, and slang, and responding quickly with stories that reflect those trends is essential. Social listening is central to that effort.

Finally, advertising remains a critical revenue stream for magazine publishers and therefore a critical focus of analysts' work. In magazine marketing, the focus is not just on attracting and retaining large numbers of subscribers. It's even more important to attract the *right* subscribers and readers in the demographics and *psychographics* that advertisers most want to reach. Additionally, because a magazine's most loyal readers age, publications that depend on advertising must continually convince younger generations that their grandparents' favorite magazine is something they also would enjoy.

The challenge is twofold. First, how do you get young people to even look at an established title to see what it offers? Second, how do you create content that still satisfies long-time subscribers but also attracts new generations of younger readers? Said another way, can an editor afford to drive away loyal subscribers in efforts to attract new and younger subscribers that appeal more to advertisers? What if the attempt doesn't succeed, and the magazine just winds up with fewer subscribers? What if it partly succeeds, but the combination of the fragmenting advertising market and declining subscriptions produces less total revenue? What if the magazine stays focused on keeping its existing readers happy and doesn't try to attract younger subscribers? Will the title die along with its aging readers? It's a constant battle.

Because consumer magazines' *lifestyle* focus appeals to advertisers, industry executives seek deep **insights** into the lives and habits of their readers. Audience research may involve paying thousands of households a year to complete a 100-page book-length survey form that asks questions not only about what magazines the respondents read and the platforms they use to consume that content—typical audience questions across all media sectors—but also what brand of beer they drink, soda they buy, snacks they eat, cars they drive, toothpaste they use, fashion labels they have in their closets, and so on. That information then is distilled so that magazine sales departments can tell a manufacturer that wants to advertise Deodorant Brand X that Magazine Title Y has the most Deodorant Brand X users in its readership, if the goal of the advertising campaign is to build brand loyalty among existing customers. But if the goal is to attract new customers, they also can tell the manufacturer that Magazine Title Z has fewer Deodorant Brand X users among its readers, but the readers' profiles suggest they might be easily converted.

So important is this type of readership research to magazine publishers that some corporations have media analysts assigned to specific advertising *verticals*—the term used for individual consumer product sectors. Automobiles might be a vertical, for example, or pharmaceuticals, cosmetics, or luxury goods that only the very richest people can afford. Analysts assigned to a vertical spend all their time sorting through audience data for the different content their media company produces, trying to find matches that will appeal to their best advertising clients.

Other advertising-related questions a magazine publisher might ask include: Which ads on which pages are readers most likely to actually read? Which ads in which magazines are most likely to result in **conversions**—that is, getting the reader to actually buy the product? How do readers of Magazine Title Q live? What are their habits and hobbies, and how might we use that information to sell advertising into the magazine? For example, do the majority of readers of a car magazine also own pets? What type of pets? Do most of them live in city centers or out in the suburbs? What types of pet-related products do car-loving dog owners who live in apartments in the city need as compared to car-loving dog owners who live in the suburbs?

Then there are questions about the match between advertising and reader interests. Cosmetics advertisers might want to buy space in a particular title—such as a yoga magazine or an organic food title that reaches mostly young female readers. But research may show that those readers are turned off by cosmetics ads because the products clash with the values the magazine represents.

Finally, in the rapidly changing magazine sector, analysts are tasked with teasing out the path to a profitable future for each title. They test questions such as which combinations of free content, subscription, and digital paywalls generate the most revenue for a given magazine, as well as which *brand extensions* are likely to prove profitable.

As always, the biggest challenge is asking the right questions of the data. A major part of an analyst's job is to help magazine executives understand what questions they need to be asking—what their benchmarks of success are in the short, medium, and long term. Then analysts translate those goals into questions that can be examined through data.

Executives' goals almost always center on maximizing revenues and profits. But in a time of change, too tight a focus on revenue can be self-defeating. For example, as a new technology diffuses through the public, at first, it won't generate much money. If the company largely ignores it because it brings in only a small share of the company's income, they may lose that entire market to a competitor if the technology succeeds. On the other hand, it's hard in a time of shrinking resources to convince senior managers to invest time and money in emerging technologies and new ideas, given that most of them will fail. In the rapidly changing publishing industries, it is a constant dilemma.

If there is one certainty for media analysts in the consumer magazine sector, it is that the goalposts for "winning" will move constantly. The *key performance indicators* (*KPIs*) that senior executives are using today will be different from the ones they asked for yesterday and from the ones they'll be chasing tomorrow. The analyst serves as consultant, counselor, and devil's advocate in the rooms where those decisions happen.

While the magazine industry is unquestionably going through a period of rapid change, retrenchment, and reinvention, it seems unlikely that audience demand for specialized, lifestyle-oriented, long-form content will disappear anytime soon. Magazines can be expected to remain a major media sector with an outsized influence on culture, trends, and consumer decisions for the foreseeable future. What form magazines will take over the next generation may be harder to predict, but that media analysts will play an increasingly important role in shaping decisions at both individual publications and across the magazine industry seems a virtual certainty.

Trade publications and newsletters

An important subsector of the periodicals industry is the *trade press*. Trade publication titles focus on covering a specific business topic or industry. In the United States, there are far more trade publication titles in circulation than consumer magazines, although most titles would not be recognized by the general public. The audience for trade publications are the executives and professionals working in the industry the publication covers or in related industries that supply it, as well as the government regulators who oversee it.

Most trade publications are heavily dependent on advertising for revenue. Many get all of their revenue from advertising, sending their magazine without charge to all key executives and professionals in the industry the publication covers. Advertisers in trade publications are business-to-business (B2B) advertisers—that is, companies that sell products and supplies to other businesses, such as manufacturing equipment, the raw materials needed to make products, business services, and office equipment and supplies.

Because trade publications are read by senior industry executives with decision authority, they deliver a very high-quality audience to B2B advertisers (Chapter 5). The trade publication sector of the magazine industry is at least as competitive as the consumer magazine sector. Most industries have multiple trade publications competing to serve them and competing for the advertisers that want to do business with their executive readers.

A further subset of the trade press sector are *industry newsletters*. Business newsletters focus on providing high-quality, industry-specific business intelligence to senior executives, and most depend entirely on steep subscription fees for revenue, carrying little, if any, advertising.

Few newsletters today are actually "print" media. The business newsletter industry was one of the first legacy media sectors to go digital. Digital delivery reduced newsletter publishers' production costs, while delivering added value to subscribers by delivering critical business intelligence almost instantly. Consequently, media analysts working for industry newsletters have a wealth of granular data on reader behavior.

Although trade publications are very different from consumer magazines, the questions publishers ask are similar. However, media analysts working for trade publications are less likely to find relevant data about their audiences and advertisers from public sources or syndicated research firms. In most cases, they would need to commission or conduct their own research to get the data they need. Other types of research important to consumer magazine publishers also is unlikely to be as relevant to analysts working for trade publications. Social media listening around a trade press title, for example, would probably not, in most cases, generate a high return on the time invested.

Academic and professional journals

The academic and professional journals publishing sector is a growth industry, as the importance of research and education to progress in every area of human endeavor becomes increasingly apparent (Johnson et al., 2018). The number of journals globally is increasing about 5% annually, an increase from its historical average growth rate of just over 3%.

Subscriptions are the primary source of revenue for journals, with sales of *bundled* journal subscriptions to libraries being an increasingly important part of journal publishers' revenue models. While subscriptions by individual readers also produce revenue, the importance of that source has been declining as more scholars gain online access to journals through digital library databases (Johnson et al., 2018). At the same time, however, the digital sale of individual articles has been a growth source of revenue for publishers. A few journals also sell advertising, and some charge authors a per-page publication fee for accepted articles.

Historically, journals have been produced in print. In recent years, however, libraries have preferred digital subscriptions, which improve public access and require little physical storage space. Many individual readers also see digital subscriptions as a way of clearing off overcrowded bookshelves. The increasing digitization of academic and professional journals means analysts have access to granular data about usage and reader behavior.

One of the fastest growing sectors of the journals industry is *open-access* publishing. Open access refers to journals that have adopted the principles set forth in the 2002 Budapest Open Access Initiative, which called for making research and knowledge free of charge and easily accessible to all users. The content of open-access journals is licensed under the Creative Commons instead of being protected by copyright law. True open-access journals—as opposed to "predatory" journals—still maintain high standards of scientific peer review and professional editing, and many are published by major educational publishers alongside their copyrighted journals. Open-access journals are funded through a variety of models, including charging authors for publication. But the open-access approach is still new, and questions about how to sustainably fund such journals without making it financially impossible for scholars from poor countries or institutions to publish their research still need to be addressed.

Publishing companies with large stables of academic journals have media analysts on the job. Because of the global market for research journals, geography is among the first questions an analyst asks: How many subscriptions does each journal have in each country and region of the world, and how many articles from that journal are downloaded in each country and region of the world? How many institutions around the world have access to the journal through subscriptions or bundled deals, and where are those institutions located? Which institutions are responsible for the most article downloads for each journal? And what are the year-to-year trends in these numbers and over the past five years?

Other questions of interest include identifying the most downloaded articles from each journal title each year. What were the topics and who were the authors? Which authors in a particular field are most cited across all academic journals in which they might publish? How is each journal promoted, and which of the promotions appear to be driving individual and institutional subscriptions? Where do the most highly used articles in each journal come from—individual submissions, as the result of an organized symposium on a topic, or from the creation of a "theme" issue for the journal with a call for submissions of research on the theme topic?

Journal publishers also want to know whether the number of citations to a journal produces more subscriptions later—or does the relationship work in reverse? Is that different for journals in one academic or professional field than it is for journals in another? What should a journal's editor be doing to raise the title's international profile and increase subscription demand?

Social media and search are other areas of interest for analysts working for journal publishers. How often do articles in a journal get mentioned on social media? Who were the authors and what were the topics? Where do those *mentions* occur and in what context? Do social media mentions result in click-throughs or in news stories about the research? If so, does that produce more subscriptions or individual article sales? How often do readers come to the journal's site as the result of searching for information on a particular topic? Which search engines refer them to the journal most often? Which search engine referrals are most likely to generate single-article sales and downloads? *Search engine optimization (SEO)* is becoming increasingly important in journal publishing.

Finally, as in most industry sectors, analysts working for journal publishers are frequently asked to evaluate the production efficiency and profitability of each journal. It is their job to identify areas where production costs could be reduced, to spot and test new opportunities for increasing revenue and profitability, and to identify strategies for increasing the global profile of individual titles. They look at questions such as what is the average time from a manuscript's submission to its publication? What is the average acceptance rate of submitted articles? On average, how long is each issue in production, based upon the number of pages, and how well is the editor staying within the allocated production budget?

With about half of all academic and professional journals produced by small companies or institutions, demand for professional media analysts in the sector lies primarily with educational publishers who produce numerous titles across multiple academic fields. The sector's global growth insures that among the larger educational publishers, there will be increasing demand for skilled analysts who understand and value the production and distribution of knowledge.

Summary and conclusion

The publishing industries are the oldest media industry sectors. Across history, publishing has been the means by which knowledge was transferred, culture influenced, business information shared, governments reformed, and human rights championed. Other media forms may seem more important or interesting in the 21st century, but none has been around long enough to challenge the centrality of print media and the publishing industries in history. Indeed, the profession of media analytics developed to create a trustworthy basis for relationships between publishers and advertisers. Later forms of media simply imitated the idea.

Today, printed media have been more disrupted by digital technologies than any other medium. Because of the comparatively high cost of producing content on paper, the fragmenting of audiences and advertisers has hit publication business models particularly hard. But predictions that publishing—and printed media products—would disappear entirely in the digital age have been discredited.

What is true is that the publishing sectors—books, newspapers, consumer and business magazines, and academic and professional journals—are reinventing themselves and now producing content in multiple formats. It's also true that at least some audience members are likely to continue to demand their books, newspapers, magazines, and journals be available in print. Finally, despite a full generation of disruption, at least two traditionally print media—books and academic and professional journals—have demonstrably thrived in the digital age, even while being changed by it.

Even so, in this time of reinvention, publishing companies are embracing media analytics with a new fervor. The major companies that publish books, newspapers, magazines, newsletters, and journals are increasingly turning to professional media analysts to help them more effectively market their publications to advertisers, more efficiently manage their production and distribution processes, more actively listen to their readers, and more creatively shape their editorial decisions.

But even as that happens, there are challenges. Newspapers and consumer magazines, in particular, are seeing their growth slowed or eroded by competition. At the same time, they are engaged in the resource-intensive process of trying to develop new products and strategies. Many are actively deploying media analytics to help, but having data is not enough. The challenge is to understand what the data is telling you and then act quickly and effectively on the findings. Having skilled media analysts on staff is crucial to that ability.

While few people think first of publications when they think about media research and career opportunities in media analytics, there are opportunities to be found in those industries. The demand for skilled analysts who welcome the opportunity to be part of reinventing the future of an industry continues to grow.

Additional resources

Alliance for Audited Media. AAM offers universities and libraries access to data for educational purposes. The website also has numerous data reports, explanations, and examples of data available to assist in discussion: https://auditedmedia.com/

Lists of the metrics AAM uses to measure audiences for different types of publications, and their definitions: https://support.auditedmedia.com/

News/Media Alliance is a nonprofit organization representing US news and publishing industries. The organization's website has articles, industry data, and other industry resources: www.newsmediaalliance.org/

Pew Research Center, Journalism & Media. The Pew Research Center has highly credible current data on the state of different news media sectors in the United States, including books, newspapers, and news magazines, as well as research on current issues and trends in those industries: www.journalism.org/

Statista. Current reports and statistics on industries in the United States and globally, including media industries. Some basic reports and data available for free: www.statista.com/

Recommended cases

These cases can be found on the textbook website: www.routledge.com/cw/hollifield

Case 11.1: Analyzing the Market Position of a Magazine
Case 11.2: Strategizing the Launch of a New Consumer Magazine
Case 11.3 (5.3): Analyzing the Automotive Vertical for a Local Newspaper

Case studies, along with accompanying datasets for this chapter, can be found on the text website. We particularly suggest the preceding cases in the order listed. See the companion website and instructor's manual for detailed descriptions of these and other relevant cases.

Discussion questions and exercises

1. The chapter outlines many of the questions and issues that media analysts in each of the publications industry sectors are being asked to answer. Look again at some of these questions. Write a list of the variables *you* would use to try to answer each of the questions, and discuss why you would pick those. How would you combine variables to get insights into the question? What controls would you use, and where might you get the data for your variables? Be realistic as you think about the questions. Approach it as if your boss just gave you this assignment.

2. Go to the AAM Website: https://auditedmedia.com/. Search the site for terms and definitions: https://auditedmedia.com/search/?term= definitions. Go through at least some of the many tables of terms and metrics used to calculate audience size in different types of publications. At a minimum, look at, compare, and contrast the "Magazine media circulation terms and definitions," "News media terms and

definitions," "B2B/Farm media circulation terms and definitions," and "Definitions of common business media digital terms." Discuss what you learn about how the print industries market their products and operate as businesses according to how AAM defines the different metrics it uses for various publication sectors. Compare the metrics across publication sectors and discuss what those differences would mean for the accuracy and size of the circulation figures presented to advertisers.

3. One of the big questions in the magazine industry is how to get young readers to even look into older, established magazines. Think about some important, well-established magazine titles that would appeal to different audience segments such as women, men, business professionals, etc. Choose titles that you would expect to have mostly an older readership—people such as your parents or grandparents. You're the analyst working for that publication. Brainstorm ways to get people in their twenties to at least look into the publication and learn about its content.

4. *Exercise: Analyzing magazine readership charts*
   Look at the three charts of data about the readers of three different fashion magazines. Do the age data for each title add up to 100%? Why or why not? Does the diversity data for each title add up to 100%? Why or why not? What does "(000s)" in the Audience Chart title mean? What is the size of the Print/Digital audience for each title? What other data, if any, might you want to use as controls for each of these charts? Why or why not?

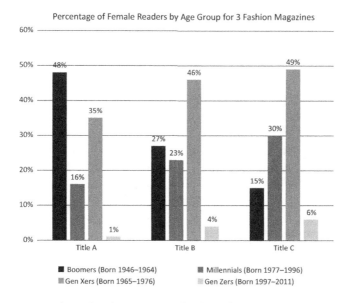

Figure 11.1 Female readers by age group for three fashion magazines
Source: Dr. C. Ann Hollifield; MPA The Association of Magazine Media

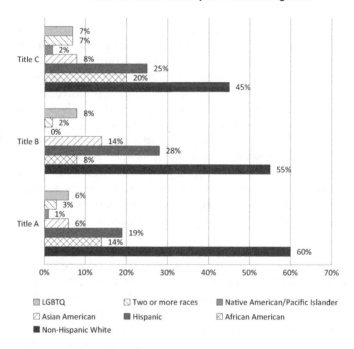

Figure 11.2 Profile of reader diversity for three fashion magazines

Source: Dr. C. Ann Hollifield; MPA The Association of Magazine Media

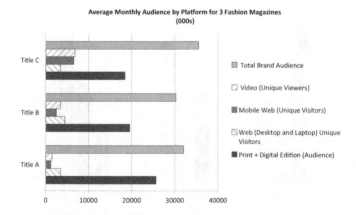

Figure 11.3 Average monthly audience size by consumption platform for three fashion magazines

Source: Dr. C. Ann Hollifield; MPA The Association of Magazine Media

Note

1. Those numbers did not include the growing market in "predatory" academic journals that purport to be peer-reviewed but, in fact, publish almost anything submitted so long as the authors pay for publication. While some credible scientific journals and most "open-access" journals also charge authors publication fees, "vanity" journal publishing of minimally verified "research" has become a global for-profit industry in the 21st century.

References

Abernathy, P. M. (2022). The expanding news desert: The loss of newspapers and readers. *University of North Carolina.* www.usnewsdeserts.com/reports/expanding-news-desert/loss-of-local-news/loss-newspapers-readers/

Alliance for Audited Media. (2022). Support center. *Terminology and Definitions.* https://support.auditedmedia.com/

Bennett, C. O. (1965). *Facts without opinion: First fifty years of the Audit Bureau of Circulations.* Audit Bureau of Circulations.

Cauhapé-Cazaux, E. G., & Kalathil, S. (2015). *Official development assistance for media: Figures and findings.* CIMA & OECD. www.oecd.org/dac/conflict-fragility-resilience/docs/CIMA.pdf

Faverio, M., & Perrin, A. (2022, January 6). Three-in-ten Americans now read e-books. *Pew Research Center.* www.pewresearch.org/fact-tank/2022/01/06/three-in-ten-americans-now-read-e-books/

Hollifield, C. A., Martin, H. J., & Ren, C. (2005, August 10–13). *The influence of newspapers on rural economic development.* Presentation to the Newspaper Division, Association for Education in Journalism and Mass Communication, San Antonio, TX, August.

IbisWorld. (2021). *Global book publishing industry (2016–2021): Market research report.* www.ibisworld.com/global/market-research-reports/global-book-publishing-industry/

Islam, R. (2002). Into the looking glass: What the media tell and why. In *The right to tell: The role of mass media in economic development* (pp. 1–23). World Bank Institute.

Johnson, R., Watkinson, A., & Mabe, M. (2018). *The STM report: An overview of scientific and scholarly publishing* (5th ed.). STM: International Association of Scientific, Technical and Medical Publishers. www.stm-assoc.org/2018_10_04_STM_Report_2018.pdf

Levin, D. (2019, October 20). When the student newspaper is the only daily newspaper in town. *New York Times.* www.nytimes.com/2019/10/19/us/news-desert-ann-arbor-michigan.html

Matsa, K. E., & Worden, K. (2022, May 26). Local newspaper fact sheet. *Pew Research Center.* www.pewresearch.org/journalism/fact-sheet/local-newspapers/

Noam, E. M. (2009). *Media ownership and concentration in America.* Oxford University Press.

Perry, P. (2019, December 9). A decade of change: Publishing industry trends in 7 charts. *Submittable Blog.* https://blog.submittable.com/publishing-industry-trends/

Pew Research Center. (2010, January 11). *How news happens: The study of the news ecosystem in one American city.* www.journalism.org/2010/01/11/how-news-happens/

Pew Research Center. (2021, June 29). *Newspaper fact sheet.* www.pewresearch.org/journalism/fact-sheet/newspapers/

Priest, C. (1994). *An information framework for the planning and design of "information highways.* www.eff.org/Groups/CITS/Reports/cits_nii_framework_ota.report.

Walker, M., & Matsa, K. E. (2021, May 21). A third of large US newspapers experienced layoffs in 2020, more than in 2019. *Pew Research Center.* www.pewresearch.org/fact-tank/2021/05/21/a-third-of-large-u-s-newspapers-experienced-layoffs-in-2020-more-than-in-2019/

Watson, A. (2019, August 27). *US magazine industry: Statistics and facts.* Statista. www.statista.com/topics/1265/magazines/

Watson, A. (2021a, September 22). *Number of magazines in the US 2002 to 2020.* Statista. www.statista.com/statistics/238589/number-of-magazines-in-the-united-states/

Watson, A. (2021b, November 11). *Annual number of books read in the US 2019–2021.* Statista. www.statista.com/statistics/222743/mean-number-of-books-read-in-the-us/

Watson, A. (2022a, January 27). *US periodical publishing revenue 2010–2020, by media type.* Statista. www.statista.com/statistics/184957/us-periodical-publishing-revenue-by-media-type-since-2005/

Watson, A. (2022b, February 10). *US magazine industry statistics and facts.* Statista. www.statista.com/topics/1265/magazines/#topicHeader__wrapper

12 Online and mobile analytics

Online media content, particularly mobile access to that content, has transformed our daily existence. As of 2022, more than half (58.9%) of global website traffic was mobile (Clement, 2022). On screens large and small, we check news headlines, weather, and traffic patterns from any location, often via installed apps. Our shopping experience has been revolutionized, from consumers' shift to online retailers and next-day delivery, to using mobile apps while in-store to evaluate products and compare pricing, to using food delivery apps to bring meals directly to our doors. Mobile phones and content now assist us with banking, transportation needs, dating, fitness and nutrition, and even health care.

Advertisers follow the audience, and digital ad spend[1] has now surpassed TV and print sectors in the United States and worldwide (Wagner, 2019). Because of the growth of these new digital revenue streams, online and mobile metrics are more important than ever. For context, many countries can be described as "mobile-first," referring to the fact that their populations never or rarely used a desktop or laptop, skipping directly to mobile phone usage for news, information, and entertainment content. Some African countries fall into this category. Mobile-first also can simply refer to the amount of time spent on mobile and the size of the country's mobile audience far surpassing any desktop preferences. Indonesia and India are two such nations, with 90% of India's "digital time" represented by mobile usage (Comscore, 2017).

Many similarities exist between online and mobile measurement. While consumers access websites from their phones and tablets (considered mobile devices) as well as from desktop and laptop computers, some differences do exist in terms of how these platforms are measured. We will discuss the measurement approaches common to both online and mobile-first and then spend some time discussing measurement aspects unique to mobile. While online measurement can encompass any media format, this chapter will focus on online measurement not related to online video or audio, which are covered in Chapters 8–10. But the two digital platforms

DOI: 10.4324/9780429506956-16

share one simple truth: Data analytics can be a bridge "to build a better connection between people that [are] creating and promoting content and the readers [users]. If you understand the [users] better, then you can create a stronger bridge or connection between the two through the data and *insights* provided," according to one top analytics executive.

One commonality to online and mobile measurement is that they are census-based, meaning that every user and their activities can be potentially counted. Because of the nature of digital devices, every user leaves a digital footprint. The activity within each website, web page, and application ("app") used can be tracked and documented. Thus there is no need for a sample of data when the complete record can be gathered and analyzed whether via mouse or screen click, time spent on page, or the like.

Online/mobile measurement providers

The online and mobile content environments have more measurement firms than any other sector, likely because these are comparatively newer platforms. Among the big names providing measurement to these sectors around the world are Comscore, Google Analytics, Adobe Analytics, Nielsen, Kantar, Ipsos, Hitwise, Parse.ly, and Chartbeat. Some of these companies provide national-level online and mobile statistics and syndicated reports, while others are services subscribed to by online publishers to better understand and optimize their own web traffic, audience engagement, advertising efficacy, or other objectives. New digital measurement companies are emerging all the time, while others disappear. We will highlight a few of the most dominant providers.

Comscore is known as a digital media measurement company and began measuring video later than Nielsen. It is recognized for online and cross-platform measurement and is used by many online publishers. Nielsen had its origins in analog video (and audio) but now measures digital media as well in order to measure the total audience. In terms of online measurement, Nielsen's Digital Content Ratings serve this purpose. They measure all digital content consumption including mobile and computer usage, of which online video is a portion. Both Comscore and Nielsen offer cross-platform measurement services.

Google Analytics is not a syndicated metrics service (which would provide aggregated data about an entire market or sector). Rather, it is a free service available to websites to measure site traffic and other attributes of individual sites. It also provides measurement for mobile devices, including mobile app user acquisition, usage, and engagement statistics (Google Analytics, 2020). Adobe Analytics is similar to Google Analytics in that it does not provide syndicated reporting. However, individual clients use it to analyze their own web traffic and audience behavior. It also offers mobile web and app measurement. There are similarities and differences between the two services (and others), but that discussion is beyond the scope of the chapter.

As we've alluded to earlier in this text, media analytics is a rapidly changing business sector, and the digital analytics space is particularly so. We've intentionally highlighted only a few of the major digital measurement providers because the names you may rely on for digital measurement today are likely to change during the course of your career and, indeed, during the life span of this text! Companies often consolidate, some are acquired, others may emerge and replace current measurement leaders, and the like. The most important thing for you as an analyst when selecting a digital metrics provider is to do your research on a measurement company's reputation, their methodology and the accreditation status of their tools, and whether the metrics they provide can help you accurately measure your objectives.

Identifying the right online metrics for the right context

Perhaps more than any other media sector, the online measurement sector suffers from definitional confusion. For instance, some terminology gets used in multiple ways. Terms like *"view," "engagement,"* and *"stickiness"* can mean different things depending on which organization is providing the metric and in what context. For instance, engagement for a brand within the advertising realm might refer to brand recall or whether there was an online purchase. However, engagement on an online news site might refer to how deeply someone read into an article, how many stories they read, how much time was spent on the site or whether they posted reader comments.[2] To complicate matters, while engagement might be used to refer to time spent on a website or an app by some companies, the terms "loyalty" and "stickiness" have been used by others to refer to the very same concept. Certainly, the online metrics industry is maturing, but definitional inconsistencies still exist.

In addition, some analysts use certain metrics simply because they are available, and some metrics are not all that useful. Avanish Kaushik, Digital Marketing Evangelist at Google, notes that too often analysts fail to measure what really matters. Pointing to social media, he notes that "vanity metrics" such as numbers of fans, *followers, posts,* or tweets can be suboptimal metrics that don't really measure success. What should be measured is what occurs *after* posts, tweets, or participation (Kaushik, 2012)—in other words, the *outcomes* of those activities. The role of the analyst, then, is to identify what success means for their organization, i.e., what are the desired outcomes? Then identify the metrics that can evaluate those outcomes. This approach goes to Kaushik's own definition of a *key performance indicator (KPI)*, which he says is "a metric that helps you understand how you are doing against your objectives" (Kaushik, n.d., "Step 3: Identify the Key

Performance Indicators" section). Are you trying to increase website traffic overall? Are you trying to make people stay longer once they get there? Are you trying to get them to visit more pages on the site? Read more deeply into articles? Post comments? Make a purchase?

Identify the metrics that will accurately match and measure those objectives, whatever they may be called. With so many online metrics providers, it is highly unlikely that there will be 100% uniformity on measurement terminology and definitions in our lifetimes! Focus on your desired outcomes and measure those.

As examples of some common metrics, refer to Table 12.1, while understanding that these terms may not be uniformly applied or used in the same contexts. Parse.ly cofounder Sachin Kamdar adds: "I think in the past, people have looked for silver bullet–style metrics, like what is the one metric that we should focus on, this one-size-fits-all thing. It just hasn't worked. And I don't think it's ever going to work. There's never going to be a single thing that makes sense for the entire industry." In addition, a

Table 12.1 Commonly Used Online Metrics

Metric	Definition	Formula/notes
Visits/sessions (daily, weekly, monthly)	Number of people who visited a website within a time period; can include multiple visits by same person).	
Unique visitors (daily, weekly, monthly)	Number of unduplicated people who went to a website within a time period.	
Page views (daily, weekly, monthly)	How many total web pages are requested within a specific time period; a measure of reach.	
Time on page/time on site	The amount of time a person spends on a particular page within a website (time on page) or the time spent on the entire website during a session (time on site).	In minutes and/or seconds
Bounce rate	Percentage of visits (sessions) on a website with a single page view (user left immediately).	(Number of visits with just one page view)/ (Total visits for a given time period)

Metric	Definition	Formula/notes
Exit rate	Percentage of users who left a website from a particular page.	(Number of people who left a website from a certain page)/(All people who entered the site from any page)
Conversion rate	Success rate of the desired outcome.	(Outcomes)/(Unique visitors or visits)
Visitor loyalty	Frequency of visits to the website during reporting period.	Number (within given time period)
Visitor recency	Amount of time since a visitor last visited the website.	Second/minutes
Length of visit	Quality of visit as depicted by length of a user session.	Length of a user session in seconds; can be represented by average time on site.
Depth of visit (sometimes referred to as "engagement" or "stickiness")	The distribution of the number of pages viewed per site visit during a specific time period.	Number of pages viewed per site visit during a specific time period.
Task completion rate	The percentage of people who are able to accomplish their intended task on a website.	The percentage of people who visit a website and are able to answer "yes" to the question, "Were you able to complete the task you came to this website to do?"
Economic value	Amount of revenue visitors add to an organization's bottom line through all the conversions they complete on its website.	Sum of the value of all financial transactions from visitors within a given time period.
Conversation rate	Rate (%) at which a company's or organization's piece of content inspired people to start talking about it; a measure of impact.	For blogs: number of reader comments per post. For Twitter: number of replies sent per day, number of replies received per day. For Facebook: Percentage feedback.

Sources: K. Arendt, personal communication, 2017; Kaushik, 2007, 2010, 2011

Note: Some terms may have multiple definitions across the industry. Where needed, definitions have been adapted for clarity.

single organization may have multiple desired outcomes, and these often change throughout a company's life cycle. For instance, a new company will be concerned about brand awareness, while an established company is more likely interested in sales, readership, or other consumption metrics.

Related to the idea of meaningless metrics is the tendency for companies and brands to chase trends in the digital space. For instance, a particular topic becomes popular or a practice trends quickly online, becoming visible due to available analytics. An erroneous tendency is for a company to be susceptible to fads and "hop on the trend bandwagon," without thinking much about whether it is beneficial for their brand to do so. Does it make sense? Is it relevant to the company? Quite often it's not, and, instead, in the words of Parse.ly cofounder Sachin Kamdar, the result is an "echo chamber around trends where people are all latching onto the hot new thing and you kind of realize, 'oh, that doesn't actually matter, and it was silly of us to kind of try to chase that trend overall.'"

Being reactionary as a result of daily, real-time dashboard metrics is not a long-term strategy, and often it leads to rash, panic-driven, and poor decision making. Such real-time metrics are a convenience and can be useful to better understand our audiences, but developing long-term strategies that connect to the bottom-line is better, and that is done by using longitudinal data and identifying patterns and trends over time.

Before metrics should even be analyzed, an organization needs to define what online success looks like for that organization and which measurement services (and relevant KPIs for the company, as just described) make sense. Too many companies are awash in information and metrics overload, leading to confusion about what real success looks like, according to Kamdar.

> I've seen a couple organizations that had like four dozen different analytics tools that they were using! And that is just so much information that . . . nobody then knows what is real, what success means, how to evaluate what's happening, because everyone will come up with their own kind of barometer. You might have someone say, "yeah, this piece of content worked really well because it drove 10,000 unique visitors to our site." And then another person comes in and says, "yeah, I don't know about that because on Twitter, I didn't see anyone tweet about it." And then another can say, "no, I think that it did do really well because we got 10,000 likes on Facebook" and then someone else says "yeah, but those 10,000 likes didn't actually drive any clicks to the website itself." And so then it's like, who's right and who's wrong in that scenario?

Kamdar says limiting the number of analytics tools will bring some consistency not only to everyone's understanding of trends and patterns but also what real success looks like for the organization.

Common online metrics

So what are some of the most commonly used metrics for the online environment? These can be found in Table 12.1. Collectively, we often see these metrics used to describe what is referred to as *clickstream data*. These metrics help tell the story of how individuals spend time online as part of their consumer journey, things like which websites they visited, which pages they viewed and for how long, and so forth. Bear in mind that no one metric will tell you the whole story, and if you have more than one objective, you probably will find yourself using a few different online metrics. Kaushik (2010), also a web analytics author and expert, says the most valuable metrics, in addition to helping you to evaluate your objectives, are those that are uncomplex, relevant, timely, and instantly useful. He also credits the former CEO of Intuit, Steve Bennett, with the notion of being able to identify the "critical few." Based on your company's or your individual objectives for your site, what would your "critical few" be? The following descriptions might provide you some clues (note: not all of them will make the cut).

Visits, visitors, or sessions

These terms are often used interchangeably and essentially refer to the same thing. How many times was someone on your website within a given time period? Note that a *visitor* could be the same person visiting multiple times. The terms "*visits*" or "*sessions*" take the human element out of it somewhat.

Unique visitors

While the previous metric could include multiple site visits by the same person, *unique visitors*, as the term suggests, eliminates duplication. It tells us how many different individuals visited a website within a given time period. No person is counted more than once, despite the number of visits each made to a site within the measured time period.

Time on page, time on site

This one is pretty straightforward, right? *Time on page* or *site* tells us the amount of time a person spends on a particular page within a website (time on page) or the time spent on the entire website during a session (time on site).

Bounce rate

This is one of the most useful metrics in terms of diagnosing a problem and being able to fix it! Basically, it tells you how often people come but leave right away. A high *bounce rate* is a strong clue that people do not like something about a website. Perhaps it takes too long to load, it is cluttered, or it is aesthetically not pleasing to most people. As Kaushik eloquently explains, "I came, I puked, I left" or more precisely, "the percentage of sessions on your website with only one page view" (Kaushik, 2010, p. 51). In order to get at this, he explains, you need the total number of visitors to the website over a given time period, as well as the visitors to the various landing pages who then clicked on another link to go to another page, something called *entering visits* (2010) by some software programs. If the percentage of these entering visits is low, that is not good! That means the bounce rate is high and that people are not sticking around. There is something about your website that people do not like, and you can now try to find out what that is. By measuring the overall bounce rate of the entire site, as well as the bounce rate of individual landing pages, Kaushik says, you can identify the pages that are sending people away at higher rates and try to find out why.

Exit rate

While this is a common metric, it is not particularly useful. As Kaushik notes (2010), it basically measures "how many people [the percentage who] left your website from a certain page" (p. 54), except the problem is that everyone leaves a website at some point and for varying reasons. That does not necessarily tell you that the page they left from was the issue. Bounce rate is a far superior metric because it focuses on the percentage of times a website is only getting one page view anywhere on the site, which can also be compared to bounce rates of individual pages. An exception to the nonutility of *exit rates*, according to Kaushik, is with *structured experiences*. In this situation, there is a multistage process or series of steps people are following in order, such as checking out of their shopping cart page, entering their shipping information, then moving on to a payment page, and so forth. An exit on any one of those pages, Kaushik (2010) notes, would indicate a bad exit and that something is wrong that needs to be fixed. But he says this is actually referred to as the *abandonment rate*.

Conversion rate

While often used to refer to sales or other financial outcomes, a *conversion* can refer to any desired outcome from a website. These conversions might include getting someone to subscribe to a newsletter, become a member of an organization, sign a petition, and so forth. Conversion simply refers to a desired outcome that you want to measure, and *conversion rate* can be calculated as "Outcomes divided by Unique Visitors (or Visits)" (Kaushik, 2010, p. 55) and is expressed as a percentage.

Visitor loyalty and recency

Taken together, this concept is defined simply as "repeated frequent visits by an individual" (Kaushik, 2011). Broken down separately, Kaushik says *visitor loyalty* can be found by asking, "during the reporting time period how often do 'people' ('visitors') visit my website?" and *recency* can be determined by asking, "how long has it been since a visitor last visited [my] website?" (2007). He explains we might expect a news site or a jobs site to have daily visitation goals. Other types of sites would not expect the recency to be as high, so a different time period could be established within which to measure repeated visits by users.

Length of visit

Length of visit probably seems self-explanatory but is defined by Kaushik (2007) asking, during the reporting period, what is the quality of visit as represented by length of a visitor session in seconds? While this is often expressed as average time on site, Kaushik explains that distribution of this metric can actually provide a better picture of what's going on, especially when one or two visitors' lengthy visits skew the average time metric (see Figure 12.1).

Depth of visit

The same can be said here, as far as avoiding averages. Kaushik (2007) refers to *depth of visit* as "during a given time period, what is the distribution of number of pages in each visit to the website?" Viewing this metric in a distribution format provides the best understanding (rather than average number of pages viewed per visit, see Figure 12.1).

Task completion rate

Kaushik (2011, "Task Completion Rate" section) explains this as follows:

> *Task Completion Rate* is the % of people who come to your website who answer yes to this question: "Were you able to complete the task you came to this website to do?" Combine that with the Primary Purpose question ("Why are you here?") and you have a gold mine of fantastic data. Why people come, how much you let them down. No guessing. No making stuff up. No inferring things from Time on Page or % Exits!

Economic value

This is truly the bottom line. Visits and time spent on our websites are great, but at the end of the day, don't we want paying customers? We

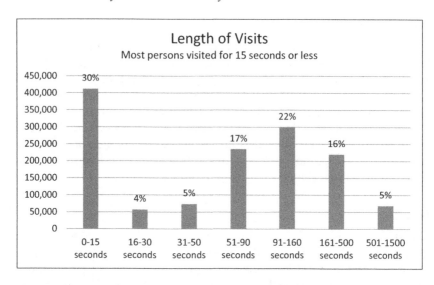

Figure 12.1 Distribution of length and depth of website visits

Source: Credit: Dr. Amy Jo Coffey (adapted from Kaushik, 2007).

hope everything leads to this. Kaushik (2011, "Economic Value" section) defines *economic value* as simply "the total $$$s (or Pesos or Rupees or Kroner) in Economic Value added to your business bottom-line by visitors to your website completing all the possible Macro and Micro Conversions."

Conversation rate

While metrics common to social media will be explored more specifically in Chapter 13, one in particular is worth mentioning here: conversation rate. Better than "likes" or posts (which are *vanity metrics*), this metric gets to the impact of your website's content because it measures how it inspired people to start talking about it. *Conversation rate* refers to comments posted on your website in response to the site's content (Kaushik, 2010); the comments may be directed specifically to the brand or be more general in nature. Kaushik (2011, "Conversation Rate" section) describes its calculation across various social media platforms: "for blogs: # of reader comments per post. For Twitter: # of replies sent per day, # of replies received per day. For Facebook: % Feedback."

Engagement

As alluded to earlier, inconsistency in defining web metrics is a recognized problem, and the definition of *engagement* may be the worst. It would be quite possible to ask ten different people—even in the measurement industry—and get ten different definitions! As noted earlier, the Advertising Research Foundation in 2006 alone documented 25 different definitions of engagement (Napoli, 2010). So why bother? Well, despite the variation in definitions, the multiple definitions are getting at something that all media and consumer sectors care about deeply, and it has to do with exciting their consumers and getting them to do something, but that "something" is where all the variation occurs. You might want to get consumers to post a comment or video, to *share* a link, to take a poll, to leave a review, or to make a purchase. Other companies might consider engagement to be how deeply someone interacts with the content, such as how long someone watches a video, how far into an article they read, or how many pages they visit within the website. Advertisers might measure engagement with things like brand recall or recollection of scenes or products within an ad. You get the idea.

Kaushik (2010) doesn't even try to define engagement. Instead, he cautions that you really need to know two types of measurement surrounding engagement: degree and kind. Most often, with online measurement, we are measuring the degree or "to what extent" someone interacted with content. This is something quantifiable. But the kind of engagement that occurred is equally important. Was it positive or negative engagement? Did someone click through every page and take actions because they were thrilled with the website and didn't want to leave? Or were they furiously clicking through every page because they were frustrated and couldn't locate the content they wanted? What were they feeling when they were on the page, and what led them to take the actions they did? These are more challenging questions to answer because they are qualitative in nature and cannot be directly known through the web metrics recorded by a mouse click.

The aforementioned online metrics are just a few of the endless digital metrics available. Your most useful or critical metric may not even be on the preceding list! Why? Because the most useful metrics are those that directly relate to your current objectives. What is your goal for the website right now? It may be different from the goal two years ago. What metric can best measure the key performance indicator (KPI) that you care most about right now? That is the metric (or set of metrics) on which you need to focus.

Measuring and reporting with purpose

To return to an earlier theme, what do you care most about? What are your company's goals and objectives? Perhaps one way to begin thinking about which metrics to use is to learn what not to use. Kaushik (2011) notes that the least useful metrics tend to be quite tactical, report "top-of-the-*funnel*" activity only (Chapter 6), require too much inference by the analyst (no direct indicators used), and focus on the "quick hit," short-term returns rather than on long-term purposes. Examples of top-of-the-funnel" activity can include things like brand recall, branded search, and general web traffic.

Vanity metrics are some of the least useful: likes, followers, fans, retweets, and so forth. They sound impressive, and many companies brag about them (hence the name), but they don't really tell us anything meaningful. Similar to an example Kaushik (2011) provides, if your company gets 25,789 likes one day and 25,924 the next, what does that slight increase mean? Is it even meaningful? What can we do with this information strategically? Not much, because we don't know what that slight increase is in response to, and whether those visitors were satisfied with their experience or not. (They may have visited the site out of curiosity because they heard how awful it was!) In addition, vanity metrics are easy to game. Anyone, even a bot, can create more likes overnight. You can even buy them!

As discussed earlier in this chapter, purposeful measurement means first understanding what success means for your organization or what its current goals are. More often than not, these goals relate to the bottom line. "If you really want to be honest about what's happening internally with your organization, you've got to find out the things that connect to the business strategy overall—such as what are we trying to accomplish over the next year or the next quarter? That isn't just representative of the company in terms of different revenue streams; it's also representative of businesses in terms of different life cycles, of where they are as a business," Kamdar explained. For example, new companies are often just seeking exposure, whereas more established companies in their growth phase may be seeking to make more money through purchases or more video views.

Using metrics to tell a story

Once you've identified your goals and objectives, you can purposefully select which metrics serve as *key performance indicators* (*KPIs*) and use those to assess your objectives. Examining these KPIs over the relevant time period for what you need to know, what story do these metrics tell? Good or bad? Is it an upward or downward trend? Have you gained or lost subscribers? What do you need to do based on these stories? These metrics are just the means to the end. Once you have the stories based on the metrics, you can use this information to make strategic decisions about next steps for your organization or website.

Other things we measure online

A/B testing

Language preference is a great example of something that might be tested using *A/B testing* methods. Online news headlines are often trialed using A/B testing. Essentially, A/B testing is an experimental process of testing in which two alternative options are evaluated by audiences, often in real time (Chapter 3). Whichever option, A or B, receives the more positive outcome, or *user experience*, would then be implemented. For instance, if Headline A receives more clicks than Headline B, then the news outlet's editors would keep Headline A for the story, as this would likely attract more readers. While the method can be used in a variety of contexts, it is used extensively in digital marketing and audience analysis.

Consumer privacy and security

Perhaps more than any other media sector, online and mobile consumers are rightly concerned about their privacy and online security. Data breaches are commonplace. Privacy and security are central to why many governments are now putting regulations into place to safeguard consumer data and privacy. Regardless of the risk, however, many consumers willingly share personal and sometimes intimate details of their lives online, whether via social media, blogs, apps, or chatrooms. Perhaps digitally native audiences are more comfortable with sharing their private lives in public spaces because they've grown up in an online environment. Or maybe many people sharing that information are simply unaware of how it is collected, shared, and used by businesses and people they don't know exist. However, privacy and security breaches can be the unfortunate trade-offs of such choices.

It would seem that consumer *identity resolution* companies[3] and third-party *data brokers*[4] would be a target for sharing details they provide about consumer identities to their clients. But in fact, some of the data broker and identity resolution companies clearly state on their websites that they are compliant with privacy regulations such as the *General Data Protection Regulation* (*GDPR*) in Europe and the California Consumer Privacy Act (CCPA) in the United States, and they even allow consumers to decide which data companies are allowed to use, share, or sell (Acxiom, n.d.; Full Contact, n.d.).

Mobile metrics

Mobile metrics, broadly speaking, refer to key performance indicators (KPIs) related to mobile device usage. Mobile metrics can include those for mobile websites as well as those for mobile applications or "apps." Most providers of such metrics include not just mobile phones in this device category but any "connected" devices such as tablets, iPads, and Kindles. Nielsen, Kantar, Comscore, Google Analytics, and Adobe are some of the well-known mobile metrics providers. Because mobile measurement is a rapidly evolving area, specific tools and product names are not listed here, as they could be different when you read this. As an example of the challenges faced by clients and analysts purchasing and using mobile metrics, we researched three providers' mobile metrics descriptions twice, a few months apart. Based on a quick glance of website descriptions, syndicated research companies A, B, and C appeared to provide the same mobile measurement. However, closer inspection revealed some inconsistencies, with clear differences in the product traits or the measurement definitions used. A few months later, the companies' definitions of what they measured changed, or the resources and descriptions disappeared from the web pages. The takeaway lesson is that it's important to do careful research and to read the fine print to understand what the data actually reflect. At minimum, the potential user would want to ask a few more questions of each provider to understand what capabilities each product offers. This is also another example of the lack of uniformity when it comes to measurement, from what is actually measured and included in the product offering, to the definitional differences of the KPIs used within the products.

Mobile app metrics

Among the various mobile metrics out there are those related just to apps. App developers or sellers may want to know how popular and profitable their apps are, among other measures. Table 12.2 shows some of the

Table 12.2 Commonly Used App Metrics

Usage and Engagement Metrics	Definition	Formula/notes
Downloads and installs	Number of people who have installed the app.	Google Analytics (iOS and Android)
App acquisition	Shows source of app downloads; in other words, indicates effectiveness of app's marketing strategy.	Google Analytics, Mixpanel
Daily active users (DAU)	Number of users who have a session with an app at least once per day.	Google Analytics, most analytics tools
Monthly active users (MAU)	Number of users who have a session with an app at least once per month.	Google Analytics, most analytics tools
Stickiness	How often users return to an app.	(Daily active users/ Monthly active users)
Average daily sessions per daily active user	How many times on average a user interacts with the app in one day.	(Number of daily sessions)/ (Daily active users)
Average session length	How much time the typical app user spends on the app during a given session.	Google Analytics or other analytics tool
Screen flow	Shows how a user interacts with each screen in the app, e.g., exits by screen, navigation path, total number of visits per screen, last screen used before exiting the app (which could suggest a problem spot).	Google Analytics
Retention rate	How many users the app retains (how many return to use it) after a set period of time.	(Number of users retained at end of time period/ Total users at start of time period)
Churn rate	How many users stopped using the app after a set period of time (the opposite of retention rate).	(1—Retention rate)
Profitability Metrics		
Average revenue per user (ARPU)	Overall value a single user provides to the app. Specifically, how much revenue is generated on average by each user (e.g., subscriptions, in-app purchases, paid downloads, ad clicks, and the like).	(Total app revenue in a time period)/(Number of users in given time period)

(Continued)

Table 12.2 (Continued)

Usage and Engagement Metrics	Definition	Formula/notes
Cost per acquisition (CPA)	How much it costs to acquire one new user.	(Total cost of marketing campaign)/(Total acquisitions or conversions)
Return on investment (ROI)	Amount of return made on the money spent building and marketing the app.	[(Gain on investment—Cost of investment)/Cost of investment]
Lifetime value (LTV)	How much value each user brings to the app; Not all users may stay with the app for same period of time, depending on type of customer.	(Average value of conversion)/(Average customer lifetime)
The "Golden" Metric	App's rating as measured by the number of stars given by reviewers in an app store (like App Store or Google Play).	Number of stars as noted in review

Source: Credit: The Manifest (Oragui, 2018)

Note: Some of these definitions lack uniformity across the industry and have been adapted where needed for clarity. Many of these metrics, such as rates, are usually expressed as percentages. This is accomplished by moving the decimal two places to the right.

most common app metrics as broken down into two categories, Usage and Engagement Metrics and Profitability Metrics (see Table 12.2). App developers are understandably interested in the number of *downloads*. However, this can be misleading and is probably the least helpful mobile app metric, as downloads do not equal usage. Many people never use the app, or they use it once and that's it. Conversely, one of the most important app metrics is *customer reviews* or *ratings*. (Think about your own habits—what is one of the first things you do when deciding whether to download a particular app?) Reviews and ratings (often depicted by numbers of stars or average rating) give you a sense of whether users are happy with their experience and, if positive, whether it will likely lead to more downloads (Vatsya, 2019).

As is true for any other kind of metric, not all mobile app metrics will be relevant for every company, as there is variation in app type, business sector, and life cycle of the app. As always, determine what your goals and objectives are first, then identify which mobile app metrics will help you properly assess those. There are different categories of metrics that may interest you. These include *acquisition, engagement, conversion, performance,* and (if interested), the so-called vanity metrics (Vatsya, 2019). But as noted earlier, be careful with vanity metrics as they are not typically indicative of much. Again, Table 12.2 provides a helpful guide.

Analytics opportunities with mobile apps

As you now know, some of the most valuable information about mobile consumers is the data that come from their smartphone apps—how apps are used, how often, and the associated geographic and other personal information they might have shared in order to access the app. As of 2022, the most popular apps by reach in the United States fell into the communications and social categories, along with entertainment and video (Ceci, 2022a). YouTube enjoyed the greatest reach of all US mobile consumers (72%) with Facebook and Gmail coming in second place (57% each). After these two apps, usage drops to 56% for Google Maps and 53% for Google Search (Ceci, 2022b).

5G and implications

5G stands for "fifth generation" wireless network and is related to the concept of the Internet of Things (IoT). Essentially, along with higher connection speeds, more types of devices can and will be connected and controlled via the internet with 5G. Due to the higher speeds, rapid downloading and page loading, greater audience content consumption is likely a result (MacDonald, 2019). More people will be accessing the web via mobile apps, and more people overall will be able to connect to the internet through their mobile phones, producing greater reach (Conway & Reynolds, n.d.). In addition, mobile experiences likely will become more immersive and interactive, as well as personalized. Such 5G-enabled experiences include augmented reality (AR) in gaming but also in retail websites, where a consumer may be able to see what they look like with certain virtual clothing or how certain furniture styles look in their home. Searches may become more voice driven rather than screen driven (Cribben, 2019; Deshpande, 2021).

Challenges of online and mobile measurement

While we've touched on some of these, one challenge still facing the online and mobile measurement industry is deduplication, that is, ensuring that unique users are indeed only counted once. Think about your own device usage for a moment. You may access a desktop computer at work but also use a laptop, a tablet, and a phone. How many other people in your workplace or household also use those same devices? It's entirely possible that two, three, four, or more people in a single household use the same device. How is a measurement company to know whose searches are whose? Which websites are used and preferred by whom? Whose usage is being counted, and how do we ensure it's not counted twice for the same person? Or whether certain searches belong to the same person but on two different devices? Also, different web browsers may be used on the same device. Because web browsers don't exchange information, one person's activities on two browsers would be measured as two different users.

This is one of the greatest challenges in online and mobile measurement. Now, some measurement firms have a solution for this using statistical modeling. Based on the types of sites visited, time of day, and frequency of usage, a firm can make educated assumptions about whether the mobile user is the 35-year-old adult or the 5-year-old child (who may have been handed their parent's phone for entertainment). Firms sometimes use the term "*look-alike*" for user assignment in such cases. That is, based upon the nature of the content and an assortment of other characteristics related to that web session, it "looks like" a 35-year-old female and not the child. Deduplication is central to the calculation of any metrics containing the term "unique," such as unique device or unique users. As part of its digital measurement standards, the Media Rating Council (MRC) states that any measurement firm using such metrics and claiming deduplication must have a clear "label on the face of any report that includes unique measurements, the basis for the calculation of the unique measurement involved [e.g., devices, users, etc.]. Discrete details of the basis of the calculation should be included in methodological supplements" (Media Rating Council, 2017, p. 31). Cross-platform, unduplicated, single-source measurement for TV and internet audience consumption continues to be a goal for the industry. Measurement companies worldwide have made strides in this area (Comscore/UKOM, personal communication, 2018; Kantar Media, n.d.; Nielsen, 2020).

Quality control for online/mobile data

As noted in other chapters, quality control is essential prior to engaging in any audience data analysis, and this includes online and mobile data. As noted elsewhere in this text, one should always be able to identify the source of the data to determine whether it is trustworthy and reliable. Beyond this, there are various quality control checks that can be performed, including checks for invalid or nonhuman traffic on websites (Fou, 2021). In addition, ensuring that a particular online or mobile measurement tool has been accredited by the Media Rating Council (MRC)[5] or similar organizations in other countries is another check. Of course, this is not required by the industry and is not a replacement for individual quality control checks.

One additional question experts recommend young analysts ask is whether the data are relevant and, depending on the objective, whether the data still will be relevant six months from now. Data can be context-specific; analysts need to know the context in which they are answering their research questions, whether the data fit the context, and what the data "expiration date" might be within that context. Finally, after filtering for all this, all data should be cleaned prior to analysis.

Summary and conclusion

As audience activity has migrated online, the measurement of this media has become increasingly important. Accurate and reliable online and mobile metrics are critical for content providers and advertisers as they conduct business in these environments. While there is no shortage of measurement firms, there is no single currency of record for the online or mobile space as is the case for the traditional media of television and radio. As a result, it continues to be not only competitive but challenging in terms of uniformity of metrics terminology. This challenge may lessen over time. Deduplication of measurement across devices also continues to be a challenge in need of a solution. Future audience analysts will face these and other measurement obstacles still unknown. However, taking on a mindset that focuses on desired outcomes and contextually appropriate metrics that matter can serve as an analyst's North Star.

Additional resources

Interactive Advertising Bureau: www.iab.com/
Mobile Marketing Association: www.mmaglobal.com/

Recommended cases

These cases can be found on the textbook website: www.routledge.com/cw/hollifield

Case 12.1: Google Merchandise Store II
Case 12.2 (14.3): Optimizing a Local News Blog
Case 12.3 (1.2): Accreditation of a New Media Measurement Tool
Case 12.4 (5.2, 6.1): Shopping for Cars

Case studies, along with accompanying datasets for this chapter, can be found on the text website. We particularly suggest the preceding cases in the order listed. See the companion website and instructor's manual for detailed descriptions of these and other relevant cases.

Discussion questions and exercises

1. What are the most strategic questions that online and mobile analysts need to answer today? What are the financial implications of the *variables* in these questions: (a) if analysts overlook such questions or ignore them? (b) if they pay close attention to these details?

2. You have been hired as a social media analyst for an online news site. Your boss tells you that your job is to double the site's number of daily "likes" for stories and total followers of the brand by the end of the year but provides no explanation or context other than that the local competition seems to have a greater social media presence. What kinds of questions might you have about your new orders? What follow-up questions might you have for your boss? What concerns might you have about the metrics she is focused on and why?

3. *Exercise: Metrics in the newsroom*

   a. You are LocalNewsToday.com. You have a great new software program that displays real-time metrics that tell you which topics and stories are trending, which ones are producing the most comments, and so on. You've noticed in the past few days that your stories about a local politician's divorce are off the charts and the audience loves to talk about it, producing a lot of online engagement and revealing a seemingly endless appetite for this topic. At the same time, the local election is next month, and people should be informed about many local ballot issues. LocalNewsToday.com has written one overview story about these important issues, and you were planning to do more about each ballot issue, but the page views were abysmal for that overview story. You could really use the advertising revenue, and you know the banner advertising surrounding another politician divorce story, based on the page-view and engagement metrics you see, would bring in ten times the amount of money a ballot issue story would. What kind of coverage decision does LocalNewsToday.com make?

   b. LocalNewsToday.com has always had a reputation for being a trusted and balanced source for news and not sensational like so many others. Yet the metrics dashboard is hard to resist. It's obvious each time one of those sensational stories takes off, and it's hard to look away! It seems so easy to manipulate and "game" the site—you could make the audience numbers increase right now in real time, just by posting more sensational stories! The dashboard is showing you the hard data and data don't lie, do they? Should LocalNewsToday.com change its strategy? Why or why not? How should the metrics dashboard be used? Explain your approach.

3. *Exercise: Optimize revenue or the user experience?*
   For each of the following exercises, assemble a brief report or write-up. You will want to first take some time to carefully think about the issues presented in each.

   a. UniSports loves catering to its soccer (football) fans. But it also wants to make money from its online content. During a recent major tournament, a UniSports.com highlight video of one of a game's biggest plays was found on Facebook—but without the game-winning goal. UniSports knows that it needs social media because many people get their content this way. Unfortunately, they only received about a third of the revenue that was generated by the highlight video because it was featured on Facebook. If people want to see the game-winning goal, the video exists on UniSports.com. As the digital analyst team leader, you just saw this second video emerge on Facebook and see the high traffic it's getting compared to your own original highlight video (with the goal) on UniSports.com. What do you do?

   b. As digital team leader, you have been asked to try to increase the revenue generated by UniSports' online video content. Currently, in one of the more popular sections of the website for daily sports highlights, all videos contain one 30-second pre-roll advertisement. You know that an easy solution would be to just increase the ad load, either adding another pre-roll or two or adding a mid-video roll or both. The display ads are already quite numerous in this particular section of the website as well, and there have been some negative viewer comments about the clutter. Depending on a viewer's internet speeds, the page can take some time to load. But the revenue potential is great, and your daily and monthly metrics for page views and engagement for this section of the website are off the charts. What is your strategic recommendation to your boss for how to maximize revenue even more for this section of the website?

4. *Exercise: Strategizing audiences' technology use*

   a. Look at the metrics in Table 12.3 showing how readers of the news blog Oconee County Observations access the content they want. Discuss how you would advise the owner of the blog (or any other content site) to use these data strategically.

   b. What do the data say about the blog's audience?

   c. What do the data *mean*, if anything, in terms of their potential relationship to the success or failure of the site?

   d. How should the owner of the blog use this information? What changes, if any, should he consider making in terms of the types of content on the blog and/or the way that content is produced, designed, and formatted?

e. If he decided to start selling advertisements around the blog, would these data have any impact on what kinds of ads he should try to sell in terms of types of companies and/or types of advertising production (text, video, audio, photographs, graphics)?

Table 12.3 Technical Profiles of Online Users on a News Blog

Online service provider	Users	New users	Sessions	Bounce rate	Pages/ session	Avg. session duration
Cable TV Company A	322	224	733	65.35%	1.90	133.69
Mobile Co. A	191	142	438	73.74%	1.64	97.03
Mobile Co. B	114	87	241	72.61%	1.54	77.23
Online operating system						
Windows	699	555	1507	66.42%	1.76	124.51
iOS	236	165	581	77.11%	1.48	79.78
Macintosh	165	126	327	71.56%	1.75	81.83
Android	28	17	47	91.49%	1.28	36.79
Online browser						
Chrome	358	259	839	76.76%	1.51	91.06
Safari	210	159	455	73.85%	1.53	68.20
Firefox	87	75	199	77.39%	1.37	128.00
Edge	60	46	86	74.42%	1.49	51.45
Mobile service provider						
Cable TV Company A	86	52	179	78.21%	1.46	54.44
Mobile Co. A	79	58	208	80.29%	1.46	80.93
Mobile Co. B	48	36	101	76.24%	1.50	95.28
Cable TV Company B.	9	2	21	80.95%	1.19	13.62
Mobile operating system						
iOS	236	165	581	77.11%	1.48	79.78
Android	28	17	47	91.49%	1.28	36.79
Windows	4	4	5	80.00%	1.20	54.80
Mobile screen resolution						
768 × 1024	179	117	468	77.78%	1.43	84.43
1024 × 1366	39	35	67	83.58%	1.25	29.96
834 × 1112	16	11	25	48.00%	3.12	176.96

Source: Oconee County Observations

Notes

1. Includes advertising that appears on desktop and laptop computers, tablets, mobile phones, and internet-connected devices (Perrin, 2020).
2. As early as 2006, the Advertising Research Foundation identified 25 different definitions of the term "engagement" by various industry stakeholders (Napoli, 2010).
3. Identity resolution is a process of matching a single user across devices and media platforms using the various identifiers used with each; such identifiers can be online or offline (e.g., email address, phone number, address, cookies). Identity resolution is central to successful marketing across today's fragmented media landscape but also helps companies in privacy law compliance (Parker, 2022).
4. A data broker, also referred to as an information broker, information product company, or syndicated data broker, is "a business that aggregates information from a variety of sources; processes it to enrich, cleanse or analyze it; and licenses it to other organizations. Data brokers can also license another company's data directly or process another organization's data to provide them with enhanced results. Data is typically accessed via an application programming interface (API), and frequently involves subscription-type contracts. Data typically is not 'sold' (i.e., its ownership transferred), but rather it is licensed for particular or limited uses" (Gartner, n.d., para. 1).
5. As with other media sectors discussed, the Media Rating Council (MRC) has been heavily involved with evaluating measurement standards in the online and mobile environments. In 2017, the MRC issued its Digital Audience-Based Measurement Standards and in 2019 took these a step further to issue the MRC Cross-Media Audience Measurement Standards (Phase 1 Video), which also applied to online and mobile through its definition of digital media platforms. These standards will likely continue to evolve along with the technology of the platforms.

References

Acxiom. (n.d.). *Privacy.* www.acxiom.com/about-us/privacy/

Ceci, L. (2022a, March 15). Most popular app categories in the United States during 3rd quarter 2020, by reach. *Statista.* www.statista.com/statistics/579302/top-app-categories-usa-reach/

Ceci, L. (2022b, March 15). Mobile audience reach of leading smartphone apps in the United States in May 2022. *Statista.com.* www.statista.com/statistics/281605/reach-of-leading-us-smartphone-apps/

Clement, J. (2022, July 20). Percentage of mobile device website traffic worldwide from 1st quarter 2015 to 2nd quarter 2022. *Statista.* www.statista.com/statistics/277125/share-of-website-traffic-coming-from-mobile-devices/

Comscore. (2017, May 9). *Which global internet markets are the most 'mobile-first?'* [Blog]. www.comscore.com/Insights/Blog/Which-global-internet-markets-are-the-most-mobile-first

Comscore/UKOM. (2018, April). Personal communication. Comscore/UKOM summary of methodology.

Conway, S., & Reynolds, E. (n.d.). *5G becoming reality*. HawkPartners. https://hawkpartners.com/strategic-communications/5g-becoming-reality-3-considerations-for-forward-looking-marketers/

Cribben, C. (2019, September 20). What does 5G mean for video advertising? *The Drum*. www.thedrum.com/industryinsights/2019/09/20/what-does-5g-mean-video-advertising

Deshpande, I. (2021, December 16). How 5G will impact customer experience in mobile marketing. *Spiceworks*. www.spiceworks.com/marketing/mobile-marketing/articles/5g-impact-mobile-marketing-customer-experience/

Fou, A. (2021, December 10). How to spot ad fraud, and how to combat it. *WARC*. www.warc.com/newsandopinion/opinion/how-to-spot-ad-fraud-and-how-to-combat-it/en-gb/4430

FullContact. (n.d.). *Frequently asked questions*. www.fullcontact.com/faq/

Gartner. (n.d.) *Gartner glossary*. www.gartner.com/en/information-technology/glossary/data-broker

Google Analytics. (2020, July 13). *Google analytics for mobile apps*. https://developers.google.com/analytics/solutions/mobi

Kantar Media. (n.d.). *Cross-media campaign measurement*. www.kantar.com/expertise/audience-measurement/cross-media-campaign-measurement

Kaushik, A. (2007, July 17). I got no e-commerce. How do I measure success? *Occam's Razor*. www.kaushik.net/avinash/i-got-no-ecommerce-how-do-i-measure-success/

Kaushik, A. (2010). *Web analytics 2.0: The art of online accountability and science of customer centricity*. Wiley Publishing.

Kaushik, A. (2011, June 28). Your web metrics: Super lame or super awesome? *Occam's Razor*. www.kaushik.net/avinash/web-metrics-super-lame-super-awesome/

Kaushik, A. (2012). Social media and business. *Vikalpa*, *37*(4), 92–97.

Kaushik, A. (n.d.). Digital marketing and the measurement model. *Occam's Razor*. www.kaushik.net/avinash/digital-marketing-and-the-measurement-model/

MacDonald, G. (2019, June 14). What will 5G mean for marketers? *LinkedIn Sales and Marketing Solutions EMEA Blog*. https://business.linkedin.com/en-uk/marketing-solutions/blog/posts/content-marketing/2019/What-will-5G-mean-for-marketers

Media Rating Council. (2017, December). *MRC digital audience-based measurement standards: Final version 1.0*. http://mediaratingcouncil.org/MRC%20Digital%20Audience-Based%20Measurement%20Standards%20Final%201.0.pdf

Napoli, P. M. (2010). *Audience evolution: New technologies and the transformation of media audiences*. Columbia University Press.

Nielsen. (2020, December 8). *Cross-media currency becomes reality with Nielsen ONE*. [Press release]. www.nielsen.com/us/en/press-releases/2020/cross-media-currency-becomes-reality-with-nielsen-one/

Oragui, D. (2018, March 29). 14 key app metrics you need to track for your mobile app. *The Manifest*. https://themanifest.com/app-development/14-key-app-metrics-you-need-track-your-mobile-app

Parker, P. (2022). What is identity resolution and how are platforms adapting to privacy changes? *Martech*. https://martech.org/what-is-identity-resolution-and-how-are-platforms-adapting-to-privacy-changes/

Perrin, N. (2020, June 23). US digital ad spending update Q2 2020. *eMarketer*. www.emarketer.com/content/us-digital-ad-spending-update-q2-2020

Vatsya, A. (2019, November 14). The 16 mobile app metrics you need to absolutely track in 2022. *WebEngage*. https://webengage.com/blog/best-mobile-app-metrics/

Wagner, K. (2019, February 20). Digital advertising in the US is finally bigger than print and television. *Vox.com*. www.vox.com/2019/2/20/18232433/digital-advertising-facebook-google-growth-tv-print-emarketer-2019

13 Social media analytics

Social media are central to media analytics across all platforms, content types, and purposes. The reason is simple: Social media are a primary source of audience and consumer data on content and product consumption for tracking the movement of content and ideas from one person to another, for identifying opinion leaders within social networks, and for gaining *insights* into individuals' personal psychology.

In short, social media are a gold mine for media analysts. They provide a nonstop stream of detailed data about behaviors and preferences of specific individuals. When aggregated, those data suggest how specific content or products are being received by customers and can signal shifting interests and emerging trends. They also allow media companies and marketers to develop detailed profiles of individual consumers, the better to target them with advertising that persuades them to buy things.

There are, however, also serious downsides to social media that professionals should not ignore. First, there are major methodological problems built into social media data that raise questions about representativeness and *validity*. Additionally, the detailed data on individual audience and consumer behavior raise issues about privacy and the potential misuse of such data. Some media companies now use social media activity in personnel management in ways that raise questions about employee privacy, discrimination, freedom of speech and action outside the workplace, and, for news organizations, journalistic priorities. Finally, social media also have proven to be a remarkably effective tool for influencing ideas and behavior across the globe—for both good and ill—a power many corporate and political actors are eager to exploit.

The use of the data generated through social media, whether for positive purposes or negative ones, depends on the skill and context with which those data are analyzed and interpreted. Thus media analysts inevitably play a central role in social media analytics and therefore in the growing storm of global controversy surrounding them.

DOI: 10.4324/9780429506956-17

This chapter will explore two different approaches to analyzing social media data: (1) social media analysis, which is the analysis of users' actions while using social media platforms, and (2) social network analysis, which is analysis of the way information moves through social media networks from person to person or from place to place. The chapter also will briefly examine some of the ways media and marketing companies are using social media analytics, as well as the methodological and ethical challenges that are built into the data.

Social media in the communication ecosystem

Social media are distinct from older media and communication systems in a number of ways. Traditional media platforms use a one-to-many communication model that, depending on the media sector, may be either synchronous or asynchronous but offers users only limited opportunities for interaction.

Social media, in contrast, are networks. A network is any system through which information or goods pass interactively—that is, back and forth—between two or more points. Highways, railways, telephone systems, email, and social media platforms are all networks.

As networks, social media companies succeed or fail on the basis of network economics. The value of any network to a user depends on how well the network connects the user to points (nodes) the user wants to reach. The airline you'll value most is the one with the best flights to the greatest number of your most frequent destinations. With social networks, you'll value the networks your friends, family, and colleagues use most often. If your most valued friends spend all of their time on Instagram or Reddit, that's where you'll be, too. If no one you like is on Facebook, you won't be there either. And who would spend time on a social media platform with 100 users, when an account on a global platform connects you to those same 100 "friends"—and several billion others as well?

Social media are different from traditional media in other ways too. They simultaneously offer users both synchronous and asynchronous communication, as well as one-to-one, one-to-many, and many-to-one interactions. The result is a platform that enables many-to-many communication, with multiple choices for feedback between communicators—called *actions*.

According to Tania Yuki, founder of Shareablee, a New York-based social media analytics company, in 2020 there were 290 billion social media actions across all of the social platforms the research company monitors (personal communication, January 21, 2021). Of those, users took almost 79 billion actions related to American product brands—including media brands and content—based on the 86 million brand-related *posts* made on the three social media platforms of Facebook, Twitter, and Instagram. Of those, 5 billion of the actions were taken on Twitter, 23 billion on Facebook, and 50 billion on Instagram.

What constitutes an action depends on the social media platform. But, in general, the term refers to anything that leaves a measurable digital breadcrumb—a reaction, a comment, a *click-through* to the content or advertisement, or a *share*, anything that proves a user stopped what they were doing and paid attention to the content of a post.

Let's pause for a moment and think about those numbers. Think about what that dataset just mentioned—covering just one year and three social media platforms—looks like. Eighty-six million posts. Seventy-nine billion actions. These don't include data from such social media powerhouses as YouTube, WeChat, and TikTok. They don't include personal posts from users. They only include posts that were related to some American brand, whether a product or a news story that a media company posted.

The social media industries

Because of user engagement numbers like those, social media has become a critically important media industry sector in its own right. Although many of the early social media platforms were entrepreneurial startups, they have grown into powerful corporations, and the social media industry is relatively consolidated. For example, Meta was started by college students but now owns the social media platforms Facebook, Messenger, Instagram, and What's App, along with many other tech subsidiaries. Alphabet (Google) owns YouTube. Microsoft owns LinkedIn. WeChat is owned by Tencent, which owns several other tech firms. New social media platforms appear regularly, while others lose popularity, so the social media industry is continuously evolving. But what is definitely, consistently growing is the demand for people with expertise in social media analytics.

Social media platforms are not, however, the only players in the social media industry. *Social media listening* and *social media monitoring* firms have sprung up around the social media industry. Such companies offer clients a wide range of analytical services and applications. As social media have become more important in advertising and public relations campaigns, advertising and PR agencies have added social media analysts to their staffs to handle client-specific needs.

Social media analytics also are now built into the media analytics on which newspapers, magazines, television, radio, and entertainment media companies depend. Thus while there are a growing number of jobs for people specializing in social media analytics, understanding social media analytics is a core skill for almost everyone working in media, advertising, and public relations research jobs. Analysts cope with a nonstop torrent of incoming social data—data that has the potential to provide enormously valuable insights but that also present enormously difficult analytical challenges. This, at least, is certain: In the world of media analytics, social media are too big to ignore. So let's dive in.

Methodological issues

To begin our discussion, it's critical for every analyst to clearly understand social media audiences and the methodological problems that plague social media data (Chapter 3). One of the most obvious problems is that, because of network economics, the users of different social media platforms sharply differ demographically.

Fragmented social media audiences

Users' preferences for different social media platforms vary sharply by age (Auxier & Anderson, 2021). New social media platforms are usually adopted first by young people and only much later, if at all, by older demographics. After age 65, social media use drops off sharply regardless of the platform. Use also varies by ethnicity, income, gender, education, and along the urban-suburban-rural divide. Social media use also fragments across political ideology, with like-minded people gathering on some platforms and their political opponents clustering on others. Finally, socioeconomic status influences usage. Only people wealthy enough to afford computers and broadband connections or smartphones and data rates can afford to be on social media. In many countries, that also means, by extension, that people considered "minorities" are underrepresented in social media data because they tend to be economically disadvantaged.

Finally, there are the social-media abstainers. It cannot be assumed that people who choose *not* to engage with social media in the 21st century are the same in attitudes and behaviors as heavy social media users.

Nor can social media activity be considered representative of any particular population—even within the population of social media users. Information scientists estimate that 90% of all social media users are *lurkers*, that is, people who read social media posts but never post or respond to anything (Nielsen, 2006). Around 1% of users are responsible for the vast majority of content and actions. The other 9% are occasional posters and commenters. These estimates have held steady across time, even as social media usage has increased.

Because of network economics and social media abstainers, "No!" is the answer to the first critical methodological question analysts must ask of every dataset they touch: "Is this based on a representative sample of the population I care about?" No single social media platform generates data representative of any larger population. Nor does combining data from multiple social media platforms.

Challenges in building datasets

Social media analytics and network analysis also introduce a separate sampling problem. Social media datasets are built by doing searches using brand names, logos, or **keywords**. Dataset quality depends entirely on how good the person who scraped the data was at picking the right keywords. Almost every keyword chosen will generate as much junk data as good data—while, at the same time, missing a lot of what the media analyst is trying to find.

Using the keyword "vaccination" in a search for social media conversations among anti-vaxxers, for example, will pull up thousands of posts and comments on dog and cat vaccinations. Similarly, if you search for posts about someone named Robert Smith, you'll miss any posts that called him "Bob" or "Mr. Smith" or anything but "Robert Smith," while pulling up thousands of posts about people named Robert Smith who are not the person you're seeking. You also might miss the fact that the news about Robert Smith that interests you went viral the day *after* the date you set as the end date for your search.

This means the completeness of the data used in social media analytics is always questionable. Dr. Itai Himelboim (personal communication, November 8, 2018), a social media expert at the University of Georgia, notes that learning how to sample social media data for network analysis is both simple and complex: "It's really learning five minutes. And practicing a lifetime . . . to really get the right data in terms of the right syntax and combinations of keywords."

Another complication is that because of the viral nature of social media activity, it's easy for a media analyst to miss the fact that some completely unrelated event is distorting their data. If a politician holds up a can of soda during a press conference, social media **mentions** of that product are likely to *spike*. But the spike doesn't tell the analyst much about actual public interest in the brand. Worse, if the analyst doesn't take the time to conduct a **spike analysis** on the dataset, she may never realize the spike was artificial and thus completely misinterpret the data.

The challenges analysts face with social media data don't end there. Different social media platforms set different limits on the amount and type of data you can access, even from your own accounts. Some platforms give you data on user demographics or location, and others don't. Platforms can change their rules about what data they will release and to whom at any time—making it hard to compare activity on your accounts across different platforms—or on any single account across time.

Even in the era of linked data, it is difficult to connect the activities of an individual user across different social media platforms and multiple usernames, if the platforms are not owned by the same company. So the analyst will find it difficult to track individual users' activities and attitudes across multiple platforms.

Social media metrics and operational definitions

Another key methodological problem comes from *operational definitions* (Chapter 3). While many platforms use the same names for the metrics they report, the terms are defined differently from platform to platform. What a user does that is counted as a *view* on one platform might be very different from how another platform counts a "view." On some platforms, video rolls are automatic and counted when someone lands on a page. On other platforms, the user must actively click on the video for a video roll to be measured. Even *emojis* mean different things on different platforms. Virtually every social media metric lacks standard operational definitions (Chapter 3).

The differences in operational definitions make it impossible to combine data from different platforms in any methodologically valid way. Thus reporting to your boss the total number of views a piece of content had across different social media platforms is likely to be misleading in terms of actual user consumption. Unfortunately, few executives or clients will welcome a lengthy report that explains the messy distinctions (Chapter 4).

Other methodological issues

As the numbers cited at the top of this chapter show, the volume of social media data can be overwhelming. Not surprisingly, analysts have been trying to apply artificial intelligence (AI) tools to the task. Results, however, have been mixed because so much of social media content is unstructured (I. Himelboim, personal communication, October 25, 2021). While machine learning has worked reasonably well when applied to coding structured content such as *time stamps* and *geolocation* data, analysts encounter *reliability* and validity issues when machines are asked to code things like the sentiments expressed in comments and emojis.

Finally, there is social media metrics fraud. *Fraud*—the deliberate creation of fake usage and engagement activity—is a major problem with social media data that costs advertisers globally billions of dollars every year. We'll discuss social media fraud in greater detail later in the chapter.

Feeling overwhelmed by this long list of methodological issues? For good reason. But despite these many challenges, social media analytics are increasingly important in media analytics and brand management because of the many insights they provide. Thus, the 21st century analyst *must* be knowledgeable about social media data. While you may not be able to safely generalize your social media data to a larger population, you can still get a very deep understanding of what the people who are engaging with a topic on a platform think. You also can observe actual behaviors, such as clicking on material, responding to posts with emojis or comments, and sharing material. That offers analysts more direct observations of people's interaction with specific content than you can get from a survey.

In research, there is no perfect research design or method. Every method has its own sampling problems and reliability and validity issues (Chapter 3). Each research method provides only part of the picture of whatever you're studying, no matter how strong your research design. The analyst's job is to understand the weaknesses in the data they're using and proceed with caution, keeping interpretations and extrapolations within the dataset's known limitations.

Social media analysis

As always, in working with any data, the first questions the analyst asks are: What do I need to know? What problem do I want to solve? What are the best KPIs to use to understand the problem? The answers to those questions determine everything that follows.

Having set the goals for your analysis and determined your KPIs, social media metrics can tell you two primary things: How much? and How good?

How much?

The first type of social media analysis is simply counting. How much of something happened? How many visitors were there? How many views? How many *followers*? How many reactions were there? How many shares? How many comments? How many conversions? Tracking the "how much" questions related to your media content or brand is known as *social media monitoring*. See Box 13.1.

Box 13.1 Key social media metrics

Term	Definition	Notes/formula
Post/tweet	The creation and sharing of any original content on a social media platform. "Tweet" is the term for a post on the social media platform Twitter.	Posting is the critical action by users because it starts the cycle of actions in any given network group.
Followers	The number of other social media users who have set their accounts to alert them if a particular person or organization posts. Followers may or may not ever see posts from accounts they follow.	A measure of interest in and loyalty to a particular social media account.

Term	Definition	Notes/formula
Actions	Any direct activity by a social media platform user including posting, commenting, sharing, clicking an emoji, watching, or converting.	Actions are the critical surrogate metric of engagement in social media analytics.
Amplification rate[a]	The number of people who share or retweet each post or tweet within a specified period of time.	(Number of shares or retweets per post or tweet)
Engagement	A term widely used across media industries to describe audience response to content. Important because engagement is believed to predict conversions. Often measured by counting user actions in response to a post or tweet.	There is no agreed-upon definition or measurement of engagement across media industry sectors, companies, or platforms.
Comment	Something that someone writes in response to a post.	Reflects a higher level of engagement than clicking an emoji. Provides detailed information that can be content analyzed.
Mention	When another user's name or username is included in a comment, a post, or a tweet.	Reflects a higher level of engagement and a stronger connection between nodes.
Like	Term used for any emoji inserted onto a social media post to signal that the reader approved of some aspect of that post or the poster.	It is not possible to tell from a "Like" emoji either how high the user's level of approval was or what part of the content pleased them.
Share/retweet	When a user reposts a piece of content to their own account so their own followers can see it or sends it by email, text, or other means to more people	Sharing/retweeting amplifies a piece of content.

(Continued)

(Continued)

Term	Definition	Notes/formula
Emojis	Any graphic symbol used to indicate a user's reaction to a piece of content; an indication of engagement.	Emojis provide no information about the intensity of the user's reaction or exactly what in a post triggered the reaction. Emojis mean different things on different platforms.
Views	The act of watching a video. Platforms vary in how much of a video must be watched by a user before it counts as a view.	Total number of video rolls.
When, or time stamp	Measures "when" social media activity occurs.	When is a post most likely to get the most or least attention? When during the day, week, year are people turning to social media and for what content or purpose?
Click-through rate (CTR)	Percentage of people who clicked on a piece of content.	
Conversation rate[a]	Amount of conversation a piece of content generated expressed as a percentage, based on the number of comments and shares. Measured differently by different platforms.	Number of comments or shares per post during a specified time period (Total number of comments or shares/ Total number of posts).
Conversion rate	Percentage of the audience that takes the action a content creator is seeking, such as clicking through to a website, buying a product, donating to a cause. A measure of the effectiveness of a post or advertisement.	(Conversions/Number of people who viewed the post or advertisement)

Term	Definition	Notes/formula
Share of voice (SOV)	Measures the visibility of a brand or product amid all the advertising or conversation competing for consumers' attention during the time period being measured as compared to direct competitors' share of voice.	Measured different ways depending on the analyst and the type of content.
Share of sentiment (SOS)	The percentage of positive and negative sentiments or actions social media users express about your brand or content as compared to your competitors'.	Measured different ways.
Share of conversation (SOC)	Percentage of conversation about your brand or content on social media as compared to your competitors' brands or content. A measure of engagement.	Measured different ways.
Watch time	The total amount of time people spend watching your ad, measured in seconds.	
Average watch time	The average amount of time viewers spent with your video ad. A measure of the effectiveness of the ad in getting audiences to engage with it.	(Watch time/Total impressions).
Node	A place on a network where traffic originates, ends, or concentrates. In social media, a social actor. Synonymous with "vertex" in network analysis.	

[a]Kaushik, 2011b

The metrics analysts track in social media monitoring go in and out of fashion. But among those most commonly used to measure the "how much" are: How many actions (reaction emojis, comments, shares, etc.) did a particular post get? How many of each type of action did the content generate? How did those numbers vary across different social media platforms, when the same or similar content was posted in different media? How did those numbers vary according to the type of content (news/entertainment; text/photo/video; comedy/drama, etc.)? How did those numbers vary according to user demographics? How did they vary by day of the week, month, year over year? How much attention was being paid to which topics and themes on social media as measured by the frequency with which certain **keywords** appeared during a particular time period? How frequently do specific keywords, such as brand names, consistently appear in social media posts?

Social media traffic, influencers, and influential users

When analyzing brand performance on social media, analysts also ask about **share of voice** (Chapter 5): How much share of voice did each brand category and each individual brand get on each platform and across all measured social media? How many actions did each brand category or brand get, and how did those numbers vary across different platforms?

A key "how much" factor in social media is the role of *influencers*. Influencers are people who are paid to post messages to social media. Research has identified at least five distinct subtypes of influencers from celebrities to people who are followed by a relatively small circle of closely connected people (Campbell & Farrell, 2020). Influencers are distinct from *influential users*. Influential users serve as experts and opinion leaders to a wide social media following but are not paid by third parties to sell specific products or ideas to their followers.

Marketers have long recognized the value of celebrity endorsements, but social media have transformed the nature and importance of influencers in online marketing. Today, there is an entire influencer industry, and many of the most successful influencers are self-created celebrities. In some cases, they achieved wide followings because of the quality of their advice on such things as makeup or fashion or, in other instances, by virtue of their comedic commentary or their cuteness. But an individual with the power to influence a large number of "friends" is too good an opportunity for marketers to ignore.

The importance of influencers in generating social media actions related to brands is clear. Research suggests that traditional advertising is less effective online because it disrupts users' goal-directed activities (Campbell & Farrell, 2020) and that marketing through influencers is seen by many social media users as less intrusive. According to one study, influencers on Instagram with between 1,000 and 5,000 followers averaged a 4.8% engagement rate from followers with brand-related content that they posted, although "engagement" was not defined (Influencer Marketing Hub & Refersion, 2022). On TikTok, influencers with larger followings were more successful, with the most widely followed influencers generating up to 14% active user engagement. Both platforms attracted the desirable under-34 demographic.

Not surprisingly, then, the influencer marketing business has grown rapidly in recent years, reaching an estimated global value of more than $16 billion in 2022 (Statista Research Department, 2022). Successful influencers are paid handsomely by consumer brands to pump products to their self-selected fans.

The role of influencers in social media marketing creates a whole new set of "how much" questions for analysts to explore. How many brand-related actions are generated by influencers, and how does that vary across social media platforms? How many influencers are there from which sources—news, TV, sports, politics, travel, food, self-created celebrities, child influencers? Which consumer demographics are more or less likely to be persuaded by influencers?

Among the challenges of measuring "how much," social media increasingly face the problem of cross-platform measurement. Many social media users—particularly the most active—are active on multiple platforms. When a client wants to track social media conversations and actions around their brand, they want to know how much conversation and how many actions were taken across as many social media platforms as possible. They also want to know how many of the conversations and actions were the same people on different platforms, and how many were unique users.

Measuring these things is challenging. First, neither operational definitions of metrics nor emojis are identical from platform to platform. Second, developing the capacity to credibly scrape and analyze the huge volume of data coming off any single social media platform requires major investments of both time and, often, money. As active social media users spread across multiple platforms, it is hard for analysts to keep up. Because social media platforms come and go in popularity, analysts have to choose wisely the platforms they're going to learn and monitor.

How good?

"How good" refers to how different elements of social media behavior relate to the KPIs that are important to you. "How good" is not only a different research question, it's a more complicated one. If a post received 10 million views, were those views that mattered? Were they the right viewers?

In fact, many of the metrics people talk about when discussing "How much" on social media don't translate to very much at all when you start asking "How good?" Analysts call these *vanity metrics*. They include such things as "likes," "followers," "retweets," etc. The numbers often look impressive, and they probably make your boss or client feel good, which is why they're known as "vanity metrics." Unfortunately, however, it's hard to know what they mean in terms of "how good."

If the likes on your post were larger this week than last, what does that mean? Did your readers like this post more than last week's? Or were more people outside enjoying nice weather last week and thus not reading social media? And does "liking" or "sharing" or "retweeting" actually translate into whatever actions or outcomes are important to your company or client? Think about your own social media behavior. How many of us have "liked" something almost out of impulse or support? You might have a lot of followers, but how often do those followers open the platform? If they do, do they see your posts? If they see them, do they read them?

Analysts focusing on "how good" ask which platforms generated the most readers/viewers for the content. Which posts generated the highest *conversation rate*—that is replies, comments, or feedback—or *amplification rate*—shares or retweets (Kaushik, 2011a, 2011b)? Which ones brought in viewers who did not just read the content but went all the way through to the original media site, generating viewers for the advertising the content producer sold instead of the ads sold by the social media platform? Which readers of which platforms were most likely to be converted into loyal—that is, returning—readers or viewers or subscribers? How many of the readers/viewers were actually the target audience or a monetizable audience?

Similarly, which keywords or themes attracted engagement with the content or brand? Which keywords were related to users' actions, what types of actions and how many? Which types of influencers, and which specific influencers, were most likely to trigger actions or conversions? Which influencers triggered actions by the brand's most valuable consumers?

Another approach to "how good" questions on social media is *sentiment analysis*. Sentiment analysis examines whether a user action on social media reflected a positive or negative attitude toward content or a brand. The analyst tries to determine whether the sentiment in a comment or an emoji was a positive or negative sentiment toward the brand or post, what type of positive or negative sentiment (love, laughing, angry), and why the person feels that way. Accurately assessing sentiments is not easy and can be further complicated by communication styles including sarcasm. Does that angry emoji mean the poster is angry at the content? Angry at the events described in the content? Or angry at the poster for having posted the content? Or something else? The reliability and validity of sentiment analysis is always questionable whether done by human coders or AI technology.

Ultimately, the question of "how good" is determined by the problem the analyst is studying and the KPIs being used as benchmarks for that problem. But here we come to a dirty little secret: Many of the assertions about why "how good" metrics are important are based on assumptions, not evidence. Does *engagement* really lead to conversions? If so, which definition of "engagement" should be used among the many used by social media platforms and social media listening companies? Does amplification really make customers think more highly of your brand? How monetizable is share of voice really and for which subcategories of brands and companies?

The truth is, in many cases we don't really know. The evidence supporting assertions about why some widely used metrics are effective for measuring "how good" is pretty sketchy.

Nevertheless, because social media data include concrete user actions and feedback, the analyst gains socioemotional insights into users that go far beyond simple measures of audience size. As a result, the questions companies want answered through social media analytics about "how good" are more and more complex.

For example, many companies are now asking analysts to plumb social media data for measures of nonfinancial performance that may ultimately affect financial performance. These include things such as the company's brand credibility with consumers, its reputation, the levels of consumer trust in the brand as compared to trust in its competitors', the strength of the brand's relationship with its customers, and their confidence in its products (Li & Stacks, 2015).

This approach to social media analysis is called *social media monitoring*. The difference between social media monitoring and *social media listening* is that listening refers to simply keeping an ear out for what's being said about topics and society in general (WorldCom, 2021). Monitoring refers to systematically identifying chatter about a specific brand or to gather insights that will help with a specific strategic business purpose. Social media listening and monitoring are becoming increasingly important parts of the social media analyst's job. They allow media companies to quickly create content of interest to a large audience, businesses to respond quickly to complaints and suggestions, and marketers to adapt their brand messaging to the moment.

In an era of intense political and social polarization around the world, backlash by consumers against brands perceived to be on the "wrong" side of important issues is becoming an issue affecting the success of both media and consumer products. Content that is out of step with public sentiment is, at best, a missed opportunity or makes a company appear tone-deaf. At worst, around highly controversial issues, it can become a choice between which customers a company is going to keep and which it's going to lose.

For company executives and brand managers, being caught on the wrong side of an important social or political issue when public opinion shifts can be career ending—literally overnight. Having analysts on board who can quickly identify changes in the public mood is critical given the lightning speed with which information and disinformation spread around the world.

Social media fraud

When asking "How good?," the social media analyst also needs to ask, "How *valid* are all these metrics? How much can I trust the numbers I'm seeing?" While data validity is an issue in all media analytics (Chapter 3), fraud in social media metrics is rampant.

There are many ways to game the social media universe, and with so much money on the table, people work constantly to invent new ones. Accounts and influencers can buy likes and followers. Many of those likes and followers are generated through the use of fake social media accounts, or *social bots*—of which there are many types employing many technologies, including humans (Gorwa & Guilbeault, 2020). The number of fake social media accounts is huge, with estimates ranging from 5% to nearly 45%, depending on the platform, the year, the topic of social media conversation, and the study. Social bots are used to boost vanity metrics or to anonymously spread misinformation, which distorts social listening metrics.[1]

Engagement pods are another way to game social media metrics. An engagement pod is a group of people—sometimes thousands of them—who band together to like and share each other's content to artificially drive up everyone's engagement metrics.

Estimates of the total size of the social media fraud problem vary, but most estimates are large. According to *PR Week*, one study found 54% of surveyed influencers *admitted* having used one or more fraudulent techniques to boost their metrics (Hickman, 2019). Since late 2018, Facebook has been taking down more than 1 billion fake accounts every quarter, with a high of 2.2 billion in the first quarter of 2019 (Statista, 2021). But many experts believe both figures are underestimates of social media fraud.

It is up to the analyst to constantly examine metrics for signs of fraud. One of the key tools for doing so is *social network analysis*, which will be discussed in more detail shortly.

Social media data interpretation

If executives' expectations of what can be learned from social media data are large, so too are the challenges of interpreting social media data. And the challenge of interpretation falls squarely on analysts' shoulders. Yes, social media metrics can provide richer insights into human responses than can traditional media metrics. But what do the data on user actions actually mean, particularly in relation to specific company goals?

For example, if a broadcast TV network promotes a new series on social media, the goal is to get people to view the series when it's released. The network may be trying to estimate *viewership* for the purpose of setting advertising prices.

But the question for the analyst is how much the social media platform's user-base overlaps with people who still watch broadcast television or subscribe to the streaming platforms the network will use for distribution. How good is the match between users of that social media platform and the network's target audience for the new program? How many of the comments the preview generates—"I can't wait to see this!" or "I love this actress"—actually translate into something the analyst can accurately report as *intent to view*? Finally, of course, how many who say they're going to watch the show actually *do* when the time comes?

Clearing the fog that clings to social media data is not easy—and not cheap. Social media measurement companies pay for large-scale public opinion surveys so they can correlate what they're seeing in chatter on different social media platforms with the trends and opinions that formal public opinion research is revealing in the larger population. They also buy consumer data to correlate actual buying behavior with brand engagements on social media platforms.

Fortunately, over time, evidence that social media metrics do relate to actual behavior has accumulated. There is, for example, some evidence from the early years of social media research that a company's reputation on social media and the trust and confidence customers expressed about it were related to positive trends in financial measures such as net income, profit margins, and earnings per share (Li & Stacks, 2015). Other research has shown that an absence of user engagement on social media in product categories lines up closely with poor sales in those categories and, conversely, higher engagement lines up with higher sales (T. Yuki, personal communication, November 3, 2018).

The harder question is how predictive such chatter really is for estimating future product sales. Are the chatterers a representative sample of customers, or are they a subsample of the product's rabid fans or rabidly disgruntled customers? Probably the latter. Then there is the question of whether users of a particular social media platform are representative of a specific product's potential customer base. Brands want positive chatter on the platforms favored by their most valuable customers. A lot of positive chatter among a group that represents only a small part of a brand's potential customer base—with silence on the platforms that attract the most likely or desired customers—is not good news. It's the analyst's job to understand that and spot the problem.

Social network analysis

The second approach media analysts apply to social media data is *network analysis*, which focuses on the user-to-user connections rather than on user engagement with content. Network analysis tracks how something moves from point to point through a network and identifies the most important *nodes*, or spots where traffic concentrates, in a given network system. Analysts want to understand how, when, and why concentrations happen around specific nodes.

Network analysis existed long before social media arrived. Transportation, communication, and utility systems depend upon it, as do such things as epidemiological studies during a pandemic, planning the shipment and delivery of global trade goods, forecasting population shifts across time and geography, and understanding people's interpersonal networks.

Understanding interpersonal networks is particularly important because it is through such networks that information, ideas, money, and power flow through communities, organizations, and societies. Research has established that an individual or community's position on social networks is related to such things as their perceived importance inside an organization, community, or society, their ability to innovate, and the likelihood that they will successfully adapt to changing conditions (Collien, 2021; Flora et al., 1992; Flora & Flora, 1993: Granovetter, 1973). In general, the more "weak ties" an individual or entity has—that is, the greater the number and more broadly spread the connections they have—the more information, influence, new ideas and power that person or organization is likely to have in their social and professional networks.

The goal of social network analysis is to identify patterns of connection among the network's users, including the subnetworks and clusters that form. The focus of interest is the relationships and patterns of interaction, not the characteristics of the individuals on the network (I. Himelboim, personal communication, November 8, 2018). Metrics measure the relative importance of individual nodes in driving activity within the network, and a visual map is created to make it easier to understand the patterns.

Based on visual mapping and the metrics on interactions, network analysis helps the analyst identify the most important individuals in the network, the connections between individuals, the strength of those connections, whether those connections are one-way or two-way, how information moves through the network, and the points where the movement stops or is blocked. See Figure 13.1. Comparing network maps can pinpoint who is responsible for creating certain types of information—factual information versus conspiracy theories, for example. It also can help identify the fastest and most efficient way to spread critically important information such as public health information or evacuation orders in the face of a looming

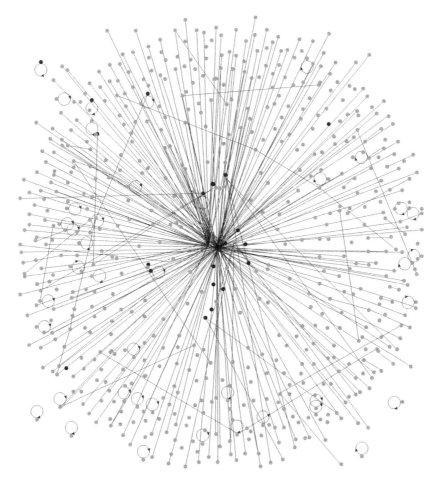

Figure 13.1 Network analysis graph
Source: Dr. C. Ann Hollifield

natural disaster. Finally, network analysis is an important tool for identifying social media fraud by making it easier to spot engagement pods and social bots.

Identifying and understanding subnetworks and clusters in social networks is of increasing interest to media companies, marketers, and social scientists because clusters become information echo chambers. People within clusters influence one another and trust one another more as sources of information than they do out-of-cluster sources. Clusters play a critical role in media content and product consumption choices—and also in the spread of information, disinformation, and conspiracy theories. Research has shown for example, that false news and information move much faster and farther—up to 100 times farther—across Twitter than truth and factual news stories (Vousoughi et al., 2018). Such analyses are critically important to know if your goal is either to stop the spread of lies and misinformation across society or to accelerate the dissemination of information important to such things as public health and safety.

As even just this brief discussion makes clear, network analysis is a complex method that requires training, practice, and skill to use effectively. Teaching even the basics is beyond the scope of this text. It is, however, important for anyone working in social media analytics to be aware of network analysis, how it differs from other types of social media analysis, and what can be learned from using it. Anyone interested in specializing in social media analytics should seek training in the network analysis research method. Information can be found in the Additional Resources section of this chapter.

Uses of social media analytics by brands and companies

We've already discussed many of the ways brands and companies use social media analytics. But there are a few specifics worth adding to our discussion.

The first set of questions is about social media in general: How much traffic is there on social media? What are the trends in that traffic? Is it growing overall year to year, and where is it growing? Which platforms are gaining and losing audience? How are user demographics on a platform changing? Which social media platforms are likely to generate consumer engagement, actions, and conversions?

Another set of questions is about what types of content engage social media audiences: video, text, pictures, graphics? Which types of content generate the most conversions? And even more specifically, what types of storylines—comedy, animal videos, political memes, etc.—generate the most actions and conversions within each type of content such as video, audio, text?

Brands also look to social media analysts for insights about their competitors. Which platforms are becoming more or less popular for posting brand-related content or advertising, and why? Which social media platforms are most popular with leading brands in the client's product category, and why? Which platforms do their direct competitors use—and why?

Share of voice is always a key question on social media, but it is measured many different ways. What the analyst finds depends on the denominator used in the equation. Are you measuring share of voice on a single platform or across all social media platforms? Is it the share of voice of your industry against other industries, of your product category against all other product categories or just related product categories, of your brand against all other brands or just against brands that are direct competitors?

Another application of social media analytics is a *social media audit* (Gattiker, 2013). A social media audit is a periodic, comprehensive evaluation of a company's social media presence and strategy. It includes but goes beyond the types of marketing and conversion metrics that have been the focus of most of this chapter. A social media audit takes a step backward and begins with larger questions: What are the reasons this company/client is engaging with social media? How do those reasons fit with the way the company or organization creates value? Given how the company creates value, what results or value does the company believe it can create through using social media? And how will the company measure the success or failure of its social media efforts? What are the benchmarks it will use?

Social media audits include questions about how much it is costing the company in employee time and money to engage with social media, and what returns on investment those efforts have achieved? Which employees are and are not engaging with social media on behalf of the company? How are they engaging with social media and with what effects—positive or negative? Are the company's social media efforts and messaging coordinated or disorganized? Are the company's social media efforts having positive or negative effects on its reputation and value?

Social media audits may be undertaken as part of a company's general management and strategic review or as part of a public relations campaign. Indeed, many public relations agencies offer social media audits as a client service. While social media audits usually are focused on larger questions of organizational management, strategy, and efficiency, they can't succeed without social media data, so the social media analyst can expect to be deeply involved.

Uses of social media analytics for media analysts

Many of the questions just discussed also are relevant for media analysts working in traditional media companies. Media companies are brands themselves. Media is a product category, and content is a consumer product. But media analysts have a somewhat different relationship to social media, which makes following social media analytics even more important. Social media are media platforms in their own right, which make them both a threat and an opportunity. They are direct competitors to legacy media for both audience time and attention, as well as for advertising. But given social media's vast audiences and interactive structure, they are becoming increasingly important to content marketing and distribution.

For the analyst working in a traditional media company, one of the key questions is *where* social media activity is occurring—that is, which social media platforms are generating the most audience for different pieces of content. Are people more likely to click on clips from a late-night comedy show on Facebook than they are on Twitter or vice versa? On which platform are users more likely to share that clip? Producers want to identify the platforms that are most popular with a show's target audiences, and where posting content is mostly like to generate actual program views. Social media analytics help pinpoint whether the audience members of Program A are more likely to engage with or buy advertised products than the audience members of Program B, even if the demographics of the two audiences are similar.

The same is true for news producers. On which platform is a newspaper story or TV news teaser most likely to be shared? Is that the same platform where users are most likely to click through to the original news organization to read that and other stories? Finally, are the demographics of that platform's users the ones most important to the news organization and its advertisers? If not, what should the news organization do differently to attract shares and click-throughs with its most valuable audiences?

It's not just the "where" of social media that is important. It's also the "*when.*" At what times of the day, on what days of the week, in which months is the target audience most likely to engage with the content a media company posts? How far in advance of the release date should a film studio or network start promoting a new production on social media to generate maximum buzz? What times of day should a news organization post headlines or teases to generate maximum audiences on its legacy and digital platforms? How do those times vary depending on the content, the news platform, the social media platform, and the target audience?

Social media data also are valuable for content development. News producers can use social media analytics to track issues and topics important to people in their markets, as well as to track the spread of misinformation they may want to address in their reporting. Entertainment producers can get ideas for new episodes or storylines from topics and trends on social media.

In addition to their value in marketing and content development, social media are an increasingly important distribution platform for traditional media companies. The amount of text, video, and audio content people are consuming through social media platforms has been rising sharply each year. That provides both opportunity and risks for the media companies that pay the costs of producing that content.

The opportunity comes from making a wider audience aware that specific content exists—boosting content discovery. The risk is that social media companies—not the content producers—will get much of the revenue from the advertising sold around the content. Monitoring how content is moving through social media and whether the result of that is revenue positive or negative for the producer is an increasingly important part of a media analyst's job.

Finally, as influencers and influential users play bigger roles in shaping the wider public's perceptions and actions, media companies need to know which ones hold most sway with the producers' target audiences and then recruit them to hype content. Media companies also want to become important themselves in the influence game, which means pushing their staff members to become social media influencers in their own right.

In other words, social media analytics now play a role in media personnel management. Newsrooms, for example, may use social media analytics data to understand which news sections—national, state, local news; business; traffic; sports; or weather—generate the largest number of social media followers, shares, or engagement. Some have experimented with using social analytics in personnel performance evaluations, tracking how often their journalists post to social media platforms about the news stories they're developing. The news director may track which journalists are most successful in getting their posts shared, which are attracting their own social media followers that the media company can convert into audience and revenue, and how successful each journalist is in using social media effectively as compared to their competitors in other news organizations and their colleagues in the newsroom. Many media companies now examine job applicants' social media use—both volume and professionalism—as part of the hiring process.

Using social media as a success metric in employee evaluations can be problematic on many different levels, including creating internal employee rivalries. Sports or weather reporters might find it easier to build their follower numbers or generate user engagement than journalists who cover news, simply because—as traditional ratings and readership research show—far more people engage with entertainment or content such as traffic and weather than with the news itself.

Pressuring employees to aggressively use social media can backfire in other ways. Social media never sleeps, so employees who post all hours of the day and night and seven days a week will be more likely to generate better social metrics than colleagues who only post during their official work hours. Encouraging or allowing such activity would, however, violate labor laws and union regulations in many countries and further erode work–life balance for the company's employees. In the long run, such policies are likely to result in high staff turnover.

Similarly, as many media professionals have learned, it takes only one careless social media post to damage a brand or destroy a reputation or career. The more pressure employees are under to post, to post first, and to post often, the more likely they are to eventually make a serious mistake that mires themselves and their employer in major controversy.

Ethical issues in social media analytics

Social media are successful because they meet a fundamental human need: human connection. But some argue that they also succeed at least in part because of the chemical responses they trigger in our brains. Research has shown that self-disclosure in conversation triggers the same pleasure and reward centers in the brain as monetary rewards, and for some people it appears to provide a greater reward than money (Tamir & Mitchell, 2012). Similarly, neurological studies of brain activity among adolescents and young adults while they used social media showed that "liking" content posted by others and receiving "likes" triggered responses in the same parts of the brain that respond to rewards (Sherman et al., 2018).

What these and similar studies suggest is that the very process of using social media may trigger impulses to disclose more about our lives, our feelings, and our attitudes to our social media "friends" than we would if we just stopped to think about it. From the social media company's perspective, that's the whole point. Their business is not about helping you connect with friends or clients. It's about selling advertising to you based on your location, your demographics, and your attitudes and selling data about you to third parties. That's the social media business model. That's why social media platforms are free to users. As Andrew Lewis (2010) observed on the community weblog Metafilter in a now famous quote: "If you're not paying for something, you're not the customer; you're the product being sold."

While users are presented with "user agreements" when they set up social media accounts, most click the "I agree" button without thoroughly reading the document. In doing so, users are agreeing to allow third parties to access and use their personal data and information in ways they can't control, with the specifics of the agreement depending on the platform and subject to change by the platform. The consequences can be dire.

Where personal data from social media becomes really powerful is when it is combined with all of the other data we generate in the digital era: location data from all the apps on our phones and in our cars that track our physical movements, our phone calls, and our personal contact lists; purchase data from our credit cards, the QR codes we use to order off restaurant menus; the scanners in stores as we check out after being asked by the clerk for our zip code and telephone numbers, even when paying with cash; voter data that show whether and how often we vote and which political party's ballot we requested in the most recent primary election; court data on every traffic ticket and legal encounter we've ever had; data from the digital devices that insurance companies now urge customers to install so they can track driving habits; and data from smartwatches and health-tracking apps, which can be sold to employers concerned about rising employee health care costs to use in hiring and firing decisions.

When you combine behavioral and lifestyle data with social media data on individuals' attitudes, emotions, and beliefs, the results raise critically important ethical questions for every analyst to consider. Most social media companies have some limitations on the personal information they sell to third parties, but the rules social media companies say they have implemented to guard users' privacy vary from company to company, are often opaque and shifting, and depend on the company itself to actually obey its own rules. Equally importantly, there have been notable security breaches on social media platforms (Cambridge Analytica and Facebook, 2018).

As the business of data analytics grows and tools of data collection expand, media analysts are going to be on the front lines of the global debate over where the line is to be drawn between economic efficiency and personal privacy. To what degree does the corporate desire to use information to achieve efficient advertising and maximum returns on investment trump the individual's right to privacy and the right to be protected from subtle, possibly even subliminal manipulation by third parties? This may be the most important and critical question facing media and audience analysts on a daily basis as they perform their roles, and social media analysts are no exception. It is truly a balancing act that is rife with ethical and societal implications.

During their careers, many professional media analysts will find themselves asked to create datasets and conduct analyses that raise serious questions about ethics and privacy. It may be necessary for the analyst to stand up to their employer or client and draw the line between what is possible—and what is right.

Social media analysts interviewed for this text say the responsibility starts when you acquire a dataset. Does that dataset contain highly sensitive personally identifiable information (PII) such as Social Security numbers in the United States, a driver's license number, or a National Identification number for citizens of countries that use those? If so, is it likely those individuals gave either implied or express consent to having that personal ID number included in *this* dataset with these other data points for *this* type of analysis? Or is it more likely that someone scraped these ID numbers off of the *Dark Web* and then built it into the dataset sold to your company? If the latter, then as an ethical professional, you should refuse to use that data.

Similarly, how are you being asked to use data scraped from social media? Are you building highly specific individual profiles that can be used to manipulate people in ways of which they are unaware, or are you examining general social trends based on the general information collected from social platforms? If you, as a social media analyst, are *not* standing up for the need to protect the personal privacy of the people who use social media, then you are part of the problem.

The European Union has led the world in writing laws to strengthen protection of personal privacy and to limit the collection and third-party use of personal data. Most of the rest of the world, particularly the United States, trail in providing legal protections for individual privacy.[2] Professional media analysts who work for transnational media companies must educate themselves about the data privacy laws in each country where their company gathers data and work actively to ensure that their employer is in compliance. That will be a continuing challenge. It is virtually certain that national and international laws on data privacy protection will evolve quickly in the next few decades—as will data collection technologies and the attempts to evade those laws.

Summary and conclusion

Experts concede that the methodological issues plaguing social media data are immense and create serious validity problems and that interpreting data from social media is a lot like reading tea leaves. They caution that perfectly accurate interpretations of data aggregated from multiple platforms will never be possible. Analysts must walk a fine line between being paralyzed by uncertainty about what the data means—and being overconfident and unrealistic about the validity of the findings. The goal is to find rays of insight in the mist, helping media executives or clients make decisions with more confidence than they could have without the data.

The key is for the analyst to approach the work not as a numbers game but as an exercise in creative strategy, taking a solutions-based approach. As with all data analysis, the key questions will continue to be: What problems do I need to solve? What information do I need to solve them? And What can these data tell me that will help answer both of those questions?

Social media analytics offer analysts several things that most other forms of media and audience data cannot. First, they offer valuable insights into human attitudes, emotions, and reactions to content. When aggregated, such information helps clarify how content preferences cluster around socioeconomic, political, and demographic groups. That can help media companies produce content that better serves people's needs. They also provide massive real-time information on emerging issues and trends, helping media producers develop content that speaks to the moment and that educates and informs about important issues of the time.

The downside is that social media also help people create their own information and disinformation bubbles, helping them to block out information that challenges what they want to believe, whether true or not. This social media capability has inarguably played a role in the increasing political polarization and dysfunction around the world (Jamieson & Albarracin, 2020; Mukerjee & Yang, 2020). When combined with highly specific personal information and identities, it also threatens personal privacy.

Finally, social network analysis allows analysts to see how information is moving through various communication networks and publics. Network analysis pinpoints how individuals are connected to one another, who influences whom, and how information moves across the globe. Those insights are almost impossible to get using other types of audience data.

While social media companies are increasingly the subject of public and regulatory critique, some forms of them are likely to remain central to communication industries for the foreseeable future. Thus there will be many career opportunities in social media analytics. Equally importantly, analysts working in other media sectors will find it necessary to work with—and understand—the constantly changing dynamics of social media data.

Additional resources[3]

Bendle, N.T., Farris, P.W., Pfeiffer, P.E., & Reibstein, D.J. (2016). *Marketing metrics: The manager's guide to measuring marketing performance* (3rd ed.). Pearson Education.

Brandwatch: www.brandwatch.com/

Cision: www.cision.com

Hansen, D. L., Shneiderman, B., Smith, M. A., & Himelboim, I. (2019). *Analyzing social media networks with NodeXL: Insights from a connected world* (2nd ed.). Elsevier.

Hubspot: www.hubspot.com

Parse.ly: www.parse.ly

Shareablee: www.shareablee.com/

Social Media Research Foundation: www.smrfoundation.org/. The open source network analysis software NodeXL can be downloaded from this site. Tutorials, newsletters, and other resources including current examples of social network analysis graphs also can be found there. NodeXL can be used to scrape social media from some platforms if allowed by the platform.

Tweetdeck: https://tweetdeck.twitter.com/

Recommended cases

**These cases can be found on the textbook website:
www.routledge.com/cw/hollifield**

Case 13.1: Analyzing Your Own Social Media Traffic
Case 13.2: Interpreting Basic Social Network Analysis Data
Case 13.3: Analyzing Twitter Data from a Local News Organization's Posts

Case studies, along with accompanying datasets for this chapter, can be found on the text website. We particularly suggest the preceding cases in the order listed. See the companion website and instructor's manual for detailed descriptions of these and other relevant cases.

Discussion questions and exercises

1. The chapter lists many questions that social media analysts are asked to answer. But the lists are only a beginning. Place yourself in one or more of the roles of General Manager, News Director/Editor, Film/TV Producer, Podcaster, Advertiser, or Brand Manager. In your chosen role, develop additional questions not already discussed in the text that you might ask a social media analyst to answer. The questions should help the company manage one or more of the following functions: strategy against competitors, content development, financial performance, customer relations. Share the questions you develop for the class to critique and discuss.

2. Revisit the questions you just developed. Explain what social media data and *variables* you would use in an analysis of each question.

    • What variables would you need to generate insight into each question?
    • Explain *why* you think those variables would be the best choice to answer a specific question, instead of the other possibilities.
    • Explain whether all of the variables can be gathered from social media, or will you have to buy other datasets and combine them with social media platform data to do the analyses?
    • Explain which social media platforms would generate data on the variables needed for each question, and which would not.
    • Discuss the methodological and validity issues you will need to consider as you analyze each question.

3. If you have a Facebook/Meta account, go to it. At your Profile, go to "Settings/Your Facebook Information." Click the view links for "Access Your Information." Under "Access Your Information," click the "Logged Information" link in the left-hand menu.
    What you will see will depend on the privacy settings you have put in place on your account.

    • Discuss with your classmates the following questions:

        • What is Facebook/Meta telling potential advertisers about you?

- How much is it tracking your online and real-world activities outside Facebook?
- How accurate are the "Interest Categories" in which you have been placed? What percentage of them are accurate, and what percentage are totally wrong?
- How do you think Facebook connected you to those categories that you consider totally wrong?
- On a scale of 1 to 10 where 10 is a completely accurate profile of you and your interests, how accurate is the profile Facebook has created of you?

- Go to Settings/Your Facebook Information/Off Facebook Activity. Scroll through all the Apps and Sites that have been sharing data about your activities on their sites with Facebook. Click the "Recent Activity" link. How far back does Facebook's tracking of your "recent" off-Facebook activity go? Discuss in class.
- Go to whatever social media accounts you have and review your privacy settings. Discuss what privacy settings you may consider changing and why.

4. Discuss the ethical issues and implications of social media analytics. How do *you* feel after reading this chapter, about how your personal data is being issued by brands, companies, and political operators? What limits, if any, do you think governments should put on the collection, aggregation, and use of individuals' social media data?

Notes

1. A study in early 2020 estimated that 45% of all of the Tweets in the United States about the Covid-19 outbreak were generated by social bots, apparently in a deliberate attempt to sow confusion, fear and political divisions among the US population (Allyn, 2020).
2. A few states in the United States—notably California and Vermont—have passed state-level consumer data privacy and protection laws. But at this writing there are no federal guidelines.
3. These resources include links to several social media monitoring and listening companies. The list is not comprehensive. They are offered as examples. Many of them have examples of the analytics they provide under "Resource" menus. Several offer the chance to subscribe to their free newsletters and blogs, a good way to learn about and keep up with this rapidly evolving area of analytics.

References

Allyn, B. (2020, May 20). Researchers: Nearly half of accounts Tweeting about Coronavirus are likely bots. *National Public Radio.* www.npr.org/sections/coronavirus-live-updates/2020/05/20/859814085/researchers-nearly-half-of-accounts-tweeting-about-coronavirus-are-likely-bots

Auxier, B., & Anderson, M., (2021, April 7). Social media use in 2021. *Pew Research Center*. www.pewresearch.org/internet/2021/04/07/social-media-use-in-2021/

Bendle, N. T., Farris, P. W., Pfeifer, P. E., & Reibstein, D. J. (2016). *Marketing metrics: The manager's guide to measuring marketing performance* (3rd ed). Pearson Education Inc.

Cambridge Analytica and Facebook. (April 4, 2018). The scandal and the fallout so far. *New York Times*. www.nytimes.com/2018/04/04/us/politics/cambridge-analytica-scandal-fallout.html

Campbell, C., & Farrell, J. R. (2020). More than meets the eye: The functional components underlying influencer marketing. *Business Horizons*, 63(4), 469–479.

Collien, I. (2021). Concepts of power in boundary spanning research: A review and research agenda. *International Journal of Management Reviews*, 23(4), 443–465. doi.org/10.1111/ijmr.12251

Flora, C. B., & Flora, J. L. (1993). Entrepreneurial social infrastructure: A necessary ingredient. *Annals of the American Academy of Political and Social Science*, 529, 48–58.

Flora, J. L., Green, G. P., Gale, E. A., Schmidt, F. E., & Flora, C. B. (1992). Self-development: A viable rural development option? *Policy Studies Journal*, 20(2), 276–288.

Gattiker, U. E. (2013). *Social media audit: Measure for impact*. Springer.

Gorwa, R., & Guilbeault, D. (2020). Unpacking the social media bot: A typology to guide research and policy. *Policy & Internet*, 12(2), 223–248. doi: 10.1002/poi3.184

Granovetter, M. S. (1973). The strength of weak ties. *American Journal of Sociology*, 78(6), 1360–1380.

Hickman, A. (2019, July 9). Majority of UK influencers engage in faker: Landmark new study. *PRWeek*. www.prweek.com/article/1590362/majority-uk-instagram-influencers-engage-fakery-landmark-new-study

Influencer Marketing Hub, & Refersion. (2022). *The state of influencer marketing, 2022*. chrome-extension://efaidnbmnnnibpcajpcglclefindmkaj/https://influencer-marketinghub.com/ebooks/Influencer_Marketing_Benchmark_Report_2022.pdf

Jamieson, K. H., & Albarracin, D. (2020). The relation between media consumption and misinformation at the outset of the SARS-CoV-2 pandemic in the US. *The Harvard Kennedy School (HKS) Misinformation Review*, 1(2), 1–16. https://doi.org/10.37016/mr-2020-012

Kaushik, A. (2011a, June 28). Your web metrics: Super lame or super awesome? *Occam's Razor*. www.kaushik.net/avinash/web-metrics-super-lame-super-awesome/

Kaushik, A. (2011b, October 11). Best social media metrics: Conversation, amplification, applause, economic value. *Occam's Razor*. www.kaushik.net/avinash/best-social-media-metrics-conversation-amplification-applause-economic-value/

Lewis, A. [@ blue_beetle]. (2010, August 26). If you're not paying for it, you're not the customer; you're the product being sold. [Post]. *MetaFilter*. www.metafilter.com/95152/Userdriven-discontent#3256046

Li, C., & Stacks, D. (2015). *Measuring the impact of social media on business profit and success: A Fortune 500 perspective*. Peter Lang Inc.

Mukerjee, S., & Yang, T. (2020). Choosing to avoid? A conjoint experimental study to understand selective exposure and avoidance on social media. *Political*

Communication, *38*(3), 222–240. https://doi/full/10.1080/10584609.2020. 1763531

Nielsen, J. (2006, October 8). The 90–9–1 rule for participation inequality in social media and online communities. *NN/g Nielsen Norman Group*. www.nngroup. com/articles/participation-inequality/

Sherman, L. E., Hernandez, L. M., Greenfield, P. M., & Dapretto, M. (2018). What the brain 'likes': Neural correlates of providing feedback on social media. *Social Cognitive and Affective Neuroscience*, *13*(7), 699–707. https://doi.org/10.1093/ scan/nsy051

Statista Research Department. (2021, January 14). Estimated cost of digital ad fraud in the United States from 2011 to 2021. *Statista*. www.statista.com/ statistics/778733/digital-ad-fraud-cost-us/

Statista Research Department. (2022, August 19). Global influencer marketing value (2016–2022). *Statista*. www.statista.com/statistics/1092819/global-influencer- market-size/

Tamir, D. I., & Mitchell, J. P. (2012, May 12). Disclosing information about the self is intrinsically rewarding. *Proceedings of the National Academy of Sciences of the United States of America*, *109*(21), 8038–8043. Published online 2012 May 7. doi: 10.1073/pnas.1202129109. www.ncbi.nlm.nih.gov/pmc/articles/ PMC3361411/

Vousoughi, S., Roy, D., & Ara, S. (2018). The spread of true and false news online. *Science*, *359*(6380), 1146–1151. https://doi:10.1126/science.aap9559

Worldcom. (2021, March 30). *The difference between social media monitoring and social listening*. https://worldcomgroup.com/insights/difference-between-social- media-monitoring-social-listening/

14 News analytics

News analytics refers to monitoring audiences' consumption of and reactions to news stories. Unlike analytics in most other media sectors, news analytics is done in real time because a single news story may be updated several times in an hour, and the entire news mix will be updated and changed multiple times a day in most news organizations. Data on audience responses are collected and analyzed continuously, with news managers and journalists deciding whether and how to allow the findings to shape their moment-to-moment editorial decisions. Moreover, in an era when the financial sustainability of news organizations that produce high-quality journalism is in doubt around the world, news analytics is becoming a critical strategic management—and survival—tool in the news industries.

For that reason, news analytics aren't just for media analysts anymore. News organizations increasingly expect individual journalists to continuously monitor audience response to their work and to use that information to improve their techniques and develop a personal fan base among readers. All of that, of course, is expected to ultimately contribute to the news organization's success. News executives say that having the skills and willingness to use audience analytics can make the difference between being hired as a reporter, promoted into management, and retained during newsroom layoffs—or not. Data analytics skills are a basic requirement for managers in many news organizations and are a fundamental tool of investigative reporting, where the use of data analysis in reporting is called *data journalism*.

While news analytics have become a fundamental professional skill for journalists, large news organizations increasingly hire full-time media analysts—often teams of them. Because of the underlying economic and product characteristics of new stories (Chapter 2), news media markets worldwide have been more disrupted than any other media industry sector by digital technology and the increased competition for audiences' attention and advertisers' revenue. Many experts believe the survival of news media organizations—particularly local news media organizations—is now

DOI: 10.4324/9780429506956-18

the biggest media management challenge globally (Albarran, 2018; Holli-field, 2019). News analytics is an increasingly important tool in addressing that challenge.

The threats facing news organizations

Let's start our discussion of news analytics with the most important point: *news content matters*. Quality journalism produces immeasurable value for society. Journalism done right is critical to maintaining transparent, less corrupt governments and businesses; democratic governmental processes; national and local economic development; peace both within and between communities and nations; and the protection of human rights (Cauhapé-Cazaux & Kalathil, 2015; Hollifield et al., 2005; Islam, 2002; National Advisory Commission on Civil Disorders, 1968).

But news industries and their ability to produce quality journalism are in trouble worldwide. To understand the management challenges facing news organizations, it's important to first understand why news industries, which flourished for centuries, unraveled so quickly in the digital age. Simply put, the economic and product characteristics of information, in general (Chapter 2), and news content specifically, interacted with digital technologies in ways that changed news markets around the world.

First, digital technologies and the internet drastically increased the competition for news audiences by making it inexpensive and easy to start new digital native news organizations. At the same time, computers, mobile phones with cameras, the internet, and social media turned billions of people around the world into content producers and distributors.

People who *post* to social media are producing content and giving it away for free, without being paid for their production time and equipment. No one would do that for any other type of product—cars, clothes, food, for example. Once produced, content—no matter what type of content it is—exists forever, potentially competing with all other news and entertainment content for audiences' time and attention (Chapter 2).

As competition has increased, audiences have fragmented, leaving most news organizations with shrinking audiences. Unlike most media sectors, it is hard for news organizations to attract audiences by differentiating their content from their competitors' because news has commodity characteristics. Commodities are products that are nearly identical no matter who produces it, such as oil, wheat, and precious metals. Breaking news stories look pretty much the same to the audience no matter which news organization or journalist reports it because the basic facts are the same. That assumes, of course, that the news organizations and journalists are all reporting the story according to professional journalistic norms and standards.

So what can news organizations do in a highly competitive business to make *their* product stand out from their competitors'? Two possibilities are content quality and packaging. Content quality means hiring the most expert reporters in specific topics such as health, politics, or international affairs or the most popular commentators for the opinion section. Packaging means hiring the most attractive anchors on television or having the catchiest slogan or the best website layout and design. But expert talent is expensive, and packaging is only a short-term fix. If it works, a competitor will copy it.

A less expensive and more successful approach that has proved effective worldwide is to abandon the 20th century ethic of journalistic balance and neutrality in favor of deliberately slanting news reporting to favor a particular ideology—political, religious, cultural, or other (Hollifield, 2006). This news product differentiation strategy succeeds because most humans avoid *cognitive dissonance*—that is, information or ideas that challenge their already held beliefs (Festinger, 1957). The problem, of course, is that when news organizations align themselves with an ideology, they may ignore negative stories about the chosen ideology and its policies and leaders, distort facts, and, in the worst cases, report information that is highly questionable factually but likely to be well received by their audiences (Baum, 2011; Cohen & McIntyre, 2019; Whitehouse & Abughazaleh, 2020).

Digital technologies have caused other audience-related problems for news industries. The growing number of digital native news and information sites has disaggregated the content bundles news producers used to attract mass audiences to sell to advertisers (Chapter 2). Audiences suddenly had multiple sources—usually free sources—they could use to get headlines, stock prices, comics, advice, birth and death announcements, weather, sports, traffic—and other information audiences they once relied on legacy news organizations to provide.

News organizations found themselves left with only a single unique product to offer their customers: reporting on hard, breaking, and investigative news. Unfortunately, there is little evidence that the audience for hard news and investigative journalism on government, politics, and business has ever been very large.

On the business side, digital technologies have created even bigger problems for news industries (Chapter 2). For newspapers, one of the worst developments was free online classified advertising sites. They effectively captured one of newspapers' most important revenue sources. Additionally, as audiences—particularly the coveted younger audiences advertisers want to reach—turned their attention to non-news content online, advertisers followed them.

Many factors influence the costs of ads and ad campaigns, including the audience quality being delivered (Chapters 2, 5), and differences in the cost of producing an ad for the platform on which it will be distributed—for example, a broadcast video ad versus an ad that will be uploaded online. But because there is an almost infinite supply of space and time available online, digital advertising rates per CPM are generally lower than advertising rates on some legacy news platforms (Bateman, n.d.). Furthermore, the majority of online advertising worldwide is bought through the major digital distribution platforms such as Google and Facebook. That means most of the revenue generated by advertising around online news stories goes to the distribution platform or search engine operators, not the news organizations that produced it. So even though television, radio, newspapers, and magazines have created online news sites, revenue from digital advertising hasn't replaced the advertising lost from traditional platforms.

All this has led to a rapidly increasing failure rate among daily commercial news organizations worldwide. The evidence is growing that, with the exception of major cities and demand for national and international news, the audience for news is not big enough in most local markets to generate the revenue needed to cover news production costs (Chapter 2). In countries like the United States, the failure of local daily newspapers across the country is creating *news deserts*,[1] areas where no independent professional news organization provides citizens with information about government decisions or community issues or serves as a watchdog over government and business actions (Abernathy, 2022; Levin, 2019).

The impact that the absence of journalism will have on democracy, local communities, and society is an issue of major concern. In some places, however, part of the gap is being filled by local news bloggers. News blogs take many forms from neighborhood websites and listservs to entrepreneurial startups that provide quality reporting about government actions and community events. Some are small revenue-producing businesses, and others are produced as a volunteer community service. But large or small, profit or nonprofit, owners and journalists in news organizations share many of the same challenges in attracting audience attention to news content.

These challenges are pushing news organizations of all types to adopt news analytics as a management tool. The use of audience research in news decisions has long been controversial among journalists and news executives, however, and media analysts working in news organizations face unique challenges from within.

Data analytics, journalism, and journalists

Although news organizations have used *circulation* and *ratings* data to sell advertising for more than a century (Bennett, 1965), using data as a basis for making news decisions is, journalistically, still relatively new (Lee et al., 2014). In news organizations, journalists and the professional culture of

346   *Media analytics across industry sectors*

journalism are often the biggest obstacles to change and innovation (Daniels & Hollifield, 2002; Hanusch, 2017; Singer, 2003). The perception that a proposed change threatens journalists' professional identities or news quality plays a big role in whether a new idea, technology, or technique is accepted or resisted by news workers (Gade & Perry, 2003; Lee et al., 2014; Massey & Erwart, 2012).

Research consistently shows journalists view the use of audience research in news decisions as a threat to editorial independence (Allam & Hollifield, 2021; Singer & Ashman, 2009; Tandoc & Ferrucci, 2017), quality journalism (Beam, 1995; Tandoc & Thomas, 2015), and professional authority and the news organization's credibility (Justel-Vázquez et al., 2016). Many journalists fear using audience data in news decisions will cause news managers to emphasize entertainment and sensational content over news and quality journalism (McManus, 1994; Tandoc, 2015). More often than not, however, journalists do a poor job of understanding their audiences' needs and interests (Justel-Vázquez et al., 2016; Lee et al., 2014; Singer, 2011). There is a disconnect between what journalists believe will—or should—interest their audience and what actually does.

In an early study of newsrooms' use of audience research, Beam (1995) found 95% of US newspapers used some type of audience research, but news executives made little use of the findings once they had them. Editors added few topics to their existing coverage based on research results, and then mostly in the entertainment—not news—sections. More recent research shows many editors still resist allowing user preferences for content to significantly influence news decisions (Allam & Hollifield, 2021; Singer, 2011).

But that resistance is showing some signs of crumbling in the face of the news industry's problems, with some journalists becoming more interested in understanding their audiences (Belair-Gagnon & Holton, 2018; Hanusch, 2017; Moyo et al., 2019; Usher, 2013). Journalists who see audience analytics as a tool for increasing their own credibility with audiences, their news organization's competitive position (Tandoc, 2015), or its financial position (Vu, 2014) are more likely to be open to applying news analytics in newsroom decisions. News managers also play a major role in getting journalists to use news analytics effectively, with journalists being more likely to adopt analytics when managers believe in their value and encourage their use (Tandoc & Ferrucci, 2017). Converts argue that journalists' relationship to audiences must evolve beyond the commonly used "active/passive/commodity" conceptions (Chapter 2) and make room for audiences to be cocreators of news in a digitally mediated conversation with editors and journalists (Lee et al., 2014).

But while many news managers and journalists now pay lip service to the benefits of news analytics, fewer actually use what they learn to shape reporting (Allam & Hollifield, 2021). Getting journalists to effectively use data on audience reactions to shape their reporting will remain an ongoing challenge for media analysts working with newsrooms.

On the other hand, media analysts shouldn't dismiss journalists' fears that constantly monitoring audiences' news consumption behaviors will produce dumbed-down reporting and *click-bait* content. Soft features and sensational content generally *are* more popular with news audiences than hard news and investigative reporting (Justel-Vázquez et al., 2016; Moyo et al., 2019). Producing primarily click-bait content is an outcome everyone in news industries—including news analysts—should want to avoid. After all, why should anyone care whether a news organization survives, if it focuses more on producing profits than it does on producing journalism that serves its audience and community, or if it willingly distorts facts or feeds societal divisions in order to grow its audiences and attract advertisers?

The job of media analysts in newsrooms is to help journalists find the delicate balance between being responsive to audiences' content interests while still providing the reporting needed to support prosperous, functional, equitable societies and informed citizens capable of self-governance. Ideally, news analytics will help journalists become more effective in turning audiences' attention to news stories that have important personal, community, or societal implications.

News analytics and journalists

News analytics are changing the profession of journalism in ways both obvious and subtle. News managers say 21st century journalists *must* be able to understand and analyze audience data and apply it to strategic thinking on behalf of their news organizations, if they hope to advance in the profession. Additionally, news executives expect journalists to use data proactively to improve their personal news judgment and storytelling. Does the journalist's story structure or style cause people to stop reading? Do audiences consistently click away after the writer uses a certain word, phrase, or trope? By examining the metrics on each story they produce and the aggregated data on their work across time, journalists might identify patterns that suggest strengths and weaknesses in their reporting and writing skills.

If individual journalists are not analyzing their own performance, their employers almost certainly are. Analytics tools allow news managers to closely examine how audiences engage with each story written by each author, as well as the patterns in audience behavior that a journalist produces across time. Metrics can be filtered by the organization's *KPIs*, so news managers can see which journalists in the newsroom are contributing most to the accomplishment of the organization's long-term, mid-term, or short-term strategic goals—and which are not.

Online audience data can be used to tease out subtle differences in journalists' performances that news managers otherwise would miss. The metrics might show that one journalist is consistently better than her colleagues at generating stories that attract visitors to the news organization's website and boost total *impressions*. But a deeper dive might show that a different journalist consistently attracts more *new* audience members, as opposed to repeat *visitors*, while a third writer excels at producing stories that, when circulated on social media, actually drive people to the news site through *referrals*. Finally, it might be another journalist entirely who consistently produces stories that audiences read all the way through, raising the news site's *stickiness* or *time spent* on page or site metrics.

How these different elements of professional performance are valued by news managers depends on the news organization's strategic priorities. But smart journalists will know at least as well as their bosses exactly how their performance stacks up in the achievement of those goals—and how they compare to colleagues' performances on all important measures.

Online news site metrics are not the only type of performance evaluation news managers are using. Managers may monitor journalists' success in employing social media to draw audiences to their stories and build the kind of personal fan bases that employers can leverage into bigger, more loyal audiences. In essence, many news organizations now expect journalists to be part of the company's promotions and marketing team. Posting headlines and story blurbs to social media is increasingly important to content promotion and *discovery*. The old philosophical question, "If a tree falls in a forest and nobody is there to hear, does it make a sound?" is increasingly relevant in the highly competitive, highly fragmented world of news. A news story that attracts no audience was a complete waste of production time, money, and resources. In the 21st century, news organizations measure how well individual journalists perform in attracting audiences.

Analytics for short-, mid-, and long-term strategic news management

Media analysts working in newsrooms are asked to answer all kinds of questions, ranging from long-term organizational strategy to the immediate problem of choosing the best headline for a story. All of these questions, however, relate to the organization's success in attracting audiences and revenue—so ultimately, most of them are about strategic management.

Strategic management refers to understanding what it will take to succeed as a business in a competitive market. It involves identifying and addressing market trends and challenges. There are three time frames in which organizations engage in strategic management: long-term, mid-term, and short-term. Technology changes so quickly in the 21st century and has such an impact on markets and business processes that experts now recommend companies limit long-term strategic plans to three years—with annual revisions.

Mid-term strategic planning refers to understanding the news organization's specific audience, including demographics, psychographics, content consumption patterns, and other important factors that are likely to impact audience size and monetization potential. Short-term strategic management refers to understanding how audiences are engaging right now with the content the news organization is producing in today's news cycle—and how today's audience engagement can be maximized.

Actively thinking about and answering questions in each of those strategic frames is critical to all organizations. But in the high-pressure newsroom environment where the demand for maximum audiences in every news cycle never ends, it can be hard to keep long-term and mid-term strategic issues in mind, much less find the time to actually try to address them. As Reid Williams, Senior Director, Storytelling Studio, Gannet Co., in the United States, advised:

> What you pay attention to is what determines your future. What gets measured is where you get your results and suddenly that drives everybody's focus. It's really important that what is being measured actually aligns with your organization's strategic objectives. So for example, you don't want to spend all of your time measuring just page views, and then at the end of a quarter or a year be asking yourself "Have we grown our subscriber base?"

Long-term strategic management

Long-term strategic questions generally center around national and international trends. These might include long-term trends in audience growth or loss in news consumption, in general, or in a particular news industry sector. So, for example, is newspaper readership growing nationwide or declining? What about the audience for local television news? Are the demographics of people who consume news changing over time and, if so, how? Are those trends different for the audiences of news produced by different industry sectors or distributed over different types of devices? What are the national trends in audience consumption of news stories in different subject areas—politics, science, business, sports? What devices do most people use to consume news? How often do news consumers visit news websites, and at what times of day are they most likely to look at news?

In what environments are they most likely to consume news—at home, at work, while commuting? In quiet environments or noisy ones?

When working on longer-term strategic management questions, analysts often use data on trends generated by large third-party research vendors, industry trade associations, government agencies, and even groups of media analysts who come together in professional teams to conduct joint research on problems of critical interest to everyone in the industry.

National and international trend data help analysts understand what they see in their own audience behavioral data. They also help organizations think about what they may need to do differently in the future.

Brand identity as long-term strategic management

Development of a news organization's *brand identity* also can be considered a long-term strategic management issue. Does the news organization want to be known for the quality of its national political reporting? Its international reporting? For its community reporting or for investigative journalism? Does it want to be known for its alignment with a particular political party, point of view, or religion? If it serves a city with a diverse population, the news organization may decide to build its brand around appealing to or providing coverage that is important to a particular ethnic or cultural group within that population.

Media analysts trying to understand and assist in the development of a news organization's brand identity will bring multiple types of research to bear on the problem. They will analyze audience data to see which audience segments are watching or reading the news. Demographic data tell the analyst who is using the content, while online data and minute-by-minute return path TV viewing data can show what stories people read or watch and what stories they ignore or quickly abandon.

Analysts often will put together *audience panels* that respond to different research questions. Panels of long-time, loyal audience members help analysts understand the organization's existing brand identity. Those panels also help the newsroom understand how loyal audiences may react to new ideas or proposed changes. Audience panels of nonreaders or viewers or of less loyal audience members help analysts identify ways a news organization might attract new audiences.

Content analysis is another critical tool analysts use to understand a news organization's brand identity. If a news organization brands itself to the public as "the source" for hard-hitting reporting on local government and community issues, content analysis may reveal that the publication or station actually runs fewer stories on local government than its competitors, which is inconsistent with its own branding. If its competitive strategy is to appeal to a particular ethnic or cultural group in the community, let's say to be the leader in serving the news and information needs of the city's African-American residents, it would be important to ask such questions as: How often do the organization's journalists seek out African-American sources for stories across all subjects? How often do we run stories on issues of specific interest or concern to African-American citizens? How often are African-Americans featured in photographs or video and in what contexts? And for that matter, how well does our newsroom staff's ethnic and racial background reflect the city's population diversity?

Finally, for many news organizations, long-term strategic management includes *forecasting*. That's done using national and organizational audience data, sometimes combined with data from audience panels or *focus groups*, to predict average news audience size several years out or around specific future events such as national elections. Long-term audience forecasting is critical to such processes as developing the company's annual and departmental budgets and hiring levels. It also is critical to setting advertising prices for the sale of spots around major events such as election seasons or the Olympics. That has to be done far in advance so advertisers can set their own budgets and ensure they reserve the advertising placements they need. A deeper discussion of the use of analytics in advertising, revenue generation, and media organization finance can be found in Chapter 5.

Mid-term strategic management

Probably the greatest number of news analytics questions fall into this category. At the simplest level, mid-term strategic questions focus on who the audience is—questions that apply to management in all media industry sectors. Mid-term strategic management issues are wide-ranging, important, and hard to answer. Analysts often must combine data from different sources; develop, test, and validate their own methods and measures; and engage in experiments and modeling. Mid-term strategic analysis requires media analysts to go beyond the "what is happening" questions to try to answer the "why is it happening" and "what will make a difference" questions.

Mid-term strategic analyses begin, of course, with: What are the demographics and psychographics of the news organization's audience? How does that audience compare to competitors'? How many audience members are repeat readers/viewers/visitors? How many are new? Are there differences between those two groups?

From there, the questions become more complex: From what other channels or apps do our audience members come to us? Do new audience members come to us from different channels than repeat readers? If so, how did they discover our content? How can we get new visitors to stay longer and dig deeper into our news site? How do we get them to come back? How do we get our regular readers to spend more time on our site, engage more with our content, and come back more often? What is our baseline for audience behavior on each question of interest—frequency, engagement, content choice, time spent with news per visit, source of discovery, etc.?

Then there are the content-related questions, which also fall under mid-term strategic thinking: Which stories appeal most to our existing audience? Does interest vary across audience demographics and psychographics? Are there differences in interest and engagement between repeat and new audience members? What types of stories generate the most engagement? In any given topical area, such as automotive, there are many different types of stories we could do—stories about car makes and models, about performance, about safety, about emerging technologies, etc. Which of those approaches generate the greatest readership? Which attracts the types of people automotive industry advertisers most want to reach?

Other content questions revolve around packaging: Does audience increase if you put a big photograph at the top of the story? To the right or left of it? What happens if you put the photograph in the middle of the story, do people read past it or stop there? Do people prefer consuming news through reading? Or through video and audio? Does that preference differ by audience demographic? What happens if you tell the story with a video insert in it instead of a photograph? How many people view a video version of a story as compared to reading a text version, if both are available online? In broadcast and cable formats, what types of news, information, and stories have the highest audience numbers? What stories make people switch to other channels or content? Do some stories hold audiences better if they are only read by the anchor or announcer, while others require video or recorded interviews to hold audiences? How do we get audience members to move on from one story to other, unrelated stories? Why did they click on a headline or start viewing or listening to a story, but then not stay to go all the way through it? How do we get them to say, "'Wow! That was good. I'll come back," so that the newsroom gets repeat visits and increased *loyalty*? What needs or uses and gratifications (Chapter 2) are different types of audiences seeking from the news?

As Reid Williams, from Gannet Co., noted, "It is really hard to figure out exactly why something did or did not happen, or why something was or was not a success."

Technology and usability questions

Technology's importance in shaping how people access and use news content means media analysts are increasingly called on to analyze technology and manage the ***usability testing*** of innovations. Technology also falls into the mid-term strategic management category. Such questions include things like what do people see first when the organization's website loads on a computer, and how does that change on different digital devices? When they look at a screen or a page, where do their eyes go first? Where does the person's eyes go after that and why? How does the pattern of their eye movement relate to what they then do—if it relates to it at all?

The list of technology-related questions is almost endless. How user-friendly is the website or news app? Is it easy for people to find the content that interests them? Is it easy for them to understand how to move around in the content and use the page functions? How likely is it that people will scroll down or swipe to get more content? Are they more likely to swipe right as compared to left, or vice versa? How can the editors make sure they know the content they have to scroll or swipe to find is even there? How do technologies like a mouse or touch screen affect the likelihood people will scroll or swipe? Is the scrolling, swiping, or touch/click function so sensitive that the reader is constantly being bounced out of the content they are trying to read to something new that they don't want?

As new technologies emerge, they're the subject of publicity and hype. For news organizations, every new technology and every new social media platform represents a new cost. As audiences and revenues shrink (Chapter 2), the cost of adopting a new technology or social media platform often comes at the expense of something else—a new hire, salary increases, resources for investigative reporting, etc. Technologies have to be paid for, integrated with existing technologies, updated, and maintained. Staff must be trained. Every minute spent using a new technology or posting content to a newly introduced social media app is time—and therefore money—taken away from an already existing newsroom process or function. Whether there will be a return on that investment in audience or revenue growth often isn't clear until after the investment is made.

Story framing

Beyond these business-driven questions, journalists also want to better understand how audiences interact with news content in ways that impact society. Word choice, for example, colors people's perceptions of news events. In 2019, management at the British newspaper, *The Guardian*, announced changes to the newsroom's stylebook to require its journalists to use the terms "climate emergency" or "climate crisis" instead of "climate change" because "climate change is no longer considered to accurately reflect the seriousness of the overall situation" (Zeldin-O'Neill, 2019). Similarly, the new stylebook requires use of "climate science denier" instead of "climate skeptic" and "global heating" instead of "global warming." Should a journalist write that President X "offered a misleading statement," or should the story say that "President X lied?"

Such questions are debated around all kinds of sensitive issues. Journalists want to know how word choices and sentence structures affect how audiences understand and interpret the news. They ask what information and emotional needs cause individuals to seek or avoid the news and how the answers to those questions differ across audience gender, age, race, sexual orientation, and psychographic *variables* such as religious and political preference. They want to learn how to use tools such as video and emerging technologies to combat disinformation and outright lies. Increasingly, journalists and news managers are turning to media analysts for help with such questions.

Short-term strategic management

In news analytics, a great deal of media analysts' work focuses on the immediate: Which stories are attracting the largest audiences today? The smallest? Which stories are getting the most social media *shares*? Which of the stories being shared on social media are people clicking through to the news site and actually reading? Which are getting the most attention from new visitors as compared to subscribers or repeat visitors? Which stories are stickiest, and which stories seem to raise the stickiness metric—average time spent per reader—for the entire site by encouraging audiences to read related stories? Which stories that journalists think are important are *not* attracting the kind of audiences the organization wants? If today is a Monday,[2] how do the different metrics today compare to averages for that metric on Mondays earlier this month or last month or during the first six months of this year?

Perhaps most importantly, journalists and news managers look at real-time metrics to see what can be tweaked to attract bigger audiences. For example, with online content, a standard technique for maximizing audiences is *A/B testing* of story headlines. Editors write two different headlines for a single story and run both. The system automatically feeds different visitors the different headlines and tracks which headline generates the most *click-throughs* to the story. Eventually, the less successful of the two headline versions is eliminated.

Search engine optimization

Another important technique for building audiences in real time is *search engine optimization* (*SEO*). SEO means making sure journalists include words in their stories that are most likely to be used by people searching for information on whatever the story is about. That involves not only identifying likely *keywords* relevant to a particular story but also related words that might be trending locally, regionally, or nationally that could be built into story texts so the stories pop up in a wide range of searches. Conversely, good search engine optimization also means understanding what topics in a news market might be the subject of frequent online searches—such as a local celebrity or rush-hour traffic. News managers might try to regularly generate stories about those topics, to increase the likelihood that people seeking non-news information will find the news site by accident.

SEO also means understanding how to design and maintain the news organization's website with SEO in mind because the search engine algorithms that determine which websites are ranked highest in a search include elements such as number of links, load speeds, and other things that require technical expertise. Moreover, search engines frequently change their search algorithms, and those formulas are never made public. Thus it takes constant monitoring and experimentation to keep track of which keywords will optimize audience discovery of the news organization's content at any given time. As a result, a large newsroom may have full-time SEO specialists on staff.

Measurement on traditional news platforms

Journalists, news editors, and media analysts monitor real-time online performance metrics constantly, making adjustments throughout the day. From the analysts' viewpoint, one of the disadvantages of traditional news platforms—print, TV, and radio broadcasts—is that they don't generate real-time data that can help identify problems so journalists can make immediate adjustments to content and content mixes. Lag times for getting audience data on traditional platforms range from several hours to months.

Even so, news managers on traditional platforms are not entirely helpless when it comes to driving audience size in real time. Newspapers historically printed "Extras!" around major breaking news events, sending carriers into the street to sell single copies to nonsubscribers. Similarly, local TV stations often try to air special stories or series likely to generate a lot of public empathy or outrage during key measurement periods, when data are most likely to be used in setting advertising rates.

News analytics data and tools

News organizations use multiple metrics to assess audience size. *Circulation* numbers are still the primary audience measure for publications (Chapter 11), while *ratings*, shares, and increasingly, impressions (Chapters 8, 9, 10) are currencies in the broadcast news industries. In the online and social media worlds, multiple measures are available—visitors, *unique visitors*, *new visitors*, impressions—amid endless arguments about which measure is most important and most valid (Chapter 12).

Just as there are multiple measures, there are multiple vendors offering audience measurement services to news organizations. Each service has its own tools and techniques, which can result in very different results even when the same audience is measured. Deeper discussions of the differences, strengths, and weaknesses of the various data collection methods and metrics can be found elsewhere in this book (see Additional Resources).

The availability of traditional measures of *audience size*, or *reach*, varies widely from country to country. Some countries do not have any vendors that provide traditional audience measurement. In other countries, the data provided are of highly questionable *reliability* and *validity* (Chapter 3) and therefore have limited value to news organizations and advertisers.

For online news distribution, Google Analytics is widely available globally. A number of specialized commercial services tools that provide real-time audience metrics are available internationally. Two well-known news analytics tools are Parse.ly and Chartbeat. Both use *dashboards* to present the data they collect. As with all commercial tools, many of the *algorithms* behind the data collection and measurement are proprietary, although in the United States and some other countries there are organizations that review and certify research vendors' methodologies so that advertisers and clients can have greater confidence in the quality of the data they are buying (Chapters 1, 11).

Dashboards for online audience data provide many of the same general metrics regardless of vendor, although the techniques for generating those metrics may vary. Total *visitors, unique visitors, page views, device* used for consumption, *location* of consumer (*geolocation data*), *day, date* and *time* (*time stamp*) of the visit, *average time spent*, referral from which the visit came—direct URL, search engine or social media platform—are all fairly standard metrics for news content sites. Most dashboards offer some level of filtering so that the data can be examined within specific contexts, such as for a particular time period. Specialized news analytics tools may offer real-time metrics, more sophisticated filters, and the ability to generate reports on specific topics, depending on the vendor.

Parse.ly, for example, allows media analysts to filter not only by time but also by posts, by author, by section, by tags, by channel, and by promotional campaign. The platform distinguishes between new visitors and repeat visitors. It can break down online activity minute by minute, as well as by hour and day, and graph current data against comparable averages or graph trends on different aspects of the audience's behavior. It can display the average time audience members spend with each post and whether they shared the story further through their own social networks. The site can track the success of a news organization's efforts to promote stories through email or newsletters, recording how many people clicked on the links or opened the email and then later visited the news site. It can help news managers spot *evergreen* content, that is stories that keep drawing audiences over time. If a news organization operates multiple news sites, Parse.ly can aggregate audience data from across all of the company's content sites, providing both total company-wide data as well as comparisons between the company's individual news outlets.

The specific functionality of news analytics tools changes constantly as vendors add features. Moreover, for all of the richness of data that they produce, no tool is perfect. While data from online measurement tools includes more variables than traditional media measurement provides, it tends to lack audience demographics. News organizations may learn a great deal about audience behavior from online metrics, but most tools generate little, if any information about who the audience is. That's a serious problem for news organizations with an advertising-based revenue model because most advertisers want to target specific demographic and psychographic segments. Matching online metrics to specific audience members is done by using audience panels, surveys, IP addresses, phone numbers, and data sources in an effort to build "big datasets" (Chapters 6, 7) that try to link the behavior of individual visitors at a news site to specific persons. The ability to accurately make those matches is imperfect, however. Similarly, it has proven extremely difficult to create cross-platform measurements that can give news organizations a true measure of their total *unduplicated audience* across all the formats they use to distribute news: TV, audio, online, mobile apps, social media, etc.

Technology-based measurement also is subject to technology failures. If a news organization's tech team miscodes something on the news site, specific metrics such as page views or visits may be under- or overcounted. Even when everything is working right, most systems will count a single person as multiple visitors, if the person accesses the news site from more than one device. Many systems will continue to count a page as active as long as it's open, even if it is running in background on a computer. That distorts metrics on content usage. Online measurement has many other such underlying problems. Often the problems are invisible until a media analyst sees something strange in the data and investigates.

News bloggers and entrepreneurs

Digital technologies have been a two-edged sword for journalists and news organizations. They have opened amazing opportunities for news entrepreneurship, helping news startups, news blogs, and news podcasts to flourish. At the same time, that additional competition has helped drastically reduce audience sizes at many existing news organizations, undercutting business models. By the end of 2019, an estimated 1,800–2000 local newspapers had closed since 2004 in the United States alone, leaving news deserts across communities and regions (Abernathy, 2022; Levin, 2019). In many smaller countries, local communities have never had local news coverage because of the economics of audience and advertising markets. But in some communities, the local news gap is now being filled by individual bloggers and even student newspapers (Levin, 2019) (see case study "Optimizing a Local News Blog" on the text website).

Research on digital news start-ups around the world found commonalities among those that succeeded—and those that failed (Cook & Sirkkunen, 2012). Those that succeeded found ways to provide content audiences truly valued and to convince advertisers and donors that the start-up was worth supporting based on those audiences. Those two requirements for entrepreneurial success are, fundamentally, the goal of all news analytics.

Summary and conclusion

The news industries have been among the most heavily disrupted media sectors in the 21st century. While digital technologies have created new opportunities for news entrepreneurship, they also have seriously fragmented news audiences and advertising markets. As a result, news organizations, particularly local news organizations, have been forced to shut down in many countries, leaving news and information deserts.

News analytics have been an increasingly important tool as news organizations fight for financial sustainability and the resources required to produce quality journalism. Digital technologies give us new ways to measure audiences and audience behaviors but have both advantages and disadvantages compared to the more traditional ways of measuring news audiences.

One of the major challenges media analysts face is simply digging through the avalanche of data that digital analytics tools provide. With so many ways of filtering and examining data, it is hard to know which audience behaviors and relationships are important. A media analyst can easily waste time and money generating analyses that produce useless information. The industry itself does not yet know whether many of the things that we can measure actually translate into bigger, more loyal, or more monetarily valuable audiences. If we don't yet fully understand the relationship between specific audience behaviors and news organizations' financial success, it is hard for media analysts and journalists to know what they should pay attention to and what they can safely ignore in the mountains of data they now have at their fingertips.

For this reason alone, it is critical for media analysts to always focus first on answering the questions mostly closely related to management's strategic priorities. The first question to be asked is what are our objectives? Such objectives should always relate to the newsroom's mission and financial sustainability, and as discussed, there must be a balance. The second question is, "What variables and KPIs best help us understand how well we are meeting those objectives?" Only after answering those questions, can media analysts or journalists identify the appropriate metrics for benchmarking and monitoring their organization's progress, and generating the most valuable *insights*.

Additional resources

Pew Research Center. "A nonpartisan fact tank that informs the public about the issues, attitudes and trends shaping the world," with a particular focus on media. Pew conducts original research and is a primary source of data on the current state of news industries in the United States: www.pewresearch.org/about/

The Poynter Institute. Newsletter, information, training on the current state of news industries in the United States: www.poynter.org/

Reuters Institute for the Study of Journalism. Connects research and practice on global journalism and facilities global exchanges. Research and reports on issues in news industries and journalism worldwide: https://reutersinstitute.politics.ox.ac.uk/about-reuters-institute

DW Akademie. Based in Germany, DW Akademie is a German NGO supporting media development and free expression worldwide. Reports, conferences, and tools supporting journalism globally: www.dw.com/en/dw-akademie/s-8120

Parse.ly.com. A leading content analytics company that provides real-time digital metrics to news organizations around the world: www.parse.ly/

Chartbeat. Another major international digital content metrics company that provides real-time digital metrics to news organizations: https://chartbeat.com/

Recommended cases

These cases can be found on the textbook website: www.routledge.com/cw/hollifield

Case 14.1: Strategizing the Future of a Local News Media Company
Case 14.2: Analyzing the Match between Newscast Branding and Newscast Content
Case 14.3 (12.2): Optimizing a Local News Blog
Case 14.4 (10.2): Evaluating a News Podcast Launch
Case 14.5 (9.3): News Viewership and Voters

Case studies, along with accompanying datasets for this chapter, can be found on the text website. We particularly suggest the preceding cases in the order listed. See the companion website and instructor's manual for detailed descriptions of these and other relevant cases.

Discussion questions and exercises

1. The chapter outlines many of the questions and issues news analysts are being asked to answer. Look again at some of these questions and pick several. Write a list of the variables *you* would use to try to answer each of the questions you've selected, and discuss why you would select those particular variables. How would you combine variables to get insights into the question? What controls would you use, and where might you get the data for your variables? Be *realistic* as you think about the questions. Approach it as if your boss just gave you this assignment.

2. The chapter talks about the challenges facing news industries worldwide. What challenges face the news organizations near you? How, if at all, do you think news analytics could help your area news organizations succeed in facing those challenges? Why? Do you think the journalists, newsroom managers, and news organization managers in the news organizations near you understand and use news analytics? Do you think that if they use them, they use them effectively? What evidence do you have for your opinions about this?

3. Of all the different metrics on audience behavior that were discussed in the chapter or that you know of, which ones specifically do you think the newsroom managers of your local news organizations should be monitoring and/or using to make news decisions? Why? What metrics do you think they should ignore? Why?

4. A key term in media analytics, including news, is "engagement." Content producers, advertisers, and donors all want evidence that audiences are not just accessing content—i.e., having the TV on in the background while you do your homework—but that the audiences are actually *engaged* with the content. But no one agrees on a single definition for "engagement." How would *you* define *engagement* as it relates to news content? What would an audience member who is *engaged* with news content look like compared to someone who also has the news app open or the TV on or the newspaper in hand but is *not* engaged with the content? Having answered that question, how do we measure your definition of engagement? Of the online metrics that are available, which, if any, would you use as a measure of engagement with news? Which metric from traditional news audience measurement, if any, would you use for measuring audience engagement? (See Chapters 8–10 and Chapter 12 for additional information and ideas.)

5. The chapter discusses how news organizations are using news analytics in their personnel evaluations of journalists and newsroom workers.

How do you feel about news analytics being used in such a way? How, if at all, does knowing this affect what you think you should be doing now to make yourself more competitive when you apply for jobs as a news analyst or as a journalist? How, if at all, does it change what you think you would need to do to be successful if you were a journalist or an employee in a newsroom? Do you think employers in other media sectors are using media analytics in similar ways in evaluating employees?

6. *Exercise: Using readers' technical profiles in news strategy*
   Google Analytics and other online metrics tools give media analysts a lot of technical data such as the abbreviated outputs from a news site shown in Table 14.1. Why? Why are these data important? How would media analysts, newsroom managers, and news organization sales departments use this information? Analyze the following information, and write a memo to the Blog's publisher with recommendations on how he might use this information in producing his blog and building its readership.

Table 14.1 Technical Profiles of Online Users on a News Site

Online service provider	Users	New users	Sessions	Bounce rate	Pages/ session	Avg. session duration
Cable TV Company A	322	224	733	65.35%	1.90	133.69
Mobile Co. A	191	142	438	73.74%	1.64	97.03
Mobile Co. B	114	87	241	72.61%	1.54	77.23
Online Operating System						
Windows	699	555	1507	66.42%	1.76	124.51
iOS	236	165	581	77.11%	1.48	79.78
Macintosh	165	126	327	71.56%	1.75	81.83
Android	28	17	47	91.49%	1.28	36.79
Online Browser						
Chrome	358	259	839	76.76%	1.51	91.06
Safari	210	159	455	73.85%	1.53	68.20
Firefox	87	75	199	77.39%	1.37	128.00
Edge	60	46	86	74.42%	1.49	51.45
Mobile Service Provider						
Cable TV Company A	86	52	179	78.21%	1.46	54.44
Mobile Co. A	79	58	208	80.29%	1.46	80.93
Mobile Co. B	48	36	101	76.24%	1.50	95.28
Cable TV Company B	9	2	21	80.95%	1.19	13.62

(*Continued*)

Table 14.1 (Continued)

Online service provider	Users	New users	Sessions	Bounce rate	Pages/ session	Avg. session duration
Mobile Operating System						
iOS	236	165	581	77.11%	1.48	79.78
Android	28	17	47	91.49%	1.28	36.79
Windows	4	4	5	80.00%	1.20	54.80
Mobile Screen Resolution						
768x1024	179	117	468	77.78%	1.43	84.43
1024x1366	39	35	67	83.58%	1.25	29.96
834x1112	16	11	25	48.00%	3.12	176.96

Source: Oconee County Observations

Notes

1. Unlike many countries, in the United States, few commercial broadcast radio stations produce local news, and only 25 radio stations in the United States were listed as "all news" in 2018 (Pew Research Center, 2019). The employment of journalists in radio dropped 22% between 2004 and 2019.
2. News content varies in predictable ways by day of the week because of the predictable patterns of human activity. In Western countries, for example, Monday is the beginning of the work week, and major political and economic announcements often occur on that day. Friday and Saturday are slow news days as people focus on the weekend. In other cultures, Friday is a weekend day. Audiences' news consumption varies accordingly. Because of the predictability of news cycles and audience consumption, news organizations compare *longitudinal* metrics by day of the week.

References

Abernathy, P. M. (2022). The expanding news desert: The loss of newspapers and readers. *University of North Carolina.* www.usnewsdeserts.com/reports/expanding-news-desert/loss-of-local-news/loss-newspapers-readers/

Albarran, A. B. (2018). Media management and economics research: A historical review. In A. B. Albarran, B. I. Mierzejewska, & Jung, J. (Eds.), *Handbook of media management and economics* (2nd ed., pp. 3–16). Taylor & Francis.

Allam, R., & Hollifield, C. A. (2021). Factors influencing the use of journalism analytics as a management tool in Egyptian newspapers. *Journalism Practice.* https://doi.org/10.1080/17512786.2021.1927803

Bateman, S. S. (n.d.). CPM advertising costs, examples and strategy. *Promise Media.* www.promisemedia.com/online-advertising/cpm-advertising-costs-examples-and-strategy

Baum, M. (2011). Red state, blue state, flu state: Media self-selection and partisan gaps in Swine Flu vaccinations. *Journal of Health, Policy, Politics and Law, 36*(6), 1021–1059. doi: 10.1215/03616878-1460569

Beam, R. A. (1995). How newspapers use readership research. *Newspaper Research Journal, 16*(2), 28–38. https://doi: 10.1177/073953299501600204

Belair-Gagnon, V., & Holton, A. E. (2018). Boundary work, interloper media, and analytics in newsrooms. *Digital Journalism, 6*(4), 492–508, https://doi:10.1080/21670811.2018.1445001

Bennett, C. O. (1965). *Facts without opinion: First fifty years of the Audit Bureau of Circulations*. Audit Bureau of Circulations.

Cauhapé-Cazaux, E. G., & Kalathil, S. (2015). Official development assistance for media: Figures and findings. *CIMA & OECD*. www.oecd.org/dac/conflict-fragility-resilience/docs/CIMA.pdf

Cohen, M. S., & McIntyre, K. (2019). Local-language radio stations in Kenya: Helpful or harmful? *African Journalism Studies, 40*(3), 73–88. doi: 10.1080/23743670.2020.1729830

Cook, C., & Sirkkuken, E. (2012). Chasing sustainability on the net: International research on 69 pure players and their business models. *Tampere Research Center for Journalism, Media and Communication*. https://trepo.tuni.fi/bitstream/handle/10024/66378/chasing_sustainability_on_the_net_2012.pdf?sequence=1

Daniels, G., & Hollifield, C. A. (2002). Times of turmoil: Short- and long-term effects of organizational change on newsroom employees. *Journalism and Mass Communication Quarterly, 79*(3), 661–680. https://doi.org/10.1177/107769900207900308

Festinger, L. (1957). *A theory of cognitive dissonance*. Row, Peterson and Co.

Gade, P. J., & Perry, E. L. (2003). Changing the newsroom culture: A four-year case study of organizational development at the St. Louis Post-Dispatch. *Journalism & Mass Communication Quarterly, 80*(2), 327–347. https://doi.org/10.1177/107769900308000207

Hanusch, F. (2017). Web analytics and the functional differentiation of journalism cultures: individual, organizational and platform-specific influences on news-work. *Information, Communication & Society, 20*(10), 1571–1586, https://doi: 10.1080/1369118X.2016.1241294

Hollifield, C. A. (2006). News media performance in hypercompetitive markets: An extended model of effects. *International Journal on Media Management, 8*(2), 60–69. https://doi:10.1207/s14241250ijmm0802_2

Hollifield, C. A. (2019). Media sustainability. In A. Albarran (Ed.), *A research agenda for media economics*. Edgar Elgar.

Hollifield, C. A., Martin, H. J., & Ren, C. (2005, August 10–13). *The influence of newspapers on rural economic development*. Presentation to the Newspaper Division, Association for Education in Journalism and Mass Communication, San Antonio, TX, August.

Islam, R. (2002). Into the looking glass: What the media tell and why. In *The right to tell: The role of mass media in economic development* (pp. 1–23). World Bank Institute.

Justel-Vázquez, S., Micó-Sanz, J.-L., & Sánchez-Marín, G. (2016). Media and public interest in the era of web analytics: A case study of two Spanish leading newspapers. *El Profesional de la Información, 25*(6), 859–868. eISSN: 1699–240

Lee, A., Lewis, S. C., & Powers, M. (2014). Audience clicks and news placement: A study of time-lagged influence in online journalism. *Communications Research, 41*(4), 505–530. doi: 10.1177/0093650212467031

Levin, D. (2019, October 20). When the student newspaper is the only daily newspaper in town. *New York Times*. www.nytimes.com/2019/10/19/us/news-desert-ann-arbor-michigan.html

Massey, B. L., & Ewart, J. (2012). Sustainability of organizational change in the newsroom: A case study of Australian newspapers. *The International Journal on Media Management*, *14*(3), 207–225. https://doi:10.1080/14241277.2012.657283

McManus, J. H. (1994). *Market driven journalism: Let the citizen beware?* Sage.

Moyo, D., Mare, A., & Matsilele, T. (2019). Analytics-driven journalism? Editorial metrics and the reconfiguration of online news production practices in African newsrooms. *Digital Journalism*, *7*(4), 490–506. https://doi:10.1080/21670811.2018.1533788

National Advisory Commission on Civil Disorders. (1968). *Report of the National Advisory Commission on Civil Disorders*. US G.P.O. www.eisenhowerfoundation.org/docs/kerner.pdf

Pew Research Center. (2019, June 29). *State of the news media: Audio and podcasting factsheet*. www.journalism.org/fact-sheet/audio-and-podcasting/

Singer, J. B. (2003). Who are these guys?: The online challenge to the notion of journalistic professionalism. *Journalism*, *4*(2), 139–163. https://doi 10.1177/146488490342001

Singer, J. B. (2011). Community service: Editor pride and user preference on local newspaper websites. *Journalism Practice*, *5*(6), 623–642. doi.org/10.1080/17512786.2011.601938

Singer, J. B., & Ashman, I. (2009). 'Comment Is free, but facts are sacred': User-generated content and ethical constructs at The Guardian. *Journal of Mass Media Ethics*, *24*(1), 3–21. https://doi: 10.1080/08900520802644345

Tandoc, Jr., E. C. (2015). Why web analytics click: Factors affecting the way journalists use audience metrics. *Journalism Studies*, *16*(6), 782–799. https://doi:10.1080.1461670X.2014.946309

Tandoc, Jr., E. C., & Ferrucci, P. R. (2017). Giving in or giving up: What makes journalists use audience feedback in their news work? *Computers in Human Behavior*, *68*, 148–156. https://doi.org/10.1016/j.chb.2016.11.027

Tandoc, Jr., E. C., & Thomas, R. J. (2015). The ethics of web analytics. *Digital Journalism*, *3*(2), 243–258. https://doi:10.1080/21670811.2104.909122

Usher, N. (2013). Al Jazeera English online: Understanding Web metrics and news production when a quantified audience is not a commodified audience. *Digital Journalism*, *1*(3), 335–351. https://doi.org/10.1080/21670811.2013.801690

Vu, H. T. (2014). The online audience as gatekeeper: The influence of reader metrics on news editorial selection. *Journalism*, *15*(8), 1094–1110. https://doi:10.1177/1464884913504259

Whitehouse, J., & Abughazaleh, K. (2020, December 30). Timeline: Fox News misinformation in 2020. *Media Matters for America*. www.mediamatters.org/fox-news/timeline-fox-news-misinformation-2020

Zeldin-O'Neill, S. (2019, October 16). 'It's a crisis, not a change': The six Guardian language changes on climate matters. (2019). *The Guardian*. www.theguardian.com/environment/2019/oct/16/guardian-language-changes-climate-environment

15 Entertainment media analytics

The term "entertainment" covers a wide range of content types and activities—far too many for any single book. This chapter will focus on how media analytics are being adopted and applied in several key areas of entertainment-oriented media.

As noted in Chapter 2, content management across all media industry sectors consists of the same five tasks: content selection, production, distribution, promotion, and evaluation. Media analytics plays an increasingly important role in each of those processes. In addition to content management, media analysts in the entertainment industries also are asked to answer questions about optimizing revenue generation, the user-friendliness of technologies and software, and the future of the entertainment business. Different entertainment industry sectors, however, value and use media analytics differently. Those differences result from the histories, economics, business models, professional cultures, technologies of production and distribution, and audience profiles specific to each sector. Because of those differences, this chapter will examine media analytics in different entertainment sectors separately.

The film industry

Media analytics in the film industry historically have focused on marketing. The primary measurements have been *opening weekend* and theater *box office*. Opening weekend is the revenue generated from ticket sales during a film's first weekend of release, while box office is the revenue generated over the length of time the film is in theaters.

Today, marketing remains the primary focus of film industry analytics, but studios are starting to experiment with other ways of applying media analytics. In the past few years, some of the oldest film studios in the business have created internal analytics teams and broadened their research mandates.

DOI: 10.4324/9780429506956-19

The film industry in the 21st century

The film industry is in the business of selecting, creating, and distributing films. Historically, the global industry has been dominated by US studios, but in recent years, other powerful centers of global film have emerged—including the United Kingdom, India's Bollywood, China, and Nigeria.

In the United States, the film industry is highly concentrated in the studio sector, with only a handful of major companies responsible for most major releases. The studio handles the finance, marketing, and distribution of a film. The studios determine which films will be financed and how big a film's budget will be, and they have a large say in many creative decisions such as choice of actors and director.

In contrast, the creative side of the industry is decentralized. Film producers contract with multiple firms to handle specific production processes such as casting, costumes, transportation, set design, or editing.

Because studios finance, market, and distribute films, that's where most media analysts in the film industry work. But other industry players—talent agencies, some types of production companies, industry consulting firms, and agencies specializing in product placement and brand integration—also hire media analysts to help them better understand and manage their sectors of the industry. The opportunities for media analysts in the film industry are rapidly rising.

The digital era has disrupted the global film industry in a number of ways. Film production is a financially risky business because of the high first-copy costs of film production and the unpredictability of audience taste (Chapter 2). While new technologies have expanded film producers' creative opportunities, they also have increased film production costs by raising audiences' expectations for production values. That means hiring expensive teams of special effects experts, computer programmers, and artists. Because of rising production costs, by the 1990s, only about 20% of Hollywood-produced films broke even through US box office, making the international audience an increasingly important factor in film industry finance (Eller, 1995) and by the second decade of the 21st century, US film studios were getting about 60% of their box office revenue from overseas (Follows, 2017).

Such financial factors affect creative decisions. Studios have become less willing to greenlight original screenplays, which don't have an existing fan base. Instead they adapt best-selling books, TV series, and comic books, or they invest in sequels and spinoffs of previous hits—anything that can bring in at least a small preexisting audience eager to see the film version of something they already love. Similarly, the industry hires known talent—directors and actors—who can draw their fans to the theater. The importance of international ticket sales means that adventure, action, thriller, drama, and other genres with broad international appeal increasingly dominate the big screen (Follows, 2017).

Box office ticket sales remain the most important source of revenue for major films. But also important is revenue from the secondary *windowing* of film rights to premium cable networks, streaming services, airlines, home video sales and rentals, and ultimately broadcast television. *Product placement*, selling the prominent placement of brand name products in films—the film industry's answer to advertising—also brings in revenue for some films, while *marketing synergies* (Chapter 2) through the secondary sale of the soundtrack from a film and other spinoff merchandise remain an important source of studio income.

Crucially, even as film ticket prices have risen to cover ever rising production costs, competition for the audience's time, attention, and media dollars has risen even faster. Premium cable channels such as HBO increasingly invest in their own original films and series as a product differentiation strategy—*Game of Thrones* being a notable example. High-speed internet diffusion makes streaming services such as Netflix and Amazon Prime Video possible, and, as their profit margins have risen, they've moved into the film and series production business.

Finally, the diffusion of high-definition television and in-home entertainment systems has narrowed the gap between the in-theater and at-home viewing experiences, further tilting film industry competition toward in-home viewing. With theater attendance declining in recent years, Hollywood has started turning to media analytics for strategic *insights*.

Media analytics and film production

Historically, the creative side of the film industry has been a business of gut instincts and personal connections. Someone has an idea for a film and is able to get the idea in front of a studio executive who has the power to greenlight it. Today, even in the data-driven 21st century media world, that reality hasn't changed much. The film business is still primarily a game of who you are and who you know. At least for now.

That said, with the investment and risks of film production rising, analysts are actively massaging film data to improve success rates. One Hollywood analyst has developed a database of thousands of creative *variables* in films: genres, subgenres, and microgenres, story elements and arcs, characters, settings, talent, effects, endings, audience feedback and box office success, to name just a few. The goal is to identify specific elements in a film early in the production process that might undercut its success with its target audiences.

Most importantly, understanding a film's audience potential is critical to greenlighting and budget decisions. Say a studio has a script it thinks might make $50 million at the box office. If the studio had a goal of a 30% profit margin, the production budget would have to be set at $35 million. But say the producers argue that given the script, another $10 million in special effects—for a total budget of $45 million—would move the film from mediocre to great. That leaves studio executives trying to forecast whether the box office potential will increase to nearly $65 million with an additional $10 million investment—and, conversely, whether the original box office potential of $50 million will be reached without it. Analytics also might be applied to see how much potential a script has for generating product placement or merchandising opportunities.

One constant danger in all creative industries is that executives will be swept away by their own confidence in a particular project. The history of Hollywood is punctuated with huge-budget films that flopped miserably with audiences, often taking down multiple careers with them. The question remains whether the film industry can develop refined-enough datasets to improve greenlighting and budgeting decisions.

The reality is that usually by the time media analysts are called in, the studio already has invested huge amounts of money in a project. The analysts are expected to work magic to maximize the studio's return on that investment through post hoc creative analysis, marketing, and distribution. Analysts in the industry are hoping better data will help them identify potential problems before filming starts, so adjustments can be made before all of a studio's competing interests—producers, writers, directors, cinematographers, editors, talent, finance, human resources, marketing, etc.—gain a voice in the process. But to succeed in the film industry, media analysts must, according to one film industry analyst, learn to strike "a balance between art and commerce" and speak the same language as the industry's creatives.

The film industry data disadvantage

Most of the media analytics action in the film industry occurs in marketing. The industry uses box office data, surveys, screen tests, and focus groups, among other methods to learn about film audiences' tastes. The industry tries to understand which groups of people have liked particular genres, storylines, and talent in the past. Better targeting means more financially efficient and effective marketing.

Research also plays a key role in developing the content used in marketing films, such as the trailers and advertisements that are released months before the film itself. Trailers and ads are screen-tested, edited, and reedited to achieve maximum impact with the target audience.

But, thanks to technology, when it comes to understanding its audiences, the film industry faces major data disadvantages compared to cable and streaming competitors. Audience members are customers, that is, subscribers, of the streaming and cable companies. In contrast, traditional film studios have no direct connection to their audiences, who are customers of the theater chains, not the studios and producers.

Cable and streaming companies have a direct, live data connection to their viewers and can gather minute-by-minute data on viewing behavior. They know what menus and carousels you scrolled through before picking what you actually watched. They know when you paused a program, went back and watched something again, or switched to something else. That allows them to build a profile that reveals your personal viewing patterns and preferences, including scenes or content that might trigger your decision to abandon a program. They know what advertisements and promotions you were exposed to before you watched something or added it to your future viewing list. All of those data points help them to better market to you, individually, through such things as recommendations.

Furthermore, when cable and streaming companies aggregate your individual-level data with the viewing and demographic and psychographic data from millions of other subscribers, they are able to greatly reduce the risks and increase the profits from the content they produce or buy.

Media analysts working for major film studios have to compensate for those gaps in their data access by building their own datasets from multiple data sources. The film studios get high-quality data on ticket sales from theater chains. That gives them an idea of the geographic areas, down to sections of each city, where a film is more or less popular. In the United States and other countries without strict data privacy laws, the analysts then combine ticket sales data with credit card data from the theaters that showed the film, identifying most of the individuals who went to a particular movie and the specific postal codes where those individuals live (Studio analyst, personal communication, November 7, 2018). That refines the understanding of audience preferences both geographically and in terms of audience demographics.

The marketing analytics teams then combine those data with their internal marketing data: Where did the studio buy billboard ads for the film in relationship to the specific zip codes or postal codes that generated the most ticket sales? On what cable channels and websites did the studio place ads for the film? Online tracking data and return path cable data can be used to determine whether a particular credit card holder was exposed to a particular ad for the film, which ad, and how many times. Similarly, credit card data also can reveal whether someone attended an earlier film where the trailer for the latest film was shown. Studios gather such data on competing films as well as their own. What is learned about the target audience for one film is applied to similar films.

The Achilles heel in this data strategy is that many filmgoers buy tickets with cash, which makes them largely invisible to analysts. Research shows cash customers differ significantly from credit card users and includes entire audience groups important to film studios, such as teenagers.

Analysts also tap other data sources for marketing, such as data from search engines on hot search topics, which might indicate interest in a subject related to an upcoming film release that could be spun into a promotion. They also track searches specifically about upcoming films. Search data combined with geographic data give film marketers insight into both audiences and locations where interest in a film or its subject area may be building—and where a little additional promotion might get more people out the door and into the theater.

Social media chatter is used in a similar way. Research has shown social media chatter, particularly prior to release, and online reviews are both predictive of a film's box office success (Gavilan et al., 2019; Gelper et al., 2018; Kim et al., 2013). Social media, however, are a two-edged sword for studios since negative word of mouth on social media has been found to undercut ticket sales both domestically and internationally. Given the importance of overseas box office receipts to film profitability, studios now release films simultaneously worldwide, in part to get ahead of any negative social media chatter.

The television and video entertainment industries

Many argue that television has entered a new Golden Age, marked by a deep pool of sophisticated, high-quality series defined by creative, ambitious storytelling (Leslie, 2017). The reliable revenue that video subscriptions provide has fueled larger production budgets, greater creative freedom, more flexible production options, and has lured top entertainment talent out of the film industry and over to television (Douglas, 2017; Katz, 2017).

Currently, three major business models are used to fund entertainment television and video: (1) Advertising only, which is the broadcast television model. (2) Subscription and advertising, a combination in which subscription is more important. That's the cable network model. (3) Subscription only, which is used for premium cable channels such as HBO, Showtime, and Starz, as well as by some streaming services, such as Netflix and Amazon.

There also are two delivery models: *linear* and *on demand*. Linear means the network schedules the programs according to programming theory, strategy, and tactics (Chapter 2), and audiences have to watch or record the program when the network schedules it. From the network's perspective, the goal is to get audiences to do *appointment viewing* of programs.

Linear programming is the primary delivery model used by broadcast networks and stations, cable networks, and premium cable networks.

The alternative delivery model is *video on demand* (*VOD*). VOD is non-linear, meaning customers can watch a program whenever they wish at the click of a button. Then there are the combinations of business model and delivery model: AVOD, which stands for *advertising-supported video on demand*, and *SVOD*, which means *subscription-only video on demand*. Free ad-supported TV (FAST) is similar to AVOD but is linear streaming through an app (Chapter 9).

In recent years, it has been common to hear younger people—and even many media professors—say "linear TV is dead. It's all online and on-demand now." Wrong. For many television companies, linear programming still attracts bigger audiences and is more profitable than on-demand programming, when the company sells both. Advertising remains the most important source of revenue for many video entertainment companies.

But it also is clear that audience preferences are tilting toward on-demand delivery and advertising-free content. However, as the number of SVOD services rises, so does competition for good content and the prices media companies have to pay to get that content. That's driving up content acquisition costs and thus subscription prices. SVODs will face pressure to become AVODs to maximize profits. Meanwhile, audiences are starting to revolt against paying ever rising subscription fees to multiple SVOD services in order to get all the content they want, as licensing rights to popular programs are increasingly scattered across multiple streaming services.

Thus while some believe SVOD will be the future in the entertainment industry, others disagree. The argument is that demand for linear advertising-supported content will remain strong because a subscription to an advertising-supported bundle of cable networks will provide better value than multiple SVOD subscriptions.

The bottom line for media analysts is this: Linear advertising-supported television is going to remain an important part of the entertainment industry for the foreseeable future, even as it takes on new forms. It will also be an important source of revenue for most companies in the video entertainment business, even those with major investments in SVOD services. Therefore, a large percentage of media analytics jobs will continue to be in linear television. Understanding the traditional media math of *ratings* and *shares*, *HUTS*, *PUTS*, etc. will be a critical job requirement for analysts.

That said, demand for SVOD services means companies have to change their strategic thinking. That means analysts face a whole new set of fascinating and challenging questions—questions with very few answers. To understand those questions, let's start by looking at research and analytics as they're used in content creation and acquisition, scheduling, and evaluation.

Research and analytics in television/video content creation

Like film, the creative side of television/video is still very much a "who you are, and who you know" business. But because of the sheer volume of TV content produced annually, research has long had a seat at the industry's creative table.

Networks are pitched thousands of program ideas each year. Before pitching a show, a producer might do *concept testing* of an idea. Concept testing involves using focus groups or surveys to ask audiences if they like the idea for a program. While helpful, the value of such feedback is limited because a program's actual success depends heavily on how the concept is executed.

The most promising concepts are further developed, and eventually a small number will be selected for *pilot testing*. Pilot testing usually involves production of an initial episode or parts of an episode to screen it for audience reaction (Eastman & Ferguson, 2013). As in the film industry, a network's final decision about whether to run with an idea is based largely on forecasts of the program's production costs and likely audience size (Chapters 2). But in linear television, other considerations also come into play that are less important to film studios—such as fit with the network or distributor's schedule and programming mix, the way a program will play against competing content scheduled against it, and the probability the program will deliver an audience demographic advertisers want to reach.

Once a network or distributor commits to a show, research continues. *Title testing* will be used to figure out what to call it. *Episode testing* may be used to gauge audience reaction to a plot line, specific characters or the performers portraying them, and the effectiveness of the script writers. *Dial testing* is one method of gathering such feedback. In dial testing, a small group of viewers turn hand-held dials to record how much they like or dislike what they're seeing on the screen. Researchers watch the group's moment-to-moment reactions in the form of two line graphs that display the aggregated reactions of, say, the men and, separately, the women in the group or of people in different age brackets or ethnic groups. Was a joke actually funny? Did one demographic find it funny, while others were offended? Are audiences turned off every time a particular actor appears in a scene?

Then there are other issues. "It's about performance—how we anticipate the programs will perform," a television programming executive said.

> But it's also about where marketing has the budget resources, and the space in the market for the content. It's about where finance says we can

take the expansion (in costs). It's about where sales say they can best monetize it. It's about how it fits into Development's production schedules. So, you're constantly playing four-dimensional chess in a competitive environment where sands are shifting beneath your feet all the time.

When developing content for linear advertising-supported television, whether broadcast or cable, the questions researchers try to answer include: (1) Will enough people like this show to generate a large-enough audience to appeal to advertisers? And (2) are the people who enjoy this show going to be people advertisers want to pay to reach?

That second question means that, in the advertising-supported linear TV world, content creation decisions are skewed toward serving some demographics and not others. People 50 years and older, low-income viewers, and even some minority groups historically have been less attractive to advertisers than younger, ethnic majority, and wealthier audiences. Therefore, producers working for ad-supported platforms create less content for audiences that are less attractive to advertisers.

Put "subscription" into the entertainment television business model, though, and the world changes. Whether you're talking about the linear subscription video business—aka premium cable channels—or the SVOD business, content creation becomes just one piece in the bigger strategic game called "portfolio management."

Content portfolio management

When customers are paying directly for content, the media company's focus changes from keeping advertisers happy to customer relations. The KPIs become **customer acquisition, customer retention**, and minimizing customer **churn rates**. The questions analysts are asked to address include things such as: How do you acquire new customers? What mix of content, services, and marketing get people to sign up? How do you keep them? What is the **lifetime value** of a new subscriber, and how can you translate that estimate into calculations of what the company can afford to spend to acquire or produce original content? Perhaps even more importantly, what types of content do you have to produce or license in order to attract new subscribers, and is that the same content mix you need to keep them subscribing once you've got them?

Said another way, in the subscription video world, the goal is no longer to maximize viewing audiences for a particular program. Instead, the goal is to get someone to give you their credit card number and the right to bill them monthly for their subscription to your service. Whether or not they ever watch the content you provide really isn't important, except as necessary to keep them from canceling their subscription.

Also different from traditional television thinking is that all potential subscribers are created equal. Audience demographics cease to matter, and the focus shifts to identifying the content mix that will attract the largest share of the population of potential subscribers. That means analysts focus on what motivates different types of households to subscribe. For example, the subscriber of record may be a 45-year-old male, but he may be subscribing to provide content for his children or elderly parents. Keeping *those* members of the household happy is what matters.

Achieving that goal is different for linear subscription video platforms such as premium cable networks than it is for SVODs. For premium cable networks, the key issues are the portfolio of content they offer subscribers and the way that content is scheduled. Premium cable networks try to buy the rights to the best newly released feature films and indie content. They then schedule it to be available at different times of the day around the 24-hour clock, on different days of the week, with different frequencies of repetition and declining frequency over time until it rotates off the schedule. The goal is to maximize the audience for each program, aggregated over multiple showings, and to minimize churn in subscriptions (Eastman & Ferguson, 2013). In contrast, in the streaming or VOD world, traditional scheduling concerns cease to be a consideration for programmers and media analysts. What matters, instead, is the appeal of the entire portfolio of content available on the service and the effects of content rotation on and off the platform within that portfolio.

Media analysts working for VOD services, particularly SVOD services, are asked to answer very different questions than in linear television. *White space analysis*, for example, means looking at the content portfolios being offered across the competing subscription services to see what types of content are *not* yet available or what audience segments seem underserved. How much inventory does a platform need to attract and keep subscribers? How long should a piece of content or series be viewable before being rotated off—a metric called *flight length*? What is the optimal *rest rate*, or time period when you take a piece of content down so audiences don't become bored with it, before putting it back up when it will seem fresh and exciting again? How many new offerings should be uploaded and in what time frame (every week, every month, some other measurement period) to keep subscribers happy? What mix of content genres works, and how much volume and variation are needed in each genre? If a service has 20 different comedy series in its portfolio, and 80% of all comedy viewing is of only four of the 20, are the other 16 necessary? What percentage of original content and what types of original content attract and keep subscribers? And, of course, while calculating all of these different factors, the all-important principle of *conservation of programming resources* (Chapter 2) means carefully tracking whether the network is "burning" all rights it paid for on each piece of content before those rights expire.

Most of these are questions of efficiency. How much inventory will actually be watched and by whom? Does certain content have to be in the portfolio to get and keep subscribers, whether or not they ever watch that content? If buying the rights to a prestigious series increased your subscriber base by 10%, does it matter that only 20% of those new subscribers ever watched the series after signing up?

Another example: Say your service is thinking about buying the rights to a long-running popular children's TV series. How many seasons do you need to buy? If the program has been on for 10 or 15 years, do you need to buy all of those rights? What will the viewing patterns be? Will today's children watch episodes from 15 years ago, or will viewing center on episodes produced in the past three years? Even if most viewing is concentrated on recent episodes, do you need the rights to all 15 years in order to convince parents their kids must have *your* SVOD service?

One of the most daunting challenges in portfolio management is figuring out how much to pay for a piece of content—a decision that has to be made prior to negotiating for rights. One metric is **cost per viewer**, which is the cost divided by predictions of audience size for that piece of content averaged over time. Complicating that forecasting game is that, as competition in the premium network and on-demand sectors grows, prices for quality content are soaring.

Finally, because of the long lead times required for both original production and rights negotiations, analysts have to project what content mix their network will need to have in place five years from now. That means factoring into their forecasting what is known about trends in audience adoption of different viewing platforms and technologies, changes in audiences' content tastes and trends, societal changes that may affect viewing preferences and habits, and long-term demographic and psychographic trends.

For media analysts tasked with guiding content portfolio management in the SVOD sector, there are still far more questions about what will work and what will be financially efficient than there are answers—and a lot of money is riding on the choices made. Analysts need to be comfortable with uncertainty, working in a high financial-risk environment with the probability of being wrong—often.

New research issues in entertainment television and video

User-experience research

As entertainment industries change, new questions arise, and new areas of research emerge. **User experience (UX)** is an increasingly important research focus in the SVOD world because on-demand delivery requires companies to build direct customer relationships with their audiences. In the past, most networks delivered content to viewers through distribution companies, such as local cable and satellite systems or broadcast stations. Those distributors handled customer relations. In contrast, streaming services have to manage their own.

UX research includes **usability testing (UI)** and **interface testing (IT)**. Usability research tests how easy it is for audiences to understand, navigate, and use a service's remote controls, visual design, content-access software, and content recommendation features (QATestLab, 2015). Interface testing examines the form and appearance of the interface and how customers respond to it emotionally. UX research also includes studies of customer satisfaction and questions about how subscribers can be encouraged to spend more time and consume more content on the platform.

Examples of UX research for an SVOD service might include how a program's position on the visual *carousel* that lists available programs influences the programs audience members notice and choose? Carousels are the SVOD equivalent of a programming schedule, except audiences choose their own adventure. So the analyst might be asked how the programs listed first on the carousel affect how long audiences stay on the platform after each sign-in and how likely they are to sample titles deeper in the listings.

Questions like these require analysts to engage in very creative thinking. Will people watch more if content is built around themes? What about if it is scheduled or rotated on the platform based on its relationship to current events and breaking news in the real world? Do viewers want to be able to contribute a running commentary on what they're watching and see what others are saying in real time? Where, if at all, does using social media fit into TV/video viewing, and what effects does the simultaneous use of the two media have on audiences' perceptions of and engagement with the video content they're watching?

Marketing research in entertainment

Marketing and promotions research is a critically important and increasingly sophisticated area of specialization for media analysts. In the linear advertising-based television entertainment world, the goal of marketing and promotions is to deliver audiences to content. In pursuit of that goal, media analysts use return path data to track which promotions for a program specific viewers saw, on what networks, around what programs, and how many times. By examining past viewing patterns, they can model an individual's likelihood of watching the network in a given time slot. With those data, they estimate the effectiveness of the total marketing campaign for a program and for individual promotional spots in the campaign.

If you always watch the network on Thursday night at 8 p.m., and that's where a new program is scheduled, then the promotions for the new program probably didn't play much of a role in getting you to watch. But if another viewer almost never tunes in at that time but was exposed to a number of promotional spots for the new show and suddenly changes her viewing habits to catch the series premiere, it's a pretty good indication the network's promotional campaign for the show was effective. While program scheduling is losing some importance due to audience time-shifting abilities via DVRs and VOD, it remains an important focus for promotion and content discovery.

Analysts gather such data over many viewers and tease out which promotional spots for the campaign were most effective in getting viewers to sample the new show or subscribe to a particular network or platform. They'll also examine how effective on-air promotions were compared with different types of off-air promotions for the show or platform—and those insights will be applied when future campaigns are developed.

Networks and platforms also invest heavily in brand research. Much of that work is done through regularly scheduled *surveys*. Sometimes those are done with audience *panels*, other times through traditional public opinion survey research. Brand research often incorporates questions such as: How do you feel about Network X? What's your favorite show? What's your favorite platform? Are you watching Network X live? Time-shifting? Streaming on your laptop or phone? When you watch TV, what networks do you consider watching and why? What types of programs do you think of first when you think of Network/Platform Z?

Analysts use the responses to develop a picture of people's brand images of particular networks and content companies. They try to understand which networks or platforms audiences think of first for original programming, sports, or movies, or for reruns of favorite series. They tease out which comedies, dramas, reality shows, or other categories come to mind first when people think about finding a particular type of program to watch—called a *consideration set*. Most importantly, they track which networks are improving or losing ground in terms of audiences' affinity toward them and, in connection with viewing data, can see which programs are driving the changes in audience's brand perceptions. That information is used in content creation and buying decisions and to make pitches to advertisers.

Other aspects of promotional research include, of course, testing the effectiveness of individual promotional spots and sizzle reels with audiences and specific audience segments before the spots or reels are released to the public. Much of that testing is now done by posting the material online and soliciting feedback from audiences or previously recruited audience panels.

The international television and video market

The market for entertainment content is increasingly international and competitive. As the number of broadcast, cable, satellite, and on-demand services has surged, so has the competition for the rights to hit programs and the prices of those rights. Thus it is vital, in the syndication market, to spot potentially successful video series as early as possible, wherever they are being developed, and to get to the producers to buy distribution rights before other syndicators become aware of the new program. Often that means spotting a new program when the concept is just being greenlighted, long before production begins.

The first step is understanding the global video market. Analysts are constantly seeking data and other information on questions such as: What program genres have the largest total global program sales? What countries have the largest total television entertainment markets? How do those two categories overlap? Are there producers or production companies who are consistently successful in a particular genre? What are current and emerging trends in audience tastes and consumption technologies around the world and, particularly, in the largest and most valuable television and video markets?

Armed with the answers to these big picture questions, analysts in the distribution sector then scour the global media industry trade press daily seeking news and gossip that might point them to a potentially valuable future project. Did someone just report that always successful producer Jane Smith was in Country X this week? Did a newspaper in Country Y report that a small rural town is being considered as the location for a new TV series? Did an industry newsletter report that ratings for a particular genre have been falling in Europe or Asia? The information that media analysts glean from reading widely across the trade press is passed on to syndication executives, helping them to spot both trends and potential hits earlier than their competitors.

The future of television and video entertainment

The television and video entertainment sector is changing so quickly that any prognostication about the future focus of research is risky. Audiences probably will continue to migrate toward VOD entertainment in the United States and many other developed nations that have the technological infrastructure to support on-demand delivery. But it also seems certain that linear television will continue to be popular with some audience segments and a lucrative industry in most countries. That means that media analysts will need to be fluent in traditional media math and analytics for some time to come.

What also is clear is that one of the key research questions analysts will be asked to address, across all sectors of the television entertainment business, will be the monetization of content. Advertising-supported linear television continues to be as, if not more profitable, than AVOD and SVOD for most television entertainment companies, according to several network media analysts interviewed. But competition for both advertising and subscribers is rising fast, particularly for publicly held media companies, where investors demand constant growth, and media companies will be seeking new sources of revenue. They will turn to analysts to determine the financial potential of each new idea.

The video games industry

The global video game industry generated around $179 billion in revenue in 2021—more than eight times the global film box office revenues for the same year (Clement, 2021; Video game industry, 2022).[1] By some projections, video game revenues may top $250 billion by 2025 (GlobalData, 2019; Video game industry, 2022).

Although video gaming emerged as a form of entertainment media in the early 1970s, not until around 2007 did the industry begin using user analytics as a key tool in game design and marketing. Today, gaming is a complex industry that includes mobile gaming—currently the largest sector—online gaming, and console-based gaming. All three sectors heavily use analytics, as do the companies that create gaming hardware such as consoles and other gamer equipment.

The research used in the software—or game development side of the industry—is similar to traditional media analytics research. The first and most pressing question is always marketing: Is there a market for a particular game concept (Ask GameDev, 2018a; Benson, 2015)? How large and appealing is that market likely to be? What are the demographics of the likely players, and are those players committed gamers or casual gamers? What is the competition for the concept? How well do existing competitors perform? For what platforms will the game need to be produced? What revenue models do similar games use? These are just some of the basic marketing questions game developers research on each new idea they consider.

Once a developer decides to actually produce a new game, research shifts to design questions. What are the *design pillars*—the design elements that define this game and make it distinctive from other games (Ask GameDev, 2018b)? Will the pillars be simple play, complex visuals, elements of humor built into the game, or some other set of features? Design pillars are the elements that define a game's brand image in the minds of players. Developers identify those pillars early in the design process, but as development proceeds, it's up to analysts to figure out whether those pillars are effective in producing a brand identity for the game with users.

The interactive nature of video games means analysts also are called in to measure the effectiveness of *game mechanics*. Game mechanics refer to how the game plays. A key element of game mechanics is the *game loop*, or what game designers call the "addiction experience" (Ask Game-Dev, 2018b). The game loop is the series of activities a user repeatedly experiences that, combined with the right incentives and rewards, keeps the player playing. Is it collecting resources, building something, and then defending it? Is it training, competing, winning, and moving to a higher level of competition?

Throughout game development, game mechanics are a major focus of research and testing. How many attempts are required for the average player to advance to a higher level (Howard, 2016)? Does advancement depend solely on luck—the software's random generation of the necessary resources? Or do players visibly progress toward advancement by building skill through playing? Then, as with other types of entertainment media, analysts also study audience reaction to such things as game characters, story arcs, and visual elements. The game development process requires a deep understanding of human psychology. Developers must figure out how to use the process of play to trigger players' emotions, engage their attention, motivate them to keep playing and buying in-game content, and move them through the game.

The data to answer such questions is generated by the actual act of play itself. Analysts work with designers to program the game to record gamers' activities at certain key points in the game. Analysts use the user data generated from play to determine whether the game actually works the way designers intended and whether the design elements are effective in attracting users and keeping them playing. As in the film industry, applying data analytics to video game design questions requires media analysts to negotiate the fraught space between data and creative personalities. Creativity-focused designers are rarely happy to hear that the data show their "baby" is ugly, and analysts working on a design team need people skills as much as data skills.

Once the game is released, the software continues collecting data on key points of play. If the game sells well, analysts will wind up with, literally, trillions of data points about how a game plays—and analysis of the game's operation continues as long as it is in the market (Howard, 2016). Findings are applied to updates, sequels, and new games under development. But the size of the datasets that gaming generates means analysts in the gaming industry need strong data management and analytical skills.

The ultimate purpose of media analytics is to improve the success and profitability of the media company for which the analyst works.

Compared with more traditional forms of media, the gaming industry has a much more diverse set of revenue models. Some companies use direct game sales for their primary revenue. Others sell monthly subscriptions to games. Some games use a transaction model, where players buy in-game content. In some cases, players may pay to acquire game elements such as weapons, real estate, or superpowers that are used in play. In others, players buy "energy" that allows the player to keep playing after a certain length of time.

Game producers also may sell ads around the content or product placement within the content, such as when a product like a specific car or recognizable soft drink brand is part of the game. As with film and television, there also are opportunities to make money by selling spin-off products such as toys, costumes, or branded clothing items—and even the concept rights for spin-off TV series or films.

Analysts in the gaming industry are asked to answer such revenue-focused questions as which audience segments are most likely to pay for games through which revenue models? To what degree can other product manufacturers leverage gamers' strong affinity for their favorite entertainment into sales of other products or spinoff products from the game itself?

The final major research focus for media analysts in the video game industry is, of course, the audience, known in the industry as "gamers". Most gamer-related questions are familiar: What types of games do different demographic segments play, and what are the platforms or technologies they use to play them? What is the relationship between a gamer's preferred platform, the types of games they play, and the amount of money they spend each year on gaming? How do different gamer segments discover games? Do they depend on friends to suggest them? Do they pay attention to advertisements? Do they read game review sites? Do they learn about new games by watching live gaming or videos on Twitch.tv, YouTube, or other sites? How important is the "perception of cool" in game choice by different audience segments? Do they follow particular game creators? Which gamer segments spend the most money on games? How does the amount of money spent differ not only by demographic segment but also across game platform, game type, and game revenue model?

Understanding gamers' behaviors is challenging. Games are played by all age groups, but the types of games played varies greatly by age and gender. There are two distinctive sectors of the gamer audience: committed gamers, who disproportionately spend the most time and money on video gaming—called "whales" in the industry—and casual gamers, who make up a much larger portion of the audience but produce much less revenue per player. Finally, children under the age of 18 are important gamer demographics, but they are subject to parental oversight in buying and playing games.

In 2019, Nielsen estimated that preteen gamers in the United States generated $2 billion in gaming revenue, despite not controlling any income themselves (Nielsen Webinar, personal communication, November 13, 2019). So how did they get their parents to spend that much money on their video games of choice? That's a key question for analysts. Just as important to gaming company revenue models is the question of *how* teens and preteens can pay for the things they want to buy, given that few have their own credit cards. Figuring out how to address such logistical issues is part of a media analysts' job.

Not all video games are considered entertainment. There are growing markets for "serious" or "applied" games. These include educational games, simulators used for training pilots and surgeons, situational simulation games used by government and business to plan responses to various scenarios, and games designed to teach skills, such as patients who need to learn how to manage chronic health problems or soldiers learning tactical skills. Developing applied games also requires the skilled use of analytics.

Video gaming is one of—if not *the*—fastest growing entertainment industry sectors globally. With that growth will come rising demand for media analysts who understand both the video gaming industry and gamers. Professional analysts in the sector address a variety of interesting questions ranging from the nature of the global gaming market to the effectiveness of the creative elements in a specific game.

Sports marketing

In 2018, sports was a US $71 billion entertainment industry in North America alone, an amount projected to grow to US $83 billion by 2023 (Gough, 2022). Media rights produced the largest part of that revenue at US $20 billion. Ticket sales were the second largest revenue source at just over US $19 billion, followed by sponsorship and sports merchandising. By one estimate, global sports revenues topped US $500 billion annually (Business Research Company, 2019).

Sports industries and media industries are highly interdependent. Sports organizations need media to draw audiences to their teams through live broadcast coverage of games and events and continual news coverage of a sport and its players. In return, sports have long been one of the most popular forms of content media can offer. Today, as large parts of the media audience have adopted time-shifted consumption, live sports broadcasts have become one of the few ways television and radio can draw predictable audiences to the real-time appointment viewing and listening that delivers audiences to advertisers.

Sports is all about marketing. Sports organizations need to sell game and event tickets. But in the past decade, the availability of big data (Chapter 7) on sports fans' behavioral and media usage has revolutionized the market-ing side of sports. Today, sports marketing is a rapidly growing industry sector in media analytics. Teams and sports organizations are hiring in-house research teams, while third-party sports marketing companies are springing up everywhere.

More a marketing than a media industry, the sports marketing industry is still attractive to many media analysts who love sports. One sports mar-keting executive says the role of the sports marketing analyst is to "think like an owner of a team," asking "what's the result that I want?" Yes, the owner wants to win the game—but also to sell tickets and sponsorships around the game, grow the TV ratings for the team's games, and sell more logo merchandise. "So if we kind of start with the 'why,' and then do all that, it's just so much fun," the executive says.

The "why" in sports marketing means understanding "*Fan DNA*," according to the executive. DNA stands for Demographics, Needs, and Attitudes. Sports marketers gather data on a team's fans through every data source available—tracking the online behavior of visitors to a team's website, Google search behavior, Gmail, social media, credit card data, choices in streamed content, etc.

With those big datasets in hand, sports marketers start thinking about the opportunities the team may be missing and the problems it needs to solve. Has the team sold 1,000 fewer tickets than expected for the upcom-ing game? How does the team get those tickets sold between now and game time? Is there a segment of the fan base that is slowly slipping away? Or one that has been building that the team has not yet recognized? What are the differences between dedicated fans, casual fans, prospective fans, and people who are totally uninterested in the team and the sport? When the team is competing for a championship or in the news for some service to the community, how many of the completely uninterested people can be converted into casual fans—and how? Once they become casual fans, how do they become dedicated fans? What keeps casual fans loyal when a favorite player leaves the team? What predicts what that departure is likely to cost the team in terms of declines in ticket sales, sponsorships, TV rat-ings, and team merchandise?

What analysts in the sports marketing industry learn from data is applied to everything from selling tickets to creating events to choosing the music played in the stadium. The questions media and consumer ana-lysts probe in the sports marketing industry include such things as: Are there fan behaviors—checking the weather report for the coming weekend, for example—that predict the likelihood that someone may buy a ticket to a game? On what day of the week does that behavior occur, and on what day of the week are fans most likely to buy tickets? How can the team most effectively communicate with different demographic segments and age groups? Does the team need to target different fan groups with different promotional campaigns, or will a single campaign fill the house? Should the team use different music in its promotional spots than it plays in the stadium during games to appeal to the fans who only watch televised games? Who buys the team's merchandise, and why?

Such analyses help sports teams increase their fan bases and their financial efficiency in marketing the team. The question for analysts is always which metric best measures the success of a marketing effort? The return on investment (ROI) has to be revenue positive to be considered successful. While that sounds simple, it's not. For example, when calculating ROI, what time period do you use? Return on a single game? Over a month? A season? A year? Three years? Efforts at understanding fan DNA or building fan loyalty are more likely to produce long-term financial benefits rather than immediate revenue increases. But then it's hard to determine which of a team's multiple promotions and campaigns was most effective in producing long-term results.

As is common in all areas of media analytics, the use of data analytics in sports is not without controversy and critics (Timms, 2018). In addition to marketing, team owners have started applying data analytics to individual athletes' and coaches' performances. Some professional athletes and fans argue that the numerical microanalysis of sports performance is making sports predictable and boring by encouraging coaches to minimize the risks they take in their use of players and their choice of plays. Critics argue that if data analytics costs sports contests their drama, in the long run, it also will cost sports teams their fans.

Nevertheless, the proliferation of sports marketing firms in recent years suggests there will be ample professional opportunities for people who understand and love data analytics, media, and sports. The key to success in the field, however, is to think like a sports executive rather than as a sports fan and develop the ability to draw creative business insights from the rich data sports teams now gather about their fans.

"There's a general feeling that in 10 years, [media analysts] are the ones to be running the team. We hear that all the time," a sports marketing executive says. "You can just see the change. You know, information is power, and these are the people with the information."

Summary and conclusion

The entertainment industry sectors covered in this chapter represent only a few of those that market entertainment. Theme parks, museums and historical sites, theater, dance and other types of cultural performances, even national and state parks, zoos, and travel companies such as cruise lines can all be considered players in the entertainment industries. Increasingly, media are being incorporated into nonmedia-related entertainment forms such as virtual reality historical experiences, multimedia performance elements, and digital online museum installations.

Regardless of the sector, entertainment media industries are growth industries globally. As they grow, however, competition for audiences' time, attention, and money between and among them also is growing.

For that reason, the entertainment industries can be expected to have increasing demand for skilled media analysts, as will nonmedia-specific entertainment organizations and industries, such as cultural organizations and theme parks. Moreover, as the success of sports marketing firms and the launch of data-driven film studios suggest, there are not only jobs but also business opportunities for analysts who are experts in specific entertainment industry sectors.

But as so many of the senior analysts interviewed for this chapter stressed, a research specialist in the entertainment world needs two critical skills: (1) the ability to think like the company CEO or team owner and to stay focused on what matters: audience growth and financial success, and (2) the ability to meld data expertise with the interpersonal skills required to work with the creatives, whose visions are the basis of success or failure.

Additional resources

Ask GameDev. (2018, May 10). *Game Design Process: Researching Your Video Game*: www.youtube.com/watch?v=utmlfUZvdJw&t=146s

Ask GameDev. (2018, May 23). *Game Design Process: Designing Your Video Game*: www.youtube.com/watch?v=2aIlRDamNT4

BEN (Be Entertainment): https://ben.productplacement.com/product-placement-an-in-depth-look-from-ben/

Benson, P. *Game Analytics and Exploratory Data Analysis*: www.youtube.com/watch?v=Ci9N7I4X_uk&t=9s Feb. 9, 2015

Box Office Guru: www.boxofficeguru.com/

Box Office Pro: https://pulse.boxofficepro.com/

CynopsisMedia: www.cynopsis.com/

GamesIndustry.biz: www.gamesindustry.biz/

Hollywood Branded: https://hollywoodbranded.com/product-placement-2/

Howard, P. (2016, July 28). *Data Science for Game Analytics at King*: www.youtube.com/watch?v=ez-4m2_jRqQ

IMDB. Film industry data: www.imdb.com/

MPAA Research and Reports: www.motionpictures.org/research-policy/

The Economist. TV's Golden Age Is Real: www.economist.com/graphic-detail/2018/11/24/tvs-golden-age-is-real

The Hollywood Reporter: www.hollywoodreporter.com/
The Numbers. *Film industry data*: www.the-numbers.com/market/
Statista.com—Statista has data on different *entertainment industry sectors*.
UCLA Film and Televisions Library: https://guides.library.ucla.edu/c.php?g=180193&p=3282127
UNESCO. Institute for Statistics. *Film and cinema data*: http://uis.unesco.org/en/topic/feature-films-and-cinema-data
VG Chartz. *Video games sales data*: www.vgchartz.com/

Recommended cases

**These cases can be found on the textbook website:
www.routledge.com/cw/hollifield**

Case 15.1: Film Industry: Deciding Where to Pitch an Original Screenplay
Case 15.2: Audience Demand for Video Games by Genre and Publisher
Case 15.3: Television Entertainment White Space Analysis

Case studies, along with accompanying datasets for this chapter, can be found on the text website. We particularly suggest the preceding cases. See the companion website and instructor's manual for detailed descriptions of these and other relevant cases.

Discussion questions and exercises

1. The chapter outlines many of the questions media analysts in each of the industry sectors are being asked to answer. Look again at some of these questions. Write a list of the variables *you* would use to try to answer each of the questions and discuss why you would pick those. How would you combine variables to get insights into the question? What controls would you use, and where would you get the data for your variables? Be *realistic* as you think about the questions. Approach it as if your boss just gave you this assignment.
2. Look at this list of questions, which are similar to some of those outlined in the chapter. Pick some to answer. Again, discuss what variables you would use to answer the question and why. Include how you would combine variables to get specific insights and where you would get the data:

   a. *Film industry.* Why was Film X twice as successful in its opening weekend box office in Atlanta, Georgia, in Christmas 2021, as it was in Seattle, Washington, as measured by its share (percentage) of total theater tickets sold that weekend in each city?

b. *Video entertainment.* What motivates people who subscribe to Amazon Prime Video but do not subscribe to HBO Max Streaming service to choose the Amazon service? What motivates people who subscribe to HBO Max but not Amazon Prime Video?

c. *Video gaming.* Children under 12 are an important target market for game companies. They spend a tremendous amount of money on games and in-game purchases, while controlling no income of their own. So what attitudes and behaviors among parents predict how much money they are willing to spend so their children can play video games?

d. *Sports marketing.* How does a team decide what music it should play in its home arena before, during, and after the game?

3. *Film industry.* Select several films currently in release. Go online and watch one trailer for each, taking notes on the key narrative elements in each trailer, the aspects of the film the trailer emphasizes, and the audience targeted in the trailer. Discuss some or all of the following questions: What audience do you think the studio is targeting with this film? What audience do you think the studio is targeting with each trailer? Why do you think the studios put together the trailer for that film exactly the way they did? Is the trailer likely to appeal to the film's target audiences? What are the strengths and weaknesses of each trailer? If you were a film industry analyst, what would you recommend to each studio after watching its trailers and comparing them to the competing trailers produced for that film or competing films?

4. *Video entertainment.* With your classmates, discuss what specific pieces of content—or types of content—each of you would consider "must have" in a new start-up VOD service, in order for you to personally decide to subscribe to it. If there is a particular series that would be important, how many seasons or episodes of it would you (and they) want the service to have available, and, realistically, how many of those do they think you and other subscribers would watch? What types of content would you *not* care about having on the service? What do you like and not like in the services you already use? Are there definable segments within your class regarding likes and dislikes in content and features? Women and men? Students from different backgrounds? Students from different geographic regions? How do you think your parents, grandparents, and friends would answer these questions?

5. *Video games.* Go to VG Chartz, the Video Games sales data site, www.vgchartz.com/. At the bottom of the page, under the link for "Latest Charts," the site offers weekly video game sales data up through 2018. Pick one week of historical data from 2018 and the same or a similar week in an earlier year. What games were selling best in 2018 globally?

What about in the United States? Europe? Japan? What changes do you see in the two weeks and years you are comparing in the popularity of games, producers, and genres? What potential explanations do you have for the trends you see in the data? What research questions do your observations raise?

If the dates or data on the site have changed, pick another year or search for video games sales data from other sources to use to think about the questions. Be sure to start by assessing the quality—*reliability* and *validity*—of the data on whatever source you have found.

6. *Sports marketing.* You are interviewing for an analyst position with a sports marketing firm. The firm's president says to you, "Our client is a semiprofessional league baseball team in a small city where there are no major professional or university sports teams." Quickly brainstorm how you would try to make attending this Saturday night's game appeal to four different age groups—Generation Z, Millennials, Generation X, and Baby Boomers? How would the messaging and the marketing outreach differ across those four groups? What data and variables would be most important to help make these decisions?

If baseball is not a popular sport in your country or region, substitute another sport that has a bigger fan base in your area.

Note

1. Estimates of industry size at the national and global levels often vary widely because the companies providing the estimates use different measurement methods and data sources. Such estimates are offered here only to provide rough comparisons of the sizes of different entertainment industry sectors.

References

Ask GameDev. (2018a, May 10). Game design process: Researching your video game. [Video]. *YouTube.* www.youtube.com/watch?v=utmlfUZvdJw&t=146s

Ask GameDev. (2018b, May 23). Game design process: Designing your video game. [Video]. *YouTube.* www.youtube.com/watch?v=2aIlRDamNT4

Benson, P. (2015, February 9). Game analytics and exploratory data analysis. [Video]. *YouTube.* www.youtube.com/watch?v=Ci9N7I4X_uk&t=9s

Business Research Company. (2019, July 17). *Increasing sports sponsorships will drive the global sports market to $614 billion by 2022* [Press release]. https://markets.businessinsider.com/news/stocks/increasing-sports-sponsorships-will-drive-the-global-sports-market-to-614-billion-by-2022-the-business-research-company-1028360019

Clement, J. (2021, November 23). Global video game market value from 2020–2025. *Statista.* www.statista.com/statistics/292056/video-game-market-value-worldwide/

Douglas, C. (2017, November 28). Finance, freedom and flexibility: How streaming platforms are luring A-List talent on and off the screen. *HuffPost*. www.huffpost.com/entry/finance-freedom-and-flexibility-how-streaming-platforms_b_5a1d9730e4b04f26e4ba9476

Eastman, S. T., & Ferguson, D. A. (2013). *Media programming: Strategies and practices* (9th ed.). Wadsworth Cengage Learning.

Eller, C. (1995, March 8). Average cost of making, marketing movie soars: Hollywood: Figure hit $50.4 million, 'a beast of a number,' says MPAA President Jack Valenti. *Los Angeles Times*. www.latimes.com/archives/la-xpm-1995-03-08-fi-40252-story.html

Follows, S. (2017, May 15). How important is international box office to Hollywood? *Stephen Follows Film Data and Education*. https://stephenfollows.com/important-international-box-office-hollywood/

Gavilan, D., Fernández Lores, S., & Martinez-Navarro, G. (2019). The influence of online ratings on film choice: Decision making and perceived risk. *Communication & Society, 32*(2), 45–59. https://doi.org/10.15581/003.32.2.45-59

Gelper, S., Peres, R., & Eliashberg, J. (2018). Talk bursts: The role of spikes in prerelease word-of-mouth dynamics. *Journal of Marketing Research, 55*(6), 801–817. https://doi.org/10.1177/0022243718817007

GlobalData. (2019, April 30). *Video games: Thematic research*. https://store.globaldata.com/report/gdtmt-tr-s212-video-games-thematic-research/

Gough, C. (2022, July 27). North America sports market size from 2009 to 2023 (in billion U.S. dollars). *Statista*. www.statista.com/statistics/214960/revenue-of-the-north-american-sports-market/

Howard, P. (2016, July 28). Data science for game analytics at King. [Video]. *YouTube*. www.youtube.com/watch?v=ez-4m2_jRqQ

Katz, B. (2017, October 19). Why more and more movie stars are heading to TV. *Observer*. https://observer.com/2017/10/mark-ruffalo-hbo-casey-affleck-alfonso-cuaron-movie-stars-tv/

Kim, S. H., Park, N., & Park, S. H. (2013). Exploring the effects of online word of mouth and expert reviews on theatrical movies' box office success. *Journal of Media Economics, 26*(2), 98–114. https://doi.org/10.1080/08997764.2013.785551

Leslie, I. (2017, April 13). Watch it while it lasts: Our golden age of television. *Financial Times*. www.ft.com/content/68309b3a-1f02-11e7-a454-ab04428977f9

QATestLab. (2015, October). *The differences between user interface testing and usability testing*. https://qatestlab.com/resources/knowledge-center/gui-usability-testing/

Timms, A. (2018, August 16). Are super-nerds really ruining U.S. sports? *The Guardian*. www.theguardian.com/sport/2018/aug/16/sports-nerds-analytics-data

Video game industry statistics, trends and data in 2022. (2022, January 18). *WePC*. www.wepc.com/news/video-game-statistics/

Glossary

A/B testing: A/B testing is an experimental process in which two alternative options are evaluated by audiences, often in real time.

accreditation: A confirmation of a successful audit indicating that a measurement tool, technology, or method has been independently reviewed and its validity, reliability, and effectiveness confirmed by an accrediting body such as the Media Rating Council.

actions: Any direct activity by a social media platform user including posting, commenting, sharing, clicking an emoji, watching, or converting.

ad injection: A type of ad fraud in which an existing ad is replaced with a new one without the publisher's consent. Digital publishers are defrauded because the fraudsters make revenue from the replacement ad's impressions.

ad stacking: A type of ad fraud similar to pixel stuffing. In this scenario, the fraudulent actor stacks ads on top of one another. As a result, users viewing the ads can only see the top ad, not the ones beneath. The advertiser will unknowingly be paying for these impressions, despite the user never seeing all of the ads.

algorithmic bias: A bias, prejudice, and/or inaccuracy that can result from historical analysis of (often unrepresentative) data or other types of analysis performed using algorithms and machine learning.

algorithms: A computational model or set of rules that can be programmed to achieve a particular outcome. Most often used today to refer to computer-mediated activity (e.g., search engine results).

amplification rate: The number of people who share or retweet a piece of content per post or tweet.

analyzed nonpaid bulk circulation: Copies of publications delivered in bulk to specific locations for redistribution to unknown readers, usually consumer magazines.

app acquisition: Shows source of app downloads; in other words, indicates effectiveness of app's marketing strategy.

audience quality: Members of the audience most likely to buy whatever is being marketed.

audience size: The most basic metric underlying media analytics: how many people/households or other unit of interest were in the audience.

audience universe: The population being referred to at a given time for measurement purposes (e.g., Women 18–49, Adults 55+, US households, etc.).

audit: The long and detailed evaluation process of a media measurement service or tool. Used to assess whether the service should receive accreditation or approval by an independent oversight body.

average active sessions: The average number of simultaneously running audio streaming sessions that are defined as active during a given time period. Calculated as (Total listening hours (TLH)/Hours in the reported time period).

average audience rating: The percentage of people who tuned into an average minute of the program. Used in national TV ratings to buy and sell advertising during a given program. This can also be reported in projections rather than a percentage that displays the number of people who were exposed to the content in an average minute.

average commercial minute ratings: The percentage of people who tuned into an average minute of a commercial airing within a program. Used in national TV ratings. Can also be reported in projections rather than a percentage, which displays the number of people who were exposed to an average minute of the commercial airing within a program.

average daily sessions per daily active user: How many times on average a user interacts with the app in one day.

average frequency: Metric that averages the frequency of individual exposure across an entire audience.

average quarter hour ratings: The percentage of people who tuned into any five minutes within an average quarter hour (15 minutes) of the program. This metric is used in local TV ratings, rather than average audience, to buy and sell local advertising during a given program. Can also be reported in projections rather than a percentage that displays the number of people who were exposed to the content in an average quarter hour.

average revenue per user (ARPU): Overall value a single user provides to the app. Specifically, how much revenue is generated on average by each user (e.g., subscriptions, in-app purchases, paid downloads, ad clicks, and the like).

average session length: How much time the typical app user spends on the app during a given session.

average time spent: The average length of time visitors spend on a site; often synonymous with "stickiness;" often calculated in relation to actions, such as average time spent on site before a conversion.

average watch time: The average amount of time all viewers spent watching a video or ad online.

beacon: A wireless transmitter that sends short-range radio signal to nearby smartphones or other mobile devices to activate various uses in location technology or "proximity marketing." Among other functions, such location information helps brands and retailers track customer location in stores and better understand browsing and buying patterns.

behavioral targeting: Uses an individual's previous buying behaviors to predict future product purchases and prepurchasing ("funnel") behaviors. Allows advertisers to serve individual consumers advertisements when they start prepurchase behaviors; maximizes the "recency" effect.

big data: Data source that is too large to be analyzed or managed using standard databases, software, or statistical methods or that exceeds capabilities of a single server or computing environment.

bounce rate: The percentage of visits to a website that had a single page view. Visitors left without taking any action or visiting any other page on the site.

box office: The revenue generated from in-theater ticket sales. A key metric used to measure a film's success; also used to compare the success of different films and of films, in general, across time.

census-level: Any measurement approach in which efforts are made to measure all units in a population. Examples: Return path data from TV set-top boxes or online. The term "census-based measurement" is also often used instead, because true censuses are rare due to technology access or failure, causing some of the population to be missing.

churn: The level of turnover among users, clients, audiences, or subscribers in any area of a media company's business. Churn increases marketing and administrative costs as customers come and go and make revenues more unpredictable.

churn rate: Percentage of users that stopped using an app, service, subscription, or brand during a set period of time (the opposite of retention rate).

circulation: Generic term for the number of copies of a publication distributed to readers. The metrics used to measure circulation for purposes of buying and selling advertising are complex and much more specifically defined.

clickstream data: A collection of metrics that describe a consumer's online journey, including but not limited to things like which websites were visited, which pages were viewed, and for how long.

click-through/click-through rate (CTR): The percentage of people who click on a link out of all those exposed to it, clicking on a link to load the linked website or content. A measure of audience engagement.

concept testing: Research on people's reactions to the overall concept, subject matter, or idea for a piece of content. Used most often to test concepts for new TV series or other high-cost entertainment content.

consideration set: The program genres, content brands, or consumer brands a person would consider when thinking about seeking content or buying something. Example: If someone is interested in watching a comedy on TV, which programs, networks, or streaming services would they search first to find something to watch.

consumer journey: The detailed step-by-step process that explains how a consumer moves toward some type of conversion decision, including marketing interactions and communications with others, both online and offline; can also be referred to as the customer or audience journey.

content analysis: A key research method used to ensure that a media company's content is in alignment with its branding.

convenience sample: A sample selected for its convenience to the researchers, not for its quality or relevance to the research question.

conversation rate: Rate (percentage) at which a piece of content inspired people to start talking about it, including comments and shares. A measure of impact.

conversion: A desired outcome or behavior that the brand wants a consumer to make (e.g., a purchase, a membership, etc.).

conversion rate: Percentage of audience that takes the action a content creator wants, such as clicking through to a website, buying a product, donating to a cause. Measurement of the desired outcome. Evidence of the effectiveness of the message.

cookies: Tracking device or data packet that can be installed onto computer browsers by websites; allows individuals' browsing histories and online activities to be tracked and monitored.

cost per acquisition (CPA): How much it costs to acquire one new user.

cost per click: Payment based on evidence that an advertisement actually was viewed because someone clicked on it. Vulnerable to ad fraud.

cost per conversion: Estimates the cost to the advertiser of each conversion achieved.

cost per thousand (CPM): Price advertiser pays to buy an ad per 1,000 impressions.

cost per viewer: The cost of the content per audience member averaged over time. Often used in estimates of future audience for purposes of negotiating the price of content rights.

cover testing: Gathering data on audience reaction to publication cover designs.

cume (cumulative audience): The estimated number of unique (unduplicated) listeners or viewers within a given time period. In radio measurement, individual listeners must have listened for at least 5 minutes in order to be included in the cume rating. Cume is most commonly used by the radio industry but is also used in television.

currency: The transactional metric(s) of record within an industry for advertising sales purposes.

customer acquisition: What it costs a company on average to gain each new customer; what strategies are effective in attracting new customers.

customer retention: What it costs a company on average to retain customers by doing what is necessary to keep them satisfied; what strategies are effective in maintaining customer satisfaction.

daily active users (DAU): Number of users who have a session with an app at least once per day.

dashboard: An online, interactive portal or user interface that continually updates various metrics; a type of data visualization.

data broker: A company that buys or collects, then sells consumer information; also known as data providers, data suppliers, or information brokers.

data fusion: A process of taking data from multiple sources with the goal of building more sophisticated models to gain deeper understanding about an audience or project goal. Often involves merging data on a single subject and combining it for centralized analysis.

data integration: A process of combining data from various sources into a single, unified view.

demographics: Personal characteristics that generally are not changeable. Gender, age, race, and income are the most important to advertisers. A factor in determining audience quality.

depth of visit: Sometimes referred to as *engagement* or *stickiness*. A term that can have multiple definitions. Usually, the number of pages viewed per visit to a website during a given time period.

Designated Market Area (DMA): A Nielsen term, these are geographic regions in the United States used for local television measurement. There are 210 DMAs in the United States. Each DMA represents a group of counties.

dial testing: A type of audience testing in which a small group of viewers twist a dial to record how much they like or dislike what they're seeing on the screen.

diary: A paper booklet used by Nielsen households in which listening choices are recorded by the household for measurement purposes. While the diary was phased out for television in the United States, it remains in some markets for radio measurement and may be used elsewhere around the world.

domain spoofing: A type of ad fraud in which a fake website is created that looks identical to a legitimate website. Advertisers unknowingly purchase and place ads on the fake site, and the fraudulent website host receives the revenue.

duplication: When audience members are counted more than once; also when an advertiser pays to reach the same people with the same message multiple times.

economic value: The total financial amount added to an organization's bottom-line as a result of all possible visitor conversion activities.

effective frequency: Measures number of times the average consumer must be exposed to an ad before a conversion occurs.

effective reach: Measures number of people reached and influenced by an ad.

emojis: Any graphic symbol used to indicate a user's reaction to a piece of content; an indicator of engagement, often used in sentiment analysis.

engagement: A term with multiple definitions across media companies and platforms. Widely used across media industries to describe audience attention or response to content. Important because engagement is believed to predict conversions. Often measured by counting audience actions in response to content.

episode testing: Used to gauge audience reaction to a plot line, specific characters, or story lines in a program episode.

exit rate: The percentage of users who left a website from a particular page.

fan DNA: DNA stands for demographics, needs, and attitudes; used in sports marketing analytics.

first-party data: Data that is generated by an organization itself.

five-minute qualifier rule: With regard to terrestrial radio measurement, in order for a listener's data to be included in an average quarter hour (AQH) or 15-minute period, the listener must be tuned in for a minimum of five minutes. If this threshold is not met, the station is not credited with that listener.

flight length: The length of time a piece of content or series is made available to audiences on a streaming service or other platform.

followers: The number of other social media users who have set their accounts to alert them if a particular person or organization posts. A measure of interest in and loyalty to a particular social media account.

forecasting: Using data and sometimes modeling to try to predict future events, such as the size of an audience for a film or series that a studio is considering developing or future trends in news consumption or technology use.

frequency: Refers to the number of times an audience member is exposed to a piece of content within a given time period.

funnel: A process of consumer thinking and action that precedes a purchase or other action. The stages in the funnel leading to a conversion are awareness, interest (i.e., consideration), desire, and action (i.e., conversion or purchase).

General Data Protection Regulation (GDPR): A broad set of consumer privacy and data protections enacted by the European Union in 2018 to protect its residents. The GDPR has served as a model for other countries when developing consumer data and privacy laws.

geofencing: A location-based technology that enables a business to serve targeted content, such as ads or coupons, to consumers who opt into the service, when a user gets within a specified distance of the business.

geolocation data: Data gathered automatically from digital devices that show a person's locations and movements across time.

granularity: The nature of data having a fine level of specificity; this level of detail and specificity is common when collecting and analyzing large datasets.

gross impressions (GI): Definitions vary, but generally, the sum of all the impressions generated by an advertising campaign; a measure of the total "weight" of a campaign; may or may not include duplicated impressions, depending on how GI is operationally defined by the user.

gross rating points (GRP): The sum of all rating points for all content within a given schedule, with one rating point equaling 1% of the total audience; a measure of the "weight" of an ad campaign, which helps advertisers understand the overall performance of their content within a market. Can be calculated as Reach × Frequency.

Households Using Television (HUT) (PUT) (PUR): The percentage of TV homes whose television screens are in use at a given time; the basis for calculating share. PUT is Persons Using Television—a measure of TV use at the individual level. PUR is used in radio.

identity resolution: A process in which first-party data are linked with external third-party data to help match individual or household. Also referred to as identification matching.

impression: A metric of reach that has varying definitions. Generally, an impression is counted when an audience member is exposed to a piece of content regardless of whether the content was actually seen.

insight: An understanding of findings from data that can be used in a way that is actionable and relevant to the business.

intention to renew: A key indicator for subscription media services; measured using multiple indicators and audience behaviors.

interface testing: Analyzes audience members' responses, including emotions, to the form and appearance of the interface they encounter when accessing content. Examples would be the program carousel subscribers use to choose and play content on a streaming service or the design of a website.

key performance indicator (KPI): A general term referring to the indicators or measurements used by a company to evaluate performance.

keywords: Words used to identify data that an analyst wants to collect through data scraping; also used by SEO specialists to help audiences discover content.

length of visit: Quality of visit as measured by length of a visitor session, usually in seconds.

lifetime value (LTV): How much value each user brings to a company through their purchases; not all users may stay with the company/brand for same period of time, depending on type of customer.

linear media: Content that is delivered according to a specific programming schedule determined by the content provider.

listener tracking (LT) method: A client-side approach to tracking audio streams by gathering data from the web-based player or mobile device. Also known as the "ping" method.

longitudinal: Longitudinal analysis looks at how data on something such as audience use or preferences changes over time. Longitudinal data-sets include data on the same variables, measured the same way, collected across multiple points in time.

loyalty: How long an audience member/consumer continues to buy/use a particular brand; returns to a particular website or channel; also emotional attachment to a brand.

marketing funnel: A concrete way to think about the consumer journey. The simplest funnel model is typically described in four stages also known as AIDA: awareness, interest (i.e., consideration), desire, and action (i.e., conversion or purchase). This four-stage process of consumer thinking and action is referred to as a funnel due to its shape when seen in diagram form. Sometimes also known as sales funnel.

mention: When another user's name or username is included in a comment, a post, or a tweet; reflects a higher level of engagement and a stronger connection between nodes.

metro (also Metro Survey Area or Metropolitan Statistical Area [MSA]): The geographic market area utilized for local radio measurement (US).

microtargeting: A marketing strategy that uses many sources of consumer data and demographics to create audience subsets/segments to target consumers or audiences at a granular, individual level.

monthly active users (MAU): Number of users who have a session with an app at least once per month.

node: A place or person on a network where traffic originates, ends, or concentrates; also called vertex.

nonlinear media: Content that does not follow a schedule created by the content distributor and tends to be accessed on demand.

opening weekend: The revenue generated from theater ticket sales during a film's first weekend of release. A key metric used to measure initial audience response to a newly released film and to predict the film's eventual overall success.

operational definition: How each variable is defined so that it can be measured; should be precise and mutually exclusive; a major issue in cross-platform and cross-company measurement, where operational definitions of the same terms and concepts often vary.

over-the-top (OTT): A method of distributing and consuming content "over" a closed traditional system, usually via a high-speed internet connection. Media delivered OTT involves neither broadcast nor cable or satellite subscriptions, instead going "over the top" of these services, hence the name. OTT is also used in voice and messaging services.

page view: In online measurement, this is generally a single instance of an individual visiting or viewing a web page. However, variations of this metric are often used, such as weekly or monthly page view, average number of page views, and so forth. Different metrics providers may have slightly different definitions.

paid circulation: Size of the audience paying to acquire a publication. Generally defined as copies of a publication sold through subscriptions and single-copy sales for a price of at least US 1 cent and not for purposes of resale.

panel: Often refers to audience panel. Usually a sample of individuals recruited to participate in audience or market research over an extended period of time, sometimes years. Panel members may be randomly selected from the population or be selected as a convenience sample, depending on the company organizing the panel.

People Meter: Nielsen tool that measures audience viewership that documents both what is being watched (tuning information) as well as who is watching it (anonymized data, demographics only) within the household.

Persons Using Television (PUT): See Households Using Television.

pilot testing: Usually involves production of an initial episode of a proposed TV series, or parts of an episode, specifically for the purpose of screening it for audience reaction.

pixel stuffing: An ad fraud technique in which fraudulent publishers place an entire ad into a condensed 1×1 pixel space, making it impossible for website visitors to see; an ad fraud common to CPI (cost-per-impressions) ads.

podcatcher: Software that automatically finds and collects podcasts and podcast episodes, making it easier for audiences to discover them and play them.

population: The group you want to study.

Portable People Meter: Individual wearable Nielsen meter that measures exposure to audio, video, and online signals. Originally developed by Arbitron, a company acquired by Nielsen in 2013.

post: The creation of a piece of content on a social media platform; a measurable action.

primary data: Data specifically collected by the researcher through a study designed to answer the question being analyzed.

print/digital unduplicated circulation: When a reader gets both the print and digital editions of a publication, it is reported in this category and not in either print or digital.

psychoacoustic masking: A type of inaudible embedded coding technology used in the signal encoding process that enables a broadcast signal to be detected by a meter, such as a Portable People Meter.

psychographics: Changeable characteristics that define people, related to lifestyles and preferences such as lifestyle, hobbies, and political views. A factor in determining audience quality.

qualified nonpaid circulation: Copies of a publication distributed to consumers without charge such as copies requested for distribution in business waiting rooms or given to students for educational use but in compliance with AAM rules.

qualified paid association circulation: When readers get a publication as part of membership in professional associations/organizations, regardless of whether the subscription is deductible from members' dues, but at least US 1 cent of the dues must go to the publication, and members must be told of the value of the publication. Used primarily to measure circulation for B2B publications.

qualified traffic: People or users (website visitors) who are not just visiting or browsing a website but who are in the market for the product or service offered on the site and most likely to buy.

rating: The percentage of the audience tuned into a particular program out of the total potential audience in the geographic area being measured.

reach: The total number of unique audience members who saw or heard certain media content at least once within a given time period. Also referred to as unduplicated audience or cume.

recency: The length of time between exposure to an ad and the consumer's likely buying decision or other form of conversion.

referral: The website or link from which an audience member arrives to another site.

reliability: Whether repeated measurements of the same population or repeated analyses of the same data produce the same results. Reliability is a necessary condition for validity. Measures, data, or findings that are not reliable cannot be valid.

rest rate: The period of time when a network or streaming service removes a piece of content from the schedule or carousel so that audiences don't become bored with it; later returning it to the lineup.

retention rate: How many users an app retains (how many return to use it) after a set period of time.

return on advertising spend (ROAS): Value of conversions generated, such as revenue from sales of an advertised product, per dollar spent on the advertising campaign.

return on investment (ROI): The percentage financial return made on the money spent building and marketing a product or service.

return path data: Data generated by user activity related to a digital device, defined by a start time and a duration that is returned to the platform provider. Example: Set-top box data.

sample: A subset of a population from which data is collected. Also the act of drawing a sample.

satisfaction: Audience attitude toward the product that predicts continued subscription or consumption. There is no single metric to measure satisfaction, but companies often combine metrics, including customer and audience reviews, into a satisfaction KPI.

screen flow: Shows how a user interacts with each screen in the app, e.g., exits by screen, navigation path, total number of visits per screen, last screen used before exiting the app (which could suggest a problem spot).

search engine optimization (SEO): The practice of making website content more discoverable and likely to appear as a top search result by a search engine by using keywords in the content.

secondary data: Data originally collected during primary research that is being reused to answer new questions by another party.

second-party data: Data that is created via data linkage or integration when two companies create a data access agreement or partnership.

sentiment analysis: Examines whether users' actions, such as comments or emojis on social media, reflected positive or negative attitudes toward the subject of a social media post or a product or brand.

session starts: The number of different digital audio sessions begun or of stream requests within a given time period.

sessions: A visit to a website or stream by an audience member.

set-top meter: A video measurement meter that sits atop a television set or nearby in a home and that records what is being watched, or at least what channel the television set is tuned to, and for how long. It does not record "who" is watching.

share: The percentage of audience tuned into content out of the total audience whose devices were in use at the time.

share of conversation: Percentage of conversation about your brand or content on social media as compared to your competitors' brands or content. A measure of engagement. Measured different ways.

share of sentiment (SOS): The percentage of positive and negative sentiments or actions social media users express about your brand or content as compared to your competitors'. Measured different ways.

share of voice (SOV): Measures the visibility of a brand or product amid all the advertising or conversation on social media that is competing for consumers' attention; measured different ways depending on the type of content being analyzed.

share (online) or retweet: When a user reposts a piece of content to their own account so their own followers can see it, or sends it by email, text, or other means to more people, amplifying the post.

social media audit: A periodic, systematic evaluation of a company's social media presence and strategy. May include analysis of a wide range of organization posts, audience activity, and conversion metrics.

social media listening: Observing broader discussions, topics, and trends on social media for purposes of identifying possible issues or content opportunities, whether or not the activity is directly related to your brand or company.

social media monitoring: Tracking the metrics of social media activity that is related to your brand or your company's KPIs.

software development kit (SDK): Software installed on digital devices to capture audience consumption data.

spike analysis: Conducting a detailed analysis to determine the cause of any sharp increase or decrease of activity that shows up in data.

stability: The consistency of data or metrics over time; often mentioned as a feature of big data.

stickiness: Term with multiple definitions depending on context. How often users return to an app or the average length of time a user stays on an app or website. Also used in the industry as a synonym for engagement or loyalty.

syndicated research firms: Syndicated research firms are independent third parties that regularly collect and distribute data and reports to clients for a fee. Example: media measurement firms.

task completion rate: The percentage of people who are able to accomplish their intended task on a website.

third-party data: Data that is commercially or publicly available from an independent entity.

time on page/time on site: The amount of time a person spends on a particular page within a website (time on page) or the time spent on the entire website during a session (time on site).

time spent: Definitions vary by platform, content, and analyst; usually refers to how long each unique person viewed a piece of content.

time spent listening (TSL): Essentially an estimate of audience loyalty, expressed in average number of hours and minutes per day, week, or other time period that the average listener spends consuming audio content from a particular source; used in reference to radio or audio but also used with television or video.

time stamp: A metric embedded in digital content recording that indicates when an audience member or user did something such as access a type of content, rolled a video, or posted a comment.

title testing: Gathering data on audience response to different proposed titles.

total audience measurement: The cumulative measurement of the audience's media consumption of a particular piece of content across all media devices and platforms; also referred to as cross-platform or cross-media measurement. Total audience measurement is often used to refer to the media industry's effort to accomplish this goal.

total average circulation—print and digital: The size of a publication's total qualified paid and nonpaid audience across all platforms.

total listening hours (TLH): In digital audio, the total number of hours listened to during active streaming sessions.

TV household (TVH): A household that has at least one TV set or screen that is able to receive audio and video signals via broadcast, cable, satellite, or the internet. Can be calculated at the national or local level and serves as a basis for other audience estimates.

unduplicated audience: The number of individual audience members or households who consumed a piece of content, with each audience unit counted only once.

unique visitors (daily, weekly, monthly): The number of different (unduplicated) people who went to a website within a given time period.

universe: As related to audience measurement, it refers to a demographic or user group such as adults 18+, men 18–49, all households in a geographic area, etc.

universe estimate (UE): The total number of households or persons in a given population. Nielsen produces UEs for total United States as well as for each of the 210 DMAs. UEs are the basis for the calculation of all audience estimates. Without an accurate understanding of the entire universe, it is impossible to understand what percentage of that universe viewed an ad or a piece of content.

usability testing: Analysis of how user-friendly different technology features, content designs, and layouts are.

user experience (UX): Any research focusing on the customer's relationship with a brand and experiences using its products; includes *usability* (*UI*) *testing*, customer *satisfaction* research, and *interface testing* (*IT*).

validity: The degree to which something such as data or analysis accurately reflects reality.

validity of inference: Validity of inference refers to whether an analyst is accurately interpreting the findings from a data analysis and their meaning in relationship to the questions being asked.

validity of measurement: Whether data accurately reflect the realities they are supposed to represent in the population being studied.

vanity metrics: Metrics that suggest popularity, such as number of likes, followers, fans, and retweets. However, these metrics are not particularly meaningful as they can be easily faked and aren't particularly helpful to a company in terms of strategy.

variables: Any factor an analyst believes is involved in answering a research question under study, whether as a possible influencing factor (independent variable) or the outcome (dependent variable).

verified subscriptions: Subscription copies the publisher designates to be read in public places or intended for individual use by recipients who are likely to be interested in the content, with or without payment; circulation metric used mostly with consumer magazines.

viewer assignment modeling: An approach to audience measurement that utilizes statistical modeling and data on the composition of audiences in geographically distant markets to estimate audience size and composition in a market under analysis.

viewership: The total number of persons who viewed a piece of video content.

views: A term with multiple definitions depending on context. The act of playing or watching a video. Platforms vary in how much of a video must be watched by a user before it counts as a view. Also used for having viewed a webpage.

visitor loyalty: Frequency of visits to a website during a given time period.

visitor recency: Duration of time that has passed since a visitor last visited the website.

visits: Number of people who went to a website within a given time period. Metric can include multiple visits by the same person. Also referred to as sessions.

wastage: Money spent on advertising that does not return conversions because the advertiser is paying for noneffective reach or frequency.

watch time: Usually the total amount of time people spent watching a video or video ad. Measured in seconds for individual videos. A metric of viewer retention and engagement as compared to a *view*, which may be measured even if a video is only played for a few seconds. Some measurement firms and platforms use other metrics, such as *time spent*, instead of watch time.

watermark: A code or hidden data embedded by Nielsen clients within the audio signal, which can be masked using psychoacoustic masking of neighboring audio frequencies so that they are inaudible. It aids in the identification of the content source.

weight: The total size of the audience reached through a particular advertising campaign across all of the different times and places that the ads in the campaign ran.

weighting: Weighting is a mathematical technique used to adjust probability samples as needed until they are representative of the population from which they were drawn. If a group is over- or underrepresented in a sample, the responses from that group are mathematically adjusted until they represent the same proportion in the dataset as the group does in the population universe.

white space analysis: Analyzing programming schedules to identify gaps in the types of content being produced or programmed so as to identify strategic opportunities in the content supply.

Index

Made in United States
Orlando, FL
09 January 2024

42274068R00239